Islands of Kinship

A Collective Manual for Sustainable and Inclusive Art Institutions

ISLANDS OF KINSHIP: A COLLECTIVE MANUAL FOR SUSTAINABLE AND INCLUSIVE ART INSTITUTIONS

PUBLISHED AND DISTRIBUTED
BY JINDŘICH CHALUPECKÝ SOCIETY
AND MOUSSE PUBLISHING CONTRAPPUNTO s.r.l.
Via Pier Candido Decembrio 28, 20137,
Milan, Italy

AVAILABLE THROUGH

- Mousse Publishing, Milan
  moussemagazine.it
- DAP | Distributed Art Publishers, New York
  artbook.com
- Les presses du réel, Dijon
  lespressesdureel.com
- Antenne Books, London
  antennebooks.com
- Idea Books, Amsterdam
  ideabooks.nl
- LibroCo. Italia, Firenze
  libroco.it

First edition: 2024

Printed in Czech Republic
by UNIPRESS, spol. s r. o.

ISBN 978-88-6749-634-1

€ 35 / $ 40

Project partners:

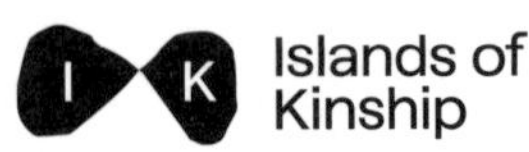

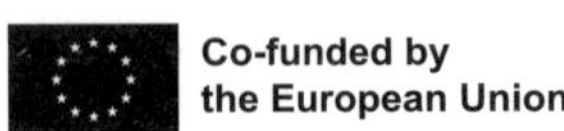

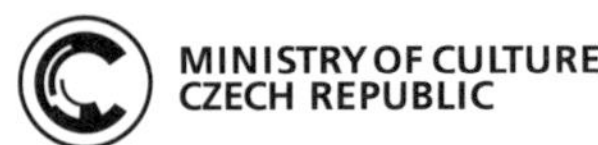

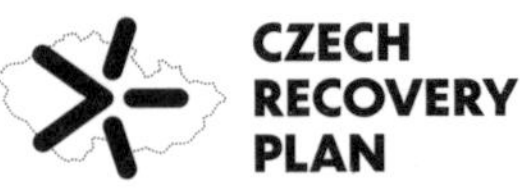

The Islands of Kinship project is cofunded by the European Union.

This paper (Munken Print White, 90 g/m²) was used from surplus stock normally destined for disposal. Manufactured in Munkedal, Sweden.

Karina Kottová, Tereza Jindrová, Nikola Ludlová, Barbora Ciprová

Editorial

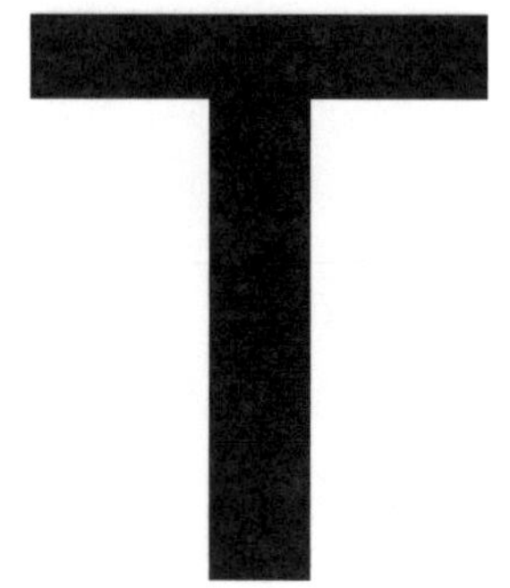

he Islands of Kinship project interconnects six midscale visual art institutions across diverse regions in Europe (Prague, Bratislava, Bitola/Skopje, Cologne, Helsinki, Riga) in an innovative collaboration model addressing issues of inclusion, kinship and togetherness, democratic exchange, and the ethics, emotions, and practical solutions for a sustainable and fair institutional operation. This publication is a result of our joint endeavors to address these themes via collaborative exhibitions, educational and public programs, co-commissioned artworks, but most importantly through smaller and larger transformative institutional experiments, aimed both at inner operation and outer collaboration and communication. The heart of this project was the possibility for each of the participating institutions to create a new job position of an inclusion coordinator. A unique group of insiders to the themes of accessibility, neurodiversity, social justice, ecological sustainability, and gender diversity was formed. Each coordinator worked both within the local context of their respective organization and engaged in an international and intersectional exchange as part of the network. Texts by the inclusion coordinators, alongside those by the project's curators and close collaborators, form the contents of this publication. We understand them as a call for wider discussion, as our means of sharing where we have come so far, acknowledging that this may only be the beginning in our attempts to lay grounds for art institutions that don't solely survive the profoundly difficult times we find ourselves in, but also create grounds for positive and possibly radical change.

The title of the publication uses the word manual, which probably evokes what we usually expect from such a form—practical guidelines containing advice about what kind of materials and services we should or shouldn't use in order to be sustainable, what kind of people we should talk to and how in order to be inclusive. We tried to step beyond these helpful but sometimes also too simplifying pieces of advice. We understand that there is more to sustainability than reducing one's carbon footprint. That environmental sustainability is deeply connected with social justice, interspecies solidarity, systemic critique, and transformative imagination. We strive to understand inclusion as so much more than audience development, or worse, an empty label attracting and justifying institutional funding and public relevance. We believe inclusion needs to stem from within, through deep transformation of the present organizational structures and mechanisms. Only then can we start to be fair and interesting-enough partners in dialogue with individuals and groups that were so far mostly excluded from the elitist world of contemporary art. The manuals written by the inclusion coordinators for this publication take various forms, from texts addressing specific fields of their expertise, through mind maps to codes of conduct, lists of principles and recommendations. They are based on our practical findings, however, they address them with sensitive recognition of broader social, political, environmental, and institutional contexts and through intersectional approaches.

The publication begins with an introductory text by Nikola Ludlová, the inclusion coordinator on behalf of the Czech organization Jindřich Chalupecký Society. Nikola summarizes and contextualizes our shared understanding of the highly discussed and charged notions of sustainability and inclusion. Subsequently, the book is structured into four major subchapters. Each contains an introductory text by one of the participating institutions' curators, manuals by the project's inclusion coordinators or guest writers, and an overview of the artwork commissions selected through a working group of the same title and presented on various occasions during the Islands of Kinship project.

The first subchapter named New Agora begins with a text by Ivana Vaseva, curator and cofounder of the Macedonian organization Faculty of things that can't be learned (FRU). Her take on the public sphere and its depoliticization in the Neoliberal era aims to display several art projects as potential efforts to revitalize the public sphere. Paulina Seyfried, the inclusion coordinator on behalf of Temporary Gallery in Cologne, presents her step-by-step manual for institutional opening through collaborative microprojects. The introductory text, containing a code of conduct for collaborative/solidary ways of working together, leads to an interactive map, in full version accessible on the Islands of Kinship website. In the second manual, FRU's inclusion coordinator Jana Brsakoska discusses the working conditions in the noninstitutional cultural sector and suggests systemic reforms, taking North Macedonia as a case study. As part of the New Agora working group, two artistic projects were commissioned: immersive installations by Dutch artist Jonas Staal and Stockholm-based Slovak artist Luki Essender. They are each presented here with accompanying texts and visual documentation.

The section entitled Family and Kinship in the 21st Century is introduced by a text by Aneta Rostkowska, director of Temporary Gallery in Cologne. The essay addresses forms of kinship, camaraderie, comradeship, and belonging outside of the social reproduction of norms entailed by the nuclear family. The following manual chapter by Fran Trento, the inclusion coordinator on behalf of Frame Finland, problematizes the notion of inclusion in regards to artistic residencies, especially addressing neurodiversity and nonfamilial modalities of kinship. The second manual is written by Katarína Slezáková,

Július Koller Society's inclusion coordinator, together with Daniel Grúň, JKS' chairman and curator. It addresses JKS's take on the archive as seen through decolonial and queering perspectives. It also outlines the institution's understanding of and caring for community and audience. This section is intersected by the presentation of two related artistic commissions—a film and installation by Feel Good Cooperative, a Rome-based collective of sexual workers, in collaboration with French artist Pauline Curnier Jardin, and a series of workshops and performances by Greek dragtivist Taka Taka.

The third section of the book is called Beyond Ecology. The introductory text by Ieva Astahovska, curator of Latvian Center for Contemporary Art, discusses how inclusion and diversity as principles undergirding the functioning of our institutions can intersect with environmental issues and how interspecies solidarity and deep ecology thinking can be inscribed into our curatorial and artistic practices. It is followed by three practice-oriented and analytical manuals. The first manual is written by Michal Klodner, Jindřich Chalupecký Society's collaborator in the field of sustainability and climate justice. His contribution centers on data feminism and technosocial feminist strands of thinking as frameworks for creating socially responsible, equitable, and decentralized digital infrastructures and spaces. Curator Aneta Rostkowska subsequently presents her take on the permacultural institution, proposing its attributes and values, as well as the needs it stems from. Karina Kottová, director of Jindřich Chalupecký Society, introduces the notion of cyclical curating—if curation in its nature cannot become slow, another form of resisting the capitalist speed might be synchronized individual and institutional cycles. The two artistic commissions created within this section are also presented here. The first is a three-channel video installation and environment by Polish artist Diana Lelonek, and second an interactive spatial installation featuring a virtual and interpersonal role-playing game by Berlin-based artistic duo Eloïse Bonneviot & Anne de Boer.

The final subchapter of the Islands of Kinship publication is entitled Inclusive (Curatorial) Strategies. Jussi Koitela, curator of Frame Finland, is once again questioning the meaning, context, and dialectics of inclusion in the sphere of art institutions and curating and stresses the need for the inclusive practices to be constantly rehearsed. In their manual on ableism and neurodiversity for art institutions, Fran Trento is providing practical guidelines for communication, hiring practices, or creating an access rider. The second manual by Paulina Seyfried is a critique of exclusion through language and explains the principles of easy and plain language. The chapter also includes a commission by Finnish artist Minna Henriksson and a commissioned series of online workshops curated by Paloma Nana and Paulina Seyfried, addressing the issues of critical whiteness, antiableist cultural work, and awareness.

By no means is this publication, or the results of the first phase of the Islands of Kinship platform, a closed endeavor. It is rather the very beginning of a long process and a moment of sharing of our initial findings, questions, successes, and failures. The collected texts, as well as the collaborative and participative structure of the publication, not only offer current examples of inclusive and sustainable practices used in the participating art institutions, but also consider the limitations within those institutions, the art system in which they operate, and the larger social and economic structures that might stand in the way of a broader and lasting change.

The graphic and print design of the book is also the result of a long process of compromises and challenges. Ecological processing and recycled materials form the basis of our efforts to be environmentally responsible, and therefore inform the design of this publication. However, we were not only concerned with purchasing commercial "eco-friendly" materials. Graphic designer Petr Knězek tried to find simple solutions that are both environmentally conscious and efficient in terms of production, logistics, and finances (e.g. by minimizing ink and material purchases, or through the layout of the book's colors and structure). We have used leftover paper from the printer's warehouse that would otherwise have ended up as waste. Each folder of the book therefore uses a different type of paper, which not only reduces costs and contributes to the vision of circular economy, but also enhances the reader's aesthetic experience.

We are aware of our responsibility for the existence of every new item on the planet and strive to minimize its environmental impact. A label placed on the back of the book encourages readers to dispose of the book sustainably after reading it, including the possibility of swapping, donating, recycling, or composting. At the same time, we do not recommend laying out the book in nature, as we are aware of the chemicals used in the colored ink.

We tremendously appreciate everyone who has been involved in the creation of this book and the project as a whole. All participants and collaborators, regardless of hierarchy or institutional background, are listed in the book, with appreciation for their individual contributions and efforts.

We sincerely hope to continue our aspirations within and beyond the network of Islands of Kinship and we are calling for allies. This publication is aimed at fellow cultural workers and representatives of art institutions of varying scales and diverse backgrounds, artists and activists, educators, students, and all those interested in arts and culture with a message. We believe the art institutions of today require profound transformation in order to become just, joyful, engaged, inclusive, and sustainable—which are some of the qualities we consider essential for becoming active players in structural change leading to the best-possible scenario of our future. We actually hope that the notions of inclusion and sustainability will disappear from our vocabularies one day, as they will just become our reality, our basic grounds. Until then, we will attempt to use them with integrity and wisely to anchor our joint efforts.

Nikola Ludlová

Introduction

Islands of Kinship: Transforming Art Institutions through the Ethics of Care

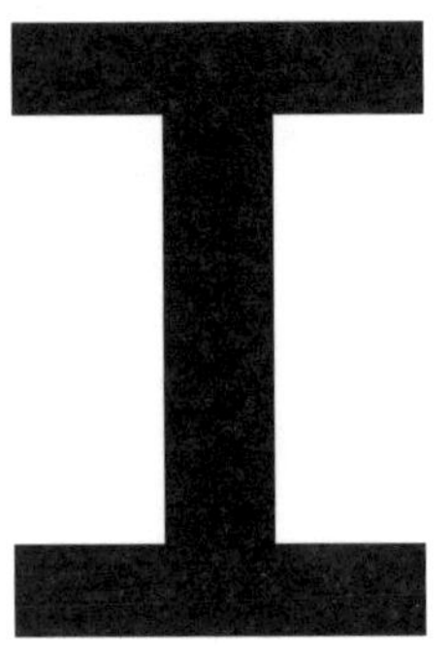

slands of Kinship (IoK) is a network of cultural workers that provides support and guidance for systemic change in our organizations and cultural and creative industries to contribute to a more just, accessible, and sustainable art system. The present publication, *A Collective Manual for Sustainable and Inclusive Art Institutions*, offers reflections of cultural workers and artists who participated in differing roles and areas in the process of instituting the change. The capacity of each organization to strive towards the aforementioned objectives was enhanced with the hiring of a new staff member who assumed the role of an inclusion and sustainability coordinator. Coming to their respective organizations as individuals with diverse personal and professional backgrounds, their primary goal was to propose middle and long-term developmental strategies, design solutions and tools, and then apply them, either individually or as a team, in the implementation of a program or the provision of services.

Apart from working in their organizations, the IoK coordinators worked collaboratively as a group, amplifying their individual knowledge capacities and augmenting human resources of the participating organizations. The meetings served as a resource for learning and evaluation of the achievements, obstacles, and failures they have encountered in their own work as well as in the work of the institution. Insights, proposals, and feedback from collaborating arts professionals and engaged communities served as another major force for change.

As public institutions, we have an ethical duty to make our programs and services as inclusive and sustainable as possible. This ethos also underlies our professional collaboration and internal operations of our staffs. What do these concepts mean in our context, though? Individual contributors to this publication ask this question repeatedly in a variety of contexts. Inclusion and the related concepts of equality and diversity have received much traction in both theory and practice in the fields of education, work, and since the 1970s also in the arts. The origins of sustainable thinking date back to the same period and the concept has had similarly wide and diverse applications and been subject of contention as to its meaning.

The critical treatment of inclusion is most developed in the field of education, where it has, during the past two decades, encountered considerable scrutiny due to its ideological ambiguity and reductionism, stemming from its foundation in sometimes antagonistic arenas: social justice, human rights, and special education. Albeit endorsed by international policy and legislation, the practice of inclusion in these critical sources has been characterized as "a neocolonial project that is embroiled in and reinforces geopolitical power asymmetries and oppressive regimes."[1] This new avenue in social inclusion scholarship identifies the enduring

1 Anastasia Liasidou, "Decolonizing Inclusive Education through Trauma-Informed Theories," *Scandinavian Journal of Disability Research* 24, no. 1 (2022): 277.

legacy of colonial perspectives[2] in academia and policy-making and calls for new theories of inclusion that would take into consideration the traumatizing effects of colonialism/ty on the "lived" realities of disabled and other disenfranchised groups of students, and address the intersections of coloniality, disability, and trauma and their impact on educational accessibility, participation, and achievement.[3]

Culture has been acknowledged in European Union's policies and funding schemes as an enabler and driver of social inclusion and sustainable development.[4] For us, the recipients of the EU subsidy programs, the policy documents and definitions are also authoritative, but only to some extent. The problem is that definitions of the concepts are framed as normative, and therefore are not problematized as is common in academic and activist contexts.[5] Although we are in agreement as to the social and political role of culture, our understanding and practice of inclusiveness and sustainability are also informed by other sources,[6] but most notably through dialogue and direct involvement of people whose access to arts and culture is difficult or nonexisting. The aim of this introduction is to make the readers aware of the contentious and historically and contextually contingent nature of the two overarching conceptual frameworks we use in this publication, and to situate ourselves in relation to them, as we want to avoid presenting them as universal, unproblematic values. The text concludes with our vision of how inclusion and sustainability may help us transform into caring institutions that we aspire to be.

2 Colonial perspectives entail in this context Western discourses and patterns of thought that have direct links with European Empire- and later nation-building, and that have been constitutive of social and public institutions that continue to characterize our culture, civic society, and nationhood.

3 Liasidou, "Decolonizing Inclusive Education through Trauma-Informed Theories," 278.

4 Based on this acknowledgement, the EU is committed to supporting and promoting culture as an essential contribution to human rights and a key element of good governance, inclusion, and sustainable growth.

5 Of course, advances in the relevant fields inform policy documents; but criticisms and new directions may run counter to the institutions' ideological foundations, and even in cases when they do not, new developments in the field are usually taken up by policy-makers at a slower pace.

6 In addition to academic sources, we specifically focus on the knowledge and expertise developed within activist groups and social change movements.

A Brief History of Inclusion

From the perspective of social history, inclusion represents one way in which societies have responded to perceived differences in the body politic, whether they are physical, mental, or cultural. Historically, the states have been seeking to isolate, or in extreme cases to annihilate "the other," or to assimilate, integrate, or include him/her/them. In social sciences, there may be differing definitions[7] of these terms as both an analytical category and the category of practice in the past and today.[8] Further, the concepts of integration and inclusion have been historically used with differing understanding and implications by representatives of various social justice movements, be it civil rights, feminist, Roma, or disability rights movements, fighting for equitable access and representation.

Inclusive Education

The concept of inclusion originated in the field of education where it designated integration (also called mainstreaming) of the disabled and nondisabled children in regular classes.

Mainstreaming required education of the teachers and changes in physical and social space to make it accessible for children with disabilities and special needs. The term has become a buzzword over the past 25 years, while the previous history of parental activism in the West that paved the way for inclusion since the 1960s has been largely forgotten. These activists based their political demands on the concept of normalization, stating that disability

7 In an article summarizing the history of the concept and the related frameworks, Morgan Friedman also corroborates the lack of consensus on the meaning of inclusion even in the intradisciplinary usage. Morgan Friedman, "Inclusion: History, Models, and Why It Matters," in *Challenges to Integrating Diversity, Equity, and Inclusion Programs in Organizations*, ed. Aaron J. Griffen (IGI Global, 2020), 150.

8 The category of analysis refers to the theoretical analytical treatment of a category in scholarly thinking, while the category of practice refers to its usage in practice, that is in political, social life between various actors, today as well as in the past. An example of this would be how certain understandings, conceptions of other groups, and self-identifications play out in social relationships and can become a source of social conflict.

does not preclude individuals with disabilities from enjoying lives comparable to those without disabilities, and therefore they should be entitled to same opportunities and rights. Normalization is one of the first conceptual frameworks that regarded people with disabilities as equals to the nondisabled.[9] Inclusion is predicated on the same belief, but it is also thought to benefit nondisabled people: first, it teaches them to communicate with and learn about and from people with whom they have previously had minimal or zero contact, and second: it has been proven that accessible and inclusive solutions that work for people with a disability are likely to also work well for people in diverse circumstances. Importantly, inclusion as a critical framework makes us sensitive to ways in which dominant ideologies (such as ableism, racism, sexism) construct normalcy.

For the East-Central European context, it is relevant to bring up the concept of integration—a Czechoslovak approach to socialization of children with disabilities in the field of special education that was introduced following institutional reforms in the educational system in the early 1950s.[10] This methodology of care was linked with the Soviet science of defectology that regarded defectivity as a disruption to the physical and mental integrity of a person. In defectology, disability was understood in social terms, yet the approach to socialization was rooted in an ableist worldview: it was dependent on the level to which an individual could be made able. Integration referred to socialization of children with physical, mental, and intellectual disabilities and making them into useful socialist citizens, and as such represented the highest stage of socialization conditioned upon the lowest possible level of disability.[11]

9 Friedman, "Inclusion: History, Models, and Why It Matters," 150.

10 Jan Randák, "Defektní a přece socialističtí? O normalitě žáků zvláštních škol v počátcích československé komunistické diktatury [Defective but Still Socialist? On the Normality of Pupils in Special Schools at the Beginning of the Czechoslovak Communist Dictatorship]," *Historie – Otázky – Problémy* [History – Questions – Problems] (2018): 52.

11 Miloš Sovák, "Základní problémy defektologie [The Basic Problems in Defectology]," *Pedagogika* [The Review of Pedagogy] 14, no. 2 (1964): 199.

This term therefore does not implicate integration of disabled and nondisabled children in an educational environment, as the former were segregated in special educational institutions. Promoted as an expression of socialist humanism and emancipation of the people with disabilities, the institutional care was paternalist and forced upon its recipients. Integration was motivated both economically and ideologically: in accordance with the socialist premise that everyone should contribute to the construction of socialism, and that whoever does not work will not eat, the state attempted to prevent economic loss by making people socially useful. This effort to make use of any available human labor force was motivated by general labor shortage in the conditions of postwar reconstruction that was caused by a marked decline in population size in consequence of the massive loss of lives at war, and postwar and post-1948 emigration. Two decades later, integration has become a policy concept guiding a new approach of the state towards the Roma, replacing the policy of assimilation. In practice though, state agents, such as scientists, social workers, and state administrators, made no distinction between these concepts (using them interchangeably) while carrying out their efforts to assimilate the Romani population.

History is replete with examples demonstrating that concepts and practices developed within communities seeking access and social justice differ from those developed by people in positions of power who have no direct embodied or mediated experience (via close relationships) with exclusion and other forms of discrimination, and who are invested in controlling access to public goods and various forms of resources (material, financial, human, social, political).[12] As described in sociological and psychological literature, the problem lies in dichotomous thinking combined with the scarcity mindset that foster out-group animosity and drive competition instead of collaboration. This dichotomous mind, resulting from the illusion of separation, is fueled by fear for one's own survival. Therefore, approaches to "difference" based on "us vs them" mentality tend to minimize it by adapting "the other" into the world of the majority.[13] These approaches are safer—as they do not pose a threat to the hegemonic power; more comfortable, because they do not necessitate engagement and transformation of the whole society, and less time-, capital-, and labor-intensive. In contrast, solutions based on the ethics of care and justice require engagement and transformation of the whole society and realization that we are relational beings whose existence is made meaningful and sustained by complex webs of relationships with other beings, entities, and environments.

The practice of inclusion has been later expanded beyond disability to accommodate other types of social and cultural differences and interests and was reframed from a civil rights issue for students with disabilities to a pedagogical methodology that ensures diversity and facilitates the overall development of all.[14] Diversity has been understood not only in terms of equitable representation, but as a societal value per se: diversity is inherent in life, and learning to reconcile differences of whatever kind is beneficial to the whole.

12 An example would be a divergence in approaches to individuals with disabilities created by policymakers, scientists, and the members of disability rights movements. Medical and charity models of disability constructed by members of the out-group, i. e. people who do not have direct experience with disability, ground integration in the ableist worldview, conceiving disability as an essential feature of identity and deviance from the norm, which ultimately relies on the humanity and generosity of the "able-bodied." Due to ideological motives, these models fail to recognize the normative power and inherent injustice of ableism, a fundamental structuring framework of the majority of social systems in the Euro-American sphere, along with patriarchy, white supremacy, classism, and heteronormativity.

13 I am leaving out from this consideration the previously mentioned pathological impulses in the society to erase difference by violent means since my focus is on efforts by hegemonic actors to remedy exclusion and/or lessen out-group hatred.

14 Friedman, "Inclusion: History, Models, and Why It Matters," 150.

Diversity, Inclusion, Equality at Work

There were other fields that battled for equity, diversity, and inclusion besides education. Classes in power have historically dominated the organization of labor, creating a system that allowed them to retain their hegemonic status by controlling access to positions and exploiting the labor of those at the bottom of the social hierarchy.[15] In the preindustrial period, in a family manufacture or a farm, labor was often divided along gender lines. Since the emergence of the laboring class during the industrialization era, workforce had been predominantly white and male. Legislation and the capitalist system taking shape in the 18th century fostered racial and gender division in the workforce by attributing a second-class status to minority groups and impinging on their citizenship and human rights. Children, women, nonwhite workers, white Irish, Italian, and East European immigrants, and workers of Jewish origin comprising a low-wage workforce represented threat to the white workers who feared being replaced by cheap labor. As a result, race and gender played a role in hierarchizing the workforce and limiting the development of class-based solidarity among the working class as well as interracial labor organizing.[16]

Also in Europe, many companies had deep-rooted histories of discrimination, and some were even implicated in genocidal politics. For instance, in Italy and Germany during the 1930s, big business partnered with Mussolini and Hitler obtaining a monopoly on the market

15 The extreme cases of exploitation include slavery, serfdom, forced labor, and modern forms of slavery such as sex trafficking, bonded labor or debt bondage, and domestic servitude.

16 Martha R. Mahoney, "What's Left of Solidarity. Reflections on Law, Race, and Labor History," *Buffalo Law Review* 57 (2009): 1515–1518. The formal equalization of the Afro-American population, following the abolition of slavery and the constitutional guarantee of basic civil rights, was affectively neutralized by the advent of Jim Crow laws in the late nineteenth and early twentieth century in the Southern United States. This ethnically selective legislation enforcing racial segregation in the public sphere aimed at keeping the economic strategy of Southern planters as close to the old system as possible. Native Americans, Latino, and Asian populations were similarly disenfranchised and excluded in the society. However, these excluded groups organized their own unions since the late 1860s, and in 1867, the National Union for Cigar Makers was the first union to accept women and Black workers.

in return for capital loans, thereby helping consolidate their power. They later prospered even more from the industrialization of death and the development of war economy by helping to construct and supply the machinery of death and utilizing forced labor.

Diversity became a part of the US labor movement vocabulary during the mid-1960s, when it coalesced with the civil rights movement.[17] The implementation of the first workplace diversity initiatives followed soon after the adoption of the Civil Rights Act of 1964. This landmark civil rights legislation, which prohibited segregation in public places and banned employment discrimination on the basis of race, color, religion, sex, or national origin, is considered one of the crowning legislative achievements of these movements.[18] The concept of diversity in the context of employment built upon the previous workers' rights effort for fair and safe working conditions and rising minimal wage, but it extended the workers' agenda by focusing on equal employment opportunities for all and addressing the underlying structural racial and gender division in the society at large. In 1973, the concept of inclusion was introduced in the Rehabilitation Act, which became the first step towards inclusivity for individuals with disabilities. In 1982, the private NYC-based newspaper, the Village Voice, granted domestic partner benefits for LGBTQ+ workers and since the second part of the 1980s, the issue of sexual harassment as a form of sexual discrimination has become a subject of working place policies in the USA and other countries.[19] Despite the historical heroic efforts and achievements of the activists and workers worldwide, inequalities based on gender, race/ethnicity, sexual orientation, disability, cultural, and other ascribed attributes continue to exist in the sphere of employment, housing, and a variety of other social domains.

17 The movements converged upon a shared understanding that there could be no civic freedom without economic security.

18 Joni Hersch and Jennifer Bennett Shinall, "Fifty Years Later: The Legacy of the Civil Rights Act of 1964," *Journal of Policy Analysis and Management* 34, no. 2 (2015): 424–456.

19 John Wills, "The Evolution of Diversity in the Workplace," *The StratX ExL*, Aug 30, 2023. Available at: https://www.stratx-exl.com/industry-insights/the-evolution-of-diversity-in-the-workplace.

Diversity, Inclusion, Equality in Visual Art

Social justice in the context of art became a concern for the Afro-American population already in the late 19th century. As mentioned earlier, the antiabolitionists specifically, but white people in general had had a hard time to accept black people's freedom and imagine them in any role other than slaves. In response, the press and public space became flooded with images of black people as subhuman and in subservient roles. Also, blackface minstrelsy became a popular form of entertainment for the white public. The proliferation of these images trafficking in harmful stereotypes, seeking to keep black people in perpetual servitude, made it painstakingly clear that access to the means of representation was an important part of the struggle for equal rights and social recognition. The reclaiming of one's image and subverting the white gaze in the field of photography expanded during the 1930s to the field of visual arts, as it gave the people a wider range of possibilities to address and heal from traumatic experiences of their own and their ancestors.[20] Upon the formation of the Afro-American Black Art Movement in the 1960s, black art became established as an identity art category.[21] The movement was part of Black Power, applying the political ideas to art and literature, also serving as a visual and publication channel for the political movement.[22]

Similar struggle against sexism in the art world was taken up by feminist visual artists since the 1970s. Building upon two decades of activism and critical scholarship produced within counterculture,

20 Elizabeth C. Hamilton, "African American Art and Social Justice," *Smart History. The Center for Public Art History.* Available at: https://smarthistory.org/reframing-art-history/african-american-art-social-justice/.

21 Black art was also a widely used category in the late 1970s and 1980s referring to artwork of British people of South Asian, African, or African-Caribbean descent. As the term was an externally ascribed collective labeling, its legitimacy has been recently disputed and its meaning reframed as a category of experience rather than identity. Rina Arya, "Rethinking Black Art as a Category of Experience," *Visual Culture in Britain* 18, no. 2 (2017): 163–75. doi:10.1080/14714787.2017.1328986.

22 Larry Neal, "The Black Arts Movement," *The Drama Review* 12, no. 4 (Summer 1968): 29.

feminist, labor, and civil rights movements, the feminists voiced critiques and advanced their perspectives via art, writing, and cultural organizing. They pushed back against the romantic notion of the art world as a heaven of freedom.[23] This romantic legacy persisted in the myth of the liberatory potential of art that can be unlocked by the exceptional talent of an individual (white male) artist. Within feminist social criticism, the myth was exposed as a legitimization of male dominance and the art system was depicted as a structure of exclusion. Women artists highlighted the disparity in opportunities for women to pursue artistic careers as well as the structural barriers and gendered norms that further constrained their choices.[24] They also brought out the disproportionality of the representation of art by women in exhibitions and collections. Another major socioeconomic and political issue was their objectification in art and simultaneous undermining of their agency as subjects by range of gendered restraints, from trivialization to violence. Women artists faced a delegitimization of their subjective experiences in art and erasure of their contribution as innovators and trendsetters by the art world establishment. They did not content themselves with critiquing the status quo though, but ventured into building institutional structure for women-centered art making, exhibiting, research and publishing, and cultural organizing.[25]

Building upon gender analysis, later criticisms expanded to encompass additional factors such as color, disability, sexuality, and class that were theorized by Kimberlé Crenshaw in her 1991 seminal article *Mapping the Margins*[26] as interlocking systems with distinctive power dynamics. The inequalities that exist in society

23 In the 18th century, freedom signified autonomous functioning of the artists without subordination to the state or church.

24 The gatekeeping was predicated on the concept of genius, which was believed to be predominantly present in men and rarely found in women. Women were effectively hindered from actively participating in the arts and culture due to the patriarchal system, which imposed on them the role of primary caregivers, resulting in a double burden.

25 Jill Fields, "Frontiers in Feminist Art History," *Frontiers: A Journal of Women Studies* 33, no. 2 (2012): 2.

26 Crenshaw, Kimberlé. "Mapping the Margins: Intersectionality, Identity Politics, and Violence against Women of Color." *Stanford Law Review* 43, no. 6 (1991): 1241–99.

came consequently to be viewed through the lens of the intersectional theory, which is a prominent framework for inclusive practice. Intersectionality sensitized the practitioners towards the negative implications of reducing a multifaceted and fluid personhood to a single identity aspect and made them prioritize the person-first approach (as opposed to identity-first approach), unless requested otherwise by the participant/recipient.

Analogical struggles for access and recognition were taken up by other oppressed groups: artists of Latino descent, First Nations peoples, Roma people, and others, who started by establishing their own institutional structures of support, but simultaneously strived for becoming part of majority institutional structures, helping to transform them into a more just and inclusive environment for all.

A Short History of Sustainability

Sustainability is nowadays used in various contexts, including the cultural sector, but its origin is linked to the concerns with environmental sustainability and economic development and the formation of the field of sustainability science in the early 1970s. In the 1980s, the term sustainable development was coined and started gaining currency in both academia and in policy making at all levels, particularly since 1987 when the World Commission on Environment and Development released its report promoting this approach. The report defined sustainable development as development that "meets the needs of the present without compromising the ability of future generations to meet their own needs" and states that "the concept of sustainable development does imply limits—not absolute limits but limitations imposed by the present state of technology and social organization on environmental resources and by the ability of the biosphere to absorb the effects of human activities. But technology and social organization can be both managed and improved to make way for a new era of economic growth."[27] In the 1980s, the idea of development in the concept of sustainable development had not yet been problematized. In contemporary discourse, sustainability has expanded to encompass not only the economy and the environment, but also the societal dimension. This entailed theorization of models of sustainable social organizing on the one hand, and incorporating social aspects into environmental and economic policies on the other.[28] The practice of compartmentalization, symptomatic of modern societies, has been supplanted by holistic approaches and interdisciplinary methods.

The proliferation of the criticism and heated debates around sustainability and sustainable development can be attributed to the vagueness and openness of the concepts, as well as the diverse range of interest groups with differing agendas. The 1972 seminal publication *The Limits to Growth*, presenting simulations of the global system's behavior modes over the next 200 years, with population growth and industrial pollution being key determining factors in a future collapse, problematized the idea of endless growth in connection with the Malthusian concern with overpopulation and overconsumption. Importantly, the term sustainable development is also applied to ongoing development projects in the Global South, which are closely connected to the ideology and agenda of developmental aid projects by Western nations, today criticized as a form of neocolonial domination. Another criticism pointed out that for societies on the verge of self-destruction, sustainability is no longer a viable framework for meaningful change. While sustainable development has been associated with the human-centered approach of shallow ecology, deep ecology overcomes the anthropocentric focus and centers

27 Philip M. Fearnside, "Sustainable Development," in *Oxford Bibliographies in Ecology*, ed. David Gibson (New York: Oxford University Press, 2019), 1.
28 An example may be an impact of economic or environmental policy on local Indigenous communities.

on degrowth, calls for multispecies justice and solidarity, and looks for forms of human and more-than-human togetherness.[29]

Environmental sustainability in the context of art institutions refers to the implementation of measures to reduce carbon emissions and energy consumption in the operation of the institution, production processes, and artistic practices. Social sustainability aims at viability of relationships, which depends on care (time and attention) and sustainable funding. Although there is disagreement about the term, we consider it to be an essential framework for our daily operations and future planning, as we face constraints in our energy, time, and financial resources.

Caring from the Inside Out: Our Vision for Contemporary Art Institutions

"No Man Is an Island," says the title of a 1970s socially critical novel by Johannes Mario Simmel that is concerned with institutional care of disabled children. Analogically, no art institution exists in isolation, but is embedded in diverse webs of relations with its environment, funders and stakeholders, collaborators and partners, artists, public, and alternatively other types of service recipients. Also internally, the institutions are formed by people in distinct positions and roles that together make the institutions alive and productive. In order to sustain the relationships and the life of the institution, these relationships need to be taken care of. Islands of Kinship is a joint project of institutions brought together by a shared interest in becoming a caring institution and applying the principles of inclusion and sustainability into our services, programming, and internal operations. This partner network realizes the projects, but simultaneously represents a larger ecosystem of care which provides resources for our individual

29 In public debates, deep and shallow approaches tend to be polarized, nonetheless, some scholars consider them rather as part of a continuum of perspectives on the environment that emerged from a long-standing critique of Western development. Merle Jacob, "Sustainable Development and Deep Ecology: An Analysis of Competing Traditions," Environmental Management 18, no. 4 (July 1994): 477.

institutional and personal development and transformation. During this two-year period, we have experienced first-hand how important it is to parallelly provide care internally, how we thrive and learn from each other when we care to talk and listen to each other in a specific set up that enables us to participate as holistic beings, not just as persons in professional roles.

The same ethics of care underlies our relationships with collaborators, audiences, and artists. We believe that inclusion and sustainable approaches form a strong foundation for building a caring institution that fosters equity, nurtures diversity, and contributes to social justice. Much care, though, needs to be invested into the relationships with groups that have been experiencing oppression and discrimination in our societies, and in consequence have been deprived of their right to culture. Seeking redress of the past and current injustice needs to take into account the socioeconomic effects of the oppression that keeps people in poverty and in the positions of powerlessness and dependency, but also inflicts trauma that negatively affects the social and mental well-being of the excluded people. In consequence, we need to build trust and awaken interest in target groups, as our institutions are seen as part of this system of exclusion, which in fact they are.

The institutional structures of the art system reflect the identities, needs, and agendas of a narrow segment of society that have had the greatest shares of power to shape it, that is predominantly white, educated, able-bodied men. As a result, these structures had been, and in most cases continue to be, inaccessible physically and socially to groups that have special access needs, such as disabled or elderly people, or who have been historically excluded on different grounds. An analogical situation exists in the present-day art institutions: there is a great asymmetry of power and resources between the people who occupy positions in the institutions and the ones we aim to attract. Inclusion and accessibility therefore require not only adjustments and transformation of the material aspects of the spaces, but also bridging social and cultural capitals to make art spaces more welcoming and appealing to groups that have been historically disadvantaged, marginalized, and disempowered. The bridging entails building sustainable relationships, learning from each other, and importantly also sharing resources to enable people to reclaim their power and decide their way of engagement with our institution.

Also, accessibility requires rethinking. It shouldn't stop at introducing practices that make content, service, and spaces accessible to a selected disabled or unprivileged audience. Rather, it should be integrated as one of the core ethical and political commitments in all areas of institutional operation and simultaneously as a critical framework assisting organizations in identifying and eliminating ableism and exclusion. As the majority of artwork in art spaces around the world is created with able-bodied patrons in mind, it is also hoped that artists, curators, and other art professionals will commit to and develop access-centered art practice and will start to consider and integrate accessibility features within the foundation of their artwork and creative practice, instead of adding them at the end. It is high time to unlearn visual primacy and prioritizing options that promote ableist concepts of normalcy.

Contemporary art institutions carry great potential for affecting social change. It is therefore vital for them to be visible and engage diverse audiences. To this effect, public programming emerges as a critical function to promote topics that have both local and global importance and relevancy. Furthermore, art spaces are increasingly serving as a kind of social spaces, where alternative practices that are transferable across different contexts can be developed and tested, and where discussions about what ethics and politics are required to eliminate societal disparities and conflicts as well as untenable human exceptionalism can take place.

This paper (Lux Cream, 90 g/m²) was
used from surplus stock normally destined for
disposal. Manufactured in Inkeroinen, Finland.

01

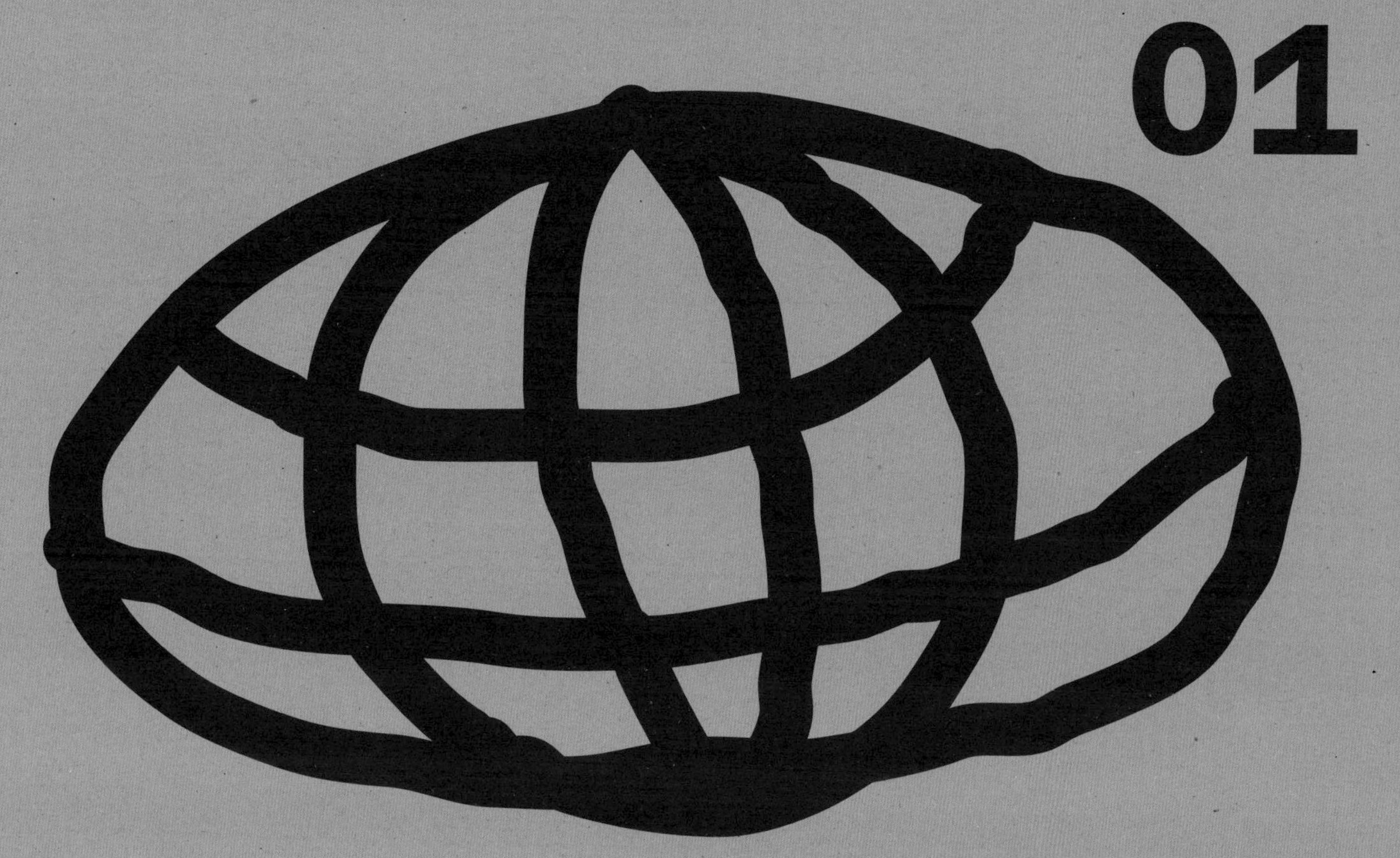

New Agora

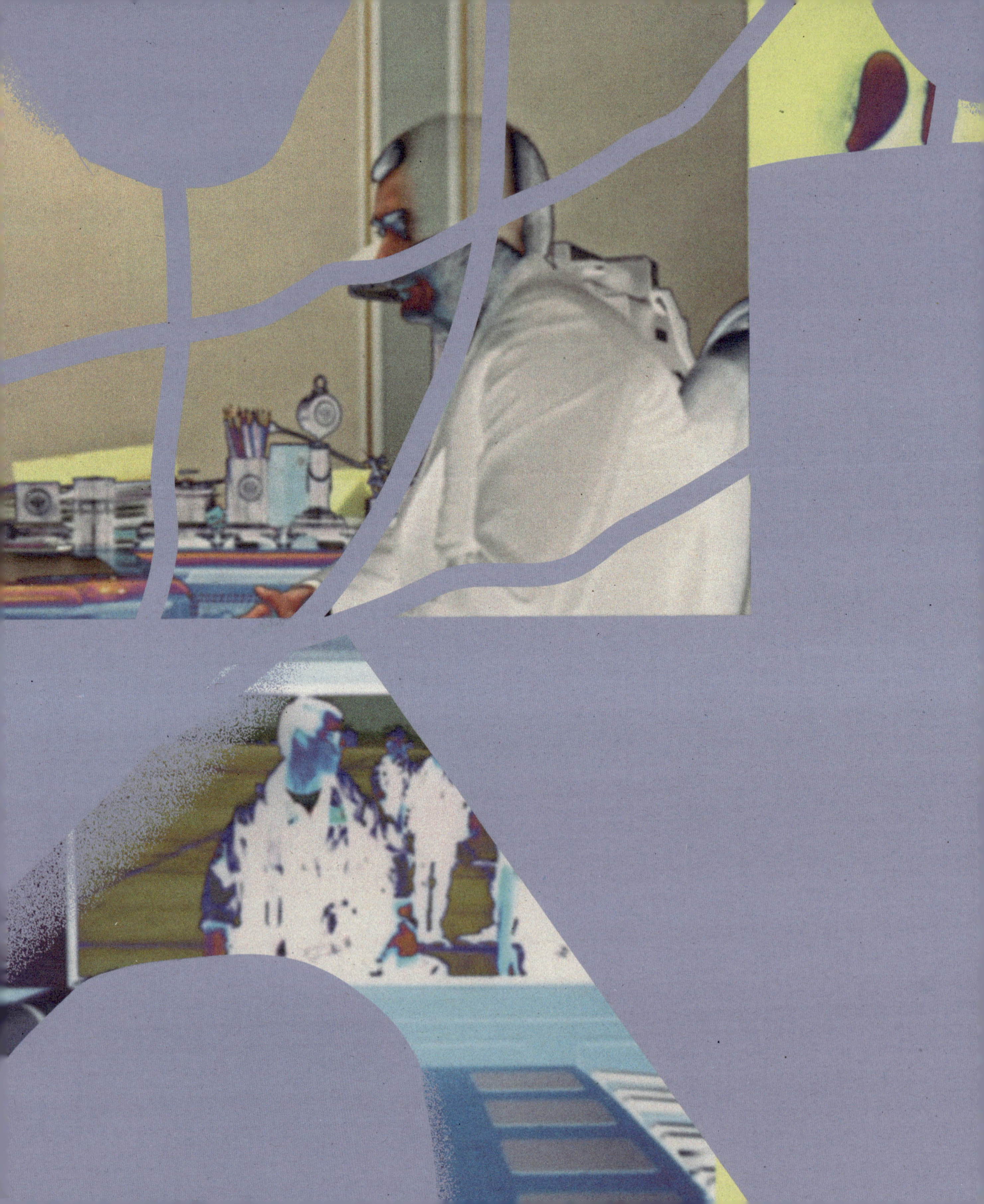

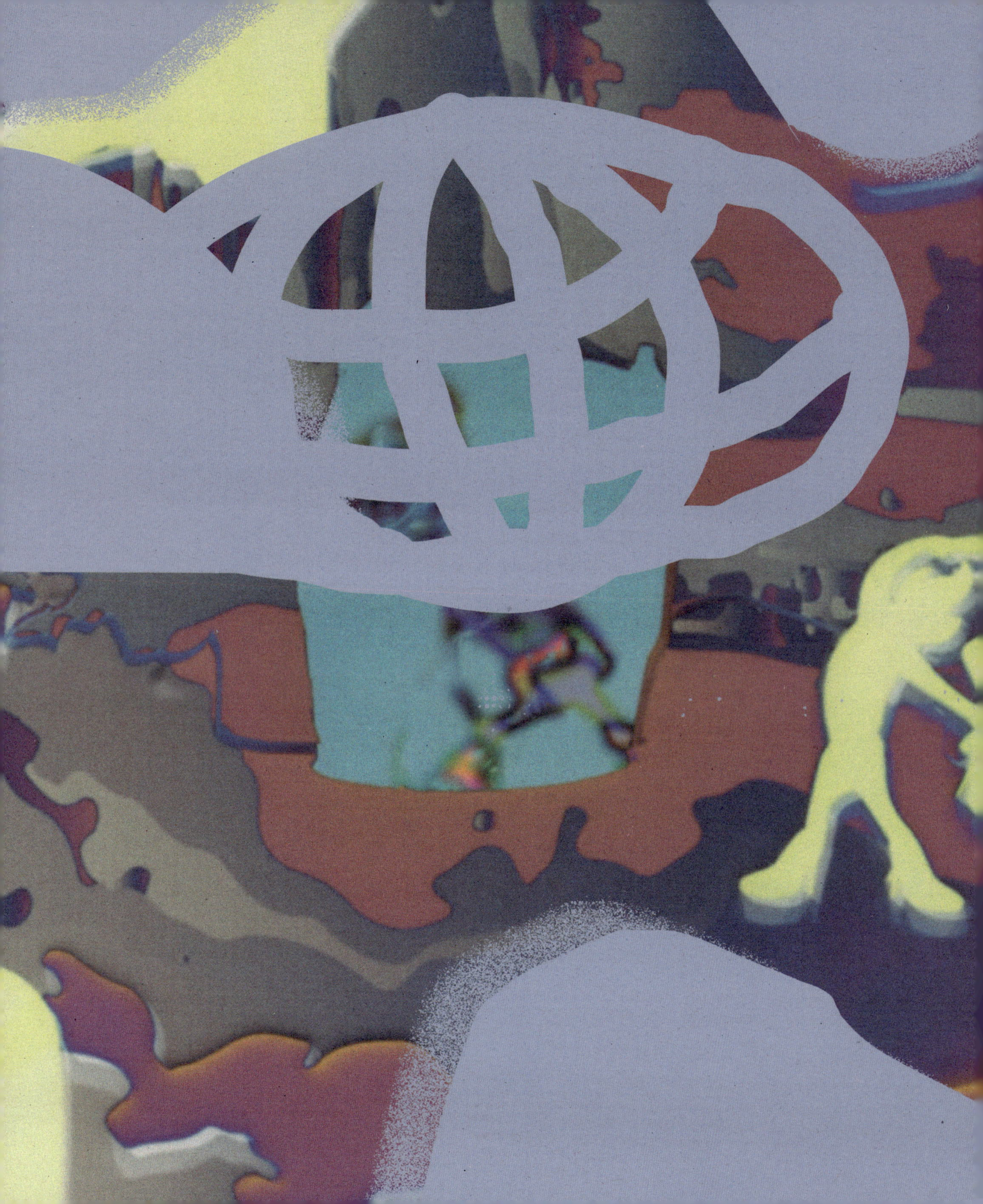

The basic goal of this program line is to treat various social phenomena primarily related to the right to use public space through education, research, and production of contemporary art. It explores especially its relation to the needs and involvement of citizens and local communities. It highlights and questions notions such as the right to

public space and public domain, free speech, access to (dis)information, and propagandist tools, generally critically reviews current socio-economic systems, and imagines emancipatory scenarios. The program line also focuses on the rights of cultural workers and analyzes the conditions under which contemporary art and culture can be produced today.

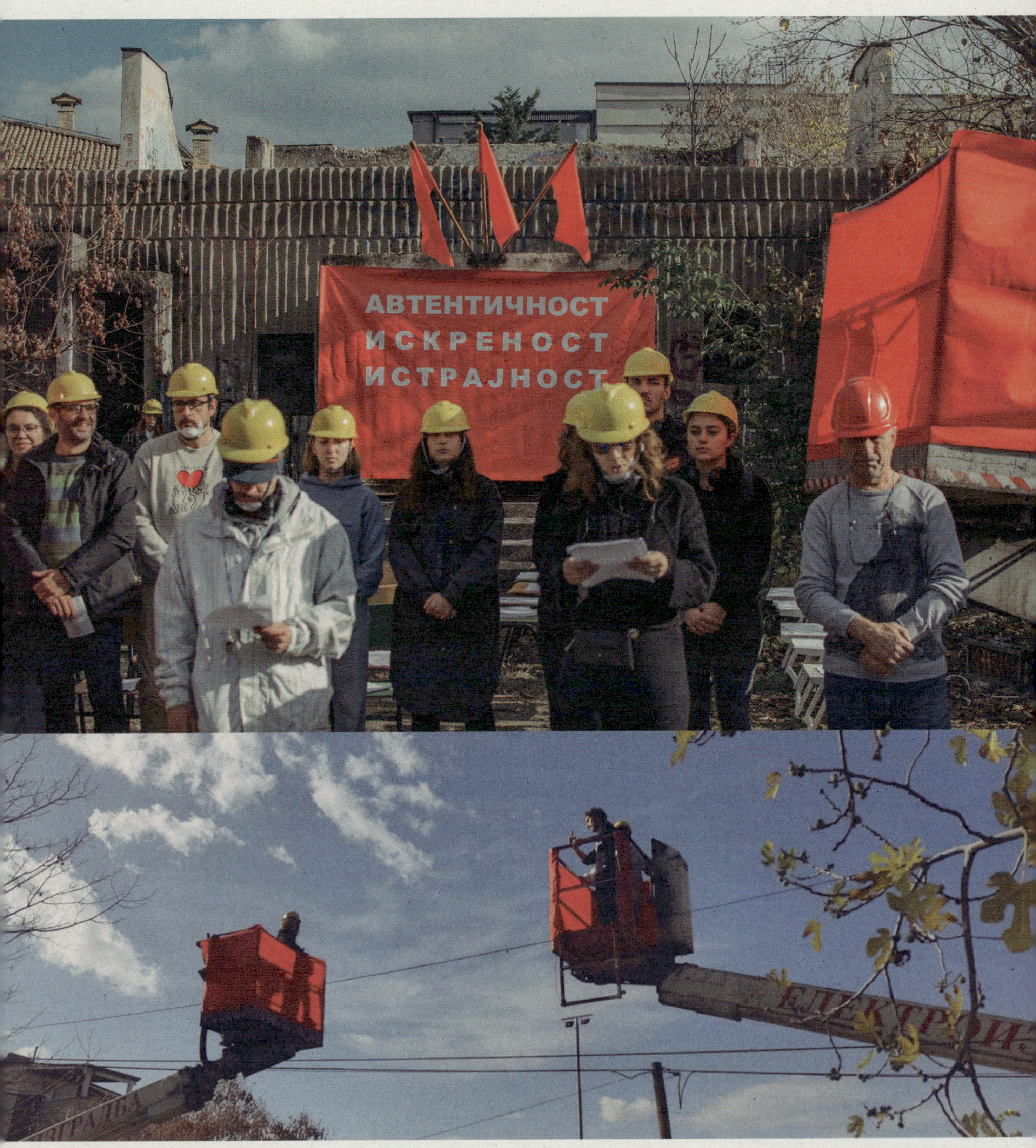
АВТЕНТИЧНОСТ
ИСКРЕНОСТ
ИСТРАЈНОСТ

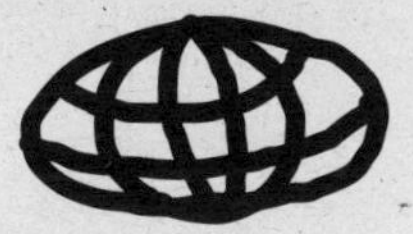

Reimagining the Agora through Counter-hegemonic Art Practices[1]

Ivana Vaseva

Public Space and Public Sphere

The public (urban) space is no longer an agora.

The public sphere is no longer a polis.

If the widespread notion of public space signifies a place of antagonisms, exclusions, and revolutions, resulting from various alliances between the state, the market, and the civil society, then public space in capitalist societies is increasingly a platform of dominance and control guided by profit-oriented strong ties between businesses and the state. The civil society in most cases is excluded or silenced, and the neoliberal urban restructuring depoliticizes, redacts, and enclosures the public space and excludes and passivizes the public sphere. In post-political conditions, the neoliberalization of public space transforms it from a place of political engagement and social interaction towards a space of spectacle that sustains consensus and creates an arena void of political deliberation and negotiation by passive consumers, usually swallowing nationalist content and rise of moral values.[2]

This process of narrowing the public by the continuous urban growth of cities in global capitalism thus leaves serious impacts on the social, political, cultural, and environmental levels and creates nondemocratic regulations and actions towards various material reconceptualizations of the public space as a demonstration of politics of power (Lefebvre, Harvey) as well as depolitization of the public sphere (Habermas, Arendt, Mouffe).

1 A variation of this text was initially written for the research Contemporary (Non)democracies made for the 16th AKTO Festival for Contemporary Arts in 2021 concentrating on one specific case—the Macedonia Square in Skopje, its almost complete privatization of the public space, and the overall research aim to stimulate the argumented debate to return to its rightful place. It was manifested through a series of posters displayed on the facade of the Municipality Center's meeting hall. Photos here: https://www.facebook.com/media/set/?set=a.4695869927100408&type=3. It later triggered the exhibition *Precarity Has a Chance: Public Spaces in Movement (Toward)* in 2023 in Gallery Structura Sofia. More at https://www.dropbox.com/s/9amehlpt0xfqjdd/%21%20KATALOG%20SOFIJA-18c.pdf?dl=0.

2 In this text, I leave aside ideas about common spaces as opposite to the public and private ones. According to Greek architect Stavros Stavrides, public spaces are always regulated and under control and supervision as opposed to common spaces or the ones that emerge in constant confrontation with state-controlled "authorized" public space. Stavros Stavrides, *Common Space: The City as Commons* (London: Zed Books, 2016).

Intro

Agoras and polises are part of our long-maintained collective imagery, of free and open physical space, accessible equally for everyone, however, more careful scrutiny reveals that there were always those rightless, unequal, and excluded from the privileged social class instead of being able to participate in democratic governance. It seems that true democracy was far more limited and smaller-numbered than imagined.

The international EU-funded project Islands of Kinship: A Collective Manual for Sustainable and Inclusive Art Institutions and especially its specifically focused program New Agora addressed art projects that confront the current politics of power aimed at reduction, control, and design of public space, and tend to spatialize emancipatory practices either in public space or in public institutions and repoliticize the public sphere. New Agora is a collaboration of small institutions in Skopje (Faculty of things that can't be learned—FRU), Prague (Jindřich Chalupecký Society), Helsinki (Frame Finland), and Riga (LCCA Riga) that envisioned education, research, and production of contemporary art.

This text is a small contribution to this specially designed chapter of the constellation of organizations across Europe and it advocates for artistic practices that try to disrupt the dominant consensus of power through emancipatory artistic strategies opening up temporary politicized democratic public spaces and discourse. It starts with the Skopje case study, or the infamous project Skopje 2014, as a grand initiative to spatialize the state-imposed narrative of mythical origins through building a new city representation[3] and strolls in different cities such as Ostrava, Riga, and Bratislava, displaying several art projects as potential efforts into reimagining and revitalization of the public sphere.

3 The Skopje 2014 project made a spatial restructuring of the physical city with a revamping of the public sphere. The public space loses its political function and the narrowing of the public space also narrows the public sphere. Both are drastically changed and a critical and argumented debate transfers to a highly antagonized and polarized voicing of opinions, etiquetting, and political parties' mishmashes in all segments: ideas, media, institutions, and (art) practices.

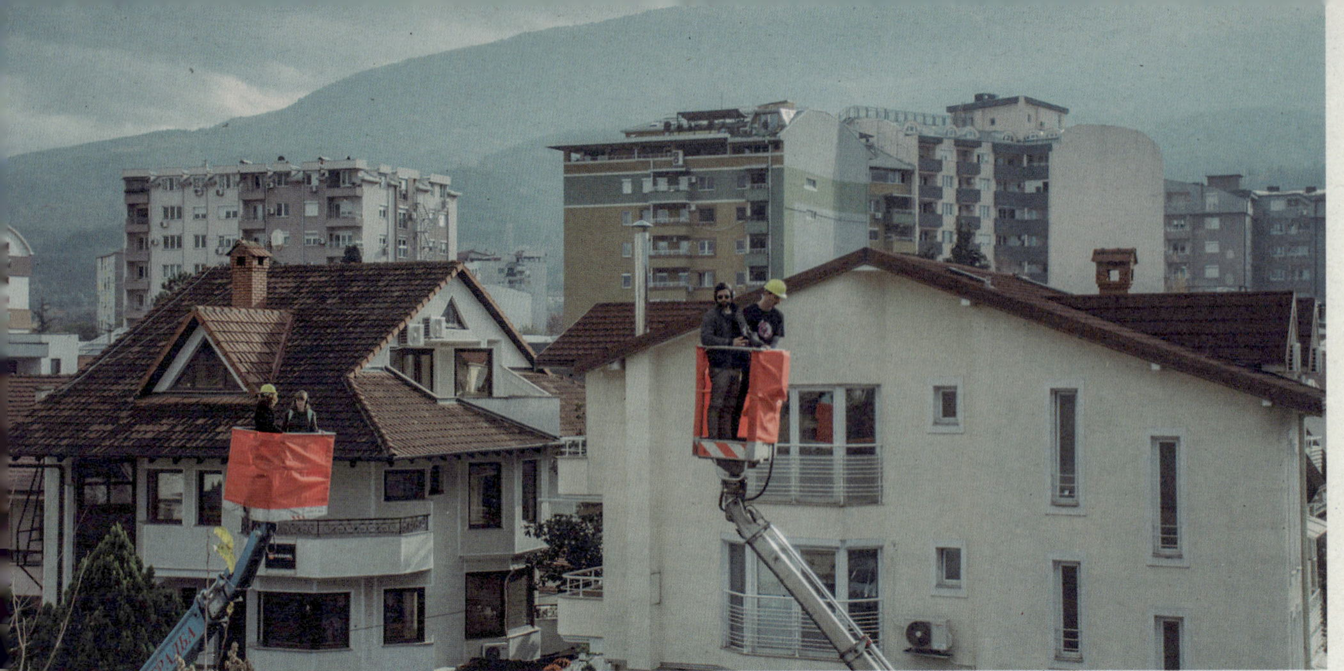

Filip Jovanovski: City as a Stage: Lost (Modernist) Utopias, Former local community center, Tavtalidze (building Domche), 2022

But firstly, what are the reasons for the destruction of the public space and how does that influence the public sphere? Why is this disappearance of public space important to democratic politics?

It is said that without public and open space for expression of public opinion, there is no public life. Or that the respatialization of the public sphere brings an opportunity for a more complete understanding and repolitization of the public sphere. As geographer Neil Smith and environmental psychology professor Setha Low wrote, investigating the means of making and remaking public space provides a unique window on the politics of the public sphere, suggesting an even more powerful imperative to the focus on public space.[4] The questions that arise from this are: How to regain and repoliticize the public sphere? How to democratize it and how to imagine different future through the reconquest of the public in the space? And what kind of art practices can help in that emancipatory endeavor? What kind of practices can subvert the existing hegemony and provide an equal ground for all the voices to take the stage and be articulated?

4 "Introduction: The Imperative of Public Space," in *The Politics of Public Space*, eds. Neil Smith and Setha Low (New York: Routledge, 2006), 7.

The public space has long been a contested notion. Philosopher and sociologist Henri Lefebvre reflected on the production of space as a result of the complex relationships and geometries of power and as a means of generalized reproduction and control. In his book *The Production of Space*, he writes that space is a complex social construction and "every society—and hence every mode of production with its subvariants (i.e. all those societies which exemplify the general concept) produces a space, its own space."[5] In that sense, societies with their spatial production essentialize their power politics, as "space is not only political but space is politics as well" and "space is not a scientific object removed from ideology or politics; it has always been political and strategic."[6] The political rhetoric being deployed spatially signifies constructing the "message" in real terms and in the public space and with that materializing of an agenda of regulation and distribution of certain aspirations. It is also important that the civil society plays a role in these entanglements, opposing the control and pushing forward the civil participation in the creation of public space, and aspiring to create a space to voice those that were shut down from the public sphere. Urban geography scholar David Harvey writes that the shaping of urban public space might influence politics in the public sphere and the right to the city as conceptualized by Lefebvre is central to global capitalist circulation. It is of utmost importance not only in the sense of having a right to inhabit the city, but also in the sense of having a role to play in giving it form. To achieve that, he writes, we need a vigorous anticapitalist movement capable of radically transforming daily life: "Only when politics focuses on the production and reproduction of urban life as the central labor process out of which revolutionary impulses arise will it be possible to mobilize anticapitalist struggles capable of radically transforming daily life. Only when it is understood that those who build and sustain urban life have a primary claim to that which they

5 Henri Lefebvre, *The Production of Space,* English translation by Donald Nicholson-Smith (Oxford, UK, and Cambridge, US: Blackwell, 1991), 31.

6 Henri Lefebvre, "Reflections on the Politics of Space," *Antipode* 8, no. 2 (1970): 33.

have produced, and that one of their claims is to the unalienated right to make a city more after their own heart's desire, will we arrive at a politics of the urban that will make sense."[7]

Considering the process of revitalization of the public sphere, on the other hand, political theorist Chantal Mouffe argues that public space is created through the constant negotiation and renegotiation of different points of view, and because of this, consensus cannot be the ideal. As opposed to the ideas of philosopher and social theorist Jürgen Habermas and political philosopher Hannah Arendt, who talk about a consensual model of the public sphere or public realm, Mouffe wrote in the agonistic model that public space is the battleground where different hegemonic projects are confronted without any possibility of final reconciliation[8] and "when conflict is not given the possibility of having legitimate channels of expression, it takes the form of violent antagonism, and this is something that we should try to prevent."[9] This is quite different from the opinion of Arendt who envisages the political space as a space of freedom and public deliberation, and the public space, like Habermas, as a space of consensus. Arendt writes: "Freedom could exist only in public; it was a tangible, worldly reality, something created by men to be enjoyed by men rather than a gift or capacity. It was the man-made public space or market-place which antiquity had known as the area where freedom appears and becomes visible to all."[10] Or, as Habermas notes, the formation of political compromises would have to be legitimated by reference to this process.[11]

7 David Harvey, "Preface: Henri Lefebvre's Vision" in *Rebel Cities from the Right to the City to the Urban Revolution* (London: Verso, 2012), 16.

8 Chantal Mouffe, "Art and Democracy Art as an Agnostic Intervention in Public Space," *Open: Art as a Public Issue,* no. 14 (2008): 10.

9 Chantal Mouffe, "Which Public Space for Critical Artistic Practices?", in *Cork Caucus: On Art, Possibility & Democracy,* ed. T. Joyce (Berlin: Revolver Publishing, 2005), 171.

10 Hannah Arendt, *On Revolution* (London: Penguin Books, 1990), 124.

11 Jurgen Habermas, *The Structural Transformation of the Public Sphere: An Inquiry into the Category of Bourgeois Society,* translated by Thomas Burger with the assistance of Frederick Lawrence (Cambridge, Massachusets: MIT Press, 1989), 232.

Counterhegemonic Narratives / Different Politics of Public Space

The contextual and critical approach of an artistic practice, beyond the purely auto-expressionist approach, is a step outside of its long-practiced autonomous social position that neutralizes and passivizes its own political potentiality. In the past but still present today, artistic autonomy is regarded as encouragement of expression of the author's personal world and research solely in artistic means as the only reason for artistic creation unburdened by its social meaning. However, the contextual and critical approach, as a reaction, intervention to, or an engagement with a certain sociopolitical context or a physical location, provides an opportunity to create new contexts, semipublic or public, or specific structures (political, sociological, artistic), elevating its heteronomous position beyond the autonomous one, according to which the work of art becomes a place for political action or social criticism.

This kind of contextual and critical endeavors signifies an intervention in reality, or as art historian and critic Claire Bishop said, is using intervention as an artistic strategy, defining it as a self-initiated and disruptive gesture in the public sphere[12] in which temporal public spaces are opened, contesting the dominant politics of power, being in constant conflict with exclusionary tendencies. This kind of art gestures detects problems and weaknesses in a given context, raises questions in terms of what should be done, and makes a proposal on how to react in order to transform. And through such struggle, usually done collaboratively and durationally, the public sphere can be recreated. For this kind of works, on the one hand, the context is not an invisible background but affects what the work wants to express, which is a critical reflection on what happens to it, in the broadest sense of the word, and on the other hand, creates its meaning as an active agent of the work itself.

12 Claire Bishop offers a historical and theoretical analysis of the "intervention" as a self-initiated artistic strategy that uses political timing, site specificity, and disruption, and has radical agency. See https://www.youtube.com/watch?v=m6DD3TOhoVI.

In various proportions, these works try to show the reasons and the ways of usurpation of the public space, as well as to offer artistic strategies for its reconquest.

Through such practices, the public space can take on the meaning of what art reveals and transform its current alienation, and, in a way, reappropriate the meaning of public space through practice. Namely, repoliticizing the public space through artistic and critical practices that try to disrupt what capitalism and the state apparatus are trying to push forward, through a public presentation of their repressive character, which would further perhaps lead to a construction of new subjectivities. Or, from Chantal Mouffe's point of view, "critical art is art that foments dissensus, that makes visible what the dominant consensus tends to obscure and obliterate. It is constituted by a manifold of artistic practices aiming at giving a voice to all those who are silenced within the framework of the existing hegemony."[13] According to Mouffe, power relations and hegemonic discourses will always exist, but they can be challenged by counterhegemonic practices, i.e., practices that will attempt to disarticulate the existing order so as to install another form of hegemony.

In such a context, if we look at the works between their critical intervention that aims to make a breakthrough to the dominant hegemony and works that display such potential, then we can distinguish two types of practices—those that directly, procedurally, and performatively enter the contested territory and affect it, thereby opening countless questions breaking through the concrete sociopolitical moment, and practices that use creative artistic solutions to express their revolt against what is placed by that same social-political moment. In both cases, they are an important response to such reality, microrevolutions, and bring the potential for its reconquest, and the constant presence, contestation, and discourse of a living and a lived public space is essential for the democratic process.

13 Chantal Mouffe, "Art as an Agnostic Intervention in Public Space," *Open/No. 14 / Art as a Public Issue* (Nai Publishers, SKOR, 2008), 12, https://monoskop.org/images/1/15/Open_14_Art_as_a_Public_Issue.pdf.

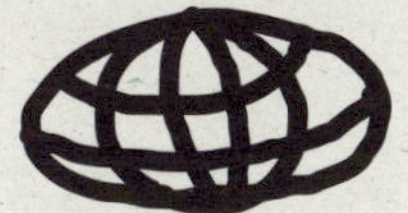

New Agora—Islands of Kinship

If the agonistic approach is particularly suited to grasp the nature of the new forms of artistic activism that have emerged in the past decades and that, in a great variety of ways, aim at challenging the existing consensus, then in this context I would like to mention several projects, like the new commission *Propaganda Station* by Dutch artist Jonas Staal, the process-based performative project *City as a Stage: Lost (Modernist) Utopias* by Macedonian artist Filip Jovanovski, the project *Of Yous* by Luki Essender, and the group exhibition *Which Side Are You On? On the Non-Aligned Decolonial Constellation*, a collaboration between FRU and Moderna galerija, Ljubljana.

Jonas Staal's practice deals with the relation between art, democracy, and propaganda and is mostly focused on stimulating temporary public spheres in a constructed setting in different venues (theaters, museums, galleries, but it can work in any public space)

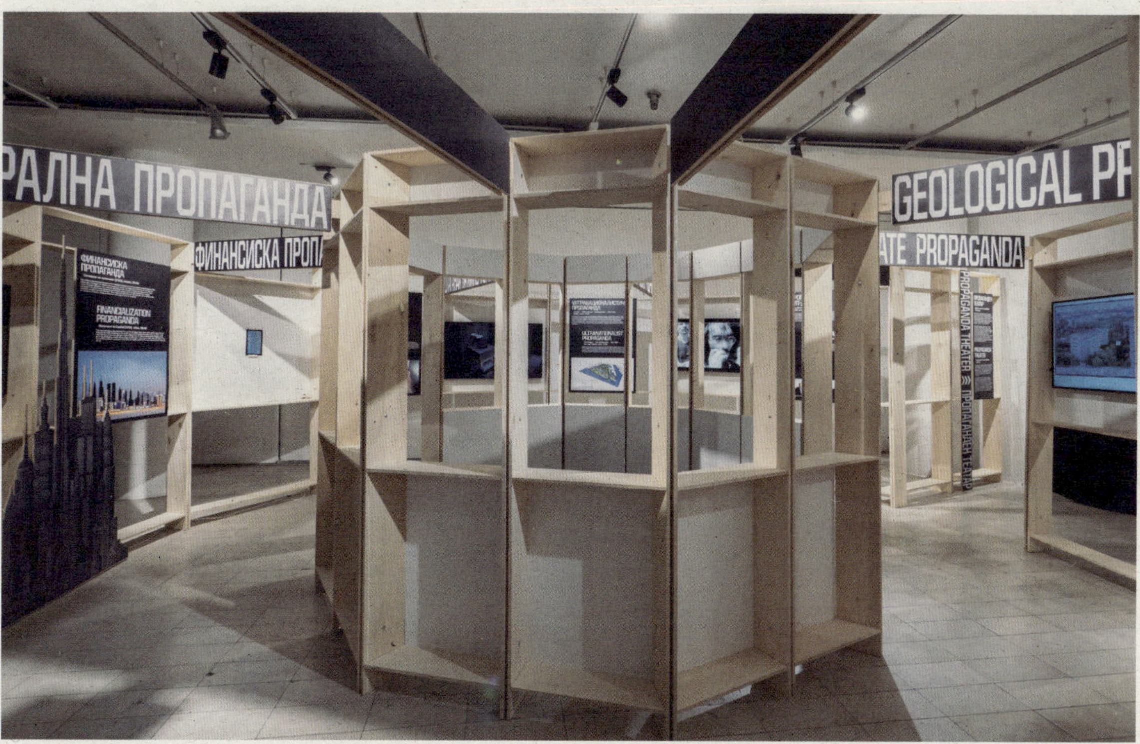

Jonas Staal: Propaganda Station,
Museum of Contemporary Art in Skopje, 2024

in voicing up stateless people and promoting stateless democracy as an option in this apocalyptic world. His endeavor is to foster emancipatory organizational structures through a specific model of assemblism. His work in the case of the New Agora segment is a new art commission titled *Propaganda Station* which gathers ten years of his propaganda research and propaganda work in a new installation and live program.

Propaganda Station researches and makes visible the role of art and culture in dominant forms of contemporary propaganda in shaping our world, on the one hand, while exploring the possibility of emancipatory forms of propaganda on the other. The project manifests as a spatial network of cells, each cell representing a different kind of propaganda—alt-right propaganda, financialization propaganda, climate propaganda—organized around the largest central cell which operates as a Propaganda School, a station for research and transmission. In this central cell, artists, academics, activists, and campaigners gather to engage in propaganda research, and explore the potentiality of emancipatory propaganda work.

Its intention is also to travel to other localities to continuously expand our understanding of the role of propaganda art—and propaganda art practice—today. This work was presented in November 2023 in PLATO in Ostrava, in March 2024 in the Museum of Contemporary Art in Skopje, in 2024 in the Museum of Contemporary Art in Zagreb, in different forms in Riga (film screening as part of the festival Survival Kit in 2023), and in Bratislava.

Filip Jovanovski creates temporary public spaces in public buildings, usually as places of confrontation between the political party, the local municipality, the businesses, and the citizens, by using the method of “reading buildings.” The intention of the various projects (in modernist buildings like City Trade Center, Railway Residential Building, The Macedonian Post Office, The Universal Hall) is to preserve the memory and heritage of architecture by alternative means and to propose common collective futures through collaborative and interdisciplinary art endeavors. In the framework of Islands of Kinship, he started his newest multiphased and durational project *City as a Stage: Lost (Modernist) Utopias* which in that stage was in collaboration with architect Miodrag Kuc and students from the Faculty of Architecture and Faculty of Drama Arts in Skopje in collaboration with the local community in Tavtalidze. It concentrated on Domche, an object/sculpture/monument with clean and clear abstract forms, cast in concrete, immersed in the community of Taftalidze. In Skopje, concrete was an expression of optimism, light, freedom of expression of the city of solidarity that had yet to be built. Today, this building is privatized and, in a sense, occupied by a political party claiming that it was the right inheritor from the former social system. The text for the performative installation was in the form of twelve stories entitled *Domche: Perhaps the Smallest Brutalist Building in the World*. The stories are written through a research process, work meetings, workshops as well as the use of archives, libraries, video and audio interviews with users of the space, conversations, archival private videos, and photos of citizens who were part of life in Domche.

Through the methodology of reading buildings, by involvement of the community and experts from different fields, and by using stage means, the project transforms the public space into a stage on which the problems of the community are "performed." This project continued to be shown in other platforms and in different forms, not as part of Islands of Kinship, but stimulated from there, at the Faculty of Architecture in Skopje in 2022 and at the Prague Quadrennial of Performance Design and Space in 2023.

Artist Luki Essender made a new installation at the Július Koller Society, which was commissioned under the Islands of Kinship project. The work of Luki Essender is situated between hints of self-portraiture and the careful analysis of phenomena, spreading out over a rich scale where the public intersects with the private. It moves on an axis between sculpture and ritual, between exactness and precision expressed in the form of strict materiality, through an open process that integrates metaphor, allusion, and transformation.

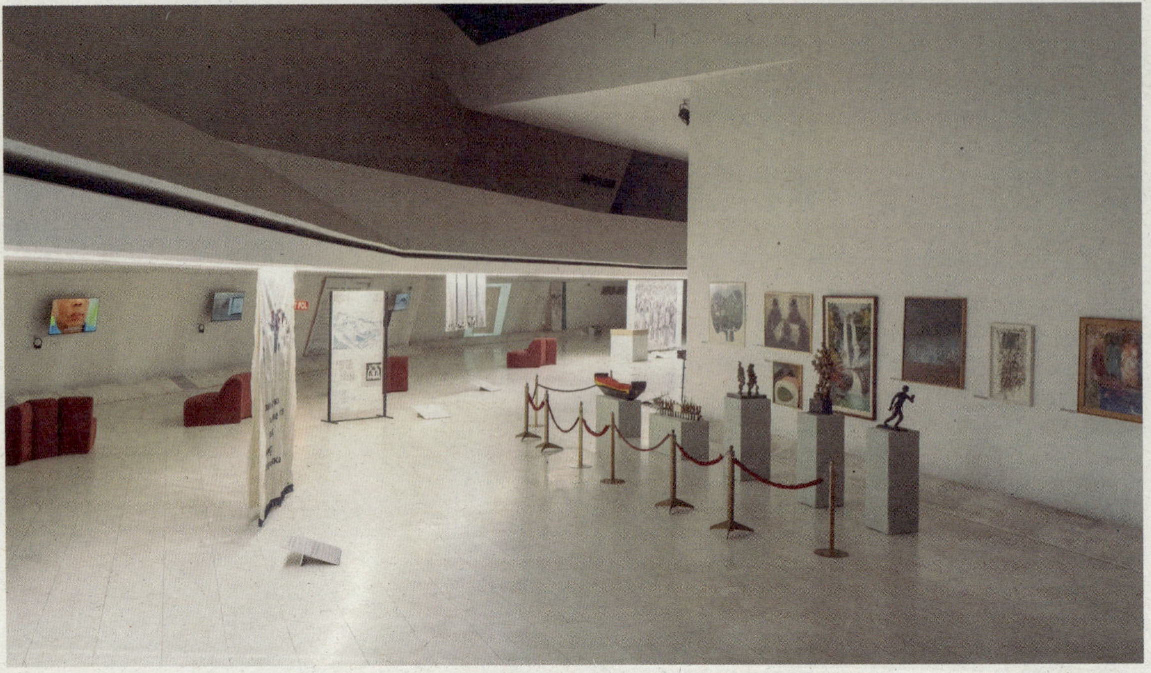

Which Side Are You On? On the Non-Aligned Decolonial Constellation, Macedonian Opera and Ballet, 2022

The abundance of inner questions, interest in language, queerness, sexuality, the public, the private, and various types of relationships on this trajectory transform into a solid and tangible vocabulary.

Creating a space for conversation and debate on the importance of rethinking the past to build a more just and equal future was raised by the international exhibition and accompanying public program titled *Which Side Are You On? On the Non-Aligned Decolonial Constellation*[14] which connected the current global geopolitical restructuring caused by the war in Ukraine with the legacy of the Non-Aligned Movement in its foundational principles—anticolonialism and (trans)national solidarity—and calls anew for a radical reinvention of the world and art within it. Alluding to Homi K. Bhabha's paraphrase of Frantz Fanon's thinking,[15] and actually one of the burning issues

14 Publication https://www.dropbox.com/scl/fi/fbm7twcxl06cpc9amf0zt/NEVRZANITE-24-11-Katalog.pdf?rlkey=d0k1dyoqedp6q805ejo5qotvh&dl=0.

15 Reference to Frantz Fanon found in the article "Threshold Thinking: Where Is the Third World?" by Homi K. Bhabha, available at https://critinq.wordpress.com/2022/08/02/threshold-thinking-where-is-the-third-world/ [Accessed 23.08.2022].

for decolonial countries in the context of the Cold War, this exhibition posed the question: Which side are we taking, in fact, when we decide to take a side and make a stand, politically and culturally? Moreover, how is it manifested today in the lives of peoples? And what can we learn from these decisions in the past?

The exhibition *Which Side Are You On? On the Non-Aligned Decolonial Constellation* broadly talks about the presence of anticolonial ideas and actions in nonaligned Yugoslavia in the very processes of decolonization, and how that legacy and knowledge of (anti)colonialism and anticolonial solidarity is neglected or even erased from today's memory. Furthermore, through the included artworks and public program, it created a vibrant and imaginative space for speculation on what the new anticolonial and anti-imperialist nonaligned world would be, politically and artistically, and how that would lay out a different prospect for the future. It is also a space for a joint effort in reinventing transnational solidarity in the current line of political events through rediscovering Non-Aligned Movement's paradigm of solidarity. It was intentionally displayed in the building of the Macedonian Opera and Ballet, a symbol of international solidarity after the Skopje 1963 devastating earthquake and a donation from the Slovenian Government.

Several Thoughts for the End

Against the neoliberalization of the public space, there are art practices accompanied by urban struggles and social movements that are trying to respond to this continually and with vigor by envisioning and testing different organizational structures and social relations creating public and urban microspaces for politicized discussion. It is our task to reconsider the public spaces together in which we can make future equal for all.

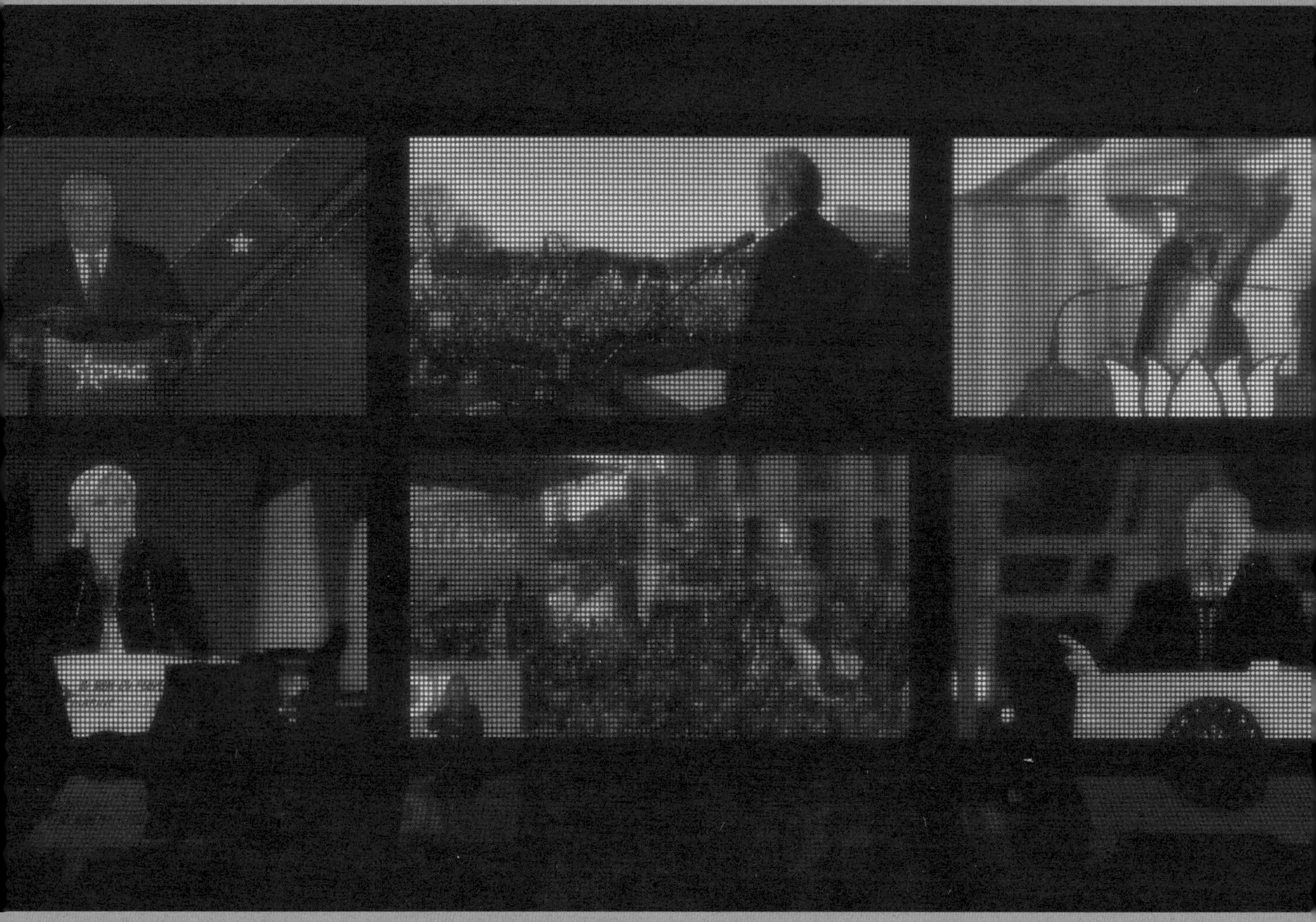

Jonas Staal: Propaganda Station

Too Much of a Role Play

Karina Kottová

Since I am raising two sons, the issues around war play come up pretty much every day. Although we try to discuss that there is actual war quite close to us (and elsewhere), with all its horrific realities, and that there are so many other games and storylines that could be explored, swords keep clanging and imaginary bombs keep flying over our garden. There is surely a lot of gender-coding and cultural transmission involved—before socializing in wider contexts, our older son just loved to play with colorful ponies, while cars, planes, and weapons were of no interest at all. This kind of stereotyping and encoding of the notion of war as something almost "natural" seems to permeate across geographies and times—boys always played with soldiers, the dominant narrative preaches (possibly girls or other genders joined them later, or exceptionally). As much as we try to break, deconstruct, or bend this narrative, it is still shaping our present, and from there it draws the future. Similar narratives program us as adults. Somewhere within us we carry our inner children, who used to play war with almost everything they found—from tree branches to paintball or computer games. The advancement of technology, of course, plays a major part in how realistic such "games" become. Yet, the process itself remains similar for centuries—we cannot really imagine ourselves without conflict, without war.

Such limits of imagination, currently driven by political and economic forces of late capitalism (which is, of course, fueled by historical systems and schemes resulting in it), are a key to the new film by Dutch artist Jonas Staal, entitled *Propaganda Theater, Video Study*. The first scene of the film is staged in a reconstruction of the White House Situation Room, where instead of projecting scenes from current conflicts and related decision-making processes, the main screen shows excerpts from Hollywood blockbuster movies, such as Top Gun or Godzilla. We get almost caught by the melody of Top Gun's notoriously romantic soundtrack and the fascinating imagery (yes, Staal's film also uses the attractive tools of propaganda to later dismantle them), when the voiceover draws us back down to earth. It reminds us of the direct sponsorship of such motion pictures by the Pentagon Entertainment Liaison Offices, which leads to script interventions and control over the "accuracy" of how the US military is portrayed. "Free ships, planes, and soldiers in exchange for providing the image of global US military supremacy," the voice comments. The film further explores computer war games, or a simulated warzone created by Hollywood studios, to finally unfold the surprisingly similar stories of two artists who have largely contributed to the public image and actions of the infamous political superstars of the USA and Russia—Donald Trump and Vladimir Putin. Their respective campaign directors and major ideologues were Steve Bannon and Vladislav Surkov, who both have had a parallel or previous background in film and theater direction. Both of them had been not only advising but also staging and directing the roles of their main protagonists before they were dismissed—possibly thanks to the growing self-esteem of their "heroes," who finally decided to direct themselves.

Jonas Staal's video study attempts to critically assess the principles of such staging, role-play, and encoding major (extremely problematic and intentionally misleading) narratives not only through mass media but also mass entertainment (while the boundaries between both keep on blurring). The spectators, Staal argues, are not only mere onlookers or consumers; they become spect-actors—active parts of the script, often without even realizing it. "Propaganda works best when it is not recognized as propaganda. It works best when the world

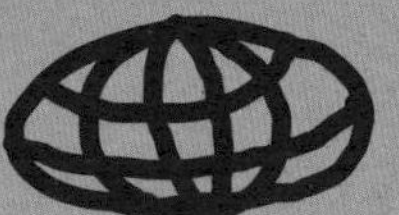

we are performing feels like our own, our home, all along," the film concludes. And this draws us back to the topic of (collective) imagination—it is not easy to start conceiving and realizing a vision of a better world when we are encoded since our childhood not to be able to see this world without war. There is an ever-growing need to keep realizing and deconstructing such narratives, and our own roles within them, in order to be able to draw an alternative, more desired, more functional picture.

The film *Propaganda Theater* is a central part of a large-scale installation *Propaganda Station,* which summarizes Jonas Staal's long-term research on propaganda and propaganda art, both critically assessing the "dark sides," and looking into the possibilities of "emancipatory" propaganda. The installation takes the form of a "reversed panopticon"—in Staal's take, the widely theorized circular prison model allowing for omnipresent surveillance of the prisoners by the guard situated in the center becomes a space for collective observation, where the "propagandists" are observed by the public. In the outer circle, earlier video works on diverse aspects and niches of propaganda are presented—from climate propaganda, through financial and liberal propaganda, to ultranationalist or alt-right propaganda, geological and empire propaganda. Propaganda is understood here not only as a historical concept referring to totalitarian regimes of the past (or those repeating similar pasts in the present) but also a quite vivid mechanism of the northern democracies. The often hidden aspects are brought to light, observed, and reassessed, in order to put our imagination back into play and discuss what kind of propaganda, as a tool used by activists, artists, and citizens, could "strike back" and help create new, more livable conditions and systems. An integral part of the installation is a live program, the Propaganda School. Local theoreticians, activists, NGO leaders, thinkers, and artists are invited to further unfold the narratives proposed by this work, bring in locally relevant issues, discuss together with the wider public and arrive at new crossovers and grounds for collective imagination and action.

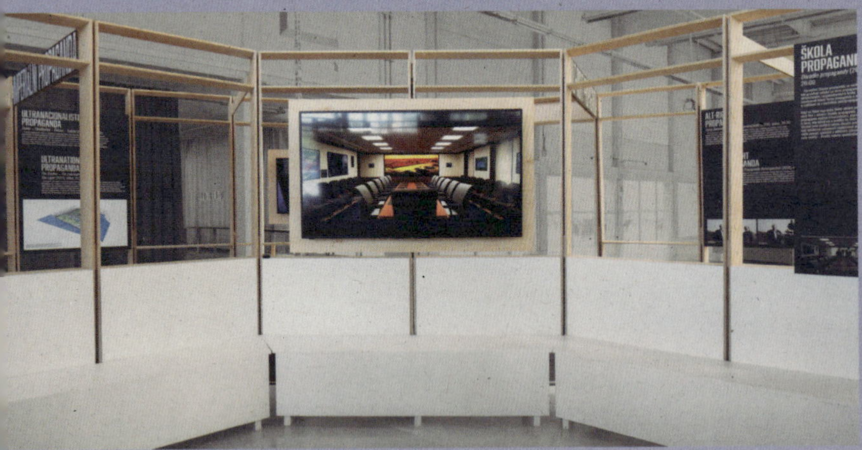

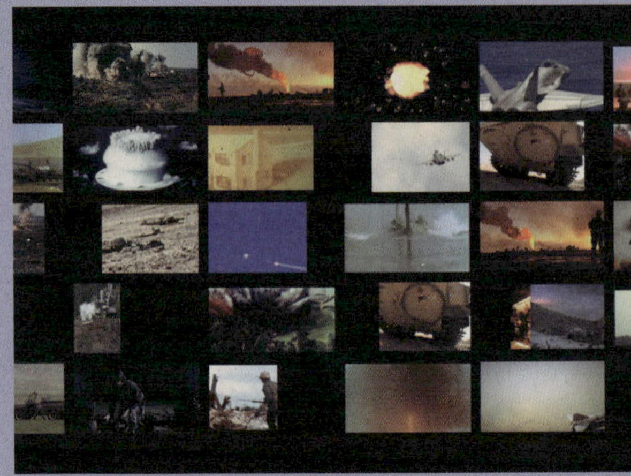

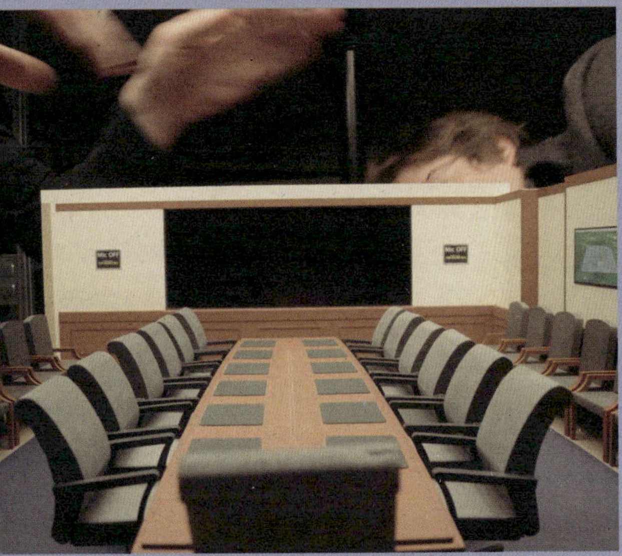

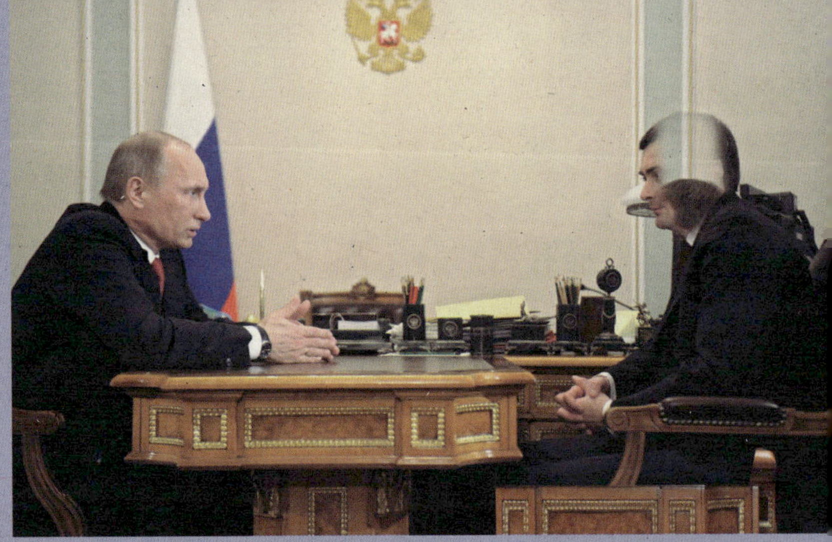

JONAS STAAL: PROPAGANDA STATION (2024)

installation and public program
2023–2024

The commission was cofinanced by Mondriaan Fund.

The commission was presented as part of exhibitions:

- PROPAGANDA STATION, PLATO Bauhaus, Ostrava, Czech Republic, November 1, 2023 – February 25, 2024, organized by Jindřich Chalupecký Society
- PROPAGANDA STATION, Museum of Contemporary Art, Skopje, Republic of North Macedonia, March 1 – August 25, 2024, organized by Faculty of things that can't be learned
- PROPAGANDA STATION, Museum of Contemporary Art, Zagreb, upcoming, fall 2024, organized by Museum of Contemporary Art

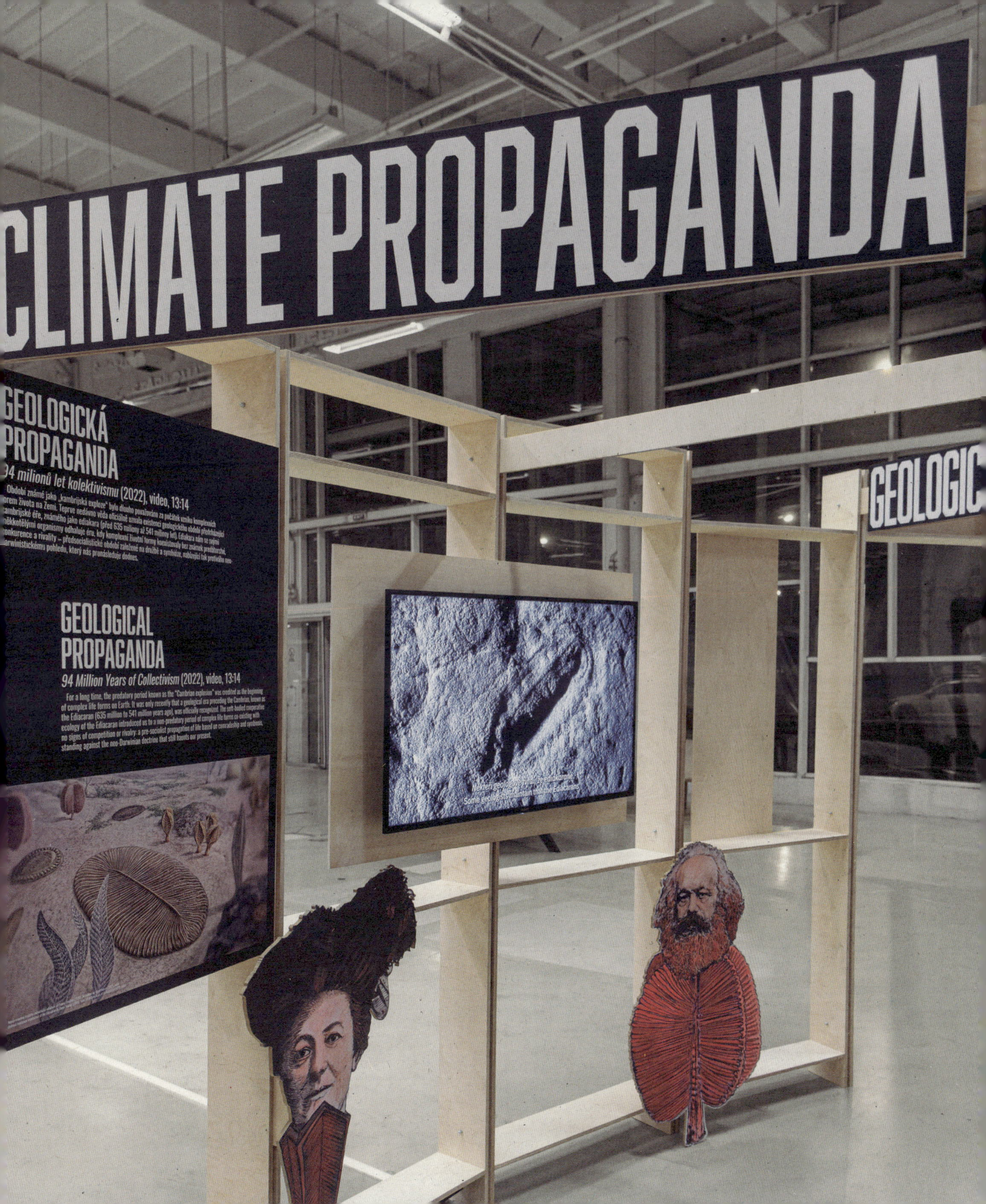
CLIMATE PROPAGANDA
GEOLOGICKÁ PROPAGANDA
94 milionů let kolektivismu (2022), video, 13:14
Období známé jako „kambrijská exploze“ bylo dlouho považováno za počátek vzniku komplexních
orem života na Zemi. Teprve nedávno věda oficiálně uznala existenci geologického období předcházející
ambrijské éře, známého jako ediakara (před 635 miliony až 541 miliony let). Ediakara nám se svými
ěkkotělými organismy odhaluje éru, kdy komplexní životní formy koexistovaly bez známek predátorství,
onkurence a rivality – předsocialistické období založené na družbě a symbióze, nabízející tak protiváhu neo-
arwinistickému pohledu, který nás pronásleduje dodnes.
GEOLOGICAL PROPAGANDA
94 Million Years of Collectivism (2022), video, 13:14
For a long time, the predatory period known as the "Cambrian explosion" was credited as the beginning of complex life forms on Earth. It was only recently that a geological era preceding the Cambrian, known as the Ediacaran (635 million to 541 million years ago), was officially recognized. The soft-bodied cooperative ecology of the Ediacaran introduced us to a non-predatory period of complex life forms co-existing with no signs of competition or rivalry: a pre-socialist propagation of life based on comradeship and symbiosis, standing against the neo-Darwinian doctrine that still haunts our present.
GEOLOGIC

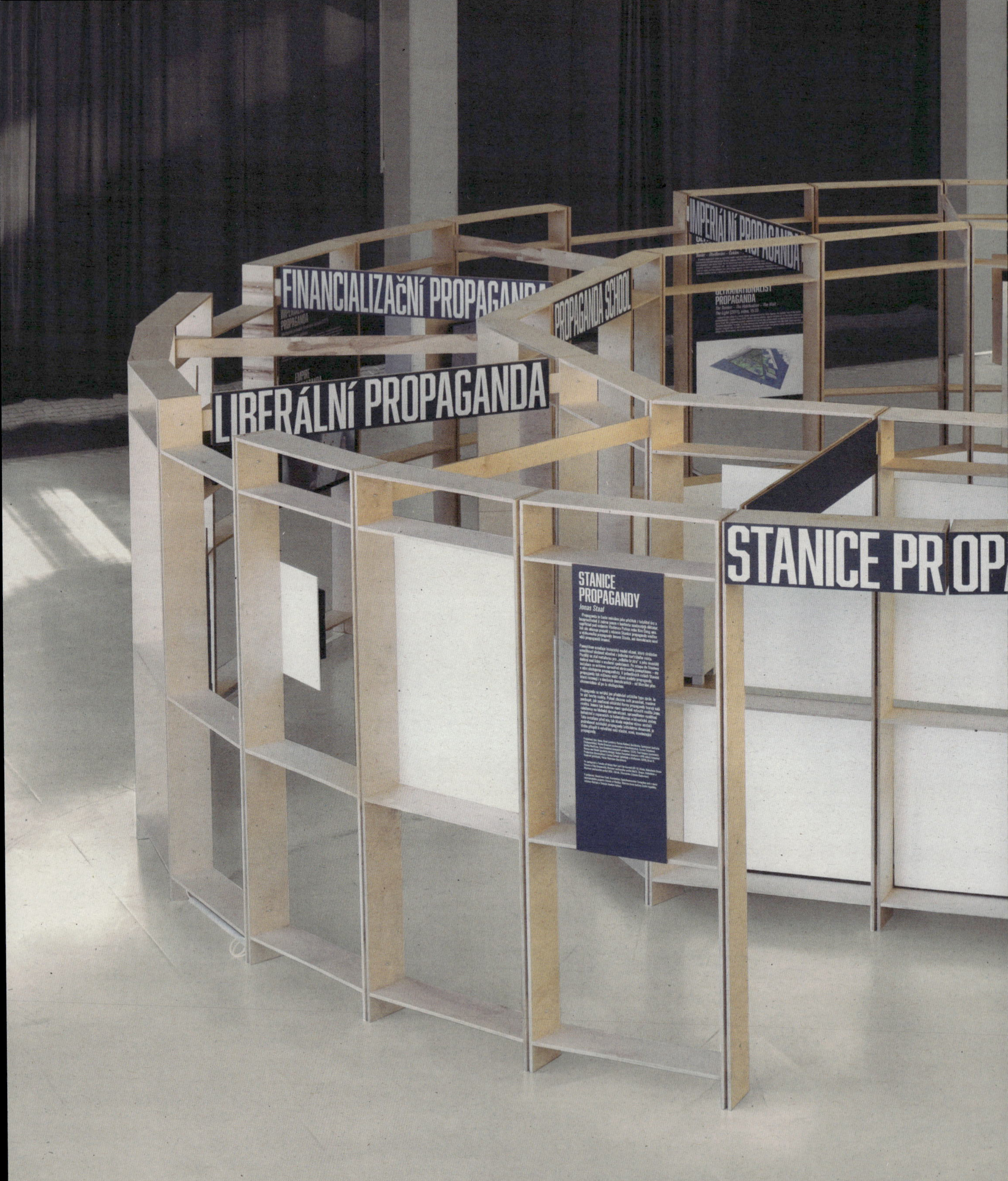
FINANCIALIZAČNÍ PROPAGANDA
PROPAGANDA SCHOOL
IMPERIÁLNÍ PROPAGANDA
LIBERÁLNÍ PROPAGANDA
STANICE PROPAGANDY
Jonas Staal
STANICE PR OPA

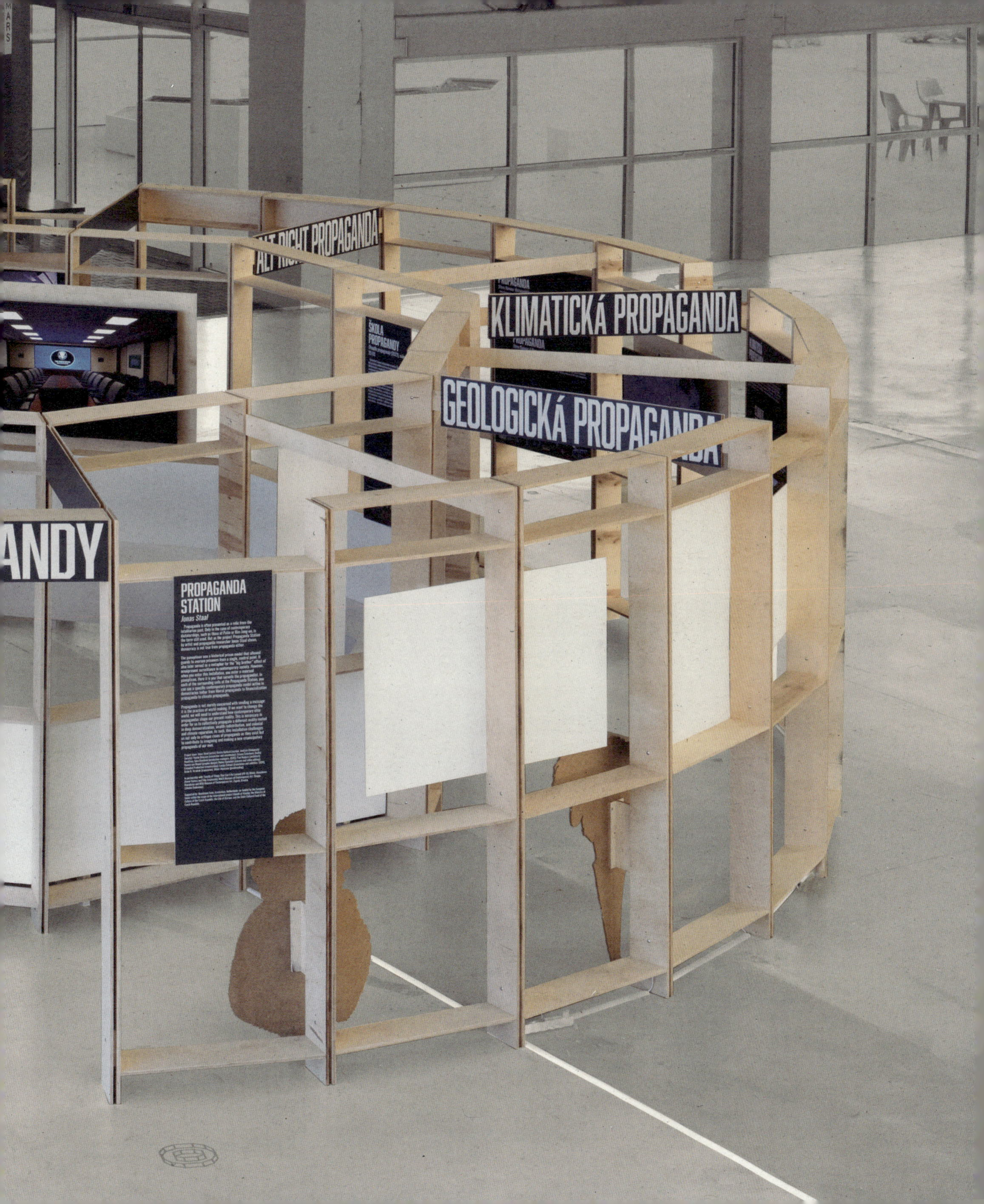
KLIMATICKÁ PROPAGANDA
GEOLOGICKÁ PROPAGANDA
ŠKOLA PROPAGANDY
ANDY
PROPAGANDA STATION
Jonas Staal

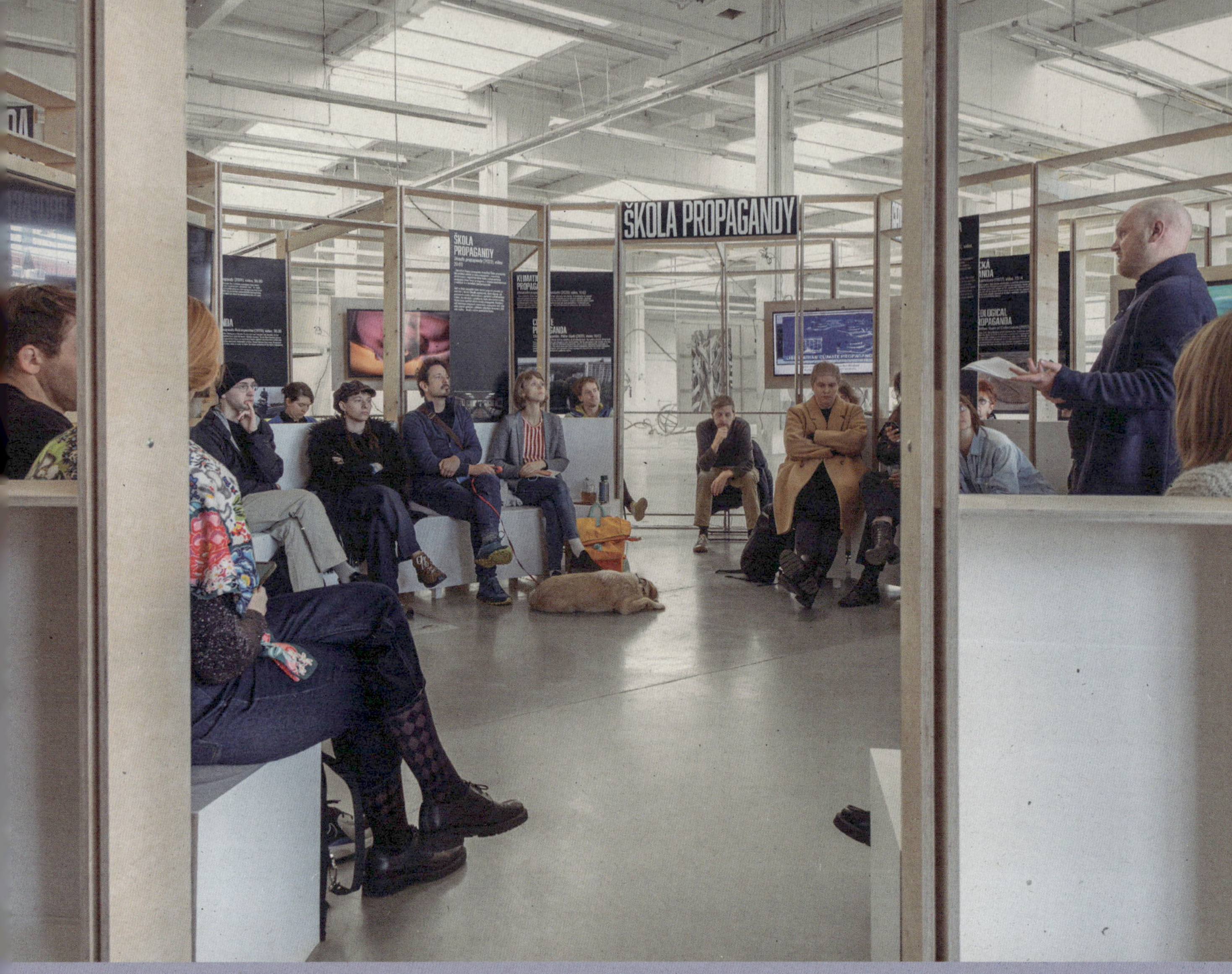

PROPAGANDA SCHOOL PROGRAM (OSTRAVA):

November 2, 2023

- **JONAS STAAL:** Art and Propaganda in the 21st Century, artist's introduction
- **ANDREA PRŮCHOVÁ HRŮZOVÁ:** Black and White Madonnas; Victims and Porters. Women, Migration, and the Media Space
- **JAN BĚLÍČEK:** Searching for a Third Way? The Czech Media Landscape between Post-Communism and Authoritarianism

December 3, 2023

- **NIKOLA LUDLOVÁ:** Introduction to the Topic of Propaganda vs. Ethnic Minorities
- **GWENDOLYN ALBERT:** Anti-Roma Propaganda
- **EDITA STEJSKALOVÁ:** Romani Propaganda

February 24, 2024

- **MICHAL KLODNER:** Media Ecology and Ecology of the Mind
- **MICHAL FELLER:** Black-Green: (Anti)Climate Propaganda in and beyond Ostrava

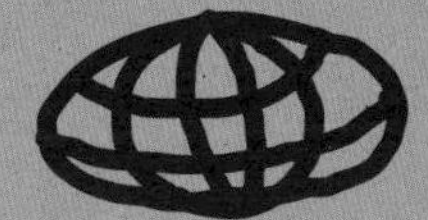

Propaganda School

At the center of Propaganda Station at PLATO Ostrava, the Propaganda School took place. Throughout the duration of the exhibition, this platform hosted meetings with propaganda researchers, activists, and organizers with the goal of jointly analyzing the tools and forms of contemporary propaganda as well as experimenting and educating ourselves in methods of (counter)propaganda.

The first section was devoted to media propaganda and disinformation, with an introduction by Jonas Staal on the relation of art and propaganda in the 21st century, followed by lectures by visual culture theorist Andrea Průchová Hrůzová and journalist Jan Bělíček. The day was concluded with a conversation between Jonas Staal and Macedonian curator Ivana Vaseva, who subsequently presented Propaganda Station in Skopje.

The second iteration of Propaganda School entitled Know Your Enemy: Hate Speech and Anti-Roma Propaganda and Counter--Propaganda Strategies was moderated by Nikola Ludlová, JCHS inclusion coordinator, with lectures by human rights activist and Romani ally Gwendolyn Albert and Roma activist and community organizer Edita Stejskalová. Their contributions analyzed the conceptual and ideological frameworks, tools, proponents, and targeted audiences of anti-Roma propaganda in comparative longdurée and geographical perspective.

The final session addressed the relationship between propaganda and climate from the perspective of media ecology and ecology of the mind as well as local climate propaganda and related activist movements. The speakers were researcher and activist Michal Klodner and Michal Feller, coordinator of the Ostrava section of the environmental NGO Hnutí DUHA.

The Propaganda School in Skopje, accompanying the exhibition at the Museum of Contemporary Art, intended to create a temporary discursive platform deconstructing the complexity of the antiquization propaganda mirrored in the project Skopje 2014. Through presentations of several theoreticians, activists, artists, and journalists from North Macedonia, this program offered interventionist contributions in the legal, media, semiotic, social, and artistic aspects of the project erected in the "captured state" and tried to ponder its future existence facing the preparations and production of the project Skopje—European Capital of Culture 2028.

After almost fifteen years since it was announced, this grandiose and controversial project, Skopje 2014, is still dwelling in the city center, reminding us how the propaganda machinery occupies the everyday, strengthening the national sentiments and traditional values through baroquization and antiquization of the city center.

Through the analysis of the tools and forms of this contemporary propaganda, the aim of this gathering at the Propaganda School was to gain a precise definition of the work of antiquization propaganda, and explore models of counterpropaganda, or even emancipatory propaganda, to reclaim public space, public memory, and the public imaginary.

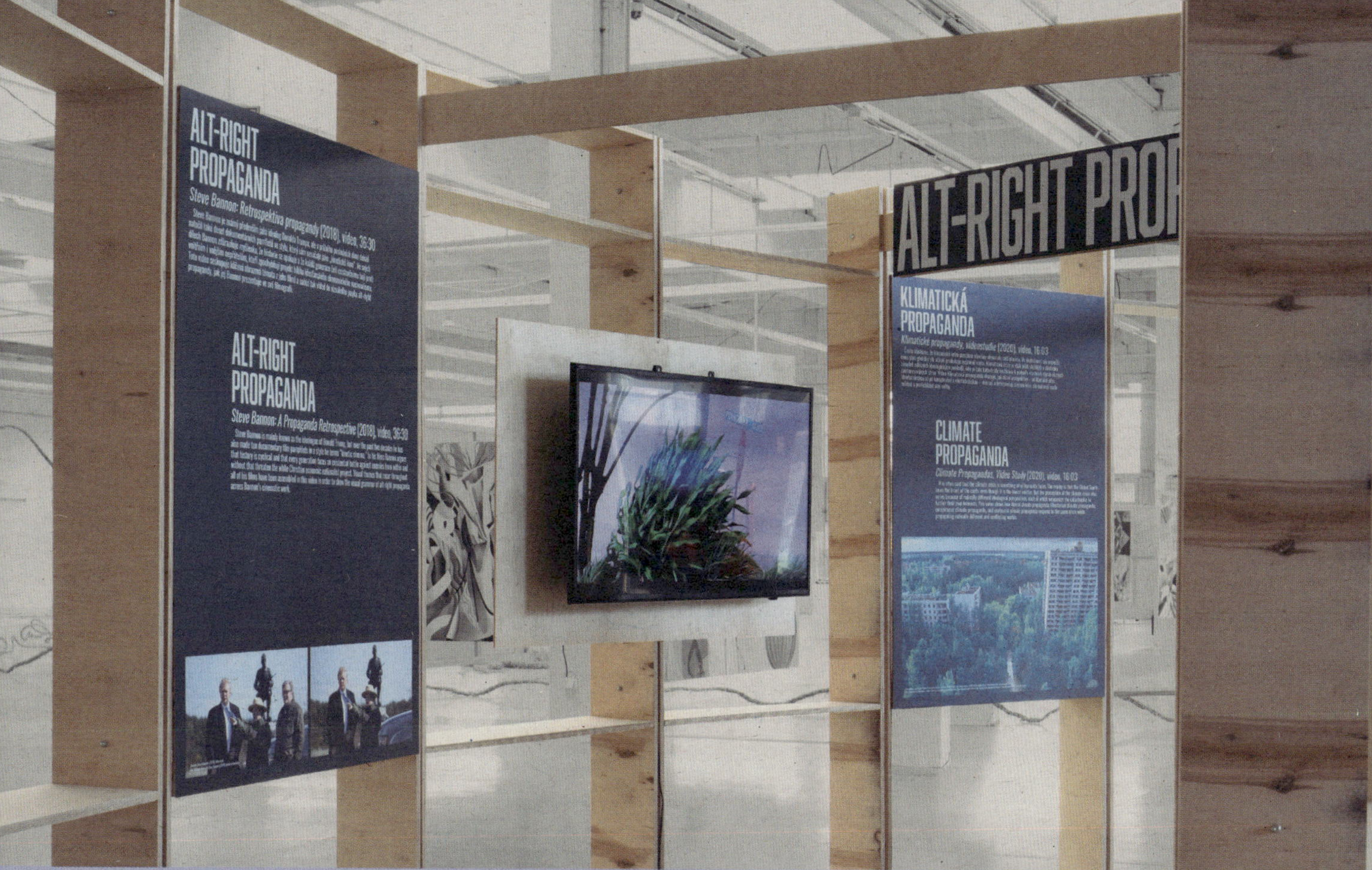

PROPAGANDA SCHOOL PROGRAM (SKOPJE):

- **IVANA VASEVA:** curatorial introduction
- **TIHOMIR TOPUZOVSKI:** Skopje: MoCA, Plans and Collaborations
- **JONAS STAAL:** Art and Propaganda in the 21st Century, author's introduction

SESSION I: ANTIQUIZATION PROPAGANDA, AN ATTEMPT AT A DEFINITION

- **KATERINA KOLOZOVA:** Self-Victimization as the Foundation of National Pride
- **BOJAN IVANOV:** Earthquake 1963–2014
- **ANA PETRUSHEVA:** Database Skopje 2014 under a Magnifying Glass
- **GORAN JANEV:** "Skopje 2014 Forever," A City Wrapped in Ethnocratic Propaganda

SESSION II: PROPAGATING SKOPJE 2028: WHAT DO WE WANT THE CITY TO BE?

- Open debate with the audience, moderated by **IRENA CVETKOVIKJ** and **JORDAN SHISHOVSKI**
- **NIKOLA NAUMOSKI:** Counter-Movements against Skopje 2014
- **NIKOLA GELEVSKI:** Architorture and Funeralization
- **BILJANA TANUROVSKA-KJULAVKOVSKI:** Imagining Skopje—With Art and Culture towards the City of the Future
- **MARJAN ZABRCHANEC:** The Public—Food for or a Trojan Horse against Retrograde Propaganda?

Manual #1

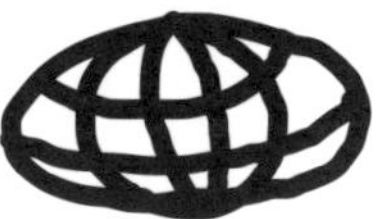

Jana Brsakoska

Institutio-nal Reforms

This paper (Vergemit White, 120 g/m²) was used from surplus stock normally destined for disposal. Manufactured in Štětí, Czech Republic.

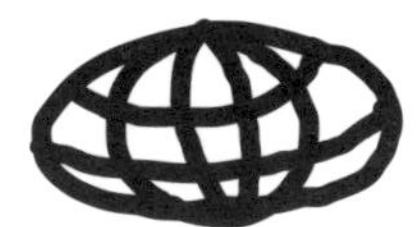

Introduction

Contemporary art thrives on diversity and creativity, and fostering an inclusive and sustainable environment is crucial for its evolution. This chapter focuses on the noninstitutional sector, a segment often neglected in terms of financial and structural support, exploring the necessity for systemic reforms. The noninstitutional sector consists of unemployed artists and cultural workers along with nonexistent support for space and operative costs, specifically in North Macedonia. The sector faces significant challenges in gaining visibility and resources. The lack of inclusivity hampers the sector's growth, limiting opportunities for artists to showcase their work and stifling the diversity that contemporary art demands. These artists struggle with operational costs, from studio space to materials. The dearth of support contributes to a cycle of limited artistic output and hinders the potential for sustainable creative practices. This refers to noninstitutional practices in North Macedonia that could be considered case studies. An important notion is providing equal access to opportunities and resources in art and cultural events, to achieve positive results in the project processes, greater institutional sustainability, and inclusivity.

This chapter should answer the following questions:

- What treatment in the way of structural support does the noninstitutional sector receive?
- What systemic reforms are needed?
- How to achieve institutional change and thus institutional sustainability and sustainable funding?
- How are inclusive practices established in the noninstitutional sector—art institutions and organizations?
- What to take into consideration for greater inclusivity?

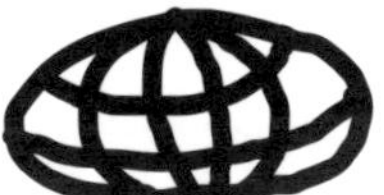

Part one gives an overview of the current relations between the system and the noninstitutional sector. It will focus on the working conditions (infrastructure and means for the production and dissemination of work), structural support in the form of space and operating costs, support on the national and local level, and the noninstitutional workers' rights vs those employed in the institutional sector.

Part two will refer to several practices by the FRU[1] organization and other examples by local organizations, elaborating aspects in close relation to the topic. Examining models of collaboration and support within the noninstitutional sector provides valuable insights. Case studies highlight the need for establishing instances where institutional reforms and community engagement lead to sustainable artistic practices. Furthermore, it identifies the major issues, resulting in the need for systemic reforms to achieve sustainability in the noninstitutional sector and greater inclusiveness.

Part three will conclude with the need for systemic changes toward the position of the noninstitutional sector in the prevailing mode of production and simultaneously elaborate on the emancipatory arts and culture that can offer systemic changes in the overall context.

1 The organization The Faculty of things that can't be learned, Skopje, Republic of North Macedonia will be further referred to by the abbreviation FRU.

Overview of the Current State[2]

The noninstitutional sector, encompassing independent artists and cultural workers (the civil sector—citizen associations, societies, informal associations and groups, and other legal forms of cultural organizations) in North Macedonia, has opportunities for public financial support for their work (programs). This support comes through the annual competition for project funding of national interest in culture at the Ministry of Culture (once a year) and calls from local municipalities (once a year), but it is limited to the project level. This funding covers costs directly related to the implementation of the project and program and lacks any kind of structural support.

Independent artists and cultural workers in this sector are often unemployed or work part-time, without any benefits of regular employment, receive fees for their professional engagement, or operate within citizen associations and cultural societies. This contrasts with artists and cultural workers who have secured employment in the institutional sector. In these competitions, organizations, independent artists, and cultural workers often receive minimal support for the realization of their projects. The noninstitutional sector lacks structural support in the form of space and coverage of operational costs for work, unlike the institutional sector which receives both programmatic and structural support from central and local authorities.

Additionally, independent artists in the country have the opportunity to cover health, pension, disability

2 Research conducted within the FRU organization concerning "The working rights of freelance artists and cultural workers in North Macedonia" developed by Ivana Vaseva and Violeta Kachakova.

insurance, and personal income tax based on the average salary from the Ministry of Culture through another annual competition. This competition is regulated by the sublaw called "Regulation for determining the criteria for the allocation of monthly allowances from the funds of the budget of the Republic of Macedonia for contributions to health, pension, and disability insurance and personal income tax of independent artists."[3] It is awarded according to criteria that consider the artistic disciplines and demonstrated activity in the last five years. Professions defined under the term "cultural workers"[4] are still not included in this favor, though inclusion is expected with the adoption of the new Draft Law on Public Interest in Culture.

This existing support is a rudimentary form received by this category of workers according to the Law on Independent Artists of the Socialist Republic of Macedonia from 1982. Some independent artists and cultural workers are members of professional associations (including the Society of Fine Artists, the Writers' Society, the Association of Architects, and the Society of Film Workers) but they do not receive protection of their labor rights from them. Despite better working conditions in the institutional sector for culture, there are also unions such as SONK and SKRM defending labor rights. However, independent artists and cultural workers are still not organized in a union/agency that will fight for their rights.

3 Ministry of Culture. "Regulation for determining the criteria for the allocation of monthly allowances from the funds of the budget of the Republic of Macedonia for contributions to health, pension, and disability insurance and personal income tax of independent artists". 2017.

4 In the current Law of Culture, there is no mention of artistic labor, nor a mention of the occupation of the "Cultural Worker" comprising the professions of curator, art theorist, art manager, etc.

Independent artists and cultural workers in the country can collaborate with state or local institutions, but only within specific projects. They do not have the opportunity to develop their programs and lack their own space for program development.

Case Studies—Organizational Practices

Challenges in Structural Support—Lack of Exhibition Spaces

Securing exhibition spaces and galleries can be challenging for independent artists or noninstitutional organizations, which is limiting their ability to showcase their work to a wider audience. Considering these challenges, the following chapter is an overview of FRU organizational practices and experiences, as well as an overview of the outputs deliberated from the Institutional Debates Report.

20 YEARS SINCE THE FOUNDATION OF THE DENES YOUNG VISUAL ARTIST AWARD IN MACEDONIA

- **ORGANIZED BY: Faculty of things that can't be learned – FRU, Skopje. In collaboration with the Center of Contemporary Arts Skopje, the network Young Visual Artists Award (YVAA), the residency program Residency Unlimited (RU), New York, and the foundation Trust for Mutual Understanding, New York. The exhibition was financially supported by the Trust For Mutual Understanding, NY.**
- **The DENES exhibition was opened by this year's winners of the award for young visual artists under 35: Gjorgji Despodov, Klelija Zivkovic, and Burju Musli.**

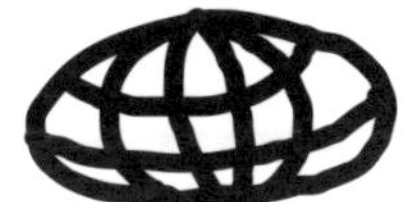

The event was held on September 14, 2023 in Chifte Amam—National Gallery of the Republic of North Macedonia. Since February 2023, the organization's main aim was to establish communication with the National Gallery of the Republic of North Macedonia to provide appropriate space for the exhibition. This was challenging since FRU is an organization that deals with initiatives organizing artistic and cultural events which are often not tied to one space.

The DENES Award was founded in 2002 but was officially awarded for the first time in 2003 to offer more possibilities for young artists to master their practice. Twenty years later, in 2023, the context still resides in institutionalized modernist frameworks and thus misses many contemporary challenges of contestation, opening, and demarginalization. There are more developed standards for the presentation, production, and distribution of art, but modernist epistemological thought and art-making still prevail. There is an abundance of improvization, a lack of funding, and experimental spaces. All of this strengthens the promotional and consumerist side of art, as opposed to its politics and criticality. However, some artists have radicalized their imagination, experimenting, fighting, and finding their ways by using alternative strategies for education (self-education) and production, and by creating new symbolic, metaphorical, and physical spaces as new public agoras. The chance provided by the DENES Award not only facilitated their emergence but also the creation of their artworks.[5]

5 FRU. New Agora – 20TH anniversary of the DENES Award_НОВА АГОРА – 20 ГОДИНИ НАГРАДА ДЕНЕС_ – FRU. (2023, September 4). FRU – Faculty of things that can't be learned. https://akto-fru.org/en/НОВА-АГОРА-20-ГОДИНИ-НАГРАДА-ДЕНЕС_new-agora/.

The 20-year celebration of the DENES Award in North Macedonia acknowledges the rare occurrences that have provided various directions in art-making and gives space to a different framework for history that differs from linear historical narration, demanding a different educational epistemological discourse and production infrastructure. Equality, antiracism, antinationalism, and sustainability are key tendencies in reframing contemporary society and art. As part of this event, there was an exhibition of photos and videos featuring past winners of the DENES Award as a commemorative ceremony, along with a presentation of the challenges they faced in the past 20 years. Additionally, a public program comprising lectures and presentations was organized by the 2023 winners Gjorgji Despodov, Klelija Zivkovic, and Burju Musli, and an exhibition of their awarded artwork.[6]

Providing Exhibition Space

Securing exhibition spaces is a critical challenge for the noninstitutional sector and organizations such as FRU, encompassing various barriers that hinder their ability to showcase their work. The lack of access to these spaces poses significant obstacles to the visibility, recognition, and sustainability of the noninstitutional sector. The challenges that FRU had to face during the negotiations for exhibition space are as follows:

6 Ibid.

Financial Constraints

Facing financial constraints while browsing and negotiating for spaces limits the ability to rent or lease traditional gallery spaces. These spaces may come with high costs, including rent, installation fees, and promotional expenses.

Competition for Limited Spaces

Intense competition for exhibition spaces, particularly in renowned galleries or cultural institutions. In this case, FRU was competing against established artists or those with institutional affiliations, making it challenging to secure slots in prominent venues.

Curatorial Preferences

Some galleries and curators have preferences for artists associated with established institutions, as this can be perceived as a marker of credibility. Independent artists may be overlooked due to these preferences, limiting their opportunities for exposure.

In the procedures for securing exhibition space, FRU needed to:

Research and Outreach

Conduct thorough research on available exhibition spaces, including galleries, community centers, alternative art spaces, and even online platforms. This involves identifying venues that align with the artist's style and thematic focus.

Proposal Submissions

These proposals typically include a portfolio of the artist's work, an artist statement, and a description of the proposed exhibition. Artists must craft compelling proposals that communicate the significance of their work.

Networking

Building relationships with curators, gallery owners, and other artists. Networking provides insights into available opportunities and increases the likelihood of being considered for exhibitions. Attending art events, openings, and artist gatherings facilitates networking.

The event was held on November 19, 2023 near the former local community center in Tavtalidze, Skopje, North Macedonia. The space provided for the artistic performance, which primarily has an activist purpose, is privately owned. The artistic performance refers to the building of the former local community, also known as Domche, which is in the same private ownership as the space around it today. The biggest challenge in the successful implementation of this project was precisely the collaboration with the owners to obtain a permit for the space near the building.

CITY AS A STAGE: LOST (MODERNIST) UTOPIAS

- **ORGANIZED BY:** Faculty of things that can't be learned—FRU
- **AUTHORS/ARTISTS:** Filip Jovanovski, Miodrag Kuch
- **PARTICIPANTS/RESEARCHERS/PERFORMERS IN THE PROCESS (2021–2022):** Miodrag Kuch, Filip Jovanovski, Jana Brsakoska, Ljubisa Arsić, Simona Dimkovska, Kristijan Karadjoski, Boris Bakal, Kulturno EHO, City Scope, Luna Shalamon, Deniz Ajdarevic, Denica Stojkovska, students from the Faculty of Architecture Skopje: Tamara Dzerkov, Dimitar Milev, Sandra Nikolovska, Bojana Isijanin, Stefan Tankov, and students from the Faculty of Dramatic Arts Skopje: Aleksandar Jovanovski, Martina Danailovska, Marija Taleska, Martina Petreska, Ivan Vrtev, Bojana Isijanin, Stefan Tankov, Martina Danailovska.
- **COPRODUCTION TEAM:** Boris Vasileski, Aleksandar Jovanovski, Deniz Ajdarevikj, Luna Shalamun
- **CURATORIAL SUPPORT:** Ivana Vaseva

Brief Overview of the Political Transition and Land Property in the Case of Skopje[7]

With the catastrophic earthquake in July 1963, Skopje became a symbol of solidarity and a representation of architectural design influenced by the socialist ideals of that time, largely shaped by the modernist style prevalent in this political context. The modernization of post-earthquake Skopje begins with the Master Plan adopted in 1965, following the winning solution proposed by Japanese architect Kenzo Tange and a collaborative team from Yugoslavia. The reconstruction of Skopje intensively begins and unfolds until the 1980s, but it fails to be fully realized, leaving many unfinished aspects that become the focus of subsequent political administrations over the next three decades.

With the dissolution of Yugoslavia and the independence of Macedonia in the 1990s, the development of the city stagnated, further affected by the transition, particularly the period of privatization in the Republic of North Macedonia. Privatization became a priority for the newly independent state, leading to the adoption of the Law on the Transformation of Enterprises with Social Capital in 1993. According to Article 1 of this law, conditions, methods, and procedures are regulated for the transformation of enterprises with social capital into entities with specified ownership. With these changes in ownership, societal interests begin to shift, affecting the use, planning, and urbanization of space. This process raises questions about public space and its utilization, as part of the vacant areas inherited from

7 Research conducted during the preparation for the project Contemporary (Non)Democracies—Disappearance of the Public Man, 2021, organized by FRU. An exhibition based on research by Jana Brsakoska, Ivana Vaseva, Filip Jovanovski, Christian Karadzovski, and Naum Trajanovski.

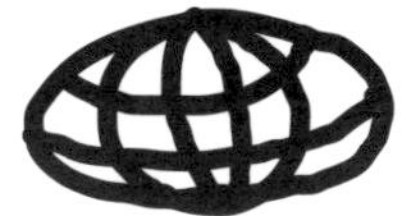

the incomplete modernization of Skopje start to become private property.

Therefore, public spaces, once symbols of representation and communication, have transformed into platforms dominated by profit-driven alliances between businesses and the state. The urban growth fueled by global capitalism has profound implications on social, political, cultural, and environmental aspects, resulting in nondemocratic regulations and actions.

Filip Jovanovski addresses these issues by creating temporary public spaces that serve as arenas for confrontation between political entities, local municipalities, and citizens. Employing the method of "reading buildings," Jovanovski aims to preserve architectural memory and heritage while proposing collective futures. His project *City as a Stage: Lost (Modernist) Utopias*, undertaken in collaboration with architect Miodrag Kuc and students from Skopje's Faculty of Architecture and Faculty of Drama Arts, focuses on Domche—a building with clean abstract forms cast in concrete, now privatized and claimed by a political party as the rightful inheritor from the former social system. Jovanovski's performative installation, titled *Domche: Perhaps the Smallest Brutalist Building in the World*, consists of twelve stories generated through research, workshops, archival materials, interviews, and community involvement.[8] The project transforms public spaces into stages where community issues are theatrically presented. Although initially part of ISLOKIN, the project expanded to other platforms, such as the Faculty of Architecture in Skopje in 2022 and the Prague Quadrennial of Performance Design and Space in 2023.

8 FRU. (2023, February 16). CITY AS A STAGE, performance_ Градот како сцена, перформанс. https://akto-fru.org/en/Градор-како-сцена_city-as-a-stage-перформанс-performance/.

Providing Exhibition Space

Securing a space under private ownership for non-formal exhibitions and artistic activism performances by the noninstitutional sector involves navigating a complex terrain that often requires careful balance between respecting private property rights and fostering freedom of expression.

Here's an elaboration on the procedures and considerations involved in this process that FRU had to face during the negotiations for this space:

Permission and Collaboration

Negotiating with Owners: This means the need to engage in open and respectful negotiations with private property owners. This involved obtaining permission to use the space for a specific period and purpose.

Collaborative Approaches: Building positive relationships with property owners. Artists propose ways in which their exhibitions or performances can contribute positively to the property and its surroundings.

Legal Considerations

Lease Agreements: In some cases, artists need to formalize their agreement through a lease or written permission. This document can outline the terms of use, duration, and any responsibilities or liabilities associated with the exhibition or performance.

Permits and Licenses: Artists are required to obtain permits or licenses from local authorities to ensure that their activities comply with zoning laws, safety regulations, and other legal requirements.

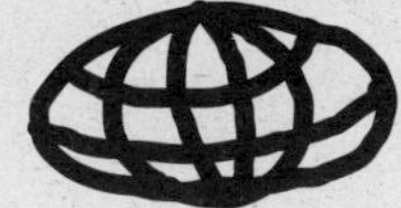

Community Engagement

Gaining Local Support: Engaging with the local community and garnering support for the artistic event. This support can act as a form of social permission and may influence the property owner's stance.

Addressing Concerns: Artists need to be prepared to address any concerns raised by the community or property owners, providing information about the positive impact of the artistic event.

Documentation and Communication

Detailed Proposals: Artists present detailed proposals outlining the nature of their exhibition or performance, its duration, and the potential benefits for the community and the property.

Communication Channels: Establishing clear communication channels with property owners, local authorities, and community representatives, where regular updates on the progress of the project can foster transparency and trust.

Risk Management

Liability Insurance: Depending on the nature of the artistic event, artists may consider obtaining liability insurance to protect themselves and the property owner in case of any unforeseen incidents.

Safety Measures: Implementing safety measures is crucial to ensure that the event does not pose any risks to participants, spectators, or the property itself.

Postevent Responsibilities

Cleanup and Restoration: Commit to cleaning up the space after the event and restoring it to its original condition. This demonstrates responsibility and respect for the property.

Institutional Debates Report[9]

As part of ISLOKIN activities, FRU has organized Institutional Debate—meetings and interviews, with cultural professionals discussing topics of inclusion according to the local context of the Republic of North Macedonia. This debate invited various representatives of local art institutions, where the main focus was on diverse speakers that are involved in different programs, that all together include intersecting social and ecological justice movements within art scenes and art institutions.

The Institutional Debate introduced four cultural professionals from four different art institutions: Cultural Echoes, Helsinki Committee for Human Rights, Tetovo Wants Park, and Museum of Contemporary Art—Skopje.

Outputs

All four interviews discuss the topic of inclusiveness within their projects, whether they are formal or informal art events, communities, or activism through initiatives.

Throughout the speakers' point of view, based on their particular experience in various fields of activity, inclusivity means involvement (engagement of stakeholders), representativeness, and arising from the needs of

9 Part of the Institutional Debates Report delivered by FRU within ISLOKIN activities. Date: 17–20 July 2023; Venue: Skopje (different venues); Activity: Interviews| Conversations.

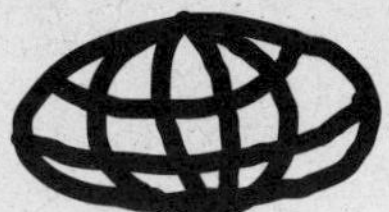

a specific community. The strategies that are implemented in all project preparations are clearly defined project goals and projected outcomes, followed by openness in access, availability in communication, collaboration, and determination.

A specific example of a clear strategy for inclusiveness implementation is given in the organization's practices of Cultural Echoes—participatory art which enables the direct involvement of the visitor in the artwork, and interaction with the artist.

The strategies and tactics through which inclusiveness can be flawlessly introduced in the realization of art and cultural events and initiatives are often directly dependent on the available financial and other resources.

In terms of media promotion and a good plan for inclusivity, every organization strives toward clear and simple graphic communication with the help of social networks, and multilingual practices in the implementation of the content.

Successfully realized inclusion results from the importance of the idea and its message from the very beginning, the availability and cooperation of key institutions, the inclusion of various groups of artists as the main protagonists who bring progress, and overcoming the conservative centers of power.

Providing adequate space is usually a challenge in the work of most art institutions, except the Museum of Contemporary Art, whose activities are carried out within the framework of one building. The Helsinki Committee directs its priorities to the community spaces, incorporating other initiatives, providing a space for socialization, a meeting place, conversation, and debate, but also an info point for foreigners and a safe place for those in danger.

However, the difficulty in providing adequate space for the quality realization of a specific event remains a challenge. It is a special challenge for organizations that deal with informal art events or initiatives to provide a space, primarily accessible to people with disabilities or handicaps, as well as a suitable space for the realization of the artists' activities.

Noninstitutional Sustainability

Achieving emancipatory arts and enhancing sustainability for the noninstitutional sector requires systemic changes that address various aspects of the art ecosystem. The following are recommendations on several potential systemic changes that could contribute to a more supportive environment for noninstitutional sustainability. Simultaneously, elaborating on the potential of emancipatory arts and culture offers insights into how systemic changes can be initiated to address existing issues and foster a more inclusive and equitable artistic landscape.

Potential Systemic Changes

Community Collaboration as a Catalyst

Engaging with communities is a transformative approach to addressing the challenges faced by the noninstitutional sector in contemporary art. Collaborative efforts between art institutions, governmental bodies, and local communities can play a crucial role in creating a supportive and enriching environment for artists. This chapter explores the significance of community collaboration as a catalyst for positive change, emphasizing its potential to alleviate financial burdens and establish networks for the exchange of ideas and resources.

Importance of Community Engagement

Supportive Ecosystem

Community engagement provides artists with access to a supportive ecosystem that goes beyond traditional institutional structures. Local communities often appreciate and value the diversity of artistic expressions, creating spaces where artists can thrive.

Diverse Perspectives and Influences

Interacting with diverse community members introduces artists to different perspectives, cultures, and experiences. This diversity becomes a source of inspiration, influencing the content and themes of their work and contributing to a more vibrant and inclusive artistic landscape.

Collaborative Initiatives

Joint Programming with Art Institutions

The opportunity for collaboration between independent artists and established art institutions results in joint programming, exhibitions, and events. These initiatives help bridge the gap between the institutional and noninstitutional sectors, fostering a sense of inclusion and shared creative endeavors.

Governmental Support and Cultural Policies

The government plays a vital role in supporting independent artists through cultural policies and funding. Collaborative efforts between artists and governmental bodies lead to the development of policies that recognize and address the specific needs of the noninstitutional sector.

Financial Benefits

Community-Supported Funding Models

Community collaboration introduces alternative funding models that rely on local support. Crowdfunding campaigns, community grants, and sponsorships from local businesses are examples of financial avenues that can help alleviate the financial challenges faced by independent artists.

Shared Resources and Spaces

Collaborative efforts can result in the sharing of resources and spaces. Community centers, local businesses, or vacant buildings can be repurposed as exhibition spaces, studios, or workshops, providing the noninstitutional sector and artists with the physical infrastructure they need.

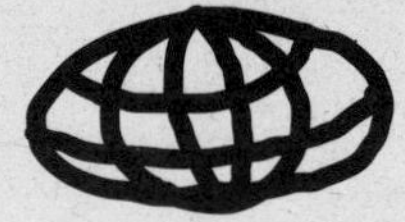

Networking and Resource Exchange

Building Networks

Community engagement facilitates the building of networks that extend beyond the art world. Collaborating with local organizations, businesses, and individuals creates connections that can lead to opportunities for exposure, collaboration, and mutual support.

Exchange of Ideas and Skills

Interaction within a community allows for the exchange of ideas and skills. Artists can benefit from the knowledge and expertise present within the community, while also contributing their unique perspectives and talents.

Case Studies and Success Stories

Showcasing Positive Outcomes

Examining case studies and success stories where community collaboration has yielded positive outcomes can serve as an inspiration and a blueprint for future initiatives. These examples highlight the tangible impact of collaborative efforts on the noninstitutional sector.

In conclusion, community collaboration stands as a powerful catalyst for overcoming the challenges faced by the noninstitutional sector. By forging partnerships with art institutions, engaging with governmental bodies, and actively involving local communities, a more inclusive and sustainable ecosystem can be cultivated, ensuring that artists receive the support and recognition they deserve.

Emancipatory Arts and Culture as Agents of Systemic Change

Challenging Dominant Narratives

Subversion and Resistance: Emancipatory arts have the power to challenge dominant narratives and resist oppressive structures. By questioning established norms, artists contribute to a broader cultural shift that questions the prevailing mode of production.

Community Empowerment

Participatory Practices: Emancipatory arts often involve participatory practices that empower communities. By engaging directly with diverse communities, artists contribute to social change, fostering a sense of agency among individuals who may be marginalized or underrepresented.

Cultural Democracy

Democratizing Cultural Spaces: Emancipatory arts strive for cultural democracy, advocating for diverse voices and perspectives. This challenges hierarchical structures in the cultural realm and calls for the inclusion of the noninstitutional sector in shaping cultural narratives.

Intersectionality and Inclusivity

Intersectional Approaches: Emancipatory arts take intersectional approaches that consider the interconnected nature of social identities and systems of oppression. This inclusivity promotes a more holistic understanding of societal issues and facilitates collaborations across diverse artistic practices.

Alternative Platforms and Networks

Building Alternative Systems: Emancipatory arts often involve creating alternative platforms and networks that operate outside traditional institutional structures. These platforms provide spaces for the noninstitutional sector and artists to thrive and connect with audiences on their terms.

Critical Engagement

Critical Dialogues: Emancipatory arts encourage critical engagement with social, political, and economic structures. By fostering dialogues and reflections, artists contribute to a deeper understanding of the systemic changes needed to create a more just and inclusive society.

Advocacy and Activism

Art as Activism: Emancipatory arts often align with social and political activism. Artists use their work as a tool for advocacy, bringing attention to pressing issues and mobilizing communities for collective action.

This elaboration informs strategies for dismantling barriers, advocating for systemic changes, and creating an environment where the noninstitutional sector can thrive as a contributor to a more just and liberated cultural landscape.

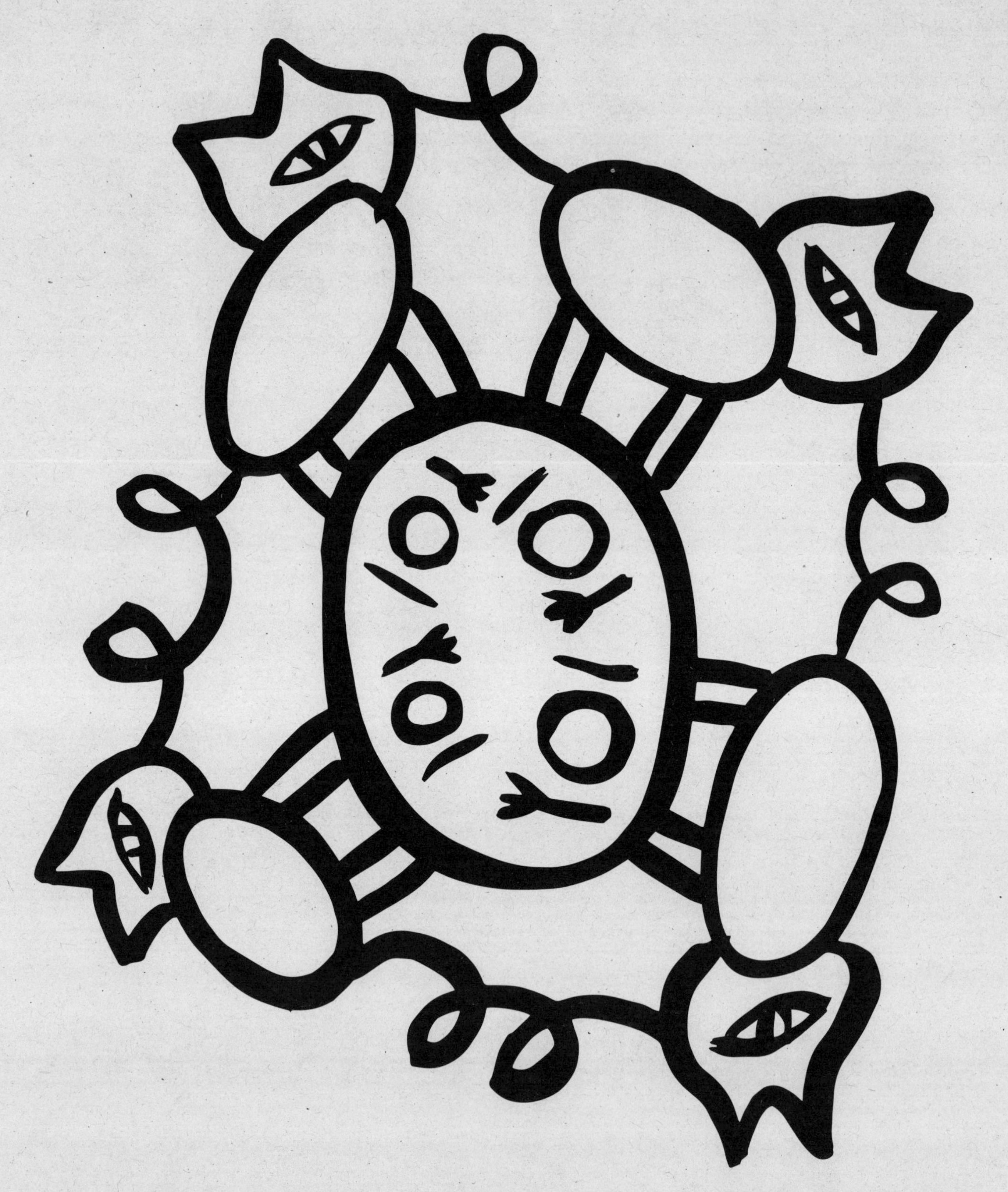

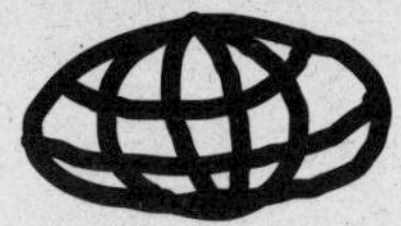

The Arena of Contemporaneity—Step-by-Step Manual to Institutional Opening through Collaborative Microprojects

Paulina Seyfried

About the Content and Intention of the Map[1]

Based on my own experiences and observations in the art field, I have been working intensively for about two years on the question of how cultural institutions can fulfill their function and responsibility[2] as public spaces. Public-funded institutions are paid by taxes, which means they are actually paid by almost all of us. The logical conclusion would then be that they are not only open to selected societal groups like a golf club or a safer space for marginalized groups. One of the possible instruments for becoming more public which I'd like to suggest here is to break down this big challenge of democratic transformation into microprojects—small-scale cultural projects which can be developed collaboratively with organizations from outside the institution. Some supposedly simple examples of these microprojects are a board of critical friends, a check-in and check-out round that frames every meeting, a working group taking care of installing gender-neutral toilets, or people initiating a sports club in the neighborhood of the institution. These examples might sound easy and also quite neoliberal, but as you will see on the map, they come with structural shifts and self-reflection tools. The following text will give background information on the research and development of the map as well as some additional material like a code of conduct draft, a glossary, and further literature.

1 The QR code for download can be found on page 103.

2 This responsibility is initially understood here in an obvious way: As state-funded institutions, they not only belong to everyone in principle, they also have the task, in whatever form, of representing and embodying their surrounding public(s).

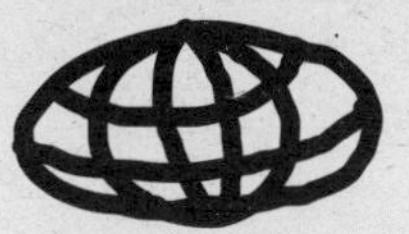

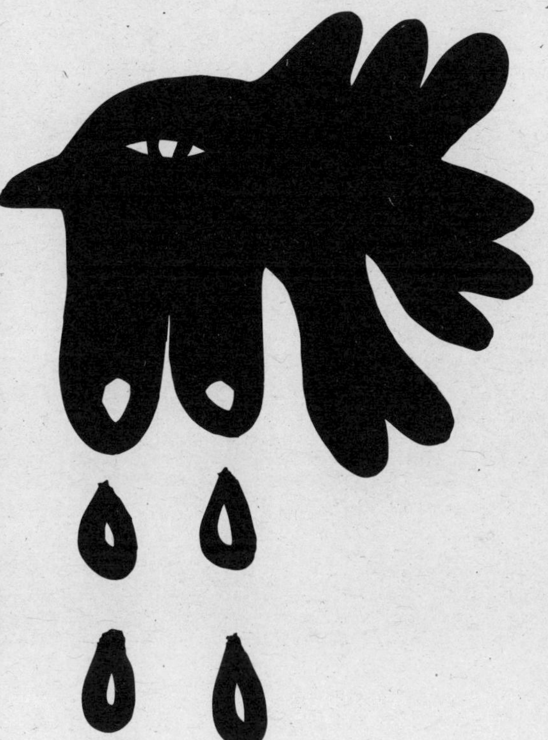

Thanks to a research grant from the City of Cologne, I had the financial security and thus the most important resource of time for an intensive examination and diverse discussions, for example with practice-based theorists Nora Sternfeld and Katrin Lohbeck, as well as physical encounters with the staff in the respective institutions. Beforehand, I studied the political theory on the concept of public sphere(s) to subsequently enter into conversational situations, for which I would like to express my sincere thanks: Freiraum at the Museum für Kunst und Gewerbe Hamburg, UZwei at the Dortmunder U, Kunsthalle Osnabrück, Kunstmuseum Bochum, Neue Gesellschaft für Bildende Kunst and Haus der Kulturen der Welt in Berlin, and Museum Ludwig in Cologne. After this discourse analysis and six interviews with representatives of different art and cultural institutions, I decided—in dialogue with designer Sophia Schach—to create a kind of a map as an illustrated bundling of the considerations.

Coming from Germany, my first research in 2021 focused on the cultural institutions and structures here. With this project in the back of my mind, in 2022, I started to work as a coordinator for institutional accessibility and local collaborations, representing Temporary Gallery—Centre for Contemporary Art in the collaborative project Islands of Kinship. In regular meetings and discussions with five other midscale visual art institutions across diverse regions in Europe, I was able to contribute and enhance my expertise in the broad field of institutional change and inclusion. In doing so, I noticed some improvements had to be made which led me to an updated and translated English version of the map. Thanks to the funding of Creative Europe, I was able to not only review the written text and translate the map but also to develop a version of the map for this joint publication which contains a QR code at the end linking to the whole map.

By reducing the text and incorporating drawings, an attempt is made to make the content more accessible; the map itself functions visually and playfully and thus represents an attempt to combine theoretical discourse and practical experience into an overall picture. Unlike a text on the issues dealt with here, the map attempts to motivate direct action in the form of microprojects as it is formulated in simple language, offering concrete steps in a more accessible way.

In particular, I would like to use this concept paper to suggest how institutional spaces can be opened up for and through collaborative knowledge generation and, above all, how internal basic conditions and understanding for this can be created. Far too often, attempts are made to integrate the institutional opening into project thinking and to deal with it once and for all within a fixed period of time. Before there is talk of giving up institutional spaces for meetings or interventions, or even converting entire parts of the institution into an "open space," a lot can already be initiated and brought closer by involving external players in program development and the orientation of the institution towards microprojects. In the long term, the map then encourages its users to involve the local community and to act as an institution beyond the linear and superficial mechanisms of representation.

The double-sided paper consists of an introductory glossary of terms relevant to this document, such as collaboration, microproject, and public space,

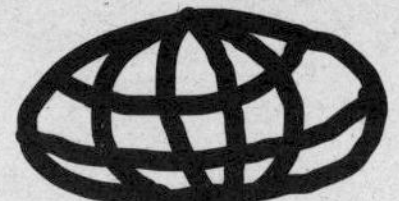

a collection of sources of inspiration and drafts, as well as references and further material. On the front page, you will find the illustrated step-by-step manual, which forms the centerpiece and is to be understood as a proposal for concrete action in the form of microprojects.[3] A sketch of a code of conduct for participants in collaborative projects is also outlined. Spaces for personal notes are just as important and present as examples and formulated proposals for solutions from a subjective perspective.

As an open-source document,[4] the map will be freely available to actors in art and cultural education, but also to other institutional and independent actors, and can be continuously supplemented and revised. The map is designed to be iterative and will hopefully reach various stages of development to reveal a diversity of attitudes. This version was created as part of the Islands of Kinship network project and is to be understood as one of many manuals for more sustainable and inclusive work in art institutions. I assume that change is possible and necessary. So let's get started and develop solutions to concrete problems and needs instead of loudly proclaiming openness yet remaining stuck in familiar power relations in the end.

3 Micropractice is understood here as the potential for structural change based on shifts in everyday practices and routines. Microprojects are therefore small-scale projects within the given structure that can lead to irritations.

4 Open source is the term commonly used to describe software whose source code is public and can be viewed, modified, and used by third parties. I imagine the handling of this first draft to be similar.

Background

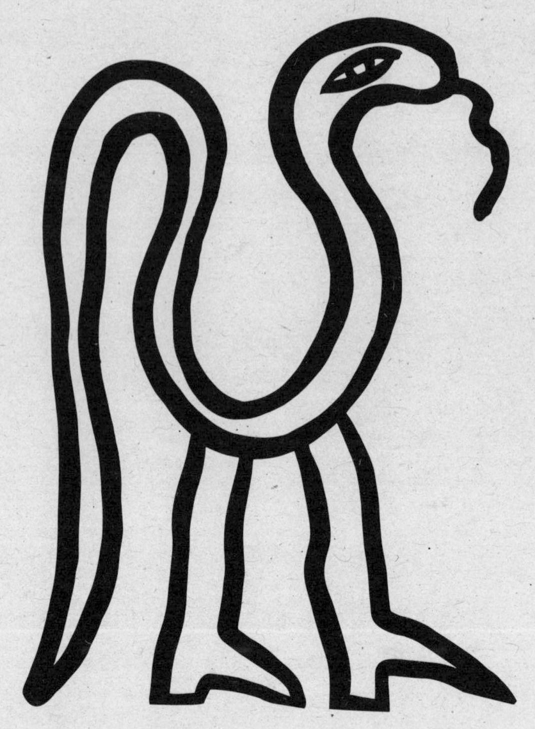

My considerations are based on the assumption that public cultural institutions need neither to be reinvented nor discarded. Rather, the underlying hope is that collaborative exchange or tandem formats, for example between the institution's staff and outsiders, can provide impulses that have an impact on the internal structures of the institutions and the mechanisms of representation, thus reversing modes of inclusion and exclusion in favor of exchange based on parity. I would like to address the (re)activation of the public function through alternative forms of coming together and cooperation between heterogeneous actors not (only) theoretically; rather, this map is to be understood as a call to action. Contrary to cluster and sectoral thinking, it is aimed at a wide variety of public, in the sense of state-funded institutions in the arts and culture sector. Above all, it is about a transformation of the self-image in working with each other and in interaction with outsiders (independent actors, visitors, sponsors). The document is therefore not intended to be used exactly in this way, but to encourage people to think differently about everyday life and thus also about appreciation for one another.

Theoretically, I start from a field-theoretical[5] understanding of the institution, according to which all actors, places, institutions, and discourses of art

5 Pierre Bourdieu, "The Logic of Fields," in *Reflexive Anthropology*, ed. Pierre Bourdieu and Loic Wacquant (Frankfurt am Main: Suhrkamp, 1996).

also shape the institution.[6] This is accompanied by a heterogeneous and dialectical understanding of the public sphere. If one follows Simon Sheikh, the public sphere is a "[...] contradictory and inconsistent conceptuality [...], and art institutions [could be] read as the embodiment of these publics [...] as a place that always becomes a place, becomes a public space."[7] The necessity of revitalizing public institutions is seen in the fact that they cannot otherwise fulfill their role as places of social norms,[8] education, and encounters, and that they increasingly lose their relevance and usefulness when they stand still. Remaining public also means staying in motion; not freezing. If we follow Oliver Marchart's discourse analysis of the concept of the public sphere, it arises "[...] wherever there is 'debate' [so that] the public space itself is not a space [...] but rather a principle: the principle of reactivation." According to this, it is about "[...] avoiding the occupation of the empty place of power, the permanent creation of closed space."[9]

What does this mean for an institution that, by its very nature and according to cultural policy, must be public? Firstly, I have observed that mediating and participatory

6 Andrea Fraser, "From the Critique of Institutions to an Institution of Critique", *Artforum* 44, no. 1 (September 2005).

7 Simon Sheikh, "Öffentlichkeit und die Aufgaben der 'progressiven' Kunstinstitution," *transversal*, no. 2 (2004), accessed October 7, 2021, www.transversal.at/transversal/0504/sheikh/de.

8 The discourse on the crisis of representation can only be mentioned briefly here. Nevertheless, it is probably one of the most important concepts in the context of questions of accessibility and participation: Who is represented how and by what? Who is given the opportunity to present something?

9 Oliver Marchart, "Kunst, Raum und Öffentlichkeit(en). Einige grundsätzliche Anmerkungen zum schwierigen Verhältnis von Public Art, Urbanismus und politischer Theorie," *transversal*, no. 1 (2002), accessed September 19, 2022, www.transversal.at/transversal/0102/marchart/de.

practices in institutions are mostly still based on the reproduction of known or predetermined discourses instead of provoking dissent.[10] The observation that institutional opening processes often function only at the content-related or temporary level,[11] but do not influence the physical interior, the team, or the structures of an institution, also led me to examine this as a structural problem: this is exemplified by the adherence to departments, fixed roles and areas of responsibility, too little exchange between departments, and, last but not least, closed doors and stereotypical representation of marginalized communities and underrepresented stories.

Becoming Active

I would like to address these problems by focusing on collaborative working methods which, in my understanding of the term, are aimed at the joint development of new content and heterogeneous systems of order and knowledge, sometimes far away from their Western understanding. As this working practice is based on debates and dissent, and necessarily involves them, the results to be achieved cannot be determined in advance. The process can be very tough and lengthy. This is precisely why shifts in practice, such as the redistribution of responsibilities, can occur during the implementation of collaborations, and also why this approach is rarely prioritized in times of increasing time pressure and persistent project logic.[12]

10 For a summary on the different levels of mediation, please see: Carmen Mörsch et al., eds., "Zeit für Vermittlung," accessed February 28, 2024, www.kultur-vermittlung.ch/zeit-fuer-vermittlung/v1/?m=0&m2=1&lang=d.

11 Here I am thinking, for example, of the increasing number of projects on the subject of care, accessibility, or the concept of open spaces as community spaces.

12 Everyday, small and large changes in hierarchies that affect power relations and the authority of interpretation should also not be ignored.

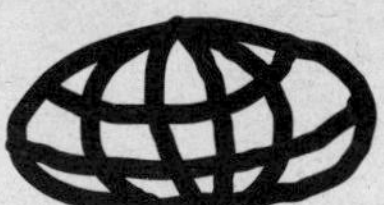

Guided by the question of what kind of spaces and structures are needed to initiate a transformation towards alternative organizational structures and openings towards the heterogeneous publics of urban society in public institutions, two theses emerged during the research, which I would like to pursue with this map:

1. Change is only possible through participation and intrinsic interest in an issue, a position, or a structural change.
2. Transformation always comes from the outside.

This is based on my basic assumption, outlined above, that what is required to share institutional spaces and infrastructures in collaborative working methods is, on the one hand, the rethinking from within, on the other hand, however, stronger impulses from the outside and acting from the needs of the respective publics instead of traditional routines. I am also convinced that diverse methods of opening up are already established in the self-organization of independent actors and that stronger networks and collaborations are therefore indispensable, especially with actors and communities outside the institution and from different fields. In such an alternative working structure, employees, independent cultural workers, and the urban community would become joint initiators, and guests (visitors) would become collaborators (participants). These considerations initially sound just as abstract and utopian as the diverse and visionary contributions to a possible future of the museum in particular and the art field in general, which have been made increasingly in recent years. The question that drove me was therefore: What could this look like in concrete terms? What are the conditions and how could we start taking action right away?

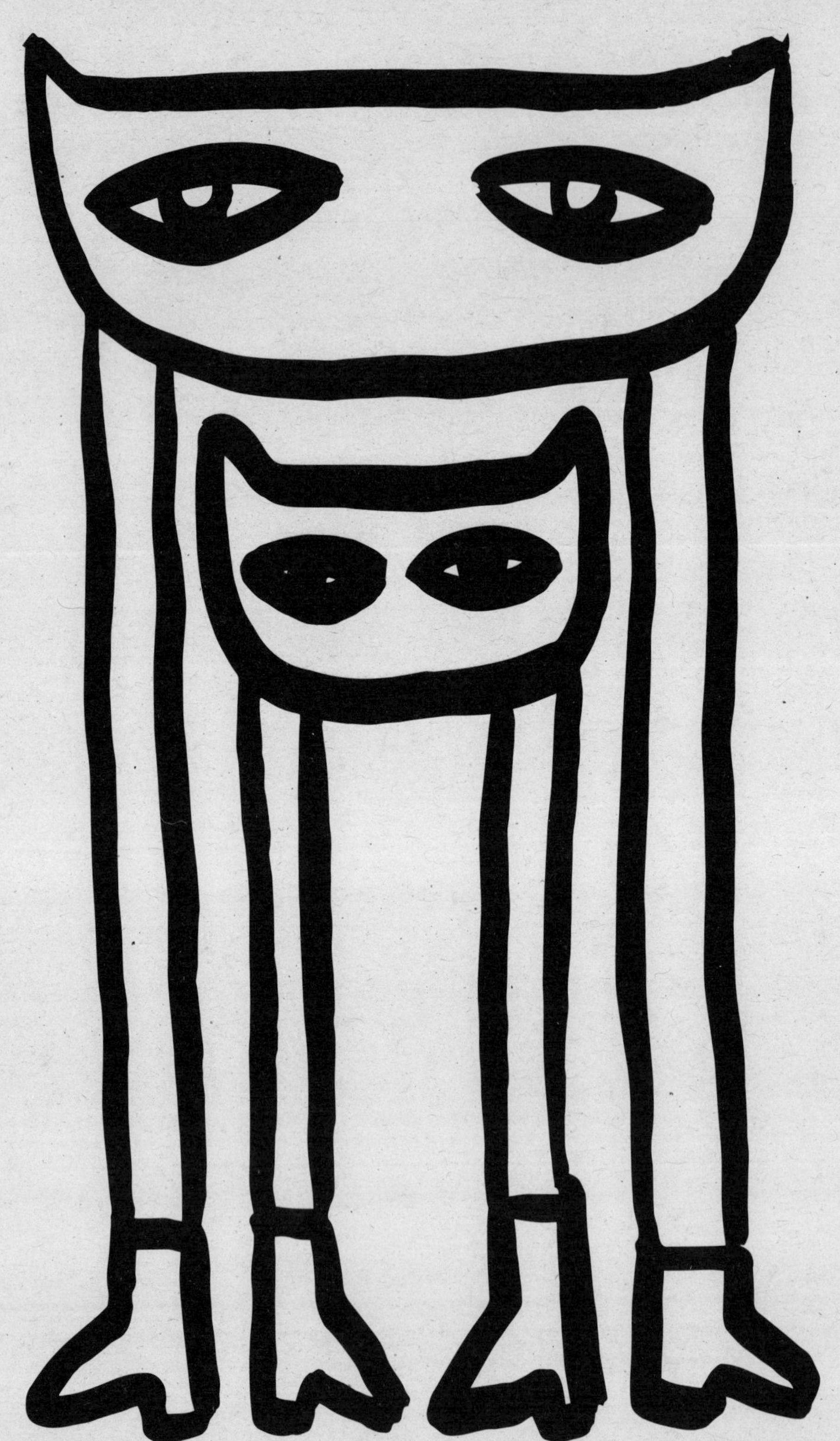

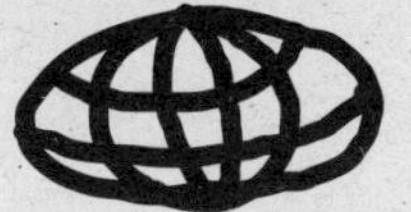

Analyses of the Discussions and Interim Results

It became clear during the interviews that the employees' ability to act initially appeared extremely limited, whether due to a lack of resources (time, financial, personnel, structural) or simply due to frustration with the large "administrative apparatuses" within institutions and cultural policy. In two institutions, close cooperation and regular exchange with outsiders were already integrated into practice. This alternative orientation and way of working slowly bore fruit there, as the institution's audience became more heterogeneous and local.

In order to achieve the long-term goal of changing institutional working methods and power relations, more time and different levels of action would be required. I quickly realized that—as is so often the case—the theory and practice of opening up institutional spaces are still very far apart. This divide can also be taken further across the board into a discrepancy between content (exhibition themes, texts, talks) and form (internal structure, working methods with outsiders, organizational forms), whereby different levels of knowledge exist here, too. The fact that change is desired, but concrete procedures are unclear, can be seen not least in the long-awaited redefinition of the museum, which was recently published and shows that change is desired:

No matter how well something can be described in words and how many exciting and innovative ideas there are in this direction, what is missing are clear instructions, assistance, or similar for, from, and in practice.[13]

13 "A museum is a not-for-profit, permanent institution in the service of society that researches, collects, conserves, interprets, and exhibits tangible and intangible heritage. Open to the public, accessible, and inclusive, museums foster diversity and sustainability. They operate and communicate ethically, professionally, and with the participation of communities, offering varied experiences for education, enjoyment, reflection, and knowledge sharing." See also: International Council of Museums (ICOM), "Museum Definition," accessed September 19, 2022, www.icom.museum/en/resources/standards-guidelines/museum-definition/.

My first wish would therefore be to take action against the buzzword attitude that has long since crept into our language and determines the content of exhibitions, publications, symposia, funding applications, and the like. Instead, I would like to emphasize work in interest-led groups and microprojects. For example, many of those involved in the discussions I initiated saw opening up as an urgent project, but this was quickly followed by a form of resignation when it came to concrete initial steps for action.

I therefore focused on the form during the interviews and asked to what extent there had been initial encounters with participatory projects, whether a distinction can be made between participation and collaboration in practice, what methodological knowledge underlies the respective work, and what kind of publics are (or should be) actually addressed.

I therefore shifted the focus from questions about solutions to needs, wishes, and challenges and quickly realized how hardened institutional structures and processes are today, and even more: how little experience and knowledge there is in terms of organizational and management-oriented methods. This led me once again to my thesis that transformation can only be driven by an interplay between those inside and outside, that impulses, irritations, and disruptions to rigid processes and routines are needed in order to be able to think and implement change again, and so are very specific further training programs and workshops. My next step in this direction has been taken and is recorded here: the development of a step-by-step guide for institutional work on microshifts in small, overarching action groups. This playful mapping of a proposed solution is primarily intended to serve as a stimulus to reflect on practice in practice and to become active through theory.

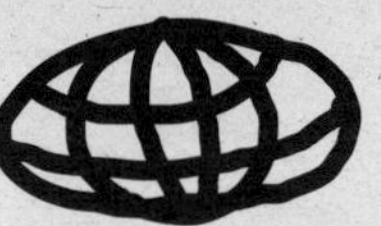

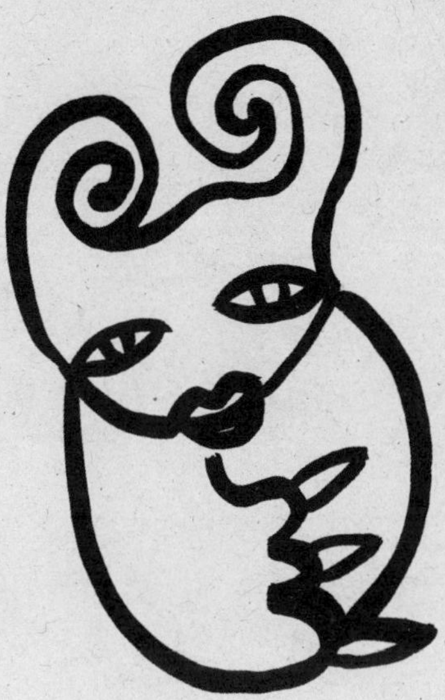

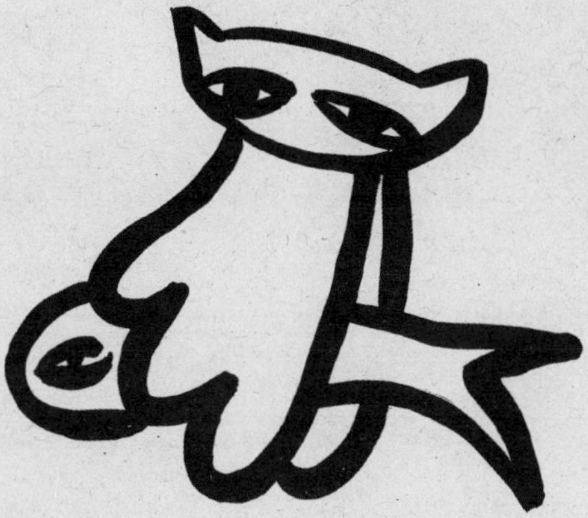

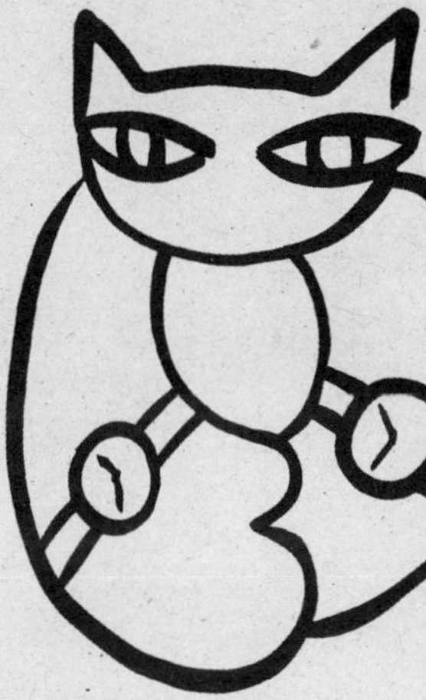

SCAN ME FOR THE MAP

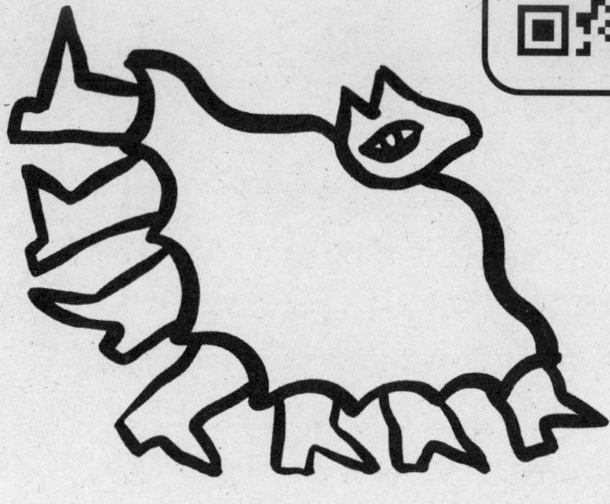

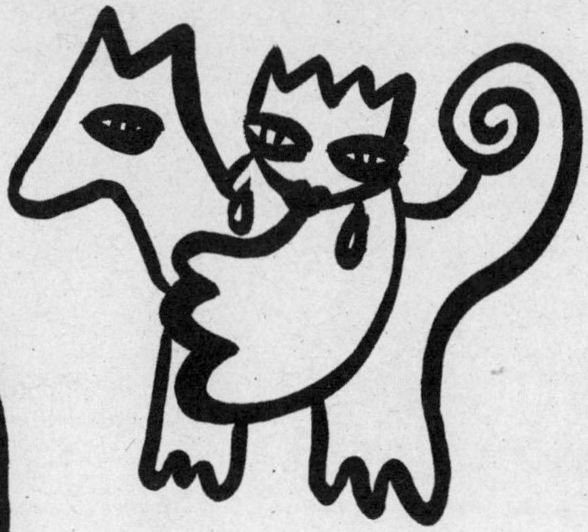

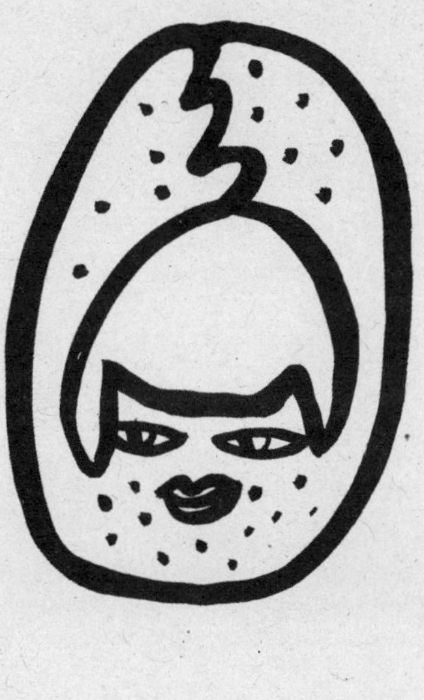

Some Thoughts on Terminology:

Collaboration

Collaboration describes an ongoing process of working together without a predefined goal or time limit, this differs from fixed cooperation.[14] The trigger for this type of collaboration is a shared dissatisfaction with a certain state or a given structure. The transformation of one's own state is part of the process, as is the generation of unknown knowledge. Collaboration can be challenging and impressive at the same time, especially in heterogeneous groups, as there are initially no fixed roles or responsibilities. In contrast to cooperation, individuals or teams work together and on an equal footing by contributing their respective expertise.

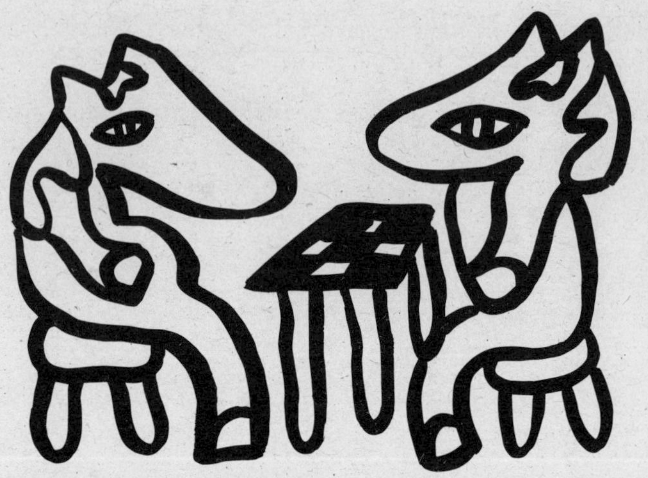

Participation

The term participation goes back to the Latin word *particeps* (taking part) and stands for involvement or inclusion. In general, it refers to the possibility of a person or group actively codesigning an event or process, but not the active contribution of their own ideas, topics, or questions.[15]

14 Florian Schneider, "Collaboration: The Dark Side of the Multitude," in *Sarai Reader 06: Turbulence*, eds. Monica Narula and Florian Schneider (Delhi: Sarai Media Lab, 2006), 572–576.

15 For example, Anja Piontek, *Museum und Partizipation. Theorie und Praxis kooperativer Ausstellungsprojekte und Beteiligungsangebote* (Bielefeld: transcript, 2017).

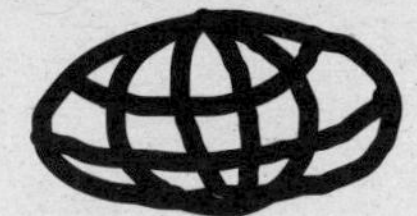

Public Space

The definition follows Oliver Marchart's view that "the public sphere arises wherever there is 'debate.' So the public space itself is not a space [...] but rather a principle: the principle of reactivation [...]."[16] If the public space is not understood as a physical space but as a space for reactivating debates, an institution can only be public if it allows dissent and friction with what it represents.

Buzzword Attitude, Or: Who Is "Everyone"? (Diversity)

For some years now, people have been talking about "everyone" as a target group for cultural institutions and programs with a buzzword attitude. It is rarely defined who is meant by this, who is being addressed. Diversity, on the other hand, is often measured in numbers: How many employees are diverse? How many marginalized groups could be attracted to the institution for an event? Here, too, the suggestion is to first look at what is there: Taking stock instead of wishful thinking, working with concrete conditions instead of numbers. It should be approached on the level of program and structure, not only on the level of marketing and funding reports.

Art Field

The term is used according to Oliver Marchart's interpretation. According to it, the art field is one of many fields of power in which hegemony is negotiated. This becomes all the clearer when he comes from

16 Oliver Marchart, "Art, Space and Public Sphere(s). Some fundamental remarks on the difficult relationship between public art, urbanism and political theory," *transversal*, no. 1 (2002), accessed October 13, 2021, www.transversal.at/transversal/0102/marchart/de.

discourse-analytical political science, and in his understanding differentiating Bourdieu's field theory with Gramsci's understanding of hegemony.[17]

Microprojects

The focus on microprojects is based on the assumption that small shifts can influence the larger structure. Especially if they are implemented collaboratively, resulting in changes in everyday routines and interactions.

Support System

Remaining in isolation is never a good idea. The support system is a kind of an advisory board, critical friends that can also actively contribute to projects of others or contribute their own. These are figures from urban society, the independent scene, local initiatives, or comparable representatives from outside, who are specifically approached depending on the project and, in the best case, sustainably tied to the institution.

Code of Conduct for Collaborative/Solidary Ways of Working Together

The Code of Conduct

can be used as a basis for internal collaboration, but above all, it can be helpful and important for working with outsiders/independent collaborators, who initially tend to have a more unstable position in terms of hierarchy and content than institutional employees. The code

17 Cf. Oliver Marchart, *Hegemonie im Kunstfeld. Die documenta-Ausstellungen dX, D11, d12 und die Politik der Biennalisierung* (Köln: Walther König, 2008), 92ff.

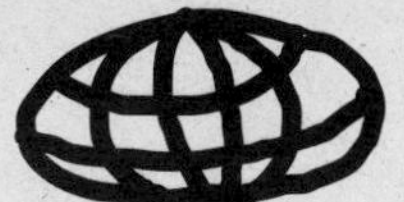

therefore replaces (or supplements) an institutional self-image and is always based on the questions of who owns the institution and who has what creative power.

All participants in a project have the same right to shape it, to take up space, and to disagree, regardless of age, gender, nationality, or level of education.

Each person brings their own perspective and therefore also a certain expertise, which should be valued equally. This is the only way to enable collaborative work between different age groups, educational backgrounds, and languages.

Internal employees offer all possible resources and create access to the institution for interested parties. They are committed to increasing awareness of access opportunities and openly communicate their ignorance and fallibility.

Understanding the museum or institution as a service provider for the various public means creating access at all levels and opening the doors as much as possible. In concrete terms, this means, for example, letting people into the depot, handing over rooms, or revealing mistakes and empty spaces.

All employees handle their language and actions with sensitivity, always with the aim of not offending anyone at any time.

Every person has different access needs, boundaries, and needs. Respecting and honoring these should be the basis of cooperation; rather than assuming things based on our own experience in our actions and communication, we should be asking the other person. Personal boundaries and social consensus should be respected.

Every type of work is valued equally and everyone involved is always mentioned.
One of the main challenges of collective or collaborative work, especially when institutional and independent people work together, is authorship. Therefore, every type of work is equally valued and all participants are mentioned.

In the case of misunderstandings or conflicts, the basic attitude is to first adopt a positive attitude towards the other person (group) instead of assuming negative intentions.
Always be sensitive in your dealings with one another. Always assume that the other person has the best intentions. Misunderstandings can only be resolved by talking things through. It is primarily about learning and unlearning together. The general principle is that the most inexperienced person sets the standard. In this context, it is necessary to discuss different types of experience, to recognize them as equally valid, and to break new ground.

Change leads to new beginnings. This can be difficult and painful; it requires patience. At the same time, this is the only way the institution can be sustainable. We are trained to acquire new knowledge and skills, but not to unlearn acquired knowledge. Unlearning can be extremely important in the context of transformation processes towards new forms of collaboration, for example when it comes to hierarchies and taking on or giving up responsibility.

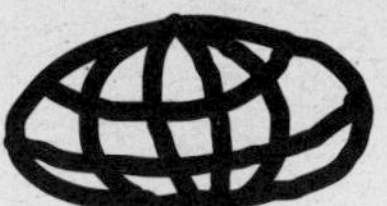

Before a project begins, a discussion round should be convened and all employees should be involved.

The entire team should be involved at the start of a new project. This includes the employees so that they can then decide to what extent they want to be involved in the project. The aim is to create a common basis (common sense) and distribute roles and responsibilities.

Dissent is important and brings new things to light. Always try to include as many perspectives as possible and do not force consensual decisions.

The more people are involved, the more perspectives there are to consider and present. Every perspective is a benefit and an enrichment.

The aim is to clarify at all times who is speaking with whom or for whom and under what conditions. Try to avoid speaking for others, give everyone space to speak for themselves.

Talk to each other, not for or about each other. A brief check-in round at the beginning of each round of talks can help, for example. Questions in such a round could be how the person is doing, how they have experienced the time since the last meeting, whether they have any new questions or needs. Each person should not speak for longer than one minute, the group listens but does not react to what is said.

Literature

- **Baur, Joachim, ed.** *Das Museum der Zukunft: 43 neue Beiträge zur Diskussion über die Zukunft des Musems.* **Bielefeld: transcript, 2020.**
- **Beitl, Matthias, Beatrice Jaschke, and Nora Sternfeld, eds.** *Gegenöffentlichkeit organisieren. Kritisches Management im Kuratieren.* **Berlin: De Gruyter, 2019.**
- **Billing, Johanna, Maria Lind, and Lars Nilsson, eds.** *Taking the Matter into Common Hands: On Contemporary Art and Collaborative Practices.* **London: Black Dog Publishing, 2007.**
- **Bourdieu, Pierre. "The Logic of Fields." In** *Reflexive Anthropology*, **edited by Pierre Bourdieu and Loic Wacquant. Frankfurt am Main: Suhrkamp, 1996.**
- **Bushart, Magdalena, und Henrike Haug, eds.** *Geteilte Arbeit. Praktiken künstlerischer Kooperation.* **Köln: Böhlau, 2020.**
- **De Wachter, and Ellen Mara.** *Co-Art: Artists on Creative Collaboration.* **New York: Phaidon, 2017.**
- **Fraser, Andrea. "From the Critique of Institutions to an Institution of Critique."** *Artforum* **44, no. 1 (September 2005): 278–283.**
- **Freire, Paulo.** *Pedagogy of the Oppressed. Education as the Practice of Freedom.* **Hamburg: Rowohlt, 1998.**
- **Gander, Robert, Andreas Rudigier, and Bruno Winkler, eds.** *Museum und Gegenwart: Verhandlungsorte und Aktionsfelder für soziale Verantwortung und gesellschaftlichen Wandel.* **Bielefeld: transcript, 2015.**
- **Gesser, Susanne, Nina Gorgus, and Angela Jannelli, eds.** *Das subjektive Museum. Partizipative Museumsarbeit zwischen Selbstvergewisserung und gesellschaftspolitischem Engagement.* **Bielefeld: transcript, 2020.**
- **Grebber, Gesa.** *Kollaboration in der Kunstpädagogik: Studien zu neuen Formen gemeinschaftlicher Praktiken unter den Bedingungen digitaler Medienkulturen.* **München: kopaed, 2019.**
- **Greuß, Fiona.** *Das dialogische Kunstwerk, Gesprächsformate und Öffentlichkeit in der Kunst von der Art Workers Coalition bis Group Material und New Genre Public Art.* **Berlin: Freie Universität Berlin, 2019.**
- **International Council of Museums (ICOM), "Museum Definition," accessed September 19, 2022, www.icom.museum/en/resources/standards-guidelines/museum-definition/.**
- **Jaschke, Beatrice, ed.** *Educational Turn: Handlungsräume der Kunst- und Kulturvermittlung.* **Vienna: schnittpunkt, 2012.**

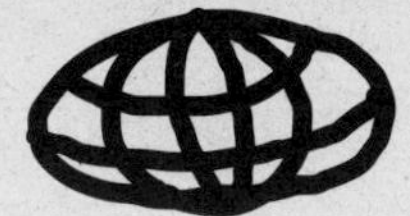

- **Kammerer, Dietmar.** *Vom Publicum. Das Öffentliche in der Kunst*. **Bielefeld: transcript, 2012.**
- **Kester, Grant H.** *The One and the Many: Contemporary Collaborative Art in a Global Context.* **Durham: Duke University Press, 2011.**
- **Marchart, Oliver. "Die kuratorische Funktion. Oder, was heißt eine Aus/Stellung zu organisieren." In** *Curating Critique*, **edited by Marianne Eigenheer. Frankfurt am Main: Revolver, 2007.**
- **Marchart, Oliver.** *Hegemonie im Kunstfeld. Die documenta-Ausstellungen dX, D11, d12 und die Politik der Biennalisierung*. **Köln: Walther König, 2008.**
- **Marchart, Oliver. "Art, Space and the Public Sphere(s). Some fundamental remarks on the difficult relationship between public art, urbanism and political theory."** *transversal* **, no. 1 (2002). Accessed October 13, 2021. https://www.transversal.at/transversal/0102/marchart/en.**
- **Marchart, Oliver. "Kunst, Raum und Öffentlichkeit(en). Einige grundsätzliche Anmerkungen zum schwierigen Verhältnis von Public Art, Urbanismus und politischer Theorie."** *transversal,* **no. 1 (2002). Accessed September 19, 2022. www.transversal.at/transversal/0102/marchart/de.**
- **Möntmann, Nina, ed.** *Art and Its Institutions: Current Conflicts, Critique and Collaborations*. **London: Black Dog Publishing, 2006.**
- **Mörsch, Carmen, Angeli Sachs, and Thomas Sieber, eds.** *Ausstellen und Vermitteln im Museum der Gegenwart. Wie verändert sich Museumsarbeit, wenn Ausstellen und Vermitteln als integriertes Konzept verstanden werden*? **Bielefeld: transcript, 2016.**
- **Mörsch, Carmen et al., eds. "Zeit für Vermittlung." Accessed September 29, 2022. www.kultur-vermittlung.ch/zeit-fuer-vermittlung/v1/?m=0&m2=1&lang=d.**

- Papastergiadis, Nikos. *Museums of the Commons. L'Internationale and the Crisis of Europe.* London: Routledge, 2020.
- Piontek, Anja. *Museum und Partizipation. Theorie und Praxis kooperativer Ausstellungsprojekte und Beteiligungsangebote*. Bielefeld: transcript, 2017.
- Plegge, Henrike, and Ina Scheffler, eds. *Umräumen. Das Moment der Veränderung bildungsinstitutioneller Räume*. Oberhausen: Athena, 2018.
- Rogoff, Irit. "'Schmuggeln.' Eine verkörperte Kritikalität." *what's next?* (2007): 259. Accessed September 29, 2022. www.whtsnxt.net/259.
- Rogoff, Irit. "The Expanded Field." In *The Curatorial: A Philosophy of Curating*, edited by Jean-Paul Martinon, 41–48. London; New York: Bloomsbury Academic, 2013.
- Rogoff, Irit. "Creative Practices of Knowledge." Lecture at the conference "Black Mountain—Educational Turn and the Avantgarde." Hamburger Bahnhof, Berlin, September 2015. Accessed September 29, 2022. https://www.youtube.com/watch?v=uCn8sq98sro.
- Schneider, Florian. "Collaboration: The Dark Side of the Multitude." In *Sarai Reader 06: Turbulence*, edited by Monica Narula and Florian Schneider, 572–576. Delhi: Sarai Media Lab, 2006.
- Sheikh, Simon. "Öffentlichkeit und die Aufgaben der 'progressiven' Kunstinstitution." *transversal*, no. 2 (2004). Accessed October 7, 2021. www.transversal.at/transversal/0504/sheikh/de.
- Sheikh, Simon. "Notes on Institutional Critique."*transversal,* no. 1 (2006). Accessed September 29, 2022. https://www.transversal.at/transversal/0106/sheikh/en.
- Sternfeld, Nora. *Das radikaldemokratische Museum*. Berlin: De Gruyter, 2018.
- Tyradellis, Daniel. *Müde Museen, Oder: Wie Ausstellungen unser Denken verändern könnten*. Hamburg: Edition Körber-Stiftung, 2014.
- Witcomb, Andrea. *Re-Imagining the Museum: Beyond the Mausoleum.* London: Routledge, 2003.
- Von Bismarck, Beatrice. *Das Kuratorische*. Leipzig: Spector Books, 2020.
- Voorhies, James, ed. *What Ever Happened to New Institutionalism?* Berlin: Sternberg Press, 2016.

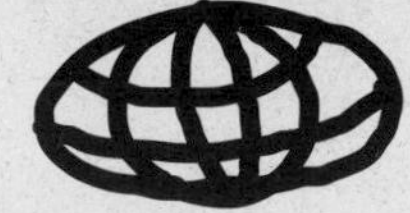

Reference Projects

- Constant Collaboration Guidelines: https://constantvzw.org/wefts/orientationspourcollaboration.en.html.
- Constant Manifestos of Care: www.constantvzw.org/p/collectiveconditions.manifestoofcares.diff.html.
- Institute for Art Education at the Zurich University of the Arts: What is Art Education? www.kultur-vermittlung.ch/zeit-fuer-vermittlung/v1/?m=10&m2=4&lang=d.
- Kollektiv Raumstation, Urban Equipe, Organize Yourselves! Changing the City Together: https://www.urban-equipe.ch/projects/organisierteuchpublikation.
- lab.Bode—Initiative to Strengthen Museum Education: /www.lab-bode-pool.de/de/.
- reflect—A Collective Journey to New Grounds: https://www.reflect-culture.de/.
- Sonja Hempel, Diana Schuster: Zine Dealing with Racialized Image Titles in Art Museums: www.diskrit-kubi.net/probevignette/probe-zinebildtitel/.
- tranzit.hu, Curatorial Dictionary: www.tranzit.org/curatorialdictionary/.

Expression of Gratitude

I want to thank the people who helped me shape this project:

Freiraum at the Museum für Kunst und Gewerbe Hamburg, UZwei at the Dortmunder U, Kunsthalle Osnabrück, Kunstmuseum Bochum, Neue Gesellschaft für bildende Kunst and Haus der Kulturen der Welt in Berlin, and Museum Ludwig in Cologne.

- SPECIAL THANKS: Katrin Lohbeck, Svenja Reiner & Aneta Rostkowska.
- GRAPHIC CONCEPT AND DESIGN: Sophia Schach
- CONTENT DESIGN AND TEXTS: Paulina Seyfried

Kind thanks to the Cultural Office of the City of Cologne for their financial support. The English version was produced as part of the Islands of Kinship project, which is funded by Creative Europe.

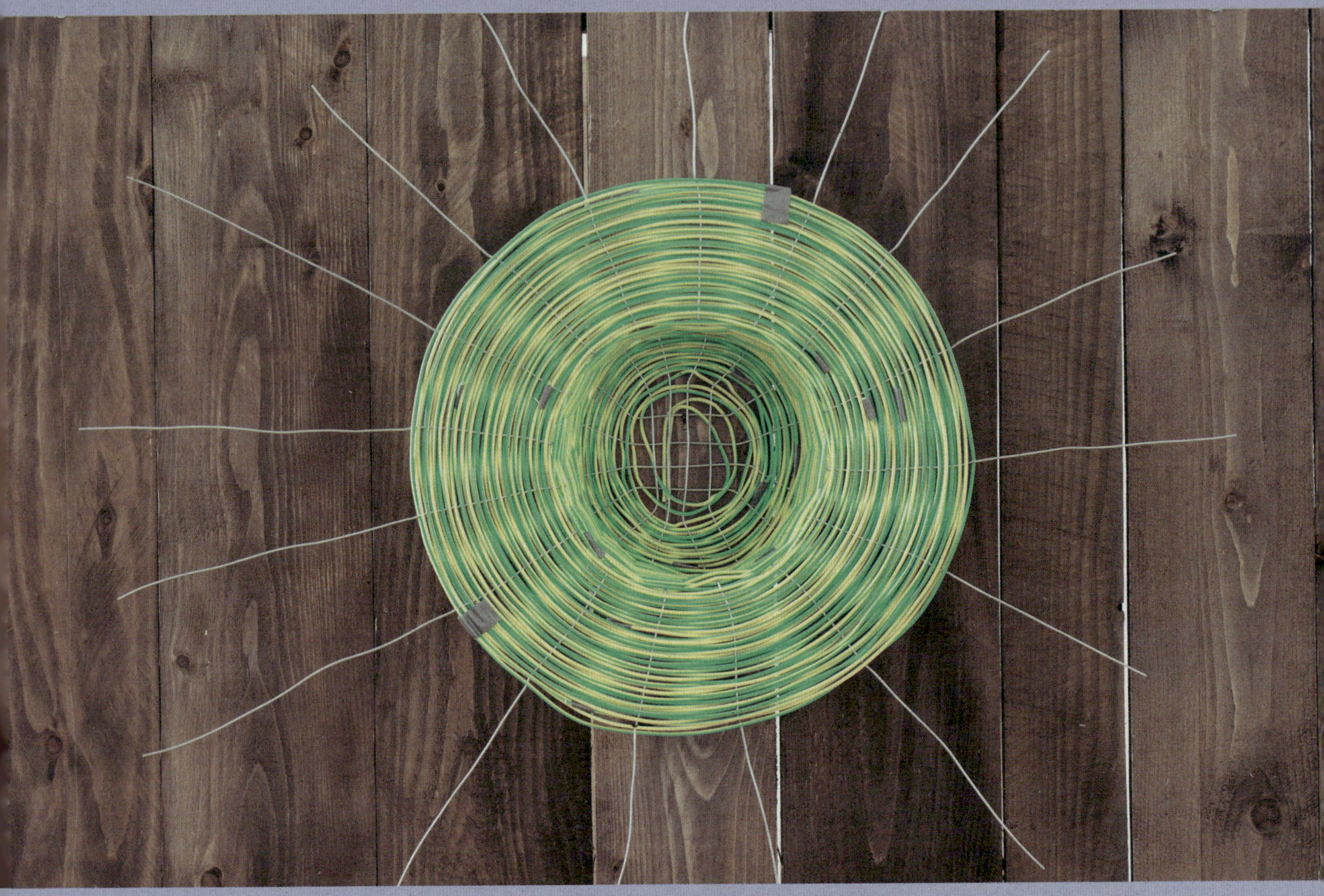

Luki Essender: Of Yous

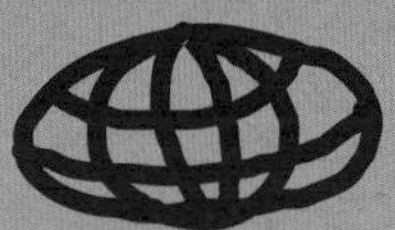

Multitudes

James Taylor-Foster

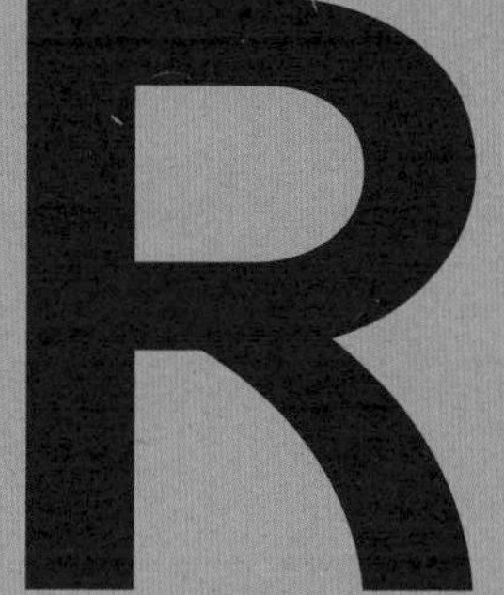eenchanting our realities with a multitude of worlds is perhaps the most pressing need of our collective now. Imagination is a personal act—a primordial part of the forever-game of human-ing. Within us are imagined figures: brief encounters, some who have grown with us since childhood, or those who have been present long before we knew to breathe. Cardinal voices that echo across our lived experience and whisper to us with intention. These imagined figures may be somehow tangible—*mom?*—or may exist far out of the habitable world. Gendered, non-gendered, wholly alien, queer-as-fuck: bodily outlines, continuously in transition, haunt and nourish our inner and outer realms. There are, I'd wager, a multitude of beings that we speak with, engage in emotional dialogue, hide from view, grow alongside and through and, perhaps eventually, reveal and give shape to. We might only glimpse them in frames, manifesting as containers or vessels: words and gestures, objects and materials, manipulations in space. Each figure seeks expression through a single body's many masks. Offering space for our many selves is muddy, vital work.

If we consider *this* world as nothing but a springboard (of infinite, gamified complexity) then we acknowledge that it can be played with or challenged. Most avenues (read: consequences) that we take are the result of choices. Making a choice is one of the basic tenets of world-glimpsing. What do I wear? Should I say these words out loud? If the act of choice-making defines the unspoken trajectories of the everyday, manufacturing a choice often feels impractical—limited to the realms of nightdream, daydream, and fantasy. Not merely making a choice, but actively creating one, untethers the self from its own sense of truth. It's an unstable condition to enter into: a space of memory, trauma, desire. It nurtures a spectral sense of who we were and how we find ourselves. It is for this reason, among many others, that world-glimpsing is not identical to world-*building*, which takes into account the realm of the nonhuman and the systems of definition that ambush us day to day. World-glimpsing centers the self as independent, autonomous, yet kindred. It makes room for the more-than-human, embraces the dissonance of it all, and concedes to the infinite malleability of things. It has no goal, nor promises resolution.

Dreamscapes, states of flow that fuse the fabulous and the frightening, are one way in which to glimpse other worlds. Dwelling in the complexity of the sleeping self unstitches a seam towards other ways of interfacing with the mystery of our psyche, and the mystery of others. If we strive to untangle our person from the carcinogen of normative behavior, we can animate our multitudinous mess of thoughts and emotions, invite others to exist beside them, and live to see what might happen as a result. We only entertain *this* world (the world I am writing from and that you, perhaps, are reading in) as *the* world because it is, as most have been taught to believe, all "flesh and blood." We crowbar our many selves into one corporeal body because it is acknowledged by others in return negatively, positively, or neutrally, and so the illusion is sustained. This world of blood and flesh consumes our scope to glimpse between and beyond. If we are to step into a landscape defined by uncertainty, a space that is sometimes overwhelming but often empowering, then we must humanize ourselves with, alongside, and for the sake of others. Without world-glimpsing, this world will be the one that ultimately liquidates our grasp of who we really are.

Kindling new narratives is a mode of world-glimpsing. Often transferred through words—written, scratched, engraved, ritually spoken or sung—works of imagination, such as stories, resonate

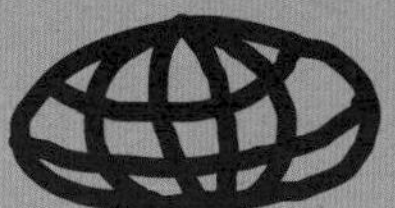

through people and places and transform, once in a while, into myth or lore. These stories are durational, built across time, and have no certain point of origin. While many stories tie us to the tangible world, some are capable of releasing us. Those able to untangle us from the taught narratives we live within are outside of linear time, detached from reality—a nebulous blend of what we can perceive with that which we yet cannot. Glimpsing new worlds through story-sharing is, at its most powerful, not a mere stumble nor the result of a coincidence. It is the carefully articulated result of a heightened attention towards the complexity of our own thoughts, our collective desires, and our interdependence to our imaginative potential.

Often connected to a place—rooms and edifices, things against our skin, images, sounds, and scents—nostalgia (a disused, dirty word) is a form of world-glimpsing that offers comfort and deceit in equal measure. It is the subliminally processed past manifesting in the present. In the steady journey towards the interior self, nostalgia can sometimes feel to be the only thing that holds our-selves

together. It is an immensely inadequate feeling. Nothing can mimic a missed sense of security, the touch of an abandoned other, or the lost rootedness of a place. Although a useful mechanism for wistful longing, or for fostering a sense of belonging, nostalgia can be far more powerful as a tool. It distorts what we remember and deforms how we recall, opening a door to the abstract and the uncanny. Autonomous from the many selves that make up who we are and who we wish to become, nostalgia invites us to imagine through our yearning, our hunger, our lust.

Reality may be irrefutable, but it is bendable. Apparitions from our pasts may be inevitable, but they are pliable. Glitches may be constant, but they are invitations. Glimpses into different worlds can be birthed through imagination: inhabited, reformed, discarded. Once alive, they live or die in the hands of their source—and in the hands of a multitude of others. It is a plurality of worlds that nourishes the world in which we find ourselves: worlds *Of Yous*.

Of Yous
Luki Essender in Cover
with James Taylor-Foster
Excerpt from a Podcast
November 9, 2023, Bratislava

Luki: I was just brainstorming in relation to my writing. I realized that I am always writing for somebody, and although it's always a singular person, in total it's a group of people, but I'm always approaching them individually. I rarely use names. I always say you, just cause it's very direct. And then I myself get lost sometimes like: "Who are you?"

James: But are you using the kind of plural you or the singular you?

L: Singular, but then it becomes this multitude *of yous*. Afterwards, after a few months or so, I tend to forget who the particular piece was for and I find it beautiful because it makes it stronger, somehow more relevant.

J: In what way?

L: It just feels firm.

J: It's defiant, right? But it's also ambiguous.

L: Yeah, exactly, both. I don't even care that I forget who the text was for, I mean, for somebody for sure, but maybe for everybody, or anybody.

J: When you make a work, are you making it for an audience?

L: No.

J: Who are you making it for?

L: Myself.

J: That's beautiful. Is that the case with everything you've done? Has that always been the reality?

L: Yeah, I'd say so.

J: So, with this work that you're opening at the JKS, who is it for?

L: It's for myself.

J: That's fascinating. It's kind of a rare position to take, from my experience.

L: I believe that if you want to start somewhere, you need to start with yourself, and you know, I haven't gotten any further than that yet. I just hope this doesn't come out like a demonstration of self-obsession because my work is not really about myself. My approach always starts with me as an individual, cause if I don't make it for myself, if I don't like it, if I don't believe, why would anybody else even care?

J: That's definitely true. So what kind of ownership do you feel over the work? Because you've done performance, installation work, you've done also more intangible and ephemeral pieces. They all have different levels of tangibility. This is a human-size installation we are talking about, so I find it interesting to talk about ownership. And the topic touches essentially the entire structure of the value around the art world.

L: I mean I take ownership. It's mine (giggles) but I want people to experience it. I want people to see it, to interact with it. I love talking about it, hearing what people think, what they feel.

J: What I understand from *Of Yous* is a very real poetic tension between the fact that it is very defiantly singular—it's aware of itself, it stands there with a certain self-assuredness, and consequently it doesn't really give a fuck about naming or promoting itself, or who exactly it is speaking to. I think that's exactly what you just described—a paradox between the idea *of you*, the creator, and a multitude *of yous*, a random horde of people that might interact with the work, followed by the fact that the work almost doesn't want, or rather doesn't need an audience or people to give it life. Does that make any sense to you?

L: Yeah, absolutely.

J: Have you ever thought about that in any really deep way or is that just simply something that's organically happening throughout your practice?

L: If you ask me who I'm making my work for, I never think of the audience. When I was in art school, it was always a question. They were encouraging us to imagine our audience. But this only works to a certain extent, you can imagine a group of people with specific attributes, but I would prefer not to. I find it rather limiting and not super relevant for myself as an artist. I don't really need to know the target group; I don't like to think in these corporate terms.

J: You and I, we've been in a rich sketchy truculent dialogue over a fairly long period of time about this work and the result is a text that is sitting alongside it. It's a sort of textual representation of the visual side of it and also my personal account, but maybe you can give us a sense of the origin of the installation from your perspective.

L: This work began with an herb drying house that I found out about through a print published by Čierne diery. I was intrigued by the structure of the object, its function, too. I thought: "Oh, this is a fun building located in the east of Slovakia." Back then, I lived in Bratislava and simultaneously I also stumbled upon a pharmacy—Lekáreň u Salvatora—a beautiful and amazing historical sight in the city center. At the time I was working on different projects, but I used to go back to the space mentally and started to develop a story between the herb drying businessman and the pharmacist in Bratislava. A fictional gay story about how they have known each other, started a business together, real love was involved, etc. I never finished the story. Maybe it was not even a story, more like a setting for a relationship that I imagined in my head. Couple of years later, I got invited to do this show with a new commission and I don't remember specifically picking this story or picking the house as a reference point but I just started making it. The way I proceed on a work of this scale is that I first start to make a 3D visualization on my computer. This is helpful not only for me but also makes the production smoother as I need help with the construction itself and when I have it in 3D it's much easier to communicate what I need from other people. So, I just started sketching and it snowballed. In the summer I then added the woven objects. It was a rough period emotionally and I remember making them intensively in my studio listening to super hypnotic synthesizer compositions by Caterina Barbieri that go on for fourteen minutes. It synced with the super repetitive weaving of electrical cables. So that emotional spiral is another layer of the project. The connection to the house was basically that I wanted to make this hybrid object that technically resembles a basket, or a hat, that people who collected wildflowers or herbs could be using or wearing. I wanted to play with the ambiguous form, that it could be a container, but it could also be a hat or, depending on how we position it in space, there can be more references. For example, during the installation process, somebody pointed out that it resembles a structure that people in Slovakia weave around big wine glass bottles, about five liters in volume. They're really beautiful, multicolored. And in my head the whole time I was thinking about these trash bins we had in our classrooms at elementary school. It looks really similar—woven with this plastic feel to it.

J: It's true that when you're in the exhibition, when you're interacting with the work, you feel this kind of strange relationship to craft, and you also have a compelling relationship to the meditative process.

That manifests most clearly through the woven works as there's a sort of tangibility of your hand there, but I think it goes throughout the whole installation material-wise. And then, these trash cans, what do you remember about them?

L: They were quite dark in color. It was one of those objects from the past, that you really did not understand as a school kid in the early 2000s. Compared to the 90s, for Slovakia it was a progressive time. We entered the EU in 2004, I felt very hopeful about the future, and it opened amazing opportunities for many. Quite contradictory to that trash can, which represented an object from a completely different, alienated regime. At the same time, it was still very present, fulfilling its function.

J: These kinds of objects have time embedded in them, there is a finality to all of it, isn't there?

L: Talking about time, I like to work with this ambiguity, when something feels familiar and confuses you at the same time. I like this metaphor of myself making a step, but I don't really put my foot on the ground to finish it. It stays hanging in the air and that's kind of my work. I can understand that some people are not comfortable with that, or they view it as not enough, unfinished, because they cannot tread on solid ground. But alienation is never anchored, and I like to work with that kind of atmosphere.

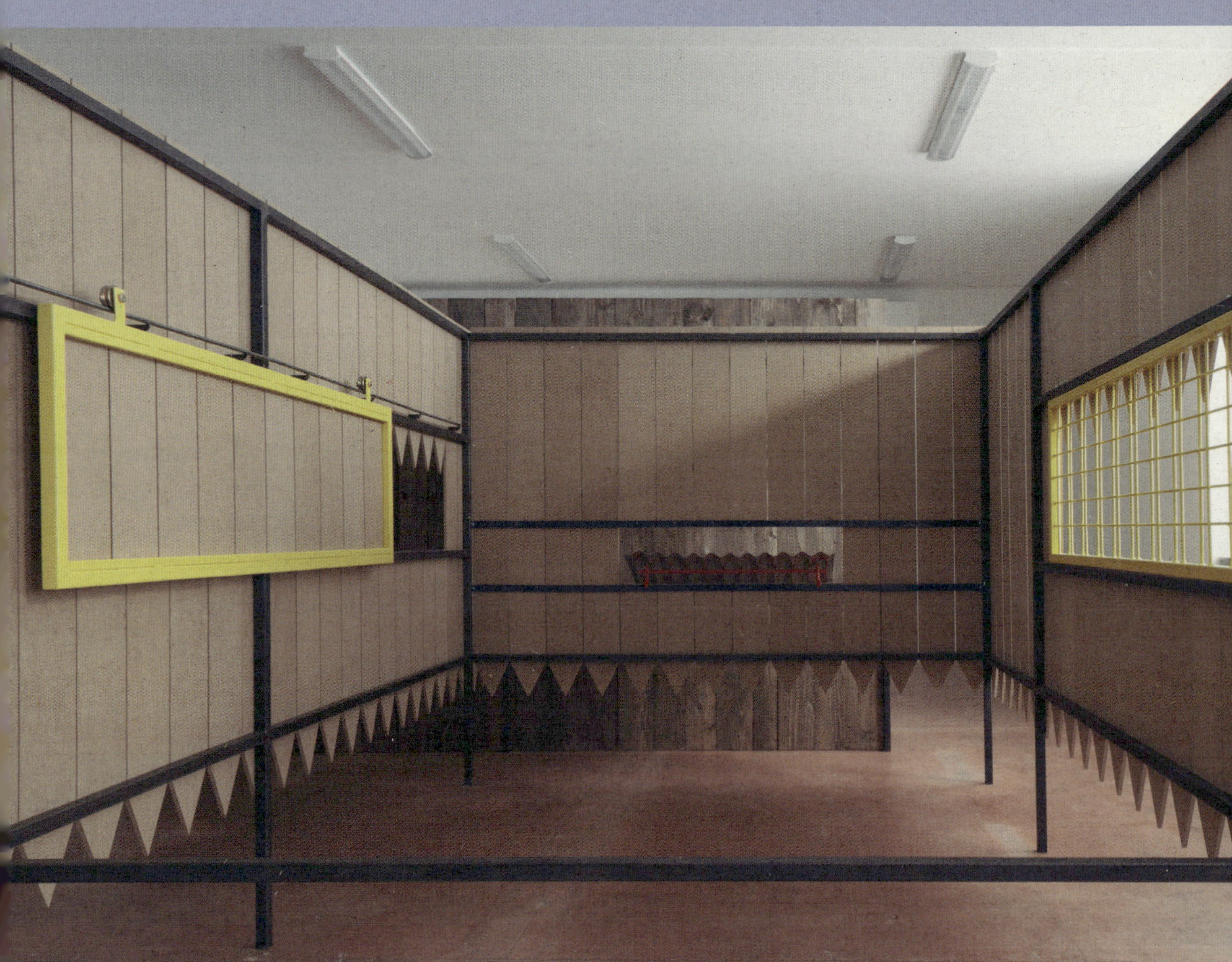

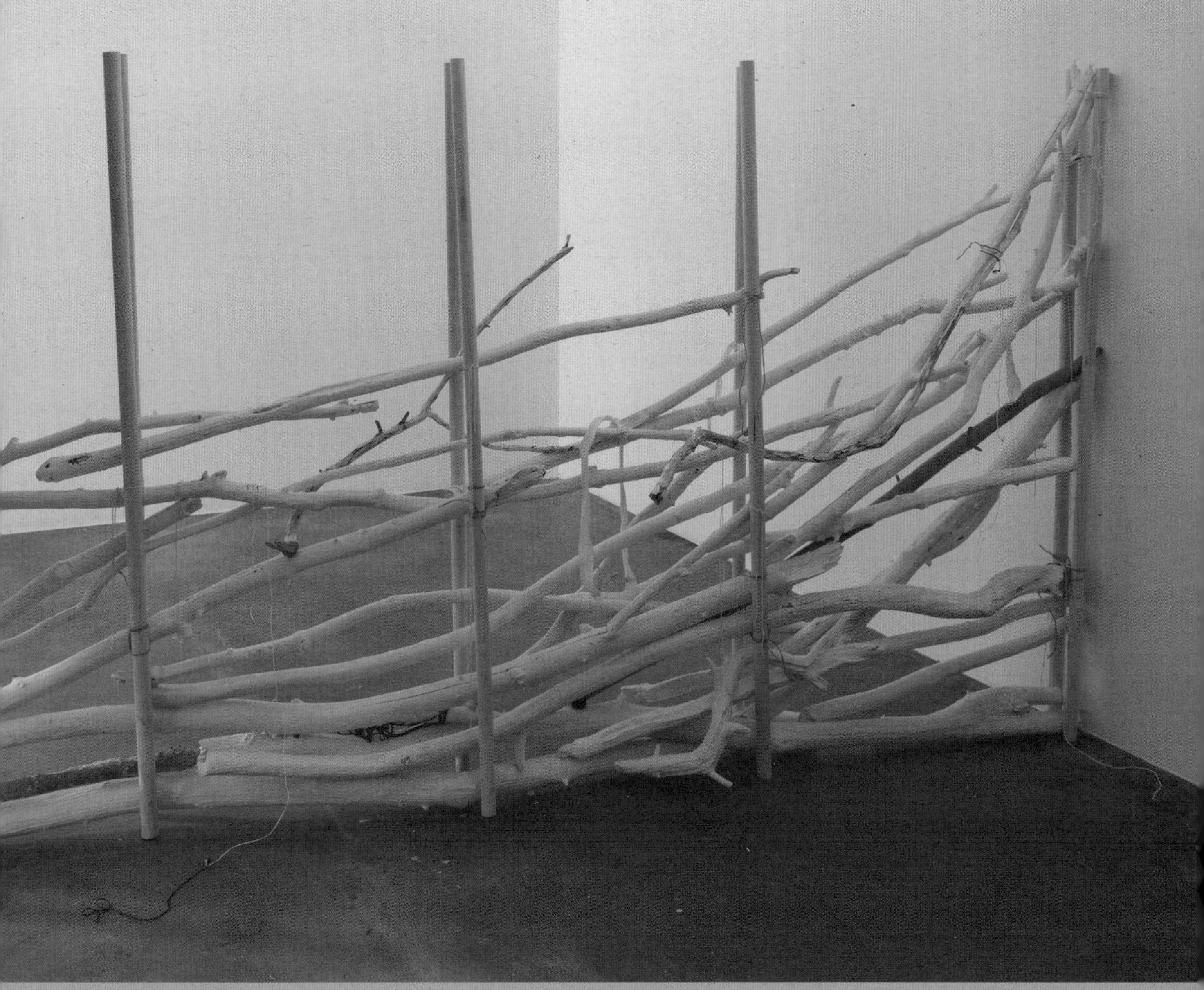

LUKI ESSENDER: OF YOUS

installation
2023

THE COMMISSION WAS PRESENTED AS PART OF THE EXHIBITION:

- Of Yous, Július Koller Society—
Nová Cvernovka, Bratislava, Slovakia,
November 10, 2023 – January 12, 2024,
organized by Július Koller Society

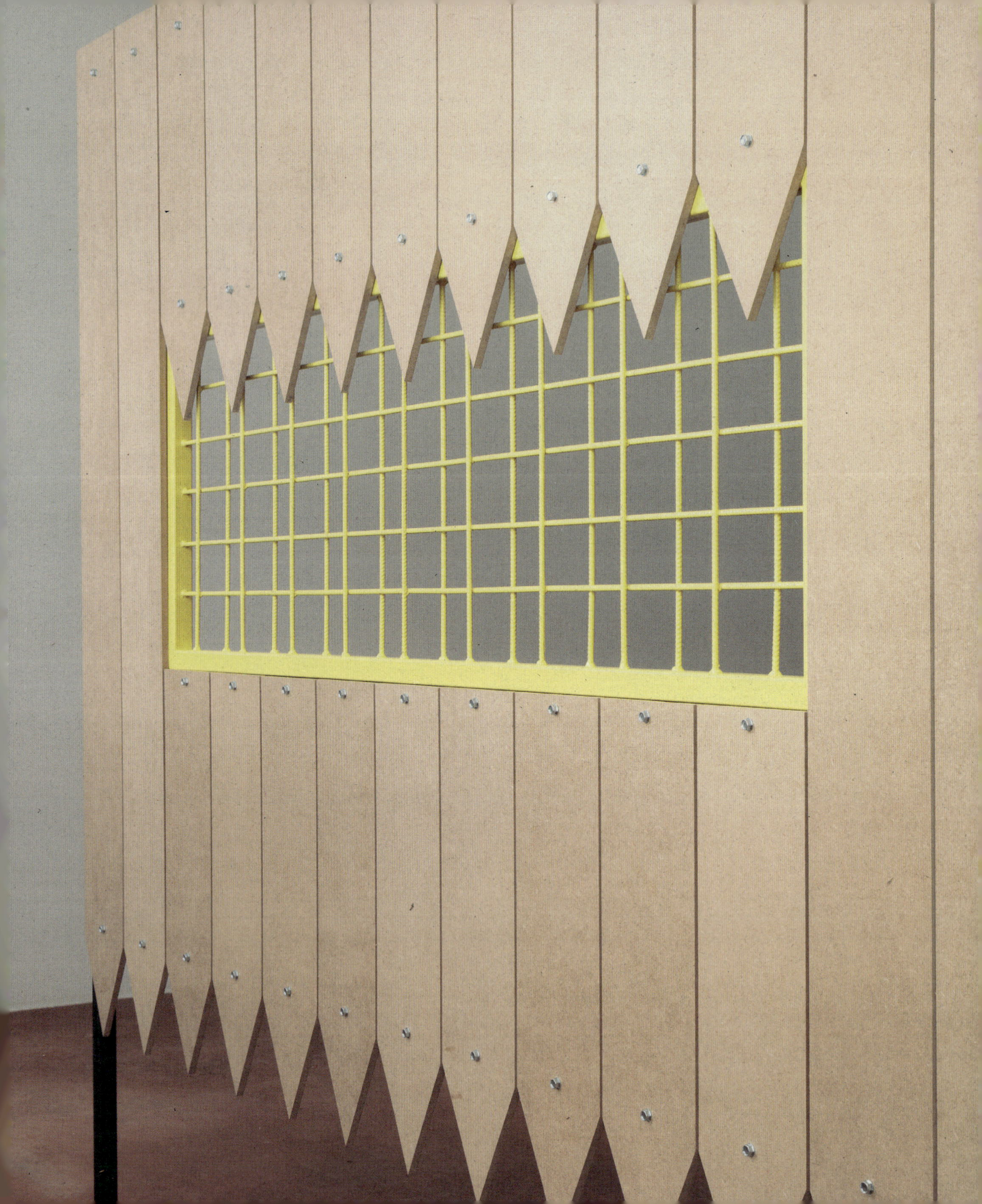

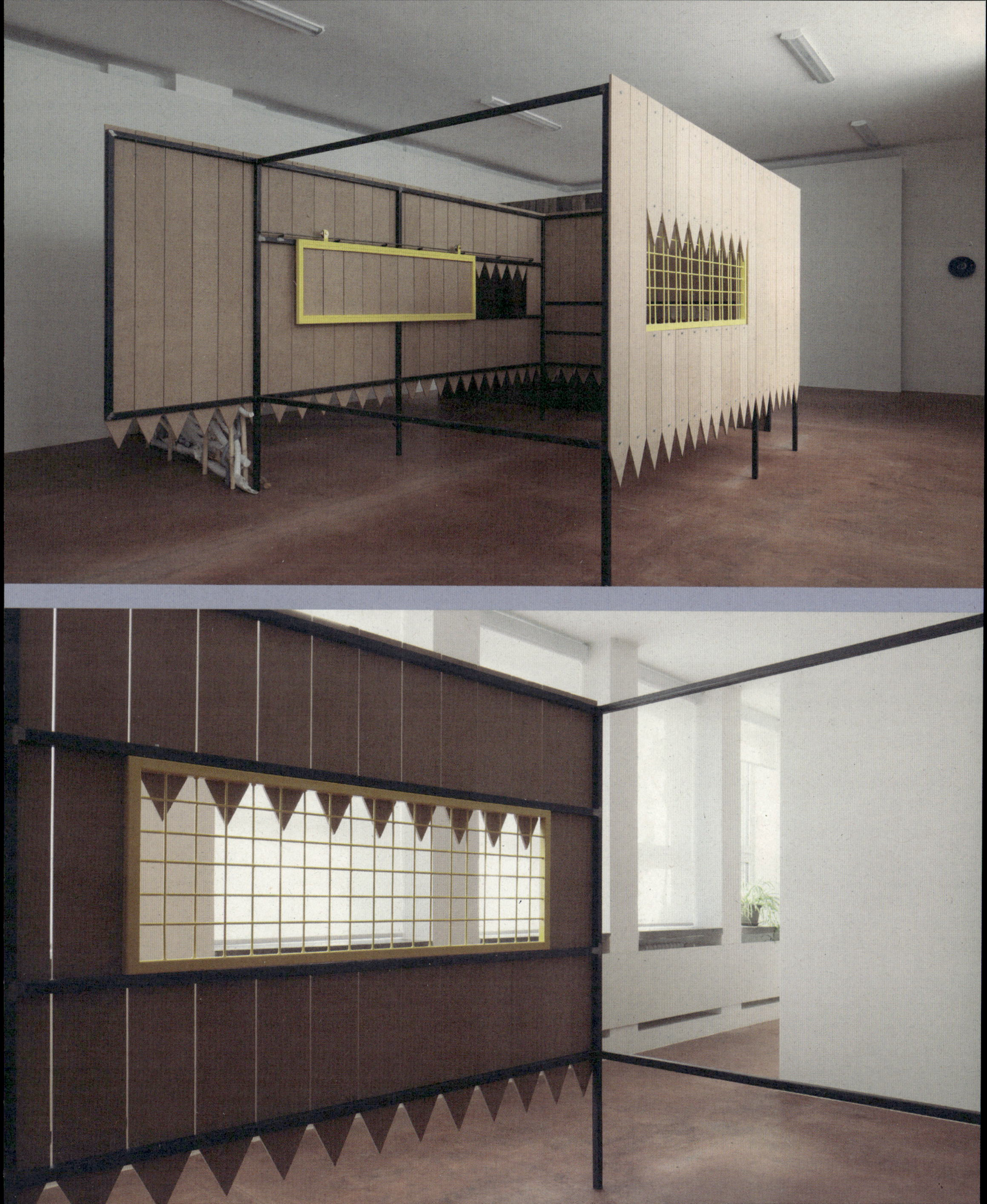

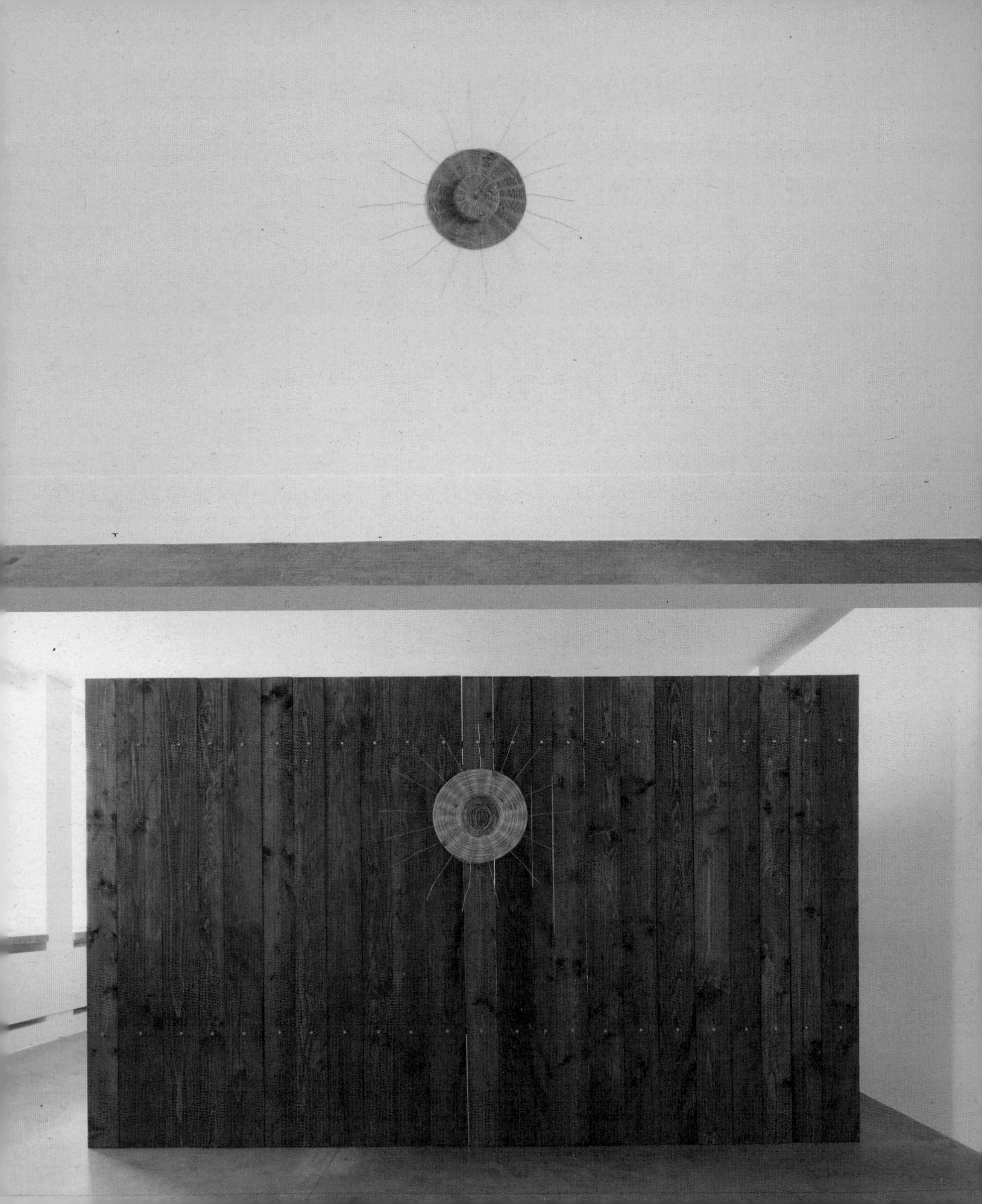

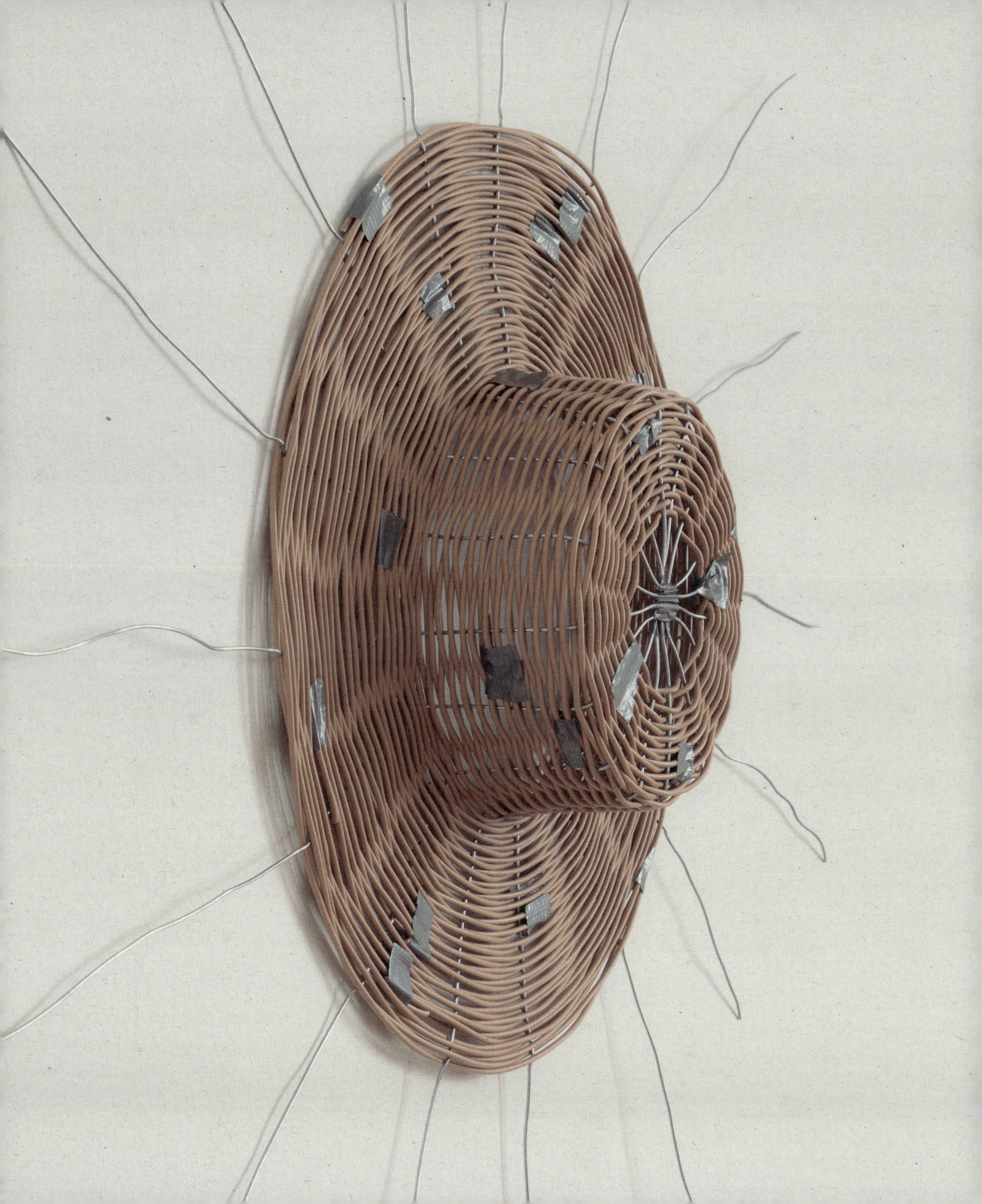

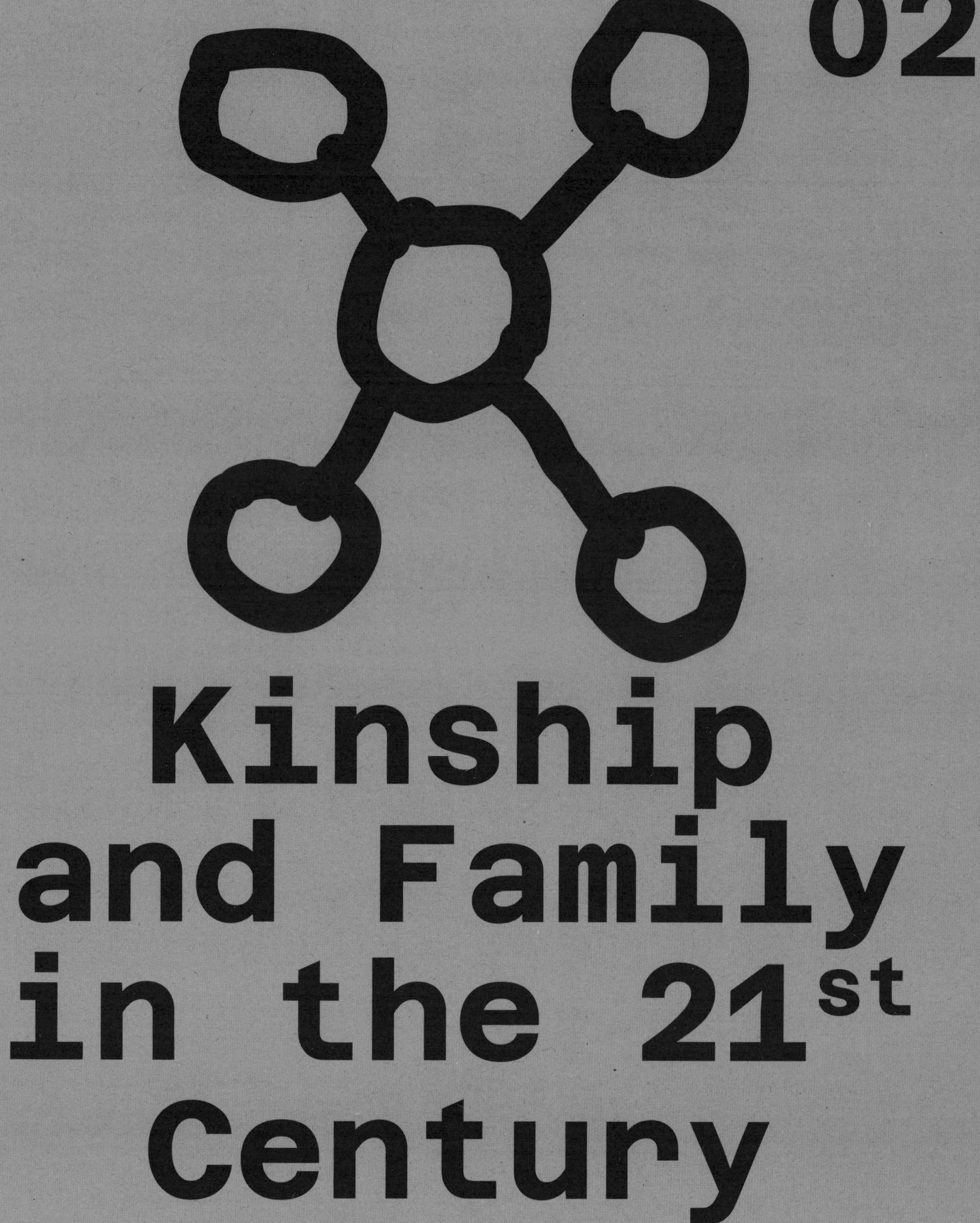
02
Kinship
and Family
in the 21st
Century

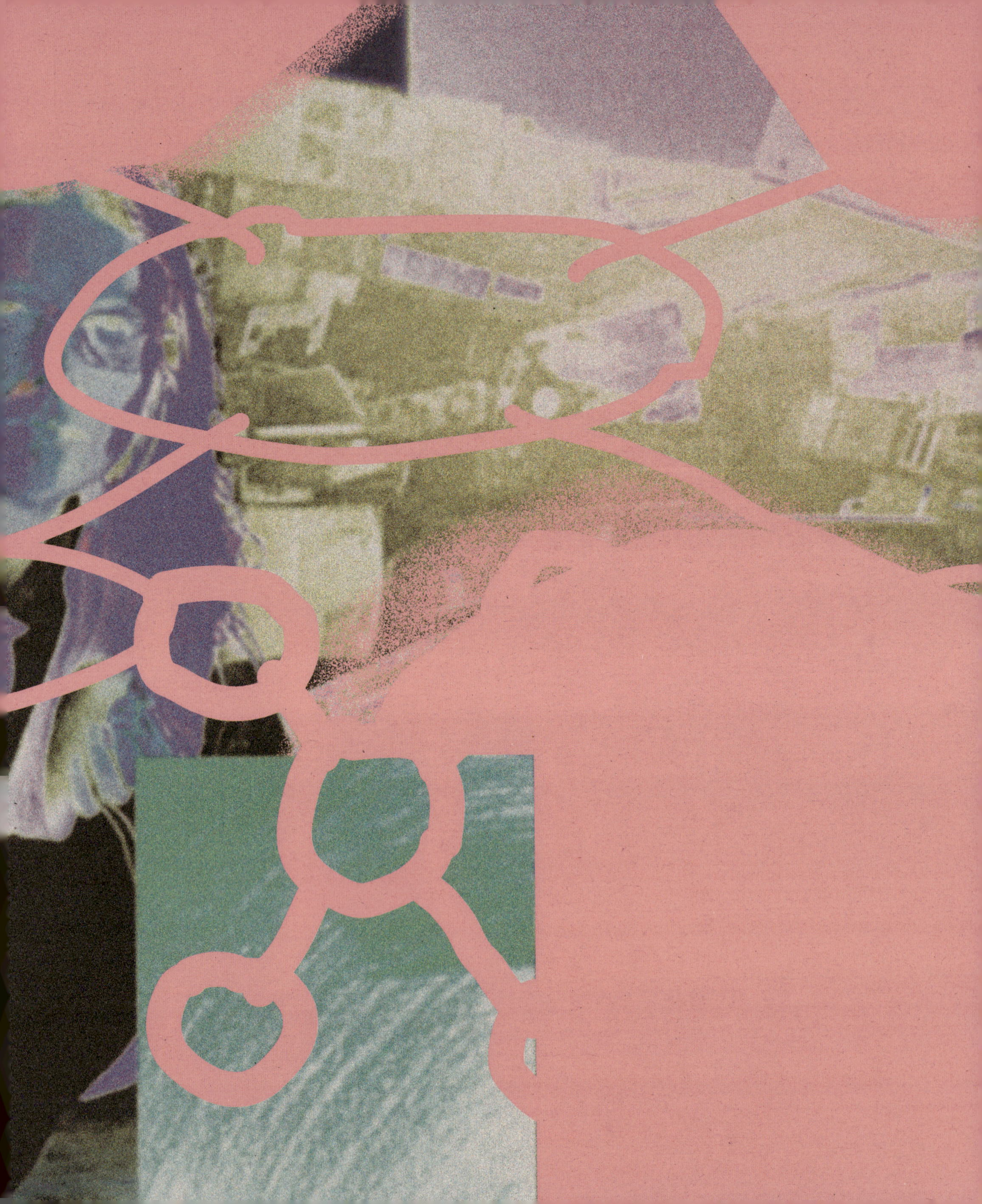

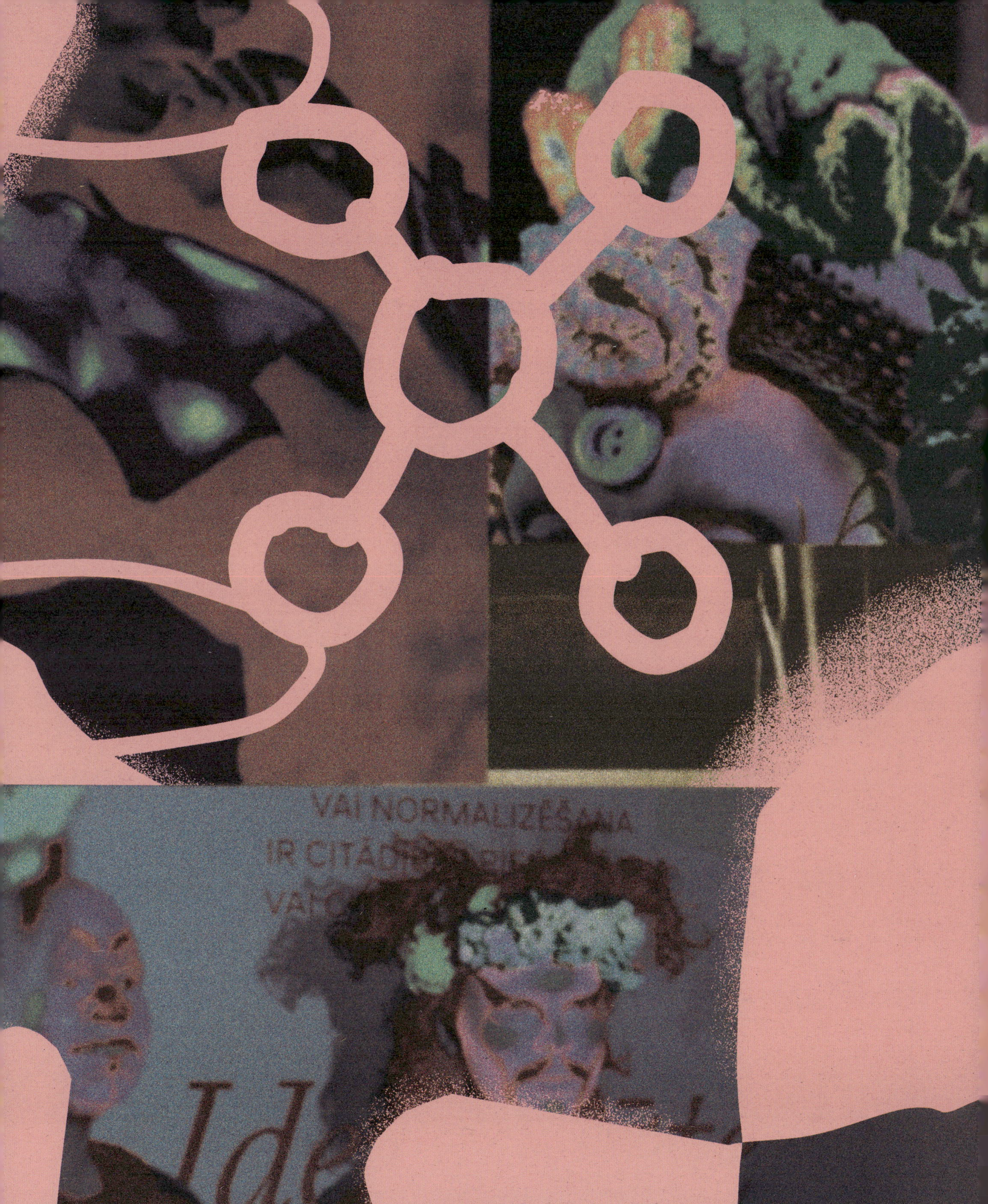
VAI NORMALIZĒŠANA

This thematic line explores and reflects intimate human relationships (such as family, partnership, or comradeship) and different modes of togetherness. Its aim is to learn about and show the diversity and richness of different ways of being and living together, question the history of the dominant ones, and advocate for emancipation of those considered as nonnormative, underrepresented, or oppressed. It challenges the (nuclear) family as a dominant paradigm for societal and economic well-being.

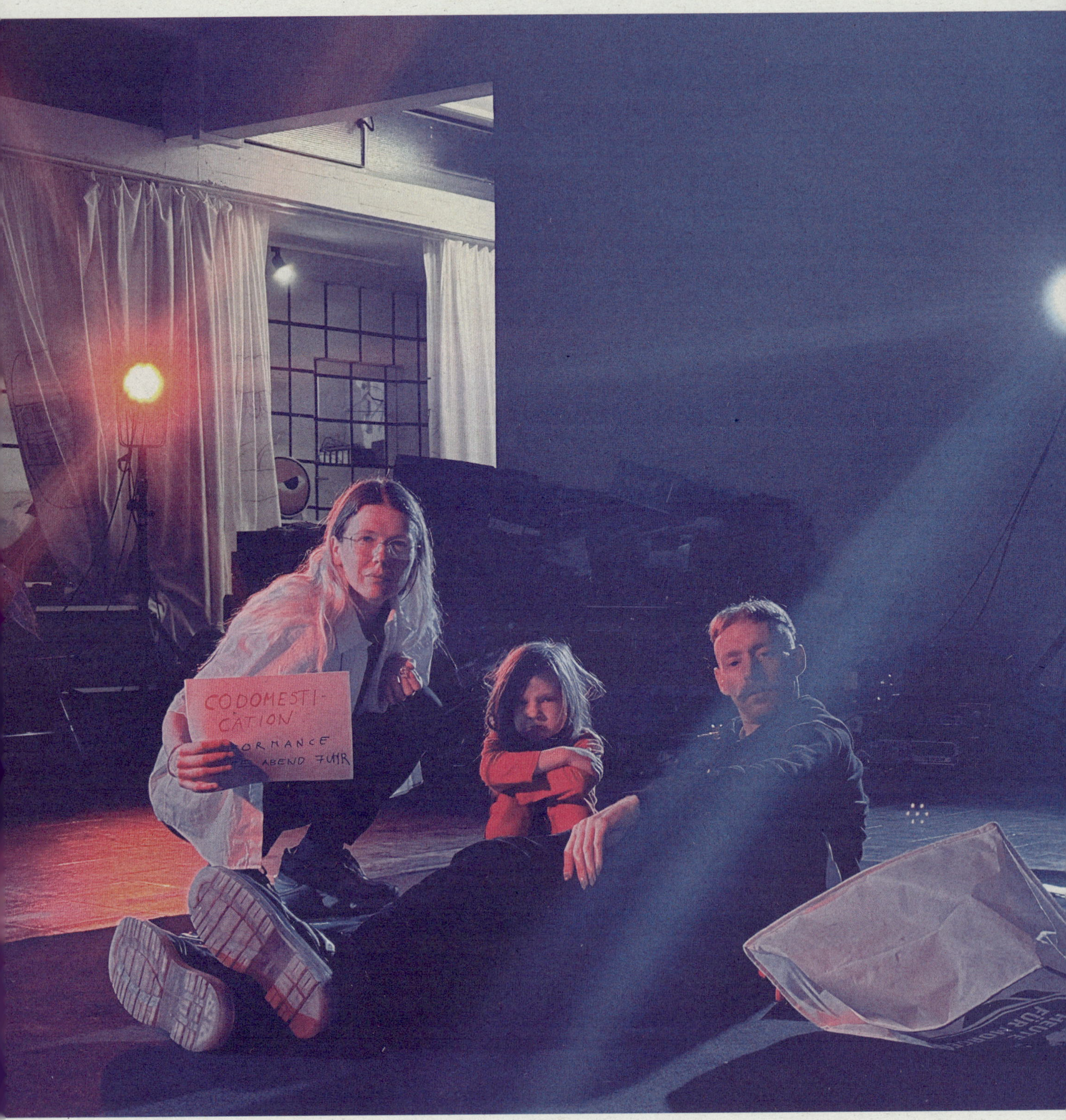

Krõõt Juurak and Alex Bailey, Codomestication.

Towards Unruly Kinships

Kris Dittel, Aneta Rostkowska

The goal of this text is to introduce the subchapter of the Islands of Kinship project, dedicated to the notions of kinship, hospitality, and care. This part of the project was realized by three art institutions: CCA Temporary Gallery in Cologne, Jindřich Chalupecký Society in Prague, and Latvian Centre for Contemporary Art in Riga. They jointly commissioned and produced two new artworks: by Pauline Curnier Jardin with Feel Good Cooperative and Taka Taka. Although many common points were present, each institution brought a slightly different perspective to the subchapter. In this text, an overall theoretical framework is sketched, followed by a brief presentation of projects at all institutions. In the last part, a comparison of all projects is provided together with some questions. The following conceptual framework is based on ideas developed within the Unruly Kinships project at the CCA Temporary Gallery by the authors of this text.

02 Kinship and Family

Kinships are often thought of as blood relations, even more often understood with reference to the Western model of the nuclear family. In this subchapter of the project, we aimed instead to contemplate and envisage various implications and forms of kinship, camaraderie, comradeship, and belonging outside of the social reproduction of norms that the nuclear family entails. What connects all of us is a belief that kinship is not given, it is to be imagined and made. And this process of kin-making involves a critical revision of the promises and fantasies of the nuclear family, as well as a collective search for new possibilities and structures that are yet to emerge. The starting point of this part of the project grew out of our personal interests and experiences, in search of a variety of ways of establishing care and love relations and imagining other kinds of sociability than the nuclear family structure. And as happens with such fundamental questions, we could not do this by ourselves or by solely relying on theoretical and discursive resources. Therefore, while considering the critique of the nuclear family, we aimed to expand this critical spirit into practices of collective learning, sharing, and contemplating being in and with the world differently. To do so, we approached artists, theoreticians, curators, thinkers, and our audiences to be our conversation partners.

"This is not an art project," we noted in our preparatory writings, and albeit this does not exactly correspond to the truth, this impulse signaled the project's nature—one that is intertwined with the personal, professional, and political. We also realized the limitations of aesthetic (re)presentations and blueprints that relations can be modeled upon. Yet we believe that kinship must be reproduced spatially, temporally, materially, in order for it to expand and affect—and art has the capacity to provide for these potentialities. We see the role of art and artists as important in this respect. Beyond bringing exposure to it, the artists in our project also consider kinship in its doing, living, and making of an unfixed web of relationality. Therefore, the project brings together a group of practitioners whose work has been consistently aligned with the aforementioned doing while being highly aware of representational regimes. This part of the project presented various temporal and spatial imaginations, disorientations and understandings of kin-relations. They prompt us to imagine the present and the future differently, to envision a world in which solidarity, interdependence, and other forms of intimate association and belonging coexist, one where we can make space and time to see one another in our abundance.

While conceptualizing this project, we had in mind the words of Judith Butler, who notes that since kinship is defined by legal, social, and economic systems, as well as religious codes and laws, norms and traditions, any effort to distinguish the study of kinship from those power relations ends in its obfuscation and idealization. Our project reckons with the fact that no ideal version of kinship exists, there is no blueprint which relations can be modeled upon. And yet it strives towards perspectives and approaches that anticipate new solidarities, affinities, and alliances, ones in which freedom in love and self-determination can be attainable for everyone. It is a leap into the unknown. How about then imagining collectively other forms of kinship? The unruly ones—not subjected to the imposed societal orders? Those which do not submit to known ways of living? They are disobedient, riotous, resourceful. How about reimagining kinship and asking again: How would we like to live? How would *you* like to live? The endeavor contemplates various possibilities of kin-making and care relations in our contemporary society. It presents various ways we relate to each other and the unexplored potentialities of these relations, starting from everyday interactions to artistic genealogies and queer lineages.

But first things first. The nuclear family, as a technology of capitalism, showed its teeth to larger parts of the population over the past few years during the global pandemic. Many articles popped up in mainstream media, pointing out the flaws of "family life" that were accelerated during the period of forced nuclear togetherness. But why this anger towards the family, you may ask. What we propose is by no means to cut ties with one's biological kin or partner, but rather to think of ways to expand those relations that are not tied by blood, inheritance, or a sense of ownership, but by a sense of justice, which demands care, love, and freedom for all. We build this critique on the work of thinkers who have been persistently calling out the injustices arising from the nuclear family system and imagining the (utopian) possibilities of expanded relations: against the backdrop of the nuclear family's privatization of care (Sophie Lewis), the institution of heterosexuality, monogamy, and compartmentalization of relations (Bini Adamczak), and by pointing at the ways we are oriented towards certain structures more than others (Sara Ahmed). These thinkers prompt a reimagining of kinship as a notion of extended (and what if, even, all-encompassing) community, one in which future forms cannot be delineated nor forecast.

All these "symptoms" might be linked to a general condition of our society which is a very narrow, standardized, and hierarchical understanding of kin-relations. This understanding reduces kinship to a relation based on blood or marriage and privileges the nuclear family (a family group of parents and children living together). The family operates on the one hand as the basic building block of capitalism, with its social relations regulated by the state, while on the other hand, it is simultaneously being undermined by the increasing demands and pressure of neoliberal forces. It is not unrelated to issues of gendered labor and its unequal distribution, domestic violence, and loneliness (it is proven that marriage separates people from their social connections), which are societal debates that have gained attention in the past years.

Of course, these issues are not new. Many have previously experienced and voiced the disappointment, discomfort, and violence of the nuclear family structure. There's an existing history and complexity to a discourse that aims to rethink the notion of the nuclear family. Many artists, theoreticians, thinkers, and writers have been expressing their ideas about multitudes of forms of kinship and care systems. For a variety of reasons, to many, the nuclear family has never been a viable option, many have faced its violence and limitations early on, or were straight up excluded from forming such relations.

The social history of the family is very helpful here as it shows that the existing situation is not a necessity: family is a historical entity taking different forms throughout the centuries. The nuclear family that is so present today is in fact more an exception than a rule. It is a result of the development of the so-called bourgeois family in the 18th and 19th centuries, itself a result of the emergence of the bourgeoisie class with its particular economic existence.

Throughout history, we have moved from bigger, interconnected, and extended structures, which protected the most vulnerable people, to smaller detached units mostly comfortable for the privileged. We do not believe in returning to this notion of the extended family, but rather seek more open and expansive structures. Even when desired, the nuclear family seems for many impossible to sustain, as contemporary sociologists and economists alarm us that the so-called "middle class" is being increasingly impoverished.

Projects at the CCA Temporary Gallery

At the CCA Temporary Gallery, the project was developed by both of us. In 2022, we formed the Forms of Kinship study group, which constituted the public research phase of the project, operating as an open research platform. The guests included writer and researcher Dr. Sophie Lewis, who spoke on the topic of family abolition and its decolonial perspective; professor Mi You (documenta Institute and University of Kassel) with whom a seminar on the social and economic history of the family was developed; Clementine Edwards who shared her research on material kinship together with Joannie Baumgärtner who spoke on the nuclear family's relation to capital; curator and LGBTQ+ activist Georgy Mamedov who introduced the radical potential of dreams; curator Khanyisile Mbongwa and healer and researcher Li'Tsoanelo Zwane who spoke about ancestral spirits and Indigenous knowledges; artist and political writer Bini Adamczak who unfolded for us the theory of polysexual economy; artistic researcher and social responsibility

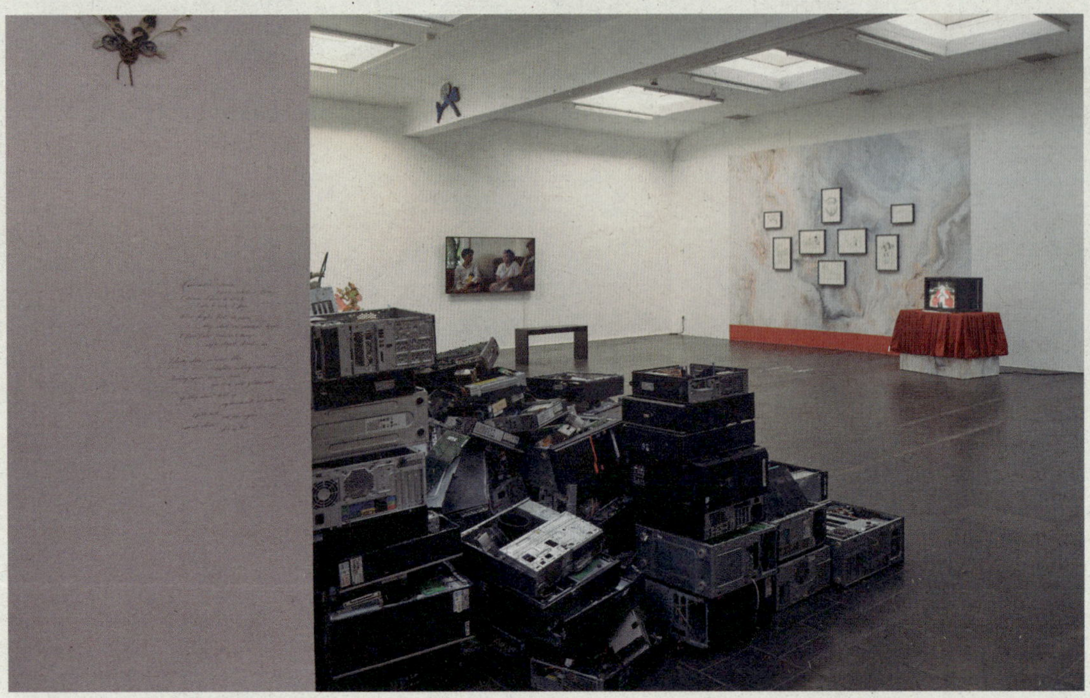

Unruly Kinships, exhibition documentation with works by Robert Gabris, Selma Selman, Lena Anouk Philips, Rory Pilgrim, Pauline Curnier Jardin, and Feel Good Cooperative

coordinator Francisco Trento who spoke about neuroqueer intimacy; and other curators from the Islands of Kinship project—Karina Kottová and Barbora Ciprová—who shared their research on the (feminist) contradictions of parenting. Many events from this series have been recorded and are available on the Temporary Gallery's YouTube channel.

In 2023, the *Unruly Kinships* exhibition was presented to the public. It gathered participants who not only rethought but also re-enacted "unruly kinships" themselves, albeit usually not in the known format of socially engaged art. They not only encourage us to reimagine existing kin-relations, they also search for different ways of sustaining them. For example, Jay Tan's large-scale sculptures, resembling an ant formicarium, housing a series of scenes dedicated to various artists, musicians, and writers with whom Tan shares a surname. The work references forms of altruism, questions of nepotism, kinship selection, and eusociality in social superorganisms like ants and humans.

Similarly, Geo Wyex in his poetic sound work draws on artistic lineages, family members, and memory objects. These “shout outs” are personal acknowledgements and public expressions of greeting and praise. In this work, Wyex asked who or what matters, and how calling things aloud might become a temporary measure of liberation.

Rory Pilgrim showed us alliances and connections between climate activists. They pointed to how climate change is forcing us to rethink the existing ways of living not only because the old ways degrade the planet (just think about the energy consumption of single-family houses in comparison to larger collective dwellings) but also because fighting anticlimate policies requires intense collective effort.

Clementine Edwards’s unfolding miniature landscape, made of rice, gold, silver, copper, and found materials, prompted us to think about the promise of the nuclear family, its unfolding, and being at peace with its possibilities and pitfalls.

Selma Selman considers what values and relations society attributes to people, labor, relations, and material objects, as she recycles scrap metal with the help of her family. Throughout the exhibition’s duration, she transformed electronic waste with the goal of producing golden earrings for her mother.

Lena Anouk Phillip’s fragile paper sculptures employ the mechanisms of the gift economy to reinforce amiable connections.

Liz Rosenfeld’s work featured holes, openings, portals, orifices, and pores that are impossible to fill. Their work explores desiring and leaking bodies through the narrative of cruising.

Pauline Curnier Jardin founded the Feel Good Cooperative together with the help of photographer and sex worker Alexandra Lopez and architect and academic Serena Olcuire. The cooperative is a space for expression, inspiration, and financial support for sex workers in Rome whose work is linked with the fragility of daily existence.

The exhibition was accompanied by a rich public program. In Krõõt Juurak's and Alex Bailey's performance, not only did their son Albert disrupt it and contributed to it, he also took an equal role in its creation. The work spoke to questions of child-parent relations, parenting, and emotional labor. iSaAc Espinoza Hidrobo and Joanna Stange offered a workshop with a choreographed ritual of care and kinship. They invited the audience to join in their dance, joy, and moment of collective transformation. Designer, artist, and researcher Yin Aiwen's live action role-playing game (LARP), a life simulation and a generative social experiment that takes peer-to-peer caring relationships as the cornerstone for a commons-oriented, caring society, unfolded over several game sessions at the institution.

The program culminated in a big, open-call-based performance and party event called Festival of Feelings and a seminar with Alva Gotby, author of *They Call It Love: The Politics of Emotional Life*. The space of the art institution became a space in which thinking about kinship develops in a collective way, a space in which kinship relations are nurtured.

In the booklet accompanying the exhibition, an infinite love letter by Kris Dittel provided a personal account of the Forms of Kinship study group series. It was followed by *Mayday* by Suzanna Slack, a fragmented memoir that touches upon the construction and violence of the nuclear family, gender, and class. Alexis Pauline Gumb's Black queer feminist genealogy put forward the concept of revolutionary mothering (in a verb form) as opposed to motherhood as a status that is selectively granted. Only when more of us pursue "unruly kinships" can a larger societal change happen. This, however, would require governments to recognize the necessity and support different ways of living on a structural level. The text by Johanna Brenner expressed in which direction this could go.

Projects at Jindřich Chalupecký Society

Jindřich Chalupecký Society developed its part of the project in the form of three chapters. The first one, Around the Family Table, took place in Berlin's alpha nova & galerie futura space in 2022 and focused on gender roles within the concept of family, the representation of LGBTQAI+ families, the concept of motherhood, and women's corporealities, as well as on other forms of communality beyond biological connections, even the absence of (or in the) family, particularly in light of the Covid-19 pandemic and its impact on the definition and (non)functioning of the family. It did this in a variety of formats, including performance, video, text, textile works, sculpture, performative readings, discussions, and research presentations.

The second, Beyond Nuclear Family: Recipes for Happiness, was realized in Prague's Display Gallery in 2022. It provided a complex artistic probe into the various ways of creating and categorizing the family, relationships, and roles that its members occupy. The exhibition's subtitle incorporated the well-established phrase "recipe for happiness" commonly used as a hyperbole, indicating the impossibility of finding a universal recipe for a happy life. By translating this phrase into the plural, the curators wanted to express the plurality of forms that different family constellations can take. By means of the installation by the artist collective Mothers Artlovers (in collaboration with the Berlin-based collective Maternal Fantasies), visitors were given specific recipes and dishes during the exhibition,

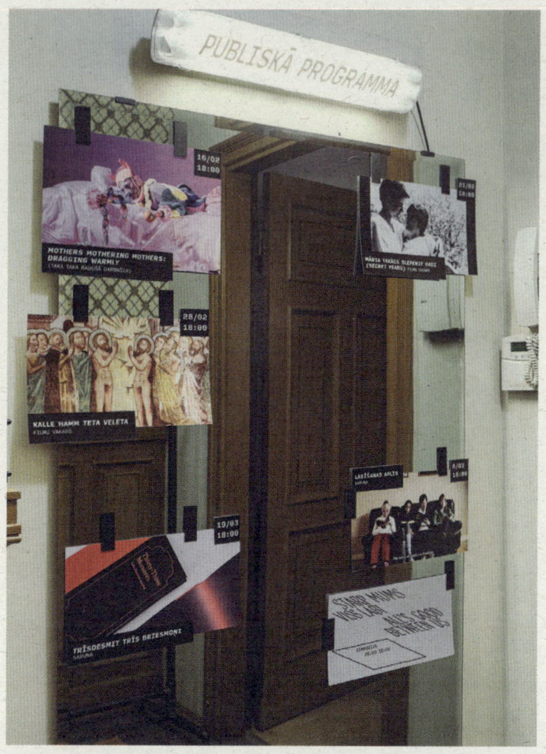

All's Good Between Us, Latvian Centre for Contemporary Art, Riga, 2024

all relating to the critique of social institutions (also including the concept of family) and relationships. The audience was able to reflect on these themes at a triangular table reminiscent of the iconic feminist work *The Dinner Party* by Judy Chicago. The other works on display—paintings, photographs, videos, texts, textiles, sculptures, performances, and arts research outputs—could also be freely read as possible recipes or (missing) ingredients for (family) happiness. In its totality, the exhibition thus presented a comprehensive and diverse "cookbook."

The third part in the form of the exhibition *Beyond Nuclear Family: Home Sweet Home* took place between November 2022 and January 2023 at the Elizabeth Foundation for the Arts in New York. It sought to provide a critical revision of the modern Western concept of the family and, through the works of more than forty international artists, explored the alternatives—historical and contemporary, geographical and cultural, utopian and fictional. This chapter wanted to redefine the questionable concept of the nuclear family and bring it back to its original "home," the U.S., where it was coined and distributed in the second half of the 20th century. This edition brought forth conversations about chosen family and queer kinship; utopian family revolutions and coexistence models; deficiency in cultural capital; fragility and ambiguity of relationship patterns; institutional childcare models; feminist chains of support; as well as familial traumas and institutional care or lack of it. Amongst existing artworks, all three exhibitions also featured newly commissioned works by six Czech artists: Eva Koťátková, Marie Lukáčová, Markéta Magidová, Vojtěch Radakulan, Jiří Skála and Martina Drozd Smutná, as well as a Family Album with small-scale commissions by the former collaborators of Jindřich Chalupecký Society, including Tai Shani, Laure Prouvost, Michelle Lévy, and Egill Sæbjörnsson, among others.

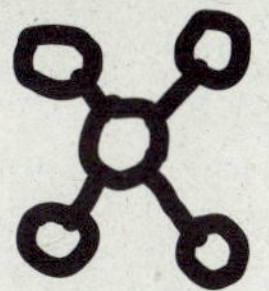

Projects at the Latvian Centre for Contemporary Art in Riga

The LCCA in Riga presented in 2024 an exhibition and public program *All's Good Between Us*, featuring artists, curators, and researchers who are currently working on gender and LGBTQ+ topics, highlighting the specifics of the region in historical and contemporary contexts. It brought gender and queer discourses into interaction with sociopolitical contexts in society, identifying cracks between identities, minorities, and different generations. At the same time, the project questioned the ways in which both individual and LGBTQ+ community histories were narrated and documented, and how ingrained assumptions normalized and justified violence and intolerance.

The title of the exhibition *All's Good Between Us* was taken from the play of the same name by Polish writer Dorota Masłowska. The play tells the story of three generations of women living in a small apartment in Warsaw, observing in their everyday lives the complex panorama of Polish history in the last century, including issues of social and national identity. Also the participants of this exhibition and public program from different generations inhabited the apartment together—the venue of the exhibition on Dzirnavu Street—communicating with each other and inviting guests to share their experiences and reflections. In March, a special symposium was organized with focus on gender, sexuality, and queer questions, analyzing them in the context of art and culture in the Baltic States and the Baltic Sea Region. It brought together cultural workers, artists, and researchers who are currently, in different projects, revising and highlighting

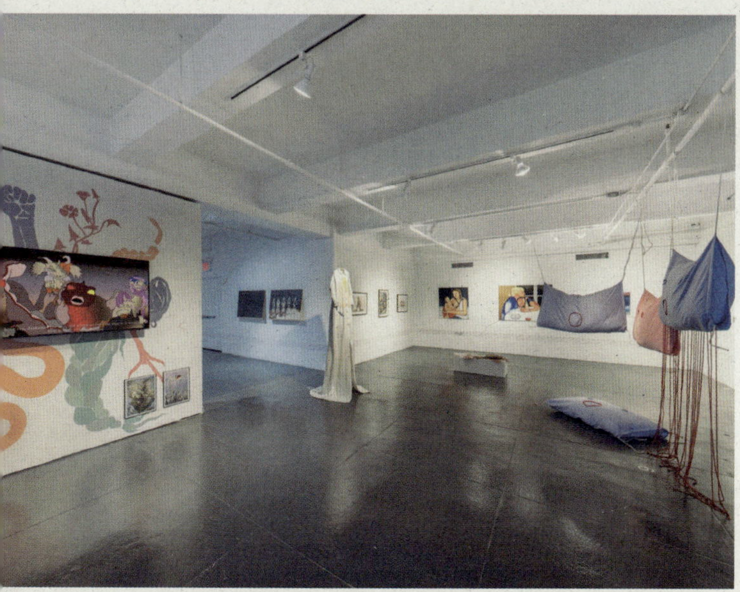

Beyond Nuclear Family: Home Sweet Home, EFA Project Space, NYC, 2023

the representation of queer history today, focusing on the documentation of stories, archival accumulation, and the interpretation of processes concerning broader social developments. For example, designer Rūta Jumīte and curator of educational programs Ieva Laube, in collaboration with critic and researcher Vents Vīnbergs, have set up a *Living Room of Stories*, which invited people to document LGBTQ+ histories in Latvia in the form of social action. A special interactive area was designed for visitors to share their experiences and record histories. The room provided tools to communicate testimonies and encourage reflection on how queer culture can be documented in both the present and the future. The room was divided in two areas: "The Living Questions Wall"' mapped personal, social, and political questions formulated in collaboration with members of the LGBTQ+ community, while "Seating Stations"' comprised furniture inviting people to stop and share their experiences—either by writing them down or telling them, inspired by the questions and stories displayed on the wall. The event explored the possibilities and limits of mediating the documentation of historical issues and how to affect social processes through this knowledge.

Although the projects had many common points, provided for example by the presentations of joint commissions by Pauline Curnier Jardin and Taka Taka, there were also interesting differences in handling the topics. CCA Temporary Gallery focused largely on collective ways of living and being in the world and aimed at broadening the notion of kinship by means of introducing the themes of kinship beyond familial relations, including with nonhumans, ancestral relations, and friendship. Jindřich Chalupecký Society dedicated more attention to artworks and projects deconstructing the notion of the nuclear family and normative kin relations, presenting a plurality of "recipes" for alternative scenarios. They were structured around several chapters devoted to forms of togetherness, being a living together in relation to architectonic spaces, gender roles, parental schemes and goals, utopian scenarios as well as through the topic of absence—whether on the interpersonal, material, or structural level. LCCA, on the other hand, focused on individual and LGBTQ+ community histories, with their historical as well as contemporary regional specifics. The projects intertwined in the understanding that kinship, comradeship, and togetherness need to be set free from the limiting notions of the "nuclear" or "traditional" family (or possibly family altogether), often reinforced by populist governments and the capitalist apparatus, limiting not only diversity and integrity, but often also the basic human right to form meaningful relations beyond a strict and redundant definition.

Pauline Curnier Jardin & Feel Good Cooperative: Roman Parties

Shimmering through Inequities

Veronika Čechová

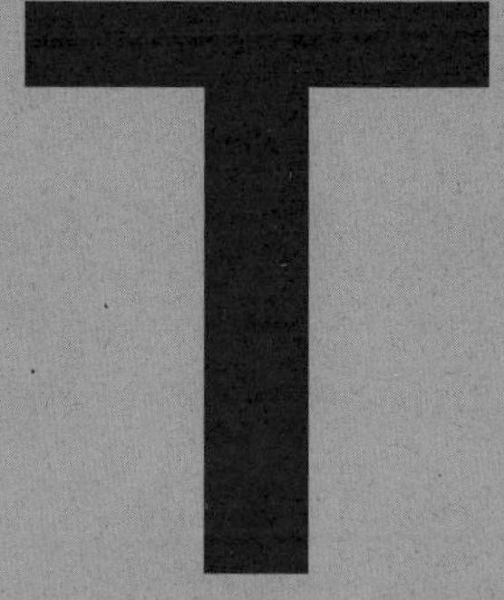

The *Roman Parties* exhibition at the Prague City Gallery presented the results of a unique collaboration between an internationally established artist, Pauline Curnier Jardin, and a collective of female sex workers, artists, and architects who, since 2020, have been performing under the collective name Feel Good Cooperative. Curnier Jardin, who lives and works part time in Rome, co-initiated the formation of the creative group, which is mostly made up of Colombian-born sex workers, during the global pandemic when a strict lockdown was imposed in Italy. This restriction had a major impact on those working in the gray economy who were not entitled to monetary support from the official structures of the state. Sex workers who depended on being able to meet their clients in person were among those at real risk of getting into material need. Moreover, they were in a particularly vulnerable position as migrant women and often trans people, without the formal entitlement to financial assistance that workers in more conforming sectors benefited from. The creation of the Feel Good Cooperative was thus an attempt to provide an immediate solution to the current crisis. Pauline Curnier Jardin, with the help of photographer and sex worker Alexandra Lopez and architect Serena Olcuire, devised a workshop for a group of female sex workers which resulted in a series of drawings depicting scenes from their everyday work interactions. These were sold for a price equivalent to the fees for their regular work. Besides directly helping in a precarious situation, this initiatory project thus created a new space for self-expression for those whose daily lives are stigmatized and ignored by mainstream society despite the fact that their activities are linked to the fulfilment of one of the most basic needs, interpersonal intimacy.

The resulting collaboration has led to several exhibition and performance projects featuring prints by members of the Feel Good Cooperative as well as art films created by Pauline Curnier Jardin and her collective. The exhibition at the House of Photography featured three films and related drawings, and for each section, a spatial and installation environment was created that resonated with the theme and atmosphere of the particular work.

The first video was a recording of a performance on October 12, 2023, when Christopher Columbus Day is celebrated in Italy and other countries around the world. The iconic position of this famous navigator and historically celebrated discoverer of the “New World” has been increasingly shaken in recent years by critical reflection on the epoch of European colonialism. Columbus’ voyages of discovery, which were a source of wealth and social prosperity for the European powers, meant centuries of enforced domination and exploitation for the Indigenous peoples of the American continent, the consequences of which can be traced back to current geopolitical conflicts. The performance by members of the Feel Good Cooperative was intended to subvert the traditional motive for Columbus Day celebrations through physical movement, sculptural intervention, and collective singing, a polyphony of yearning bodies, so as to change the meaning of sites in the public space that symbolize exploitation and power. The event was situated in the EUR residential and commercial district of Rome, originally chosen as the site for the 1942 World Expo, which Benito Mussolini planned to open as a celebration of twenty years of fascist rule. EUR offers a large-scale image of what Italy might have looked like if the fascist regime had not fallen: wide, axis-planned streets and austere buildings. Pauline Curnier Jardin and members of the collective prepared for the public an exploratory tour through the past, present, and speculative

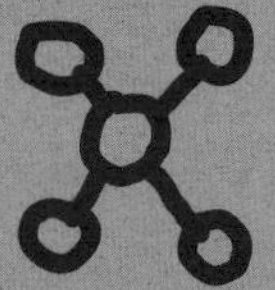

future of Christopher Columbus Boulevard, including its colonial phantoms.

The second film in the exhibition was also documentary in nature. It depicted a January 2023 trip to the Vatican when members of the Feel Good Cooperative—as well as a total of 195,000 Christians from around the world—went to bid farewell to the late Pope Emeritus Benedict XVI during the funeral display of his body in St. Peter's Basilica. The half-hour film *The Day We Saw Him Dead* followed members of the collective in their everyday clothes and makeup walking through the breathtaking interiors of one of Catholicism's holiest sites. Along with other visitors, they were smoothly led past the memorial at a pace set by the obviously well-coordinated organizers, which gives little opportunity for quiet reflection. The visit is rather reminiscent of a mass tourist attraction in the way it progresses and in the subsequent celebrations after the memorial service.

After watching the film, viewers were allowed to enter an imaginary sacristy, but instead of the devotional objects and vestments, there was an installation of prints from the *Death of the Pope* series—the result of another creative workshop in collaboration between Curnier Jardin and the Feel Good Cooperative. In a uniquely apt, humorous, and narrative way, the drawings captured scenes and impressions from the visit to the Vatican, blending the worlds of religiosity, mass tourism, female sexuality, and carnality.

The last part of the exhibition featured a 2021 film, the first ever produced by Pauline Curnier Jardin and the Feel Good Cooperative. The mysterious video, entitled *Fireflies*, featured the now familiar figures at night, in a flicker of shadows and lights along the roadside on the outskirts of Rome where they usually work. Once upon a time, there were indeed fireflies here, but they have disappeared along with the changing suburban landscape around them. Today the car headlights of potential clients in search of a one-off pleasure illuminate like searchlights faces and bodies—the faces and bodies we already know from the previous two film encounters.

Here, however, another level of communication flashes in the darkness besides the acknowledged and provocative physicality. A metaphor in which the fireflies are the women and trans people who appear at night but are invisible during the day, lacking social recognition and support, and who are, not only in times of the pandemic, precarious and vulnerable. But the Feel Good Cooperative's artworks and projects show them in an emancipatory light, as strong, beautiful, and remarkable women. They are an inspiration for a more adequate and fair integration of sex work into the economic and political system, for improving the rights and conditions of female sex workers, and for a broader social debate on related issues in general.

PAULINE CURNIER JARDIN & FEEL GOOD COOPERATIVE

The Death of the Pope
graphic prints
2023

The Day We Went to See Him Dead
video, 33:28 mins
2023

The commission was presented as part of exhibitions:

- ROMAN PARTIES, Prague City Gallery, Czech Republic, November 14, 2023 – February 25, 2024, organized by Jindřich Chalupecký Society
- UNRULY KINSHIPS, CCA Temporary Gallery, Cologne, Germany, February 4 – April 30, 2023, organized by CCA Temporary Gallery

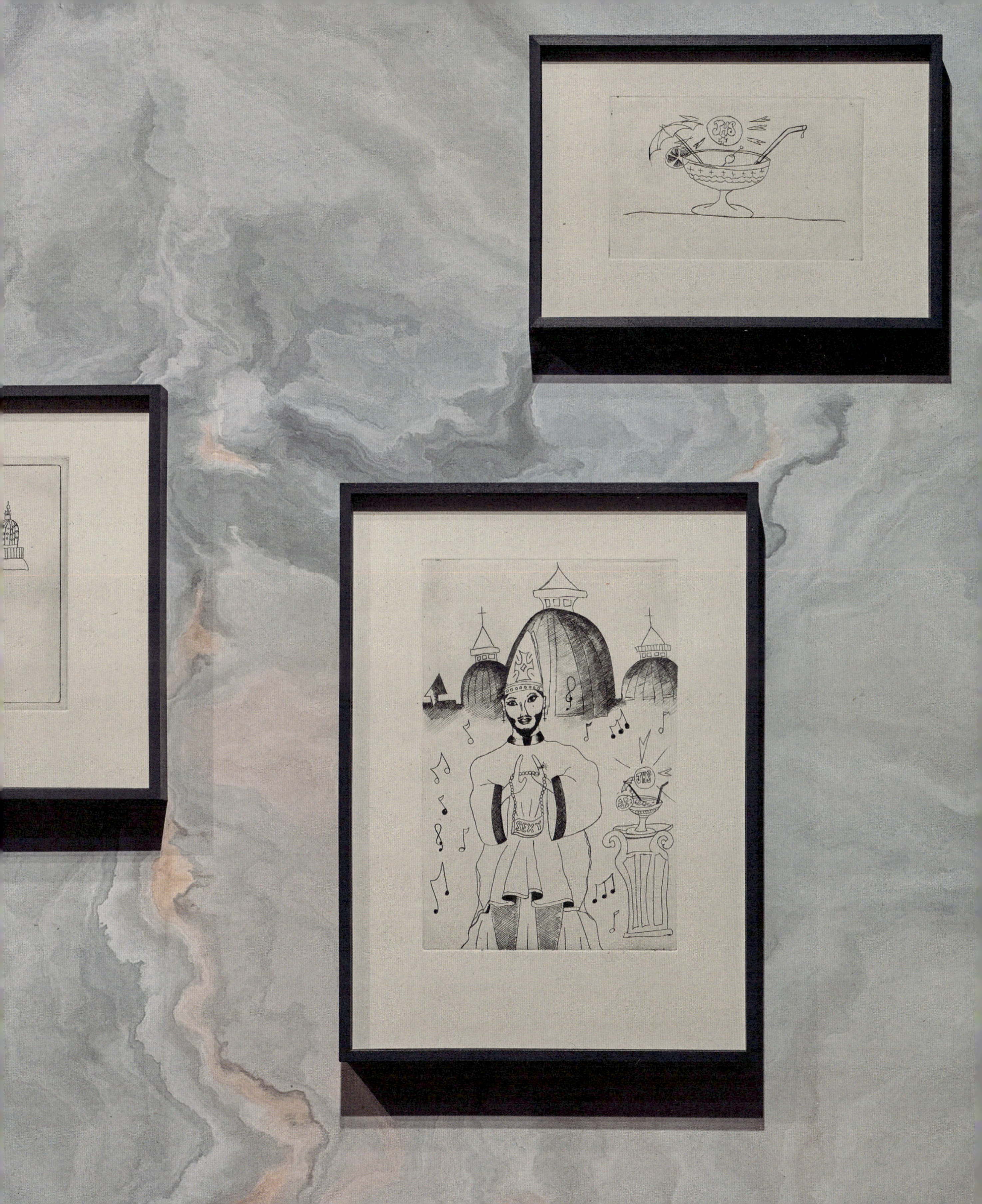
SEXY

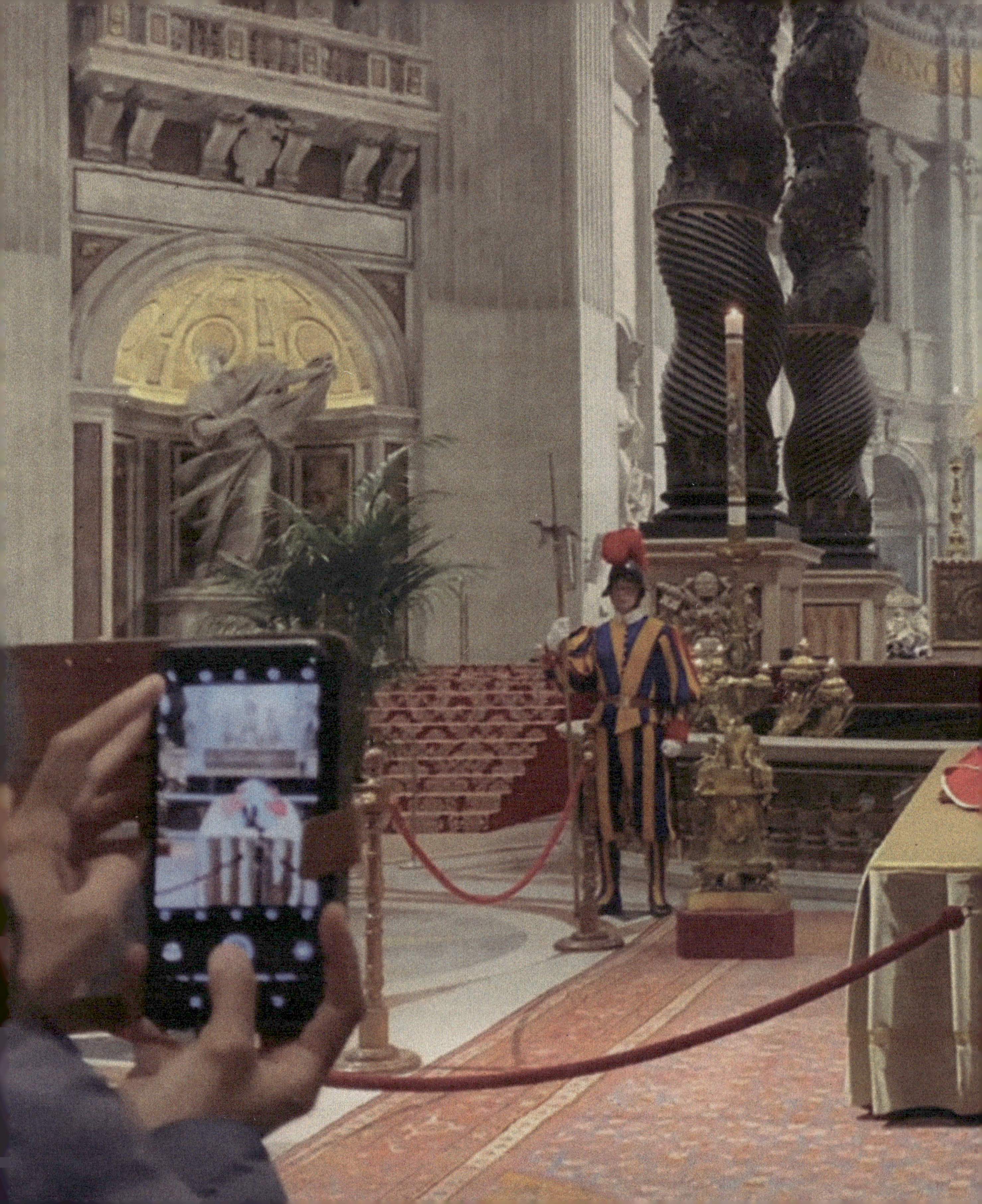

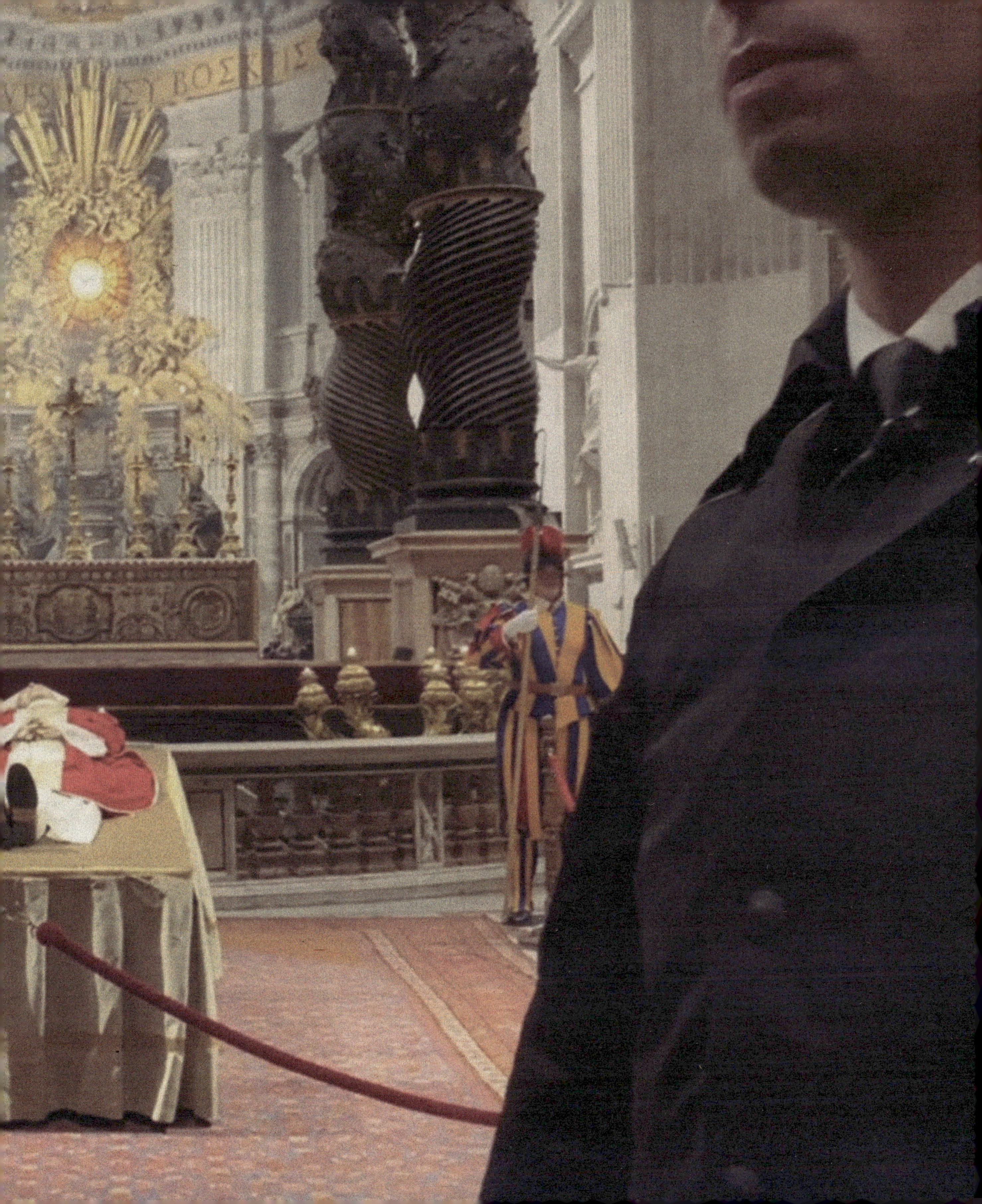

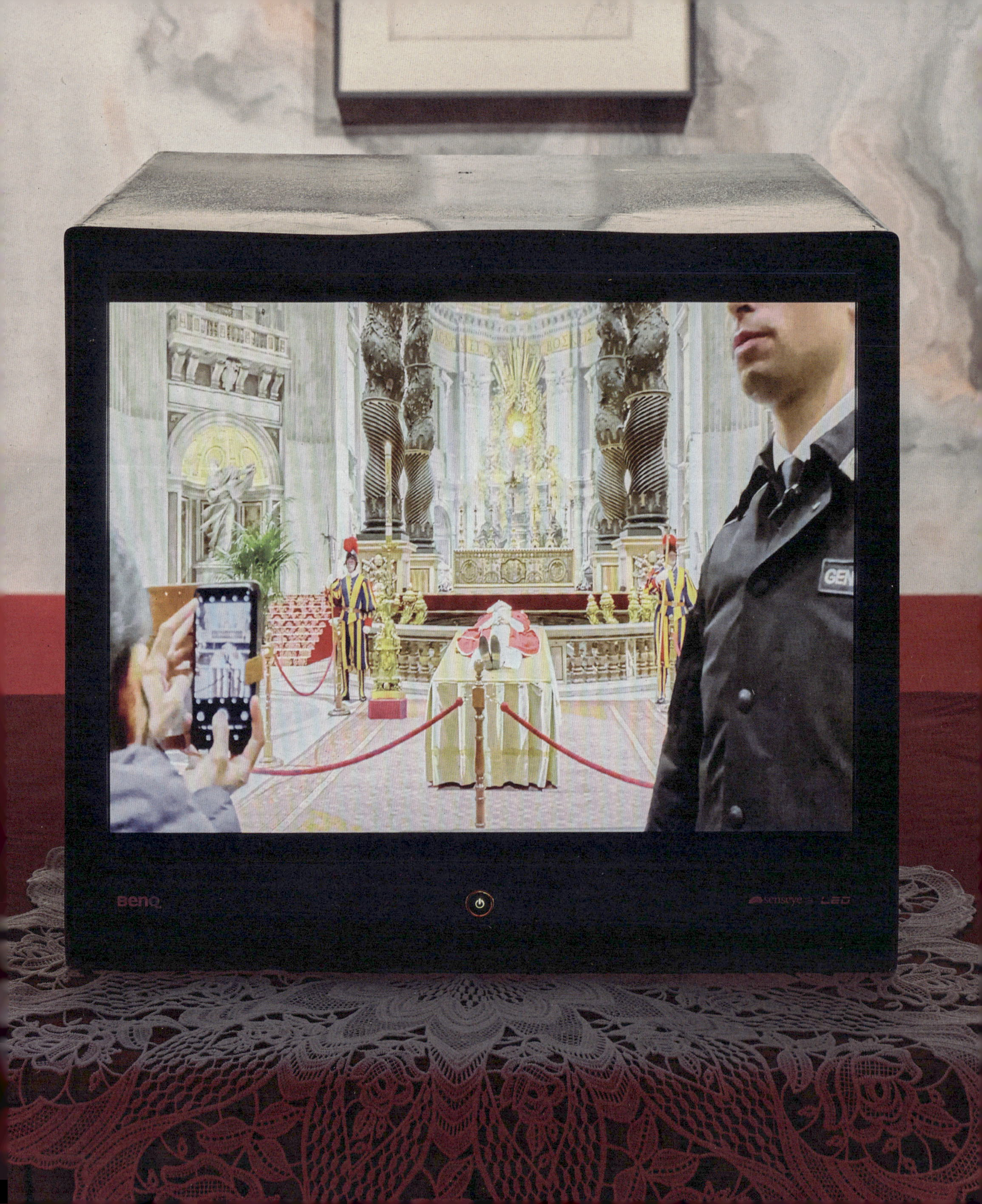
GEN
BenQ
senseye LED

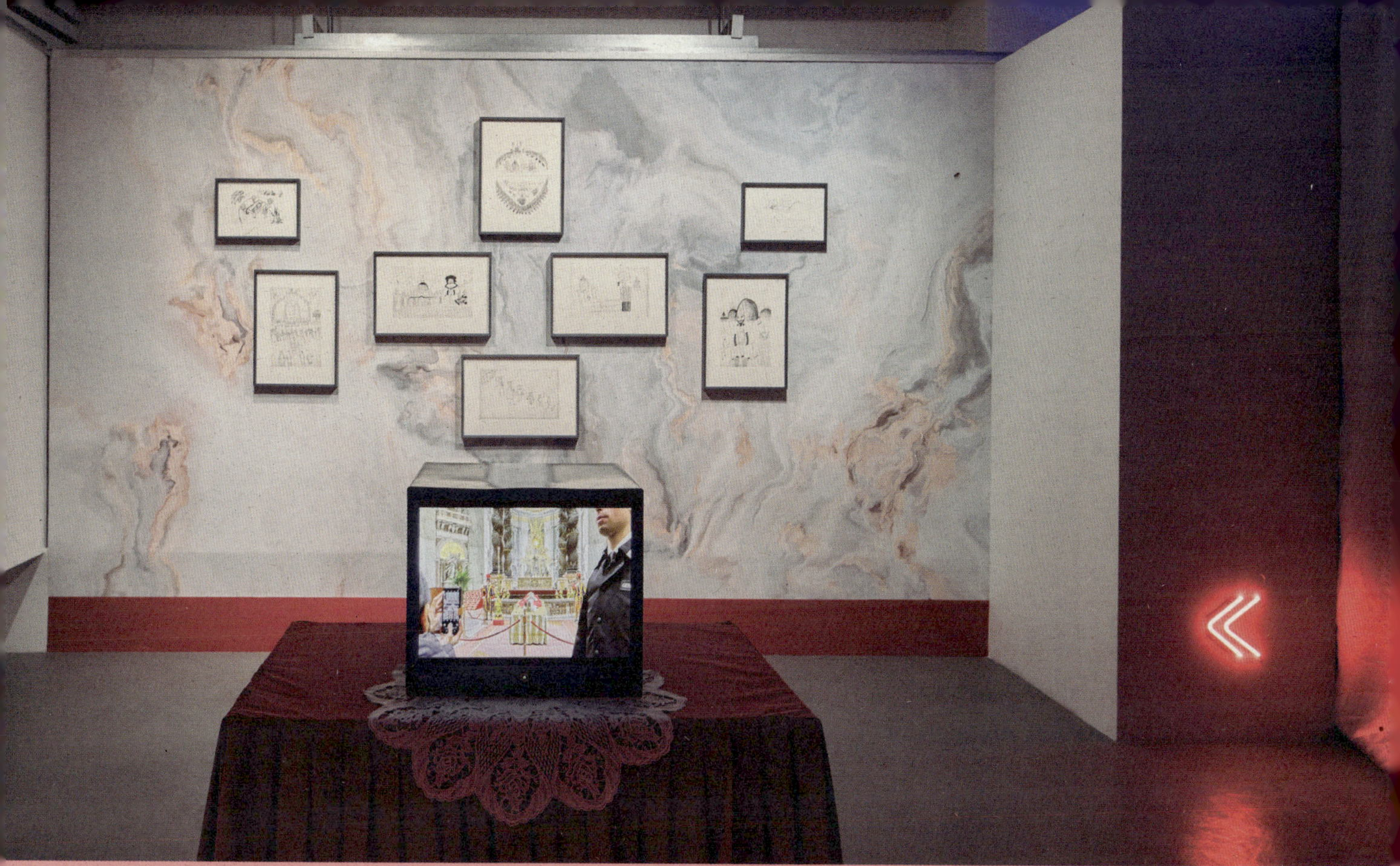

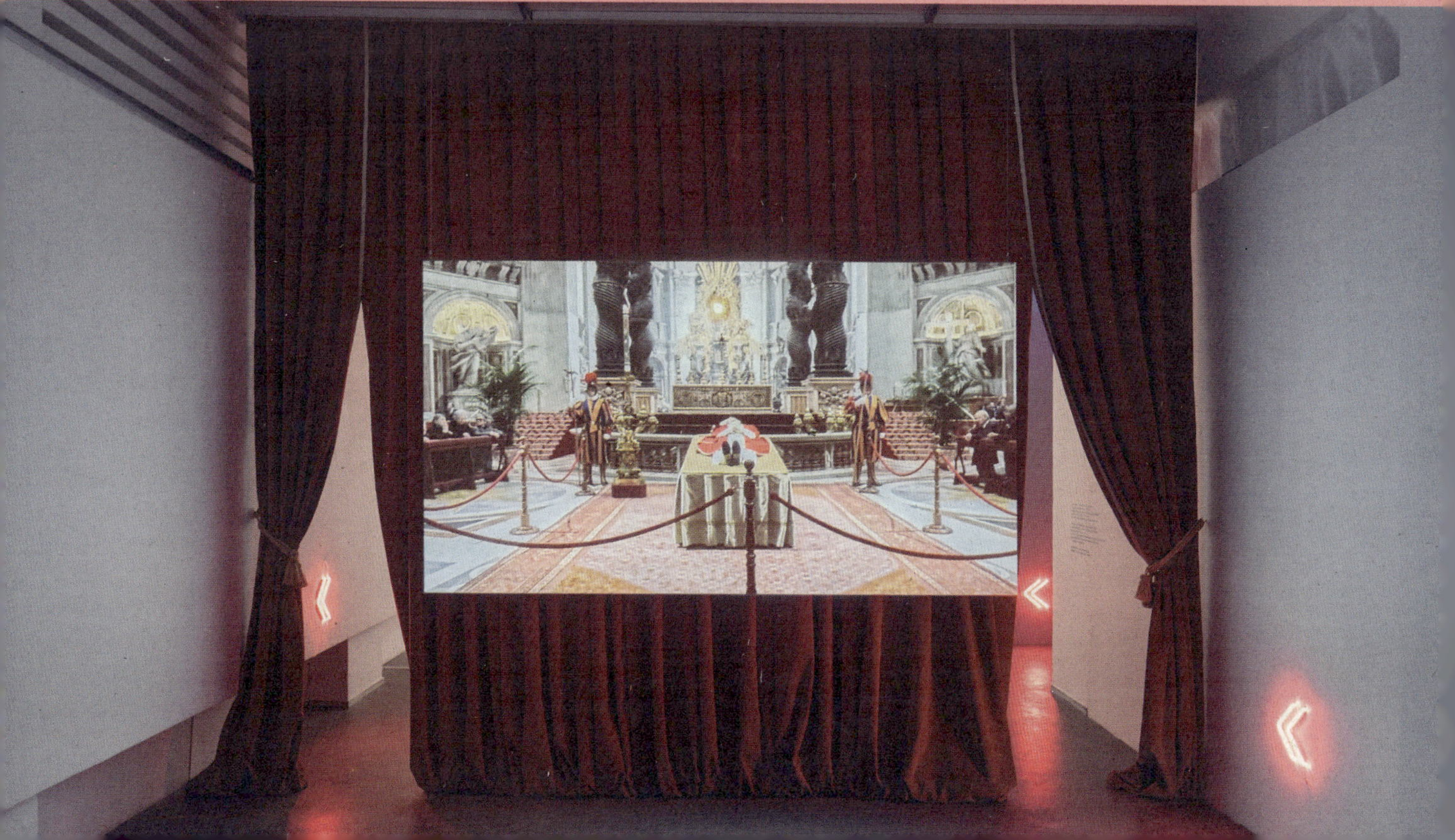

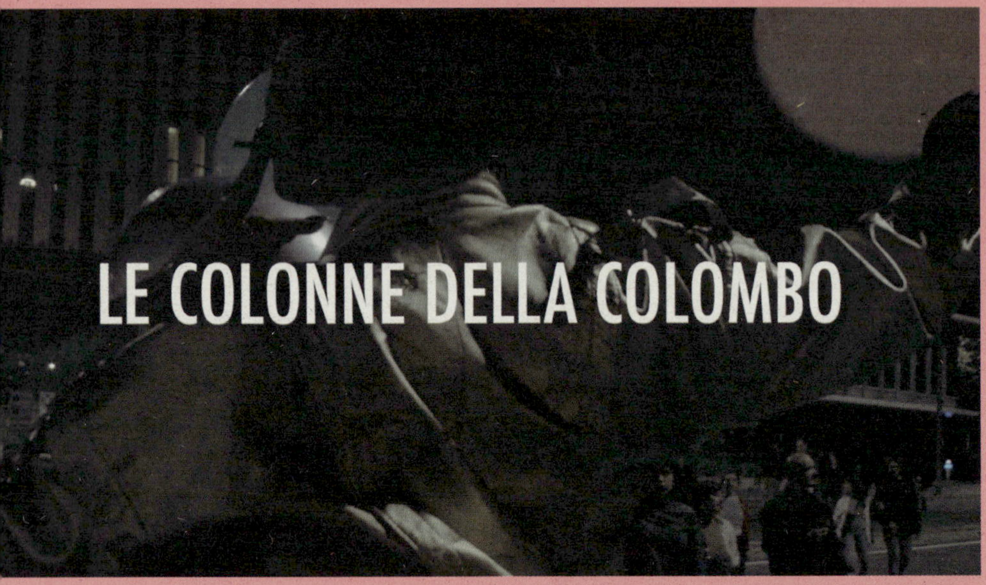

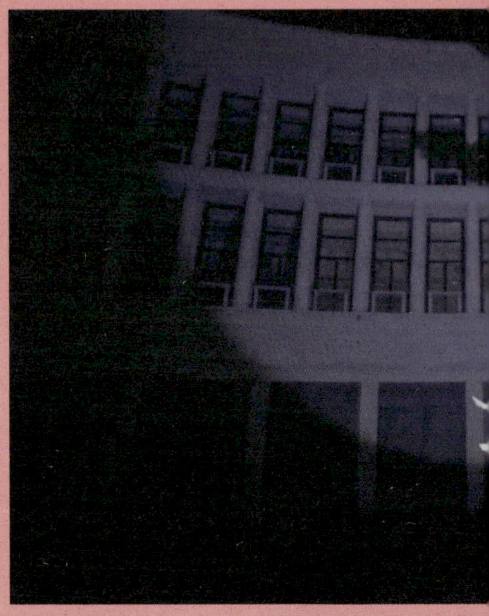

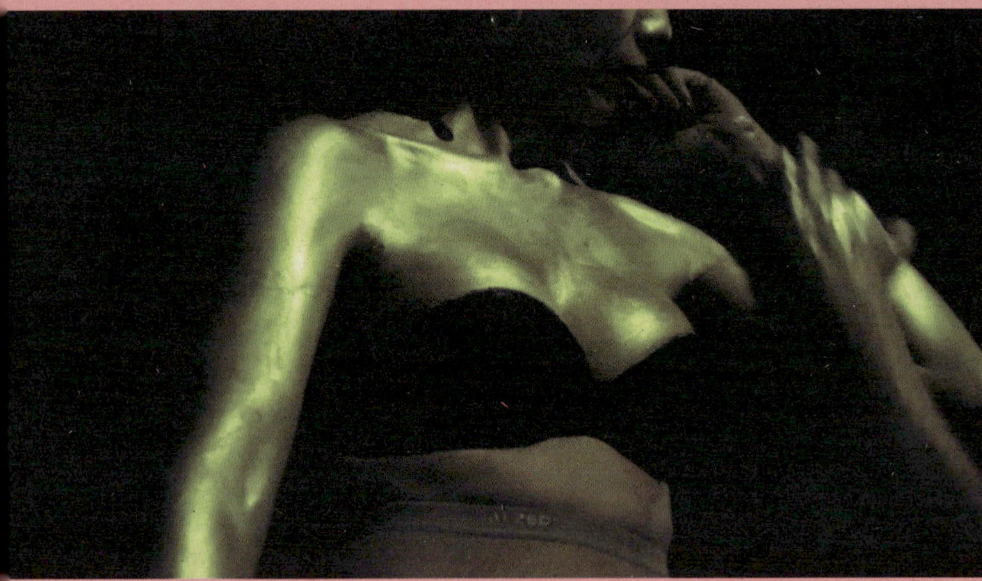

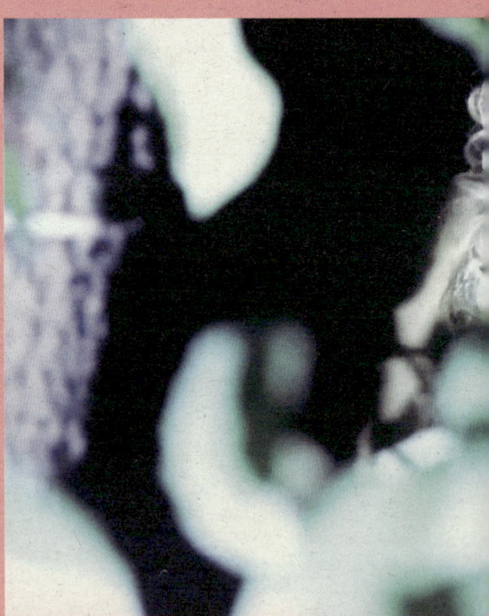

PAULINE CURNIER JARDIN
& FEEL GOOD COOPERATIVE

Le Colonne della Colombo: A Teaser
video, 3:20 mins
2023

courtesy of the artists

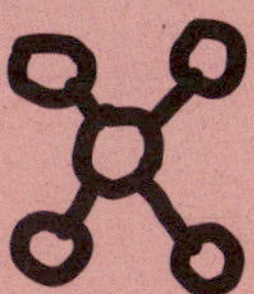

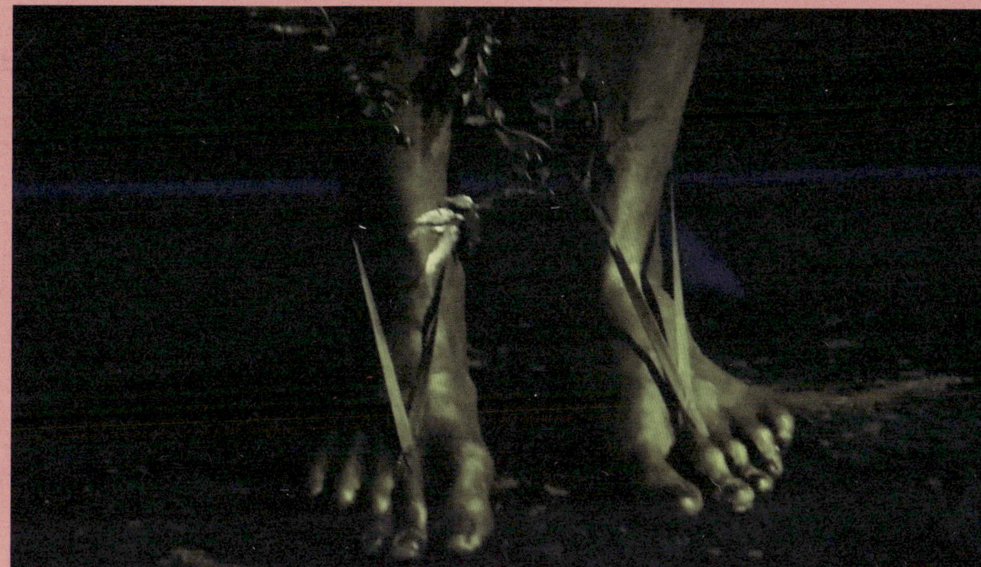

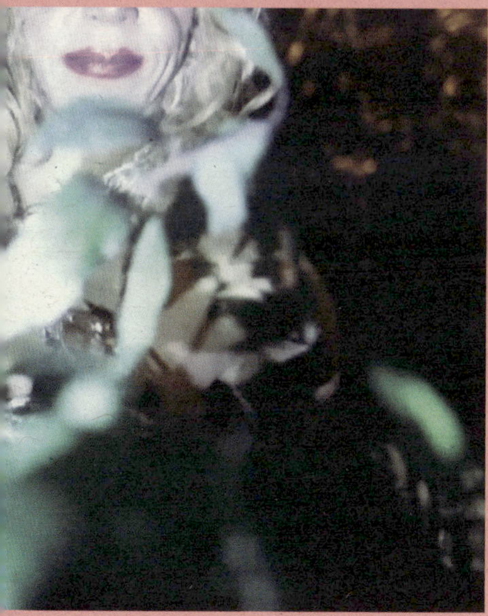

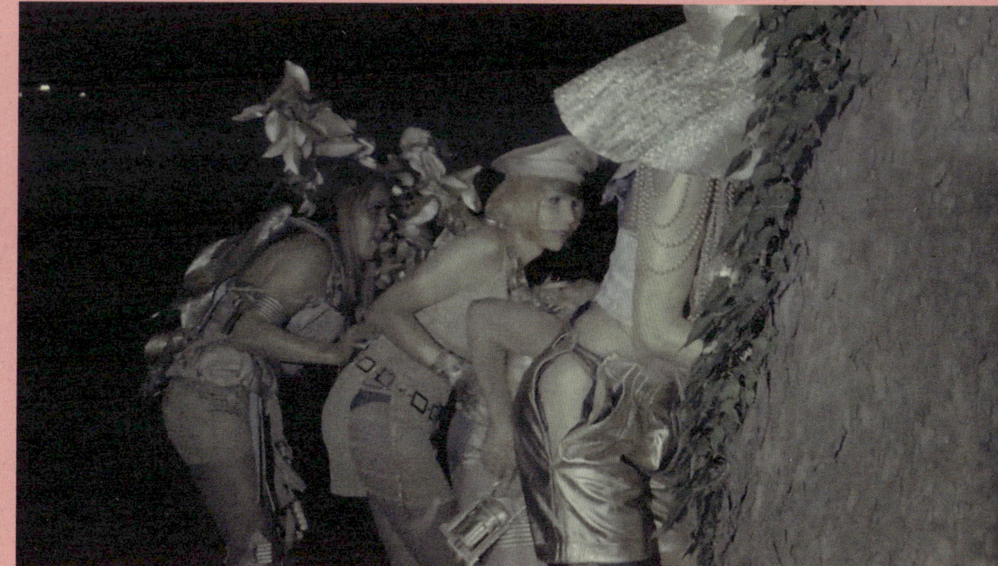

Thinking Kinship beyond Coupledom and Neuro-diversity in Artistic Residencies (And Other Settings)[1]

Fran Trento

In this text, I problematize some of the assumptions often taken for granted in our societies and cultures and how they affect access and inclusion in artistic residencies. I will focus on two aspects of human (and nonhuman) diversity that are generally disregarded or marginalized, particularly in artistic residencies: neurodiversity and nonfamilial modalities of kinship. This text also tangents my practice as Frame Contemporary Art Finland's social responsibility coordinator within the Islands of Kinship project. A manual holds performative power in that it can influence the practices of the ones who may read it. This post is not a manual but aims to *poke* institutional practices embedded with a normativity that interdicts the thriving of diversity within artist residencies.

Neurodiversity is a term that describes the natural diversity of human brains and minds and a perspective that values this diversity as a source of richness and strength. It is also a social movement that was initiated by autistic people in the 1990s and that advocates for the acceptance and inclusion of people who have different ways of thinking, learning, and acting from the norm, such as those with autism spectrum disorder (ASD), attention deficit hyperactivity disorder (ADHD), or learning disabilities. Neurodiversity challenges the idea that there is one "normal" way of being human and that any

1 This is an expanded version of the text "Discussing Artist Residencies' Underestimated Normativities" published at the *Reside/Sustain* platform. https://www.residesustain.art/en/articles/artist-residencies-underestimated-normativities.

deviation from this norm is a disorder or a deficiency that needs to be fixed or cured. Instead, it recognizes that differences are not problems but rather part of the natural human variation that contributes to human evolution and innovation. Doing this shifts normalcy from the center of human experience and questions the power structures that privilege certain ways of being over others. Instead of viewing these bodyminds as flawed and missing something that makes them unsuitable for social environments, neurodiversity proposes that material and discursive structures should be modified to accommodate and welcome all differently shaped and abled bodies.

However, many people who are neurodiverse face barriers and discrimination in accessing arts-based spaces, particularly artistic residencies, which are often designed for neurotypical people or conforming to the dominant expectations of brain functioning and behavior. For example, some residencies—and, in a broad sense, most open calls in the arts field, including exhibitions, awards, and job positions—may require applicants to submit lengthy proposals, portfolios, or CVs. The lack of openness can be challenging for people who feel more comfortable communicating in other modalities of expression than writing or expressing themselves in nonlinguistic ways. Some residencies may impose strict deadlines, schedules, or rules, which can be stressful or overwhelming for people needing more flexibility or support. Some residencies may also expect residents to participate in social events, workshops, or presentations, which can be uncomfortable or inaccessible for people with sensory sensitivities or anxiety. When one thinks about accessibility in artist residencies, what often comes to mind is the physical accessibility for wheelchair users or the height and weight of specific building structures, but not accessibility for neurodivergent persons, even though physical accessibility goes far beyond wheelchair access. What are the potential aspects of the residence's space that may cause sensory to overwhelm, how flexible are their schedules for cleaning and reporting, and what are the procedures in an emergency? In a text published in 2021 in the *Ruukku—Studies in Artistic Research* journal issue about slowness and silence, I discuss a few of these concerns. The text was written during my stay as a resident in ÖRES (Örö Fortress Island Residency Program).[2]

To address these issues and create more inclusive and welcoming spaces for neurodiverse artists and artistic researchers, I will draw on the concept of neuroqueerness, as defined by the autistic critical disability studies scholar Remi Yergeau. According to Yergeau,[3] a neuroqueer is someone who identifies or disidentifies as queer and neurodivergent; identifies as neurodivergent but not as sexually queer yet sees their neurodivergence as queering their embodiment; and occupies spaces between and among these various positions. The concept of neuroqueerness is also a political affirmation against outdated behavioral psychology discourses that falsely connect autism to extreme maleness. In truth, the number of neurodiverse persons who do not identify with binary genders and are not heterosexuals is more significant than that of neurotypicals.

2 Fran Trento, "A Diary on Slowness at Örö Fortress Island," In *RUUKKU - Studies in Artistic Research* (Issue 15), 2021. Society for Artistic Research. https://doi.org/10.22501/ruu.831242.

3 M. R. Yergeau, (2018). *Authoring Autism: On Rhetoric and Neurological Queerness* (Duke University Press: 2018).

Studies have found that people who do not identify with the gender assigned at birth are three to six times as likely to be autistic as cisgender people are.[4] Queering is also a way to play with the refusal of fixed identities, as constant stereotyping classifies and identifies autistics sometimes as too able to develop some tasks but not able enough to develop others.

In other words, a neuroqueer is someone who challenges and disrupts the norms and expectations of both neurotypicality and heteronormativity, as somebody who cannot fully attune to the normative understandings of what being rhetorical and communicative means. That means that some neurodiverse people may feel and behave differently from what a normative society expects, for instance, by feeling overstimulated by sounds, crowds, particular colors, tastes, and smells, but also by stimming, stuttering, or understanding phrases literally. It is vital to agree that the misunderstandings of the meanings in shared conversations are not the fault of neurodiverse people. Instead, the double empathy theory describes how autistic and nonautistic people may have problems understanding each other. It suggests that these problems are not because autistic people lack empathy or social skills but because autistic and nonautistic people have different ways of communicating, thinking, and experiencing the world. The theory was outlined by Damian Milton,[5] an autism researcher who is also autistic.

4 L. Dattaro, (2020, September 14). The largest study to date confirms the overlap between autism and gender diversity. Spectrum | Autism Research News. https://www.spectrumnews.org/news/largest-study-to-date-confirms-overlap-between-autism-and-gender-diversity/.

5 D. E. Milton, “On the Ontological Status of Autism: The ‘Double Empathy Problem,’” *Disability & Society*, 27(6), 2012, 883–887.

Researcher Emily Stones, in a recent article published in *The Palgrave Handbook of Disability and Communication* (2023), argues that when people with different neurotypes interact, the neurodivergent person is often blamed for the confusion, even if both parties have limitations in understanding each other.[6]

By applying this concept to artistic residencies, I will suggest ways to make them more open and responsive to the needs and desires of neurodiverse artists, curators, and other cultural workers. Again, sometimes simple and uncostly changes are effective, to name a few; employing online forms for applications instead of requesting emailing a private person—many open-source alternatives for this do not necessarily go through big tech companies. As a neuroqueer person, I refuse to apply to jobs, residencies, or open calls that require sending an email because it personalizes the process, and I start feeling that the process is already a piece of social interaction that can drain my energy. Also, forms often send an automatic email confirmation showing that the application went through—with some rather obscure exceptions, such as when I filled out a form for manifesting my interest in attending a conference in the last weeks. The website response page had the text "Thanks for the application. We won't send a confirmation email," which in practice sounds like the worst nightmare to me. Giving feedback to rejected applicants is also important, and it is not only a courteous gesture but also a beneficial practice. Feedback can help artists and researchers prepare for future opportunities.

6 E. Stones, Cross-Neurotype Communication Competence. In *The Palgrave Handbook of Disability and Communication* (45–65). Springer International Publishing, 2023. https://doi.org/10.1007/978-3-031-14447-9_4.

It can also enhance your reputation as an organization that cares about its applicants and values their time and effort. By giving feedback to rejected applicants for art residencies, grant calls, or other programs, you can build trust, loyalty, and goodwill.

Another issue commonly present not only in open calls for residencies but also in open job positions within art organizations is the lack of clarity in the hiring/application processes. Often one applicant realizes that their application was rejected only when the official news about the person selected reaches the media, and there is no clear communication about the rejection at the right time. This generates a feeling of stuckness and anxiety in which the person that applied is held in a position of uncertainty regarding their near future, making it difficult for them to properly plan their schedules and, if necessary, prepare applications for other positions/residencies. It is understandable that arts-based organizations are often short-staffed and lack resources, but communication about positive or negative decisions should be made a priority, as commonly, artists/curators are living in precarious economic settings. In particular, neurodivergent individuals may feel even more intensively stuck without knowing the outcome of their applications—as for some of us it is essential to concentrate on one task at a time and we are in the need of closure.

The second aspect of human diversity I will discuss is kinship, with the understanding that kinship can include nonhuman entities. Kinship refers to the relationships and connections people form with others based on blood ties, romance, sex, adoption, friendship, care, or affinity. Kinship shapes our sense of identity, belonging, and responsibility. However, not all forms of kinship are equally recognized or valued in our society.

There is a dominant assumption that the nuclear family—consisting of a heterosexual couple and their biological children—is the natural and universal form of kinship. The queer activist Robinou, who developed the concept of queer communal kinship (QCK), pointed out that "only forty-three of 238 human societies have monogamy as their ideal. If monogamy persists in our society, it is because of its ideological function raising romantic love crystallized in the dyadic figure of the couple as the only possible prospect of well-being."[7] This assumption has been historically imposed by colonial institutions such as the Christian churches (although not restricted to them). It continues to influence our laws, policies, and practices. One may better understand that many human assemblages can thrive together by creating strategies that denaturalize the couple form, as well as monogamy and nonmonogamy.

A few examples can be listed. First, when it comes to the practical consequences of the current and limited status quo, residencies, for instance, often do not welcome children with their parents and partners on their premises, restricting the artist's agency. In many cases, there is no concrete explanation for why an institution welcomes people who will sleep in the same bed and often occupy the same room, as there is no physical burden to the building itself and its safety. An artistic residency is often seen only as an (important) moment of solitude and self-reflection (while complete isolation is ontologically impossible as we tend to value human relations but conveniently forget the intermesh of thingies and nonhuman animals that make kin with us). Still, there is a diversity of arrangements that one person may need.

7 Robinou, (2023) *Queer Communal Kinship Now!* (1st ed.), Punctum Books: 59).

These must be discussed without exotifying any structure or subjectivity that defies the able-bodiedness perception and the overly sacred family.

At the same time, a paradox emerges: artistic residencies and other structures are not even ready to receive the most traditional family arrangements on their premises and programs. The issue is often also highlighted by the need for more clear communication from the institutions. Suppose something hinders the participation of nuclear and nonnuclear families in their programs. In that case, these should be clearly mentioned in their websites and communication materials instead of starting from the assumption that persons live alone and do not need the support of other bodies in an artistic residency. The same applies to other questions of accessibility concerning visibly and invisibly disabled bodies and the lack of accessibility should not be a surprise to be unveiled the moment one has already traveled to another city, remote location, or even a different country.

Many people are involved in modalities of kinship that defy or challenge the supremacy of the nuclear family and coupledom. For example, some people may have multiple partners or lovers; some may raise children with friends or relatives; others may form intentional communities or networks based on shared values or interests; others may choose not to have children. These forms of kinship are often marginalized or stigmatized by society, and people attuned to them are constantly subjected to affective inequalities. Artistic residencies often exclude or ignore them, usually being designed for individuals or couples—both in terms of physical spaces and institutional mindsets.

To address these issues and create more inclusive and welcoming spaces for diverse forms of kinship in artistic residencies, I will draw and return to the concept of queer communal kinship proposed by Robinou. According to Robinou, queer communal kinship is "a mode of relating that challenges heteronormative assumptions about what constitutes a family; that values nonbiological ties based on care, solidarity, and mutual support; that resists hierarchies based on gender roles or generational status; that fosters affective abundance rather than scarcity; and that promotes ecological sustainability rather than consumerism." In other words, queer communal kinship is a way of living together that celebrates diversity, interdependence, and social justice by thinking together about a future outside the oppressive practices of the family. Residencies should be spaces where one can thrive, and understandably, there are material and economic limits to accommodating different beings and their lovers/partners/nonhuman companions/thingies. Still, the measures often do not significantly burden the institutions' budget if discussed respectfully and outside the perspective of exotifying everything that does not fit the behavioral parameters of normality.

This paper (Vanguard, 80 g/m²) was used from surplus stock normally destined for disposal.
Manufactured in Burneside, United Kingdom.

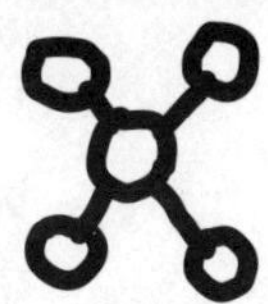

Katarína Slezáková, Daniel Grúň

Queering the Archive

What We Do

The Július Koller Society (JKS) is a nonprofit association established in 2008 in Bratislava, Slovakia. The purpose and objective of the association is to promote the works, artistic and cultural achievements of Július Koller1 as well as to enhance exchanges in contemporary arts and strengthen local and international cultural dialogue. A collection site and archive of the artist's work, a research and study unit, as well as a place for public debate and reflection, the JKS organizes domestic and international projects and activities in the areas of fine arts, art history, visual studies, and cultural theory. JKS resides within the Nová Cvernovka community and cultural center in the outskirts of Bratislava. We have our own exhibition space in which we organize contemporary art shows, usually in cooperation with external curators. In addition, we participate in exhibitions in other institutions that relate to the work of Július Koller, and we also engage in publishing activities. At the moment, the Society is run by a small team of five people, which is the largest in its history thanks to the Islands of Kinship project. At the same time, none of the team members are in full time positions. The team is interdisciplinary in its expertise, including the perspectives of art history and theory, linguistics and literary studies as well as sociology.

1 Július Koller (Piešťany, 1939 – Bratislava, 2007) is a cult figure of the postwar avantgardes on both sides of the former Iron Curtain. From the early 1960s, Koller occupied a marginal position in communist Czechoslovakia, developing his work from the sidelines. Since he was rediscovered in the 1990s, he has become an important source of inspiration for artists and intellectuals around the world. Július Koller worked with radical artistic methods that distanced his work from art's formalisms and from all kinds of aestheticism; instead, he was creating "new cultural situations." His art aimed at a "new life, a new creativity, and a new cosmo-humanistic culture." His strategy was to use real objects and real life as his program of permanent operations, challenging the present so as to open up opportunities for alternative futures. In all his works, he therefore avoided any form of technical mastery.

The core of our work is concerned with archiving practices. In 2009, the JKS obtained license rights for disseminating the works of Július Koller together with the extensive archive of the artist, which the organization has been gradually researching and publishing. This was made possible by a donation from Květoslava Fulierová. The archive has over ten thousand items including pictures, newspaper clippings, artworks, notes and mosaics—all collected personally by Július Koller. This extensive archive documents his lifelong obsession with acquiring and classifying curious evidence of the socialist world in which he lived. At the same time, it offers a key to understanding his artistic practice. He systematically reacted to the reality around him and, using a specific taxonomy, organized, manipulated, and transformed media images, advertisements, and various everyday objects.

The archive was kept in the household he shared with his partner Květoslava Fulierová and now serves as a time capsule, providing a fascinating panorama of visual cultures on both sides of the Iron Curtain. Koller's work hybridizes high and low art and fetishizes worthless packaging of consumer products. Text collages, letters, notebooks, and translations all form an integral part of the archive. Layers of documents and translations illuminate Koller's practice of receiving and transmitting signals. He used them to comment on information and disinformation spread by power-controlled media, and to deny (to everyone) seemingly clear ideological divisions, blurring their sharp boundaries.

Our Main Mission

Discussing and reflecting on inclusion within the IoK project[2] granted us an unusual chance to look at ourselves in the context of other similar institutions while building from the concepts that were present in Koller's works and manifestos.

We accept *amateurism* as Koller understands it. *Antihappening*, which Július Koller defines as a "system of subjective objectivity," denies the exclusivity and closed nature of art. Therefore, the sphere of his activities precisely became culture in its entire "*cosmohumanistic*" breadth, which indicates a field of action that will constantly relate to the negated sphere of art in such a way as to show possible alternatives to it. Koller's performative "operations," "orientations," and "organizations" may be considered by some to be fictitious constructs. In fact, the U.F.O. (1970–2007) represents a distinctive system in which Koller creates his own medium of communication, and every contact with him is an impetus for archiving. Recurring question mark motifs, plus and minus, above and below, nets, playing fields and playgrounds, and their simple layout all create an expressive instrument in a spectrum of simple and interconnected symbols that not only encrypt, but help understand the hidden meanings of the world.

We understand art as inextricably intertwined with the broader social structures that shape access to power and resources. Nevertheless, we have experienced art that creates a counter current or a new wave to be eye-opening and sensitizing. It also initiates detours able to shift the existing social structural patterns,

2 Islands of Kinship: A Collective Manual for Sustainable and Inclusive Art Institutions, co-financed by the European Union. https://islandsofkinship.org/

as they are not given, but rather constructed. However, we do not seek to place art on a pedestal. We want to use the existing tools of art to problematize it, because for it to serve its social role, it needs to be able to deviate from the established tracks, to create *meanders*. A meander is not only a deviation of the water flow from a straight direction in the form of an arc, it also forms and encloses a territory that connects with the rest of the land. It's not land and it's not an island either. But it is also a repeating pattern of ornament. A parasite on the surface of things.

Elusiveness and ambiguity are both present in another one of Koller's concepts—the U.F.O., as it never stands still, it is mobile. Such nature brings a certain type of excitement and playfulness that can be neither captured nor recorded, it can only be felt. All human experience is created in relationships—with each other, but also with things, nonhuman beings, matters or ideas, thoughts, philosophies, and feelings. These encounters pave the way for thus far unexplored ways of thinking which stem from chance, alchemy, corporeality, and interaction. What we aim to do is in essence to vibrate and excite bodies, to make them *feel*. Therefore, JKS does not need to grow, it needs to *move*.

Experiences are a source of new ways of thinking for us: it is about chance, about searching, about alchemy and about science—but it is definitely about nonhierarchical relationships and about pedagogies. We want to bring new types of knowing, leading and feeling—we consider this the main role of art. Bodies/corporeality as a tool for experiencing, knowing, leading, and feeling bring excitement and vibrate.

What Inclusion Means to Us

Inclusion is a very popular word nowadays. It is used and discussed often, yet many still struggle to grasp its meaning. Alternatively, people do not bother with any conceptualization, thus emptying the term completely and focusing only on its trendiness. We do not want to be yet another art organization that talks inclusion and ends up tokenizing marginalized peoples, only scratching the surface of social inequalities and ignoring the need for in-depth reflection and awareness that can bring real change—change in how we *do* things, not only in how we speak of them.

There are many definitions of inclusion that come from academics, researchers, artists, and institutions. However, we are convinced that it is impossible to simply accept the existing conceptualization without "translating it" to our context: cultural, institutional, and material. Thus, we wanted to have our own definition—a definition that suits the specifics of JKS, people in it, and one that also *feels* right. Our understanding of inclusion heavily relies on *doing*. We believe it to be a process, a constant effort, and an ever-present perspective. It means creating a space*community*collective[3] that can reflexively look at itself and respond to the changing needs of the individuals who are a part of it, while creating easy access for anyone who wants to get involved (examples of good practice are discussed further below). It is about disrupting power hierarchies, recognizing nonacademic knowledge, inventing new pathways and walking them,

3 We use these three terms interchangeably in this text. Community, space, and collective are in no means synonyms, but they complement each other. Since we have not found a language to name these three dimensions in one word (so far), we choose to use them all together or, to save space, each separately with an asterisk to remind us of the other two words that complete this assemblage of meanings.

as well as about imagination. It is also about fair access to resources, sustainability, and mental health. There is also one basic element that cannot be missing—accountability. We believe that the community* has responsibility towards individual people, but also that every person has responsibility towards others and towards the collective*.

The Archive

Memory stands at the center of culture, humanities, and social sciences. These explore the narratives created through human and nonhuman practices as well as networks of actors created *by* these practices. However, the matter is quite important in forming a collective memory. This most notably translates into human efforts to retain certain artifacts, items, buildings, or even pieces of nature that they find worthy, while letting other things deemed as worthless decay and perish. Some things, people, or events might be considered better forgotten, either consciously or subliminally. This dismissal is interwoven into culture, humanities, and social sciences that all put the white straight masculine narration of history front and center and deem it as universal. Whiteness, masculinity, and heterosexuality are associated with reason, science, enlightenment, objectivity, (high) culture, and advancement. Their victories have been the greatest and suffering the most unbearable. This universal understanding of Western-centric experience pushes away and even erases what does not fit the mold. This can be observed on a global scale through the decolonial lens and queering perspectives. Understanding the global motions is essential for understanding our local life and ultimately for understanding oneself.

We wish to think about and explore these forgotten and suppressed narratives. Not only because Koller's legacy and archive incite us to do so, but also because we find true value in exploring these stories so that we can imagine different futures as well as an alternative present. Such visions require unlearning what we know—quite a task since most of the essential knowledge and values that structure our thinking are employed automatically. For example, when we walk down the street, we automatically ascribe gender to everyone we meet. This is not even a conscious thought, we don't say to ourselves "this is a man, this is a woman"—we just sort them this way. Only when this automatism is disrupted, imaginations can be set free.

The archive represents Július Koller's concrete, materialized, and categorized legacy in numbered and labelled boxes. Linking the archive with JK's manifestos makes it possible to perceive meanings in the accumulated documents, to see the system where associativity seems to rule. This does not mean the archive and Koller's work in general is to be revered and glorified—quite the opposite. Archives are not neutral; they embody the power inherent in gathering, collecting, and hoarding, as well as the power that comes from mastering the vocabulary and rules of the language. We desire for the archive to be questioned, juxtaposed, reinterpreted, criticized, and queered.

We strive to share, manage, and protect the archive. We archive, hence we are archivists. We perceive it as an *archive of the commons* and on this basis we cooperate with artists and curators, we expand and rearrange original meanings with current readings, and project our fears, ideas, and relationships onto it. For us, the JK archive is a place for discussing, negotiating, and searching for potential. The archive is an opportunity to create cultural situations by layering and reinterpreting its contents from contemporary standpoints—perspectives that are hidden, marginalized, ignored, and obscured—all in order to deviate from the established ruts. The archive is a source and a cornerstone for the effort to forge alternative versions of the future as well as to form new paths of thought. We break away from reality, not in an attempt to escape it, but rather to imagine new worlds.

In reference to JK, we feel like we curate the archive; we imagine the archive as a discursive posthuman bodymind of a cyborg; we also perceive it, us, and our activity as a U.F.O.—ambiguous, situated, mysterious, elusive, unpredictable, and out of focus. The U.F.O. archive does not provide eternal truths, it appears and disappears, and is a projection site for blind spots.

What We Look for in the Archive

The archive is a starting point around which relationships are created. In the spirit of *amateurism,* we want to form (knotted) points of connectivity, a network open to interactions from the outside (*antiarchive*). That is why we are looking for a community in the archive: we ask ourselves the question of language and communication with different target groups. Our activity is bridging individuality and community, criticism and imagination. Art should communicate with other disciplines and vice versa. We attempt to *meander* existing discourses. Moreover, we wish to initiate new ones—even if for an instance, here and now, recorded only by the bodies present. This process is only possible in relationships and communities*—in discussions about priorities and values, while abandoning the idea of definitive truths, highlighting the neglected, the blind spots, and the shadows; interacting where there was no interaction before.

Where the Archive Leads Us

Since decolonial and queering practice emphasizes the need to deconstruct and question structures of power such as an archive, let us summarize this using two of its main terms: archival care and archival concern.

The Greek word "ἐπιμελία" (epimeleia) can be translated into English as "care," but also "concern." It can be understood as a call for reflection, for the rediscovery and reevaluation of inherited stereotypes. Archival care goes beyond the physical preservation of records and extends to ethical, legal, and administrative aspects of archives.

Care differs from concern in the sense of nurture, such as securing the common good, creating safe spaces and inclusive practices as well as sensitizing relationships. Care and concern/responsibility are closely related, but concern/responsibility goes beyond caring about what we might characterize as fears, doubts, and mistrust of the cultural, social, and economic structures built on the legacy of the nation-state. Care, together with the adjectivized "radical care," appears more and more often in discussions about art, work, and collective efforts.

In connection to the right of self-determination, the concept of self-care presents itself, which could otherwise be defined as a parallel to decolonial practice. It means questioning our deeply held patterns and beliefs, rethinking our role in the systems that sustain capitalism and nationalism as well as developing awareness of heightened sensitivity to language and dialogic forms of exchange. The concept of self-care is also associated with collective therapy, in which artistic activities can function and at the same time support historical awareness and cultural self-governance.

It may seem to some that care precedes an archive, as if it were an integral part of the creation of archives in their systematic classification and organization which culminates in the archival order. The connection between the practice of contemporary art and archival care is therefore significant in that the result is not necessarily some kind of archival order. The described interest in an archive, relationships, meandering, and unfolding can be called a decolonial practice, because an archive as such is a colonial project and this interest also represents a preoccupation with violence, on which the existence of an archive is based.

Examples of Good Practice

At the very beginning of the IoK project, a kick-off meeting was held in Bratislava, part of which was devoted to a workshop on conceptualization of inclusion (lead by Zuzana Jakalová and Katarína Slezáková, who later became inclusion coordinator at JKS). During the session, we have set dimensions of inclusion that draw away from focusing on marginalized groups and towards the institutional structures: programming, internal processes and relations, community and audience.

The first two are self-explanatory, so let us focus more on the difference between audience and community. Audience includes all people who regularly or occasionally visit our space for exhibitions and events. They can follow our social networks to get information about the upcoming program and invitations to events. Their involvement in JKS is ad hoc based on our initiative to create spaces where they can enjoy themselves.

The community consists of people who are regularly involved in the JKS and outside the program, such as artists, curators, art historians, theorists, art journalists and other collaborators, art students, members of the JKS board of directors as well as people employed in cultural and artistic institutions that we cooperate with. It also includes our partners outside of art institutions, our neighbors in Nová Cvernovka and friends of society, researchers, academics, performance artists, writers, poets, and others who are interested in the activities of JKS and have a closer relationship with the institution.

These dimensions guide our institutional transformation towards more inclusive and sustainable practice. We made efforts in each of them, although, considering our approach to archiving and art elaborated above, we focused on the audience and community especially, looking for ways to initiate experiences in nonhierarchical settings. The choice is to do less standard exhibitions, keep the shows on for longer periods, and open up space for community gatherings and new audiences that are not typically drawn to fine art. We also aim to explore evaluations that consider the quality of relationships and connections over sheer numbers. In the following section, we attempt to provide a peek at some of the good practices we developed on the way.

Programming

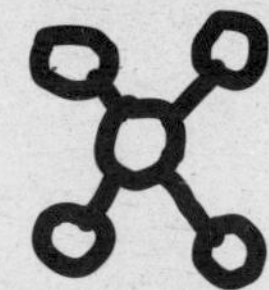

In the first part of this manual, we elaborate on our approach towards archiving, culture, and fine art. Then we give two examples how this translates into our programming practices.

Between Earthly Beings and the Unknown Cosmic World: The Continent

The exhibition was initiated by Canan Batur reaching out to JKS with interest in working with the archive. Canan came to visit us in person and spent time in the archive with Daniel's guidance. As a result, she came up with an idea for a show that would reinterpret and problematize imaginative utopias and cosmic worlds present in Koller's works. *The Continent* explored the engaged and contemplative practice(s) of Julius Koller and the poetics of his imagination for a more politically just and ecologically sound worlds. The exhibition provided a decolonial perspective by involving a group of artists that have roots outside of the European cultural circuit. This approach embodies what we want the archive to be—a starting point, base, inspiration, as well as a question, statement that can be discussed here and now by sharing experience.

Hungry Is My Favorite Word

This group exhibition curated by Nora Swantje-Almes was our first attempt at making our practice more sustainable and true to our mission as described above. The show itself dealt with queer existence and experience in heteronormative structures of history telling and pop culture. By exploring moments that became part of the cultural archives, the exhibition also rediscovered what was left out of these narratives. It speculates about what could have been if history was written by queers. Besides the themes of the show, the format is different from the exhibitions we did previously. It lasted almost five months and the live program was designed as an integral part of the exhibition—including the U.F.O. sessions (discussed below). It included performances and art events, but also community sessions that were prepared in cooperation between the curator and the inclusion coordinator. The vision was blurred, not only concentrated on the exhibited works. Engaging in different formats allowed us to connect to our audience and community in a way that is not possible through a solitary visit of the show. Community is created and experienced here and now in the space of the exhibition. It might be fleeting (like a UFO) but is always remembered. Individuals can carry this experience and return to it again and again in memory and emotion.

Internal Processes and Relations

The JKS team consists of five people with different backgrounds, most of us in precarious situations juggling multiple jobs and studies, with part of the team not even living in Bratislava. At the very beginning of the IoK project, there were only two people at JKS: Zlatka who is in charge of production, and Daniel in a position that can be best described as art director and archival researcher. Katarína, the inclusion officer, joined the team at the beginning of 2023 and brought the perspectives of sociology to the table. In May of the same year, Kata, a writer and a linguist, took over our communications and promotion. The last addition to the team was Aliza, an artist based in Nová Cvernovka, who assists with the day-to-day management of the institution. These developments mean that the team more than doubled in the short span from the beginning of the project. This is a welcomed progress. However, it also means challenges. We grappled with the position of an inclusion coordinator, as we were not sure what their position in an institution should be. Also, communication issues arose—how do we meet, how often, how do we communicate on day-to-day basis. We had to establish communication channels and regular meetings—both in person and online.

Strategic Sessions

We realized that not only the strategy of conduct, but the mission of JKS is rarely verbalized, said out loud, and discussed. The most important thing we did was to set aside time to discuss broader matters beyond the day-to-day operations, such as our mission, vision, approach to art, culture, and the archive. There was a tendency in the JKS team to assume that our individually set visions of JKS are aligned and we didn't feel the need for such debates, but more so, there is often no time, space, and capacity for discussion. For example, we used the time of relative calm over the summer and organized a full-day team session during which we did not discuss any day-to-day technicalities. Us taking a step back from the enmeshment in crisis mode, typical for the active months outside summer season, enabled us to take a break and explore retrospectively the strategies we as a collective intuitively choose.

A part of the day was focused on planning, as we had to prepare for the local funding scheme that would co-finance the project in the upcoming year and possibly could allow us to add further activities not foreseen in the original

IoK proposal. We also prepared for the visit of Nora Swantje Almes, the curator of a group exhibition planned for the spring of 2024. However, most of the day was an in-depth reflective session. For this session, we did the 4 (or whatever number) WHYs technique to explore our mission. It is a really easy technique that can help deepen thinking about the mission statement of an organization. You just repeatedly ask the question "Why do we (as a group or organization) exist in the world?" Before every repetition, the facilitator sums up what has been said and the main points and asks "why" again. The outcomes of this session served as a basis for this manual as well.

Community

Studio Visits

We set out to engage with the young and up-and-coming artists, especially with local art students from marginalized groups. Due to recent political developments in Slovakia, culture is understood as a tool of propaganda, so it is to be controlled and molded. With antigender forces being on the rise, some of the topics we explore in our programming, such as queerness, decolonization, sustainability, and posttruth, are not preferred by the government funding bodies. Thus, we find it especially pressing to engage with art students, who organize to protest these developments, but also provide them with the opportunity to engage with curators and institutions that explore the same themes in their work. To foster these connections, we organized two rounds of studio visits with curators Canan Batur and Nora Swantje-Almes, who cooperated with us on the exhibitions mentioned above. We proposed this as part of our broader cooperation. The aim was not only to connect international curators with art students from marginalized groups, but also possibly seek ways to engage (some of the) young artists in the shows. In both cases, we were successful.

Although JKS has been present in the fine art landscape for some time now, these were our first experiences in organizing studio visits. Both curators met with five young artists that were preselected by the JKS team, based on our knowledge of the local art scene. We have picked artists that we felt could communicate well with the curatorial approach, and in case of Nora Swantje-Almes, we considered the themes of queering in their works. Not all the artists have their own ateliers, thus some of the visits took place in our space. Each meeting was about an hour long and held in person when the curators were visiting JKS.

After the first round with the curator Canan Batur, we discussed the selection internally and it seemed to us that a certain type of privilege might have played a role— the artist selected to participate in the exhibition was the most privileged as they were the laureate of a young artist award and studied abroad. The other artists were less experienced in networking and communicating with curators and potentially less comfortable expressing themselves in English. This does not mean that the choice was not based on the quality of the artwork, or that it was not well deserved, but it made us think. We decided it should be our responsibility to try to level the playing field, so the less privileged artists have an equal chance to succeed regardless of their language and presentation skills. In the attempt to reduce the influence of these factors on the course of the visits, it was decided that it would be for the best that the inclusion officer partakes in the visits. So, Katarína joined Nora for the studio visits—as an explorer, learner, occasional interpreter as well as a sociologist with a deeper understanding of the local context. It turned out to be beneficial that she is not that deeply immersed in the art scene. It meant no bias when meeting the artists, no preconceived notions about their artwork (or art in general). This allowed the inclusion coordinator to have a more neutral position, not favoring any person in particular, and just provide context, translation, or explanation where necessary. The second round of studio visits resulted in two young artists, who thematize queer existence in their work, taking part in the live program for the exhibition *Hungry is my favourite word*. Michael Dore performed his songs for the first time ever at the show opening. Aliza Orlan, who typically focuses on graphic works and is venturing into the performance territory, had a performance as part of the live program in May 2024.

Audience

Nová Cvernovka (the community center where JKS resides) brings together a variety of actors, from artists and their ateliers, to freelancers, architects, NGOs, kindergartens, schools, and small businesses. JKS is however the only fine arts institution with public programming in the center. As regards audience and community generally—typically, a person is an audience member first and potentially becomes part of the community. In our case, it sometimes happens the other way around, since we intentionally choose to find collaborators that reside in Nová Cvernovka. However, they are not always interested in fine art and our activities—thus, we face the question in reverse—how do we make our community into an audience?

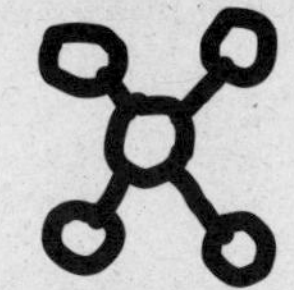

sUstainable-Feminist-Operation (U.F.O.) Series

On top of our work in programming, we wanted to go the extra mile to reach the community in Nová Cvernovka with topics of inclusion, in a way that is accessible for anyone, without any prior knowledge in fine arts. All the events within this series are related to current program/exhibitions, but only loosely. The aim is to bring perspectives outside the art world to discuss topics tackled within the main program, which are also relevant for inclusion and sustainability of art practice.

We set out to discover formats that go well beyond discussion and lectures, that dissolve the hierarchical differences between the facilitator and the attendees. For the *Continent* exhibition, we prepared a workshop on imagination in crisis in cooperation with NaZemi, an organization concerned with the economical concept of degrowth and its promotion. The workshop lasted half a day and employed participatory methods and imaginative exercises.

As was stated above, with *Hungry Is My Favourite Word*, we took matters a step further and the live program was prepared together with the curator of the exhibition and became its integral part. The live program had two lines—performances on one hand, U.F.O. sessions on the other. Our aim was to open up the gallery space towards the local queer communities preparing a combination of activities. We cooperated with queer activist spaces, collectives, and individual people. Three community sessions took place. In February, a very informal networking meetup under the name Coffee&Cake Intergeneratioal Queer Storytelling took place. Together with the student queer association Light* and the Brno (Czech Republic) based collective Plusko+, we explored the current possibilities of warm activism, talked about individual intergenerational experiences, what we have in common, and what can be built on. The event commenced with a guided tour of the queer exhibition, followed by an informal workshop for queer people of all generations. The workshop used simple art methods such as collages to explore the possible queer utopias of the future. In March, a queer-feminist diaries writing workshop took place. In the workshop, the participants were urged to see journaling as a tool that transforms our individualized perspective into collective thinking and systemic understanding. In April, a walking tour in Bratislava with Jana Zezulova focused on the history of local queer activism, and in May, Luki Essender held a reading from his artist book.

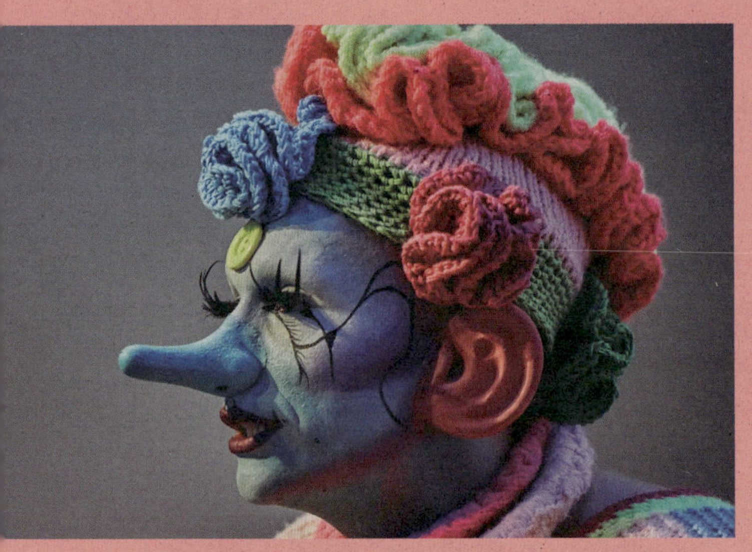

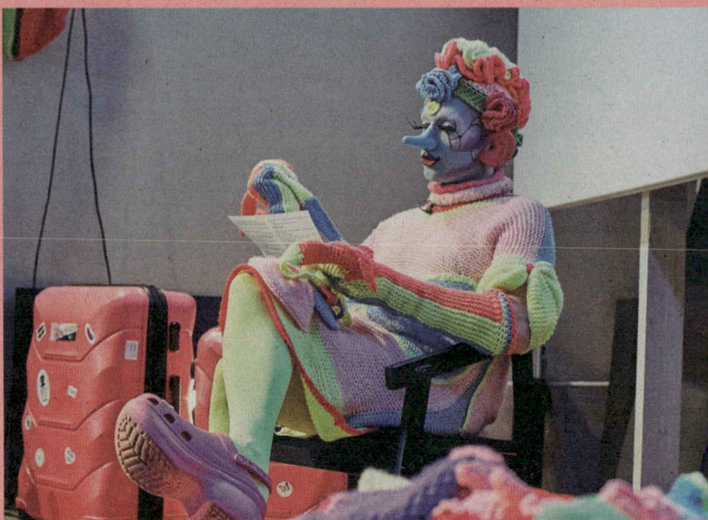

Taka Taka: Mothers Mothering Mothers: Dragging Warmly

Nonuniversal Drag Values

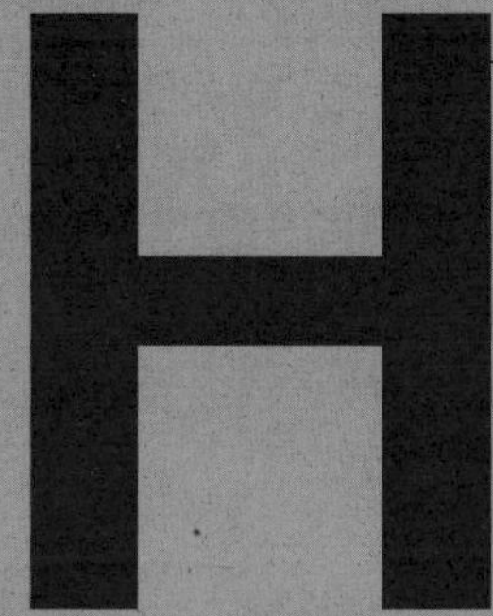

i, I am Taka Taka and the following lines are my transcription of the Drag Mothering values and tools that have been directly taught to me by Jennifer Hopelezz or indirectly by experiencing Jenny transmitting them to my siblings and learning from the relationships within the House of Hopelezz. These tools are generated in the local context of Amsterdam, and they are founding stones for me as the drag mother for the House of Løstbois.

Basics

Curiosity, acceptance, empathy, patience, listening, transparency (among us), honesty. Empowering their urgency, desire, need, affinity.
Eliminate my expectations.
Trust and doubt your drag mother.
End of violence—creation of joy.
A house is not a homogenous dance company, it's forever, but nothing lasts forever.
A tent for two people is also a house.
Laughter as a mode of resistance.
Every house can have multiple mothers.
The more houses, the better.
Every drag local community is entirely different from another.
Do not compare but actively try to understand them.
Every drag performer is doing drag for different reasons.
Drag has been written on the streets before it was written in the books.

Queer is not a look, neither a clear identity, but rather a subjective, lived experience in constant transformation.
Entitlement is for the real queens.
Drag is breaking gendered rules, it's not making new ones.
Pay your dues to the community—don't expect only to get paid.

For Freedom

Intersections have no red lights or stop signs.
We are not heroes; it is sad we need to fight for our rights.
Make fun of the morals of your freedom.
Dragxicity = drag toxicity from other people or drag queens in the scene is a construct of insecurity, just ignore it.
Becoming ourselves by not assimilating.
A drag producer who wants to change your drag character is not producing you but is killing your character.
Define your relationship with your community personally.
Accept every subjectivity as a complete incomplete.
Love the mean siblings and maybe a year later, they will not be mean anymore.
Soft is stronger.
Be humble.
Freedom is not a candy store; it's based on how much you resist the restrictions placed on you.
Depending on the country, politicians tend to want a drag queen next to them. The question is what do you want from them?

For Queer Entertainment

Don't set yourself or others on fire (literally).
All makeup and wigs from the cheapest to the most expensive look good on you and they can catch fire easily.
Sunglasses on stage block gaze exchange.
The gaze of a queer audience is a healing gaze.
The gaze of a heteronormative audience can be dehumanizing, be prepared.

Commission #4

Camp is not an aesthetic style but a subcultural heritage.
Pop star was never the goal.
If you want to become famous and rich, most likely you have chosen the wrong path. Infamous is sometimes more effective than famous.
Queer nonconforming entertainment is a visual language made from and for queer people. Welcome biographical elements and mix them with fiction for social commentary beyond commentary; bio-fictional drag.
Be approachable to everybody from your queer audience.
Lip-sync and dance ain't the only format of drag expression.
Public messages for your community can create adverse effects, the tone of addressing them is equally important to the message.
Know "her-story."
Showtime is rehearsal time and the best time to try something new.
Drag singers who cannot hear their own voice when singing live usually come out cacophonic.

> That is a charisma, not a disadvantage.
> Just don't take yourself too seriously on stage, it makes you look silly.

(Almost) never give critical feedback when a sibling has just finished performing.
Making a show in six minutes is equally relevant to working on one for six months. Clubs are not Broadway.
Address your audience in the eyes.
Always be sure to have a light on you while performing, even if it is a torch light.
Birthday cakes on stage should always fall on the floor before the sibling blows the candles.
If you do not like your show, feel free to stop the music and walk away with charm or run away.
Do not try to save the show. Welcome all of its randomness.
Help your siblings when you finish your show.
Queer public is more important for you and more important than you.

Bartenders and garderobe workers are the DNA of the party, respect them.

Aim to create queer aesthetics based on urgent subjects of your community.

Makeup is not a quality of excellence but a skill that might help.

More than 40 minutes of makeup is a waste of time.

What you want to say with your drag is equally important to what you look like.

Be calm and respectful to others backstage.

Take your wig off on stage once per while; it's good for your drag ego.

If your show offends your queer public (not their morals), be sincere, discuss it, and apologize. Keep the drama on stage.

If a producer approaches you for a project about visibility and inclusion, examine their motives and strategies closely.

Shy people are great performers, too. Allow time to develop.

For House Internal Communication

To solve a communication problem between sisters is not the goal, it is rather a chance to find out how to talk about it.

Each one is a complete character with their own set of aesthetics and needs.

Queer coexistence is learned every day.

Your siblings are your mentors.

Do not be jealous of your new siblings, actively support them, and share all of your skills with them.

Our differences in our subjectivities are our strength.

A group always has a black sheep, do not slaughter it but paint it all pink together.

Treat your kids and siblings better than how you expected to be treated by them.

Ask your kids how they arrived at their drag instead of where they are going with it.

Being all together instead of on your own makes it easier to hit the streets in drag.

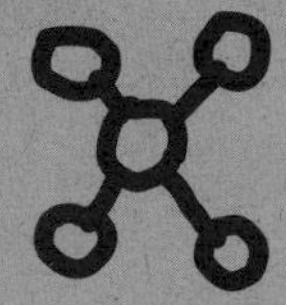

Somebody who is new to drag should be respected equally to somebody who is drag royalty.
You do get along differently with every family member.

Queer Self-Care

Drugs ain't going to treat your trauma.
Uncontrollable drug use shortens your drag life, alcohol is also a drug.
Drag is not a sprint, it is a marathon.
If everybody in the house says you might have a behavioral problem related to drugs, it's the time we need to intervene and for you to take action.
We learn queer self-love every day.
Choose your battles in the streets wisely and always have a pair of sneakers with you. Avoid walking alone at night.
Always ask if there is available budget for a taxi.
If a taxi driver does not accept you, don't report them personally but expose the policy of their company and demand active change.

Be wary of some journalists, they might seem to care about you, but they do like to racialize incidents of bullying.

Every form of violence, including public shaming and bullying, has to be immediately reported to authorities, not only on social media.
Authorities can also be dangerously ignorant.
Forgive your bloodline parents when necessary.
Freaky is an excellent quality.
Always be sweet to parents and kids on the street even when they seem to be afraid of you. Break the promise of bitchy drag, especially in front of kids on the street.
Still, “queer-read” the parents and put them in their place when necessary.

Welcome the unknown you.

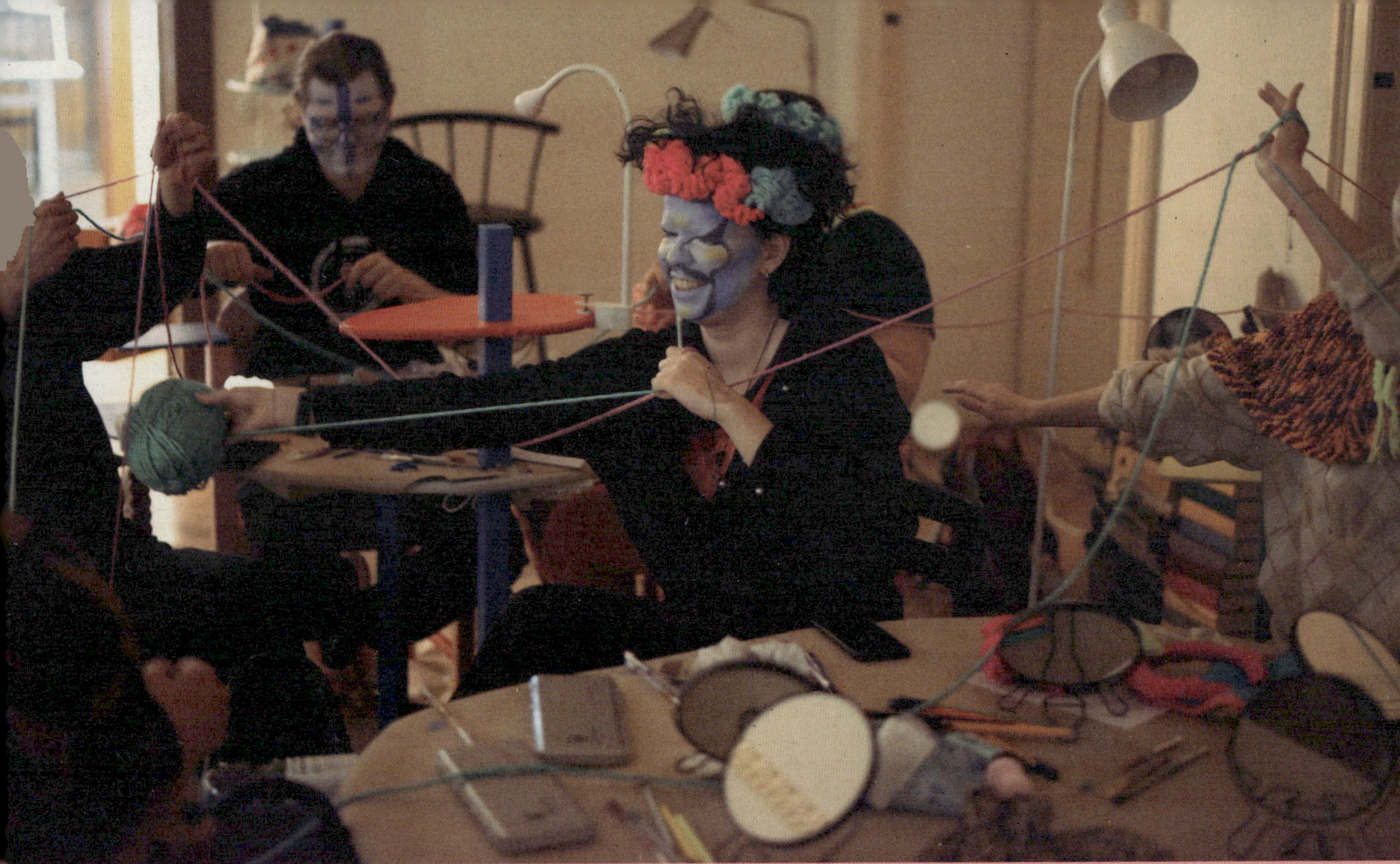

TAKA TAKA:
MOTHERS MOTHERING MOTHERS:
DRAGGING WARMLY

workshop and artist lecture
2022, 2024

The commission was presented as part of exhibitions:

- **BEYOND NUCLEAR FAMILY: RECIPES FOR HAPPINESS**, Display Gallery, Prague, Czech Republic, October 13 – November 27, 2022, organized by Jindřich Chalupecký Society
- **BEYOND NUCLEAR FAMILY: HOME SWEET HOME**, The Elizabeth Foundation for the Arts, New York, USA, November 17, 2022 – January 7, 2023, organized by Jindřich Chalupecký Society
- **ALL'S GOOD BETWEEN US**, Latvian Centre for Contemporary Art, Riga, Latvia, February 15 – March 31, 2024, organized by Latvian Centre for Contemporary Art

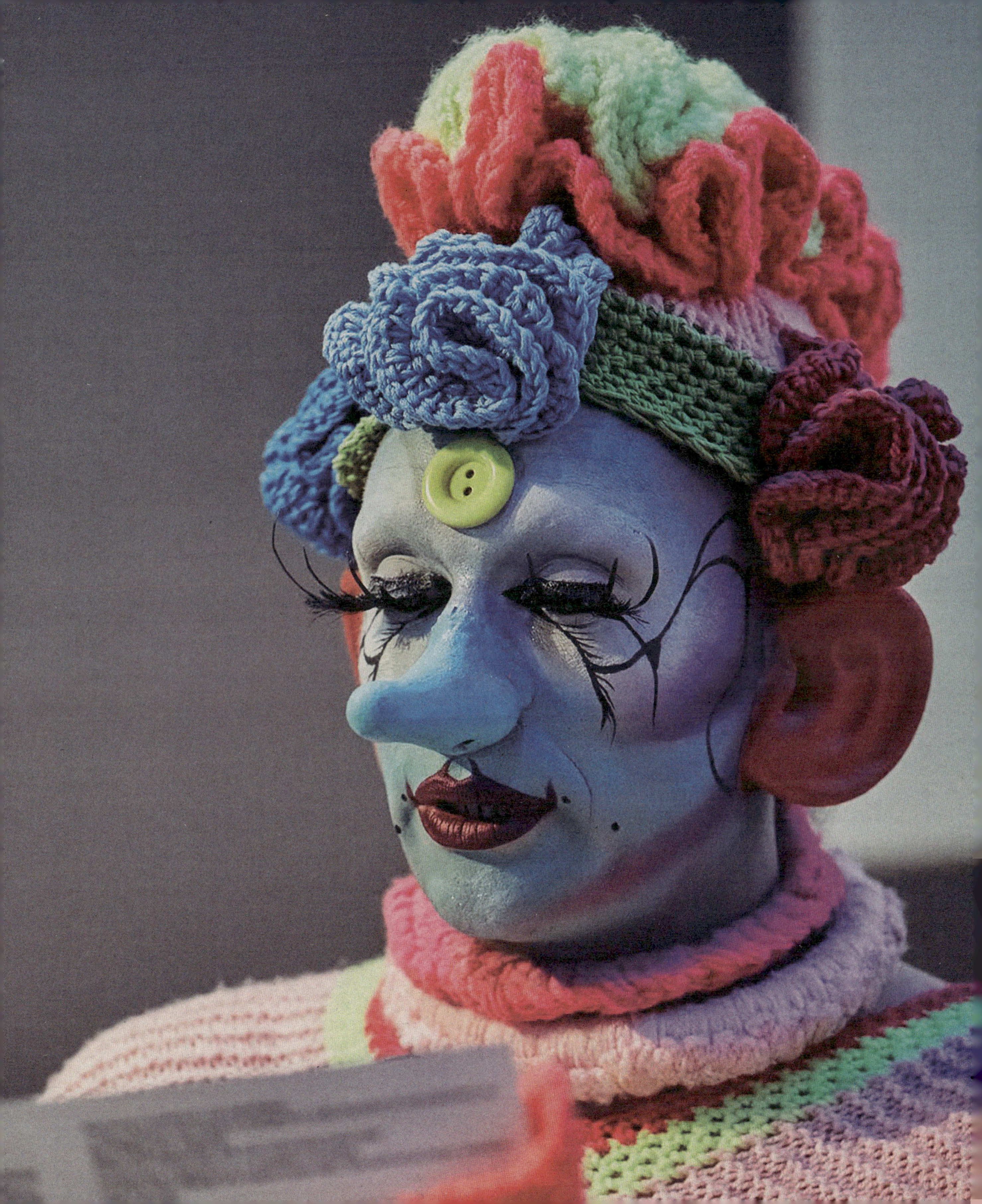

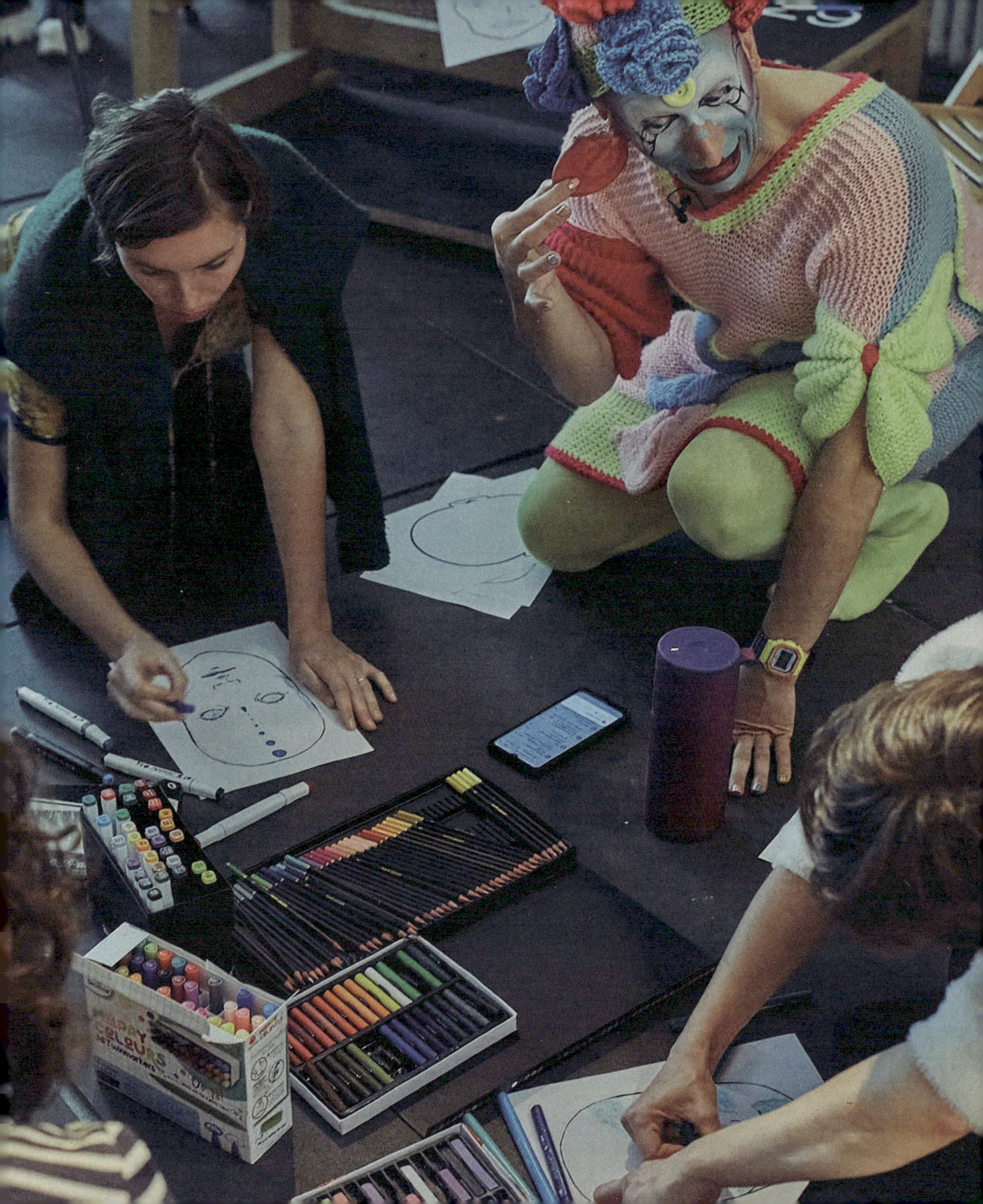

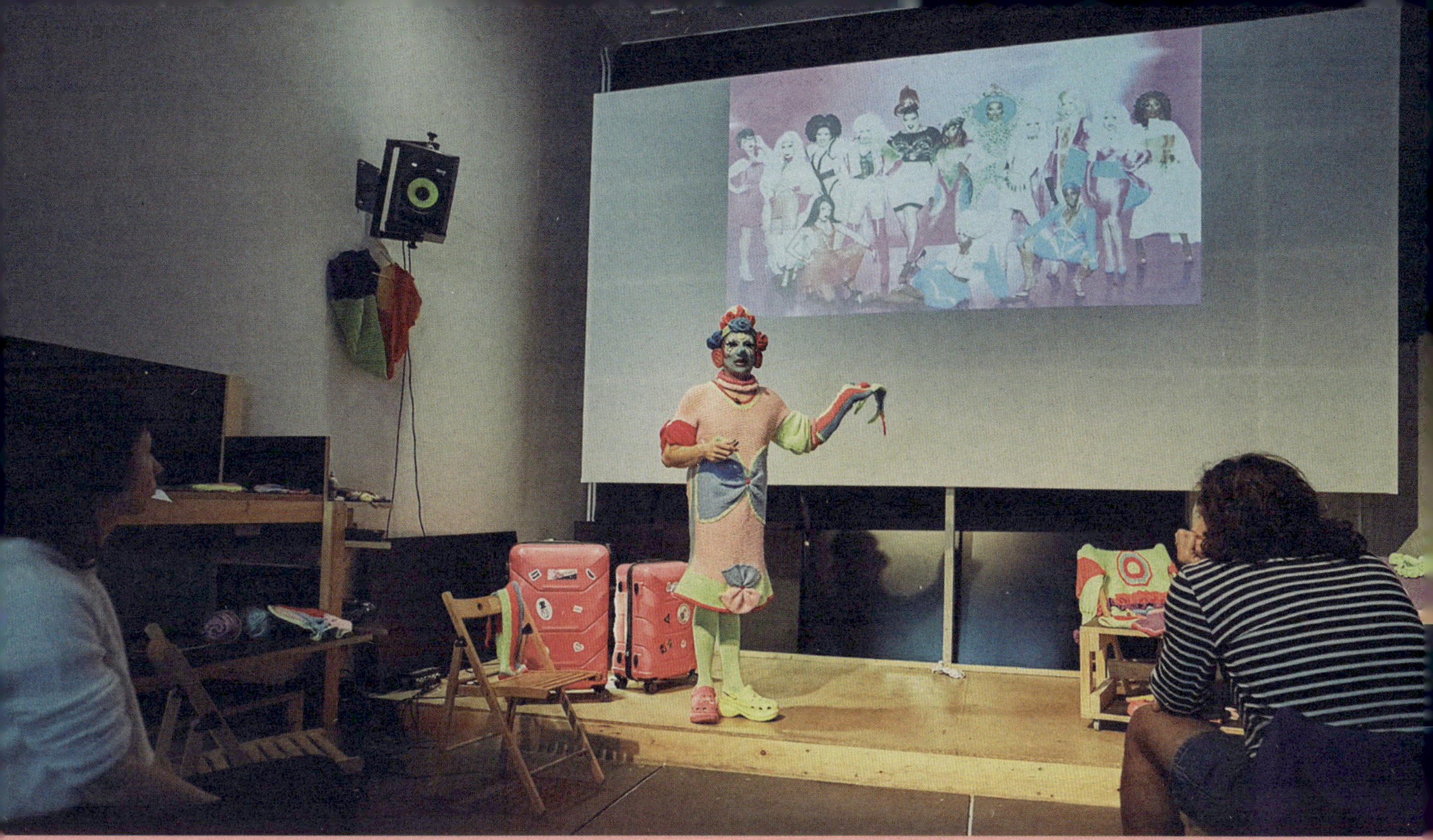

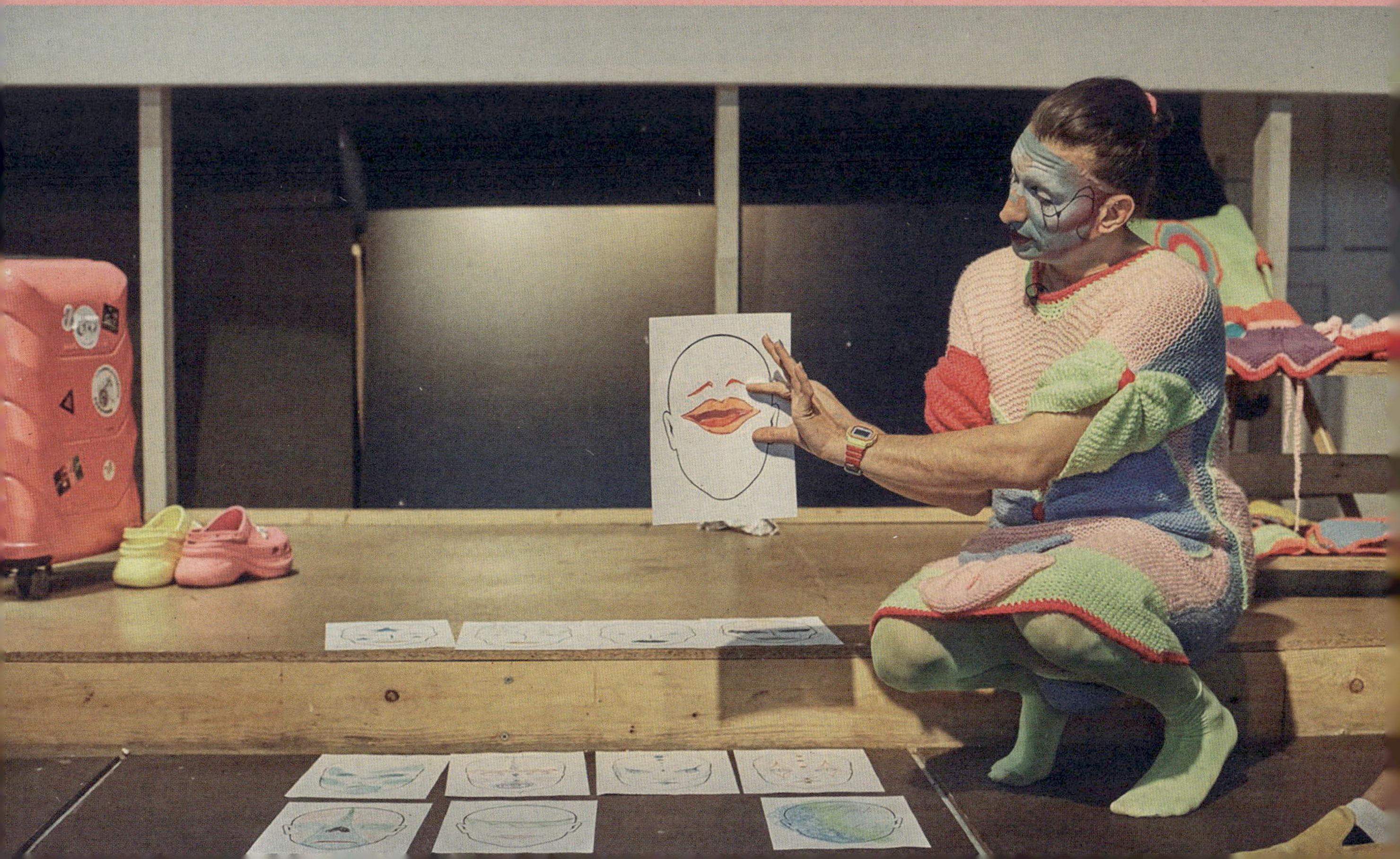

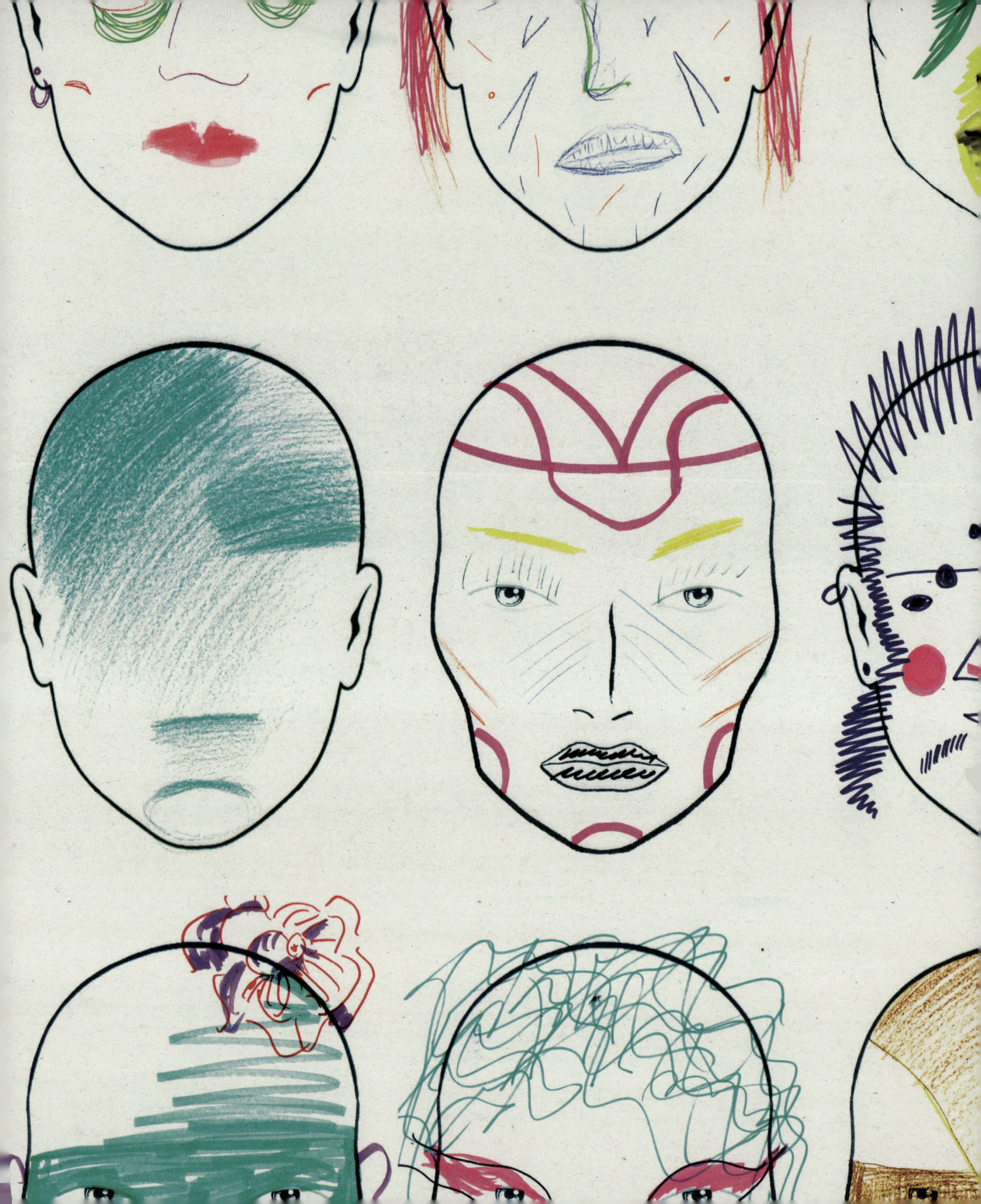

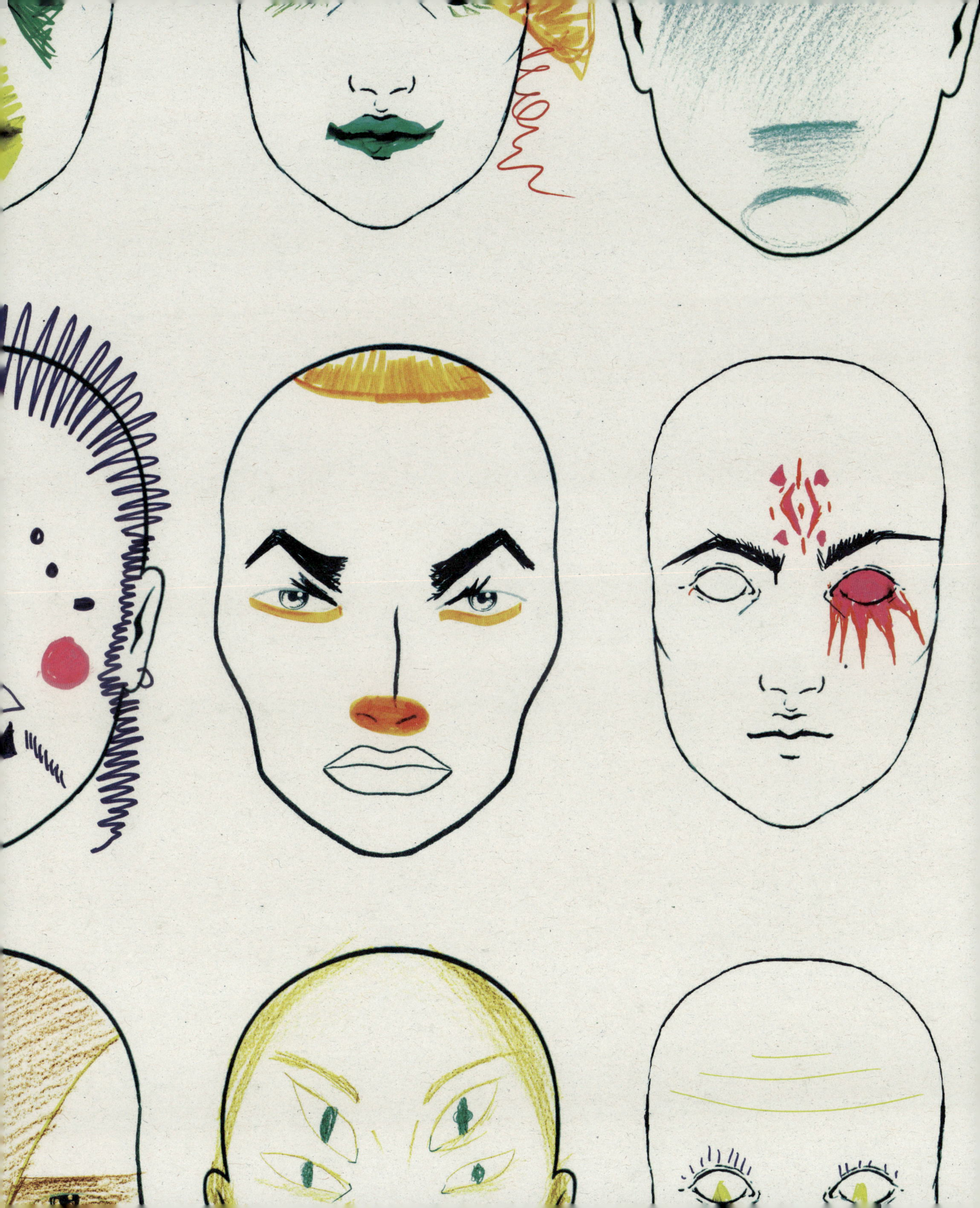

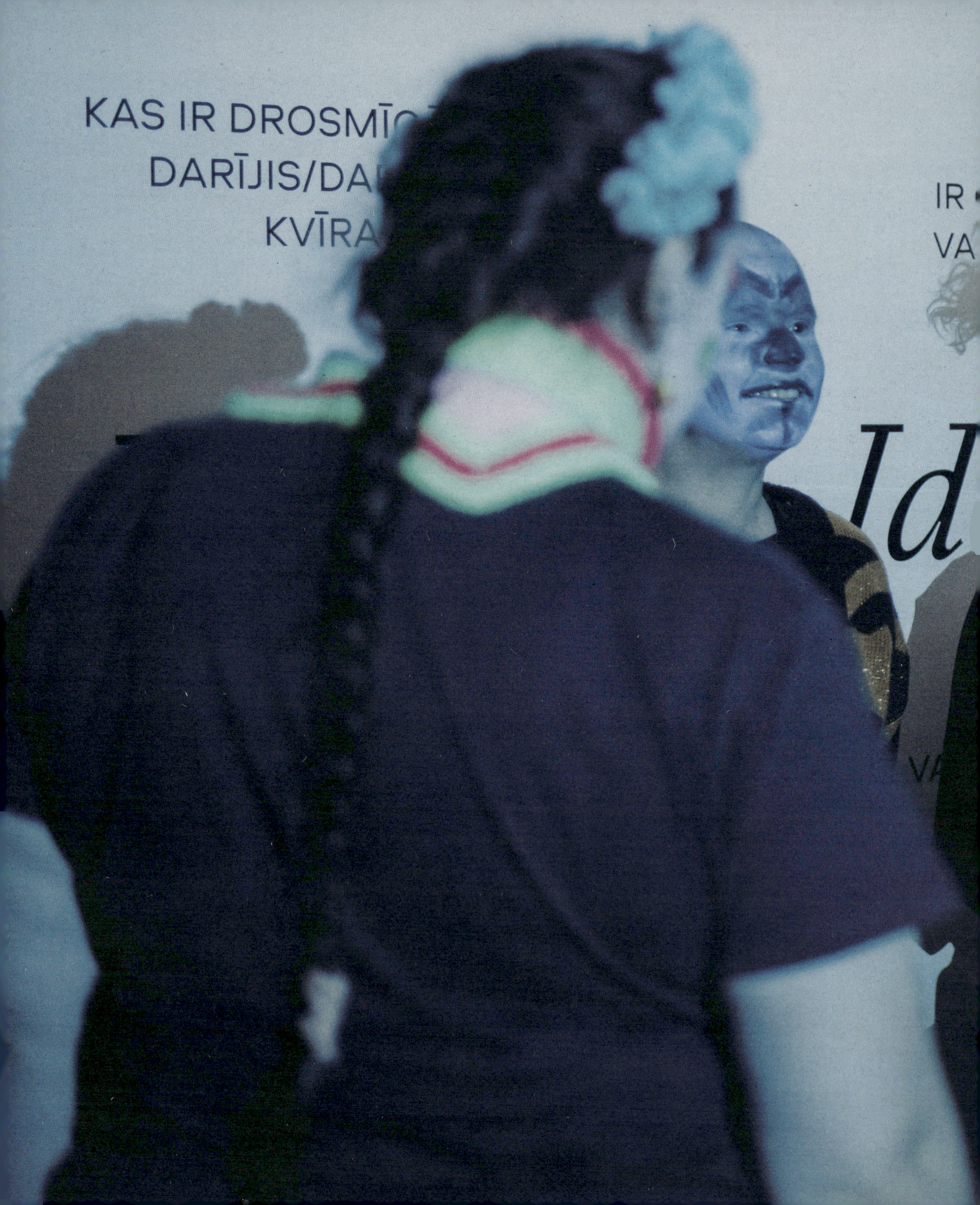
KAS IR

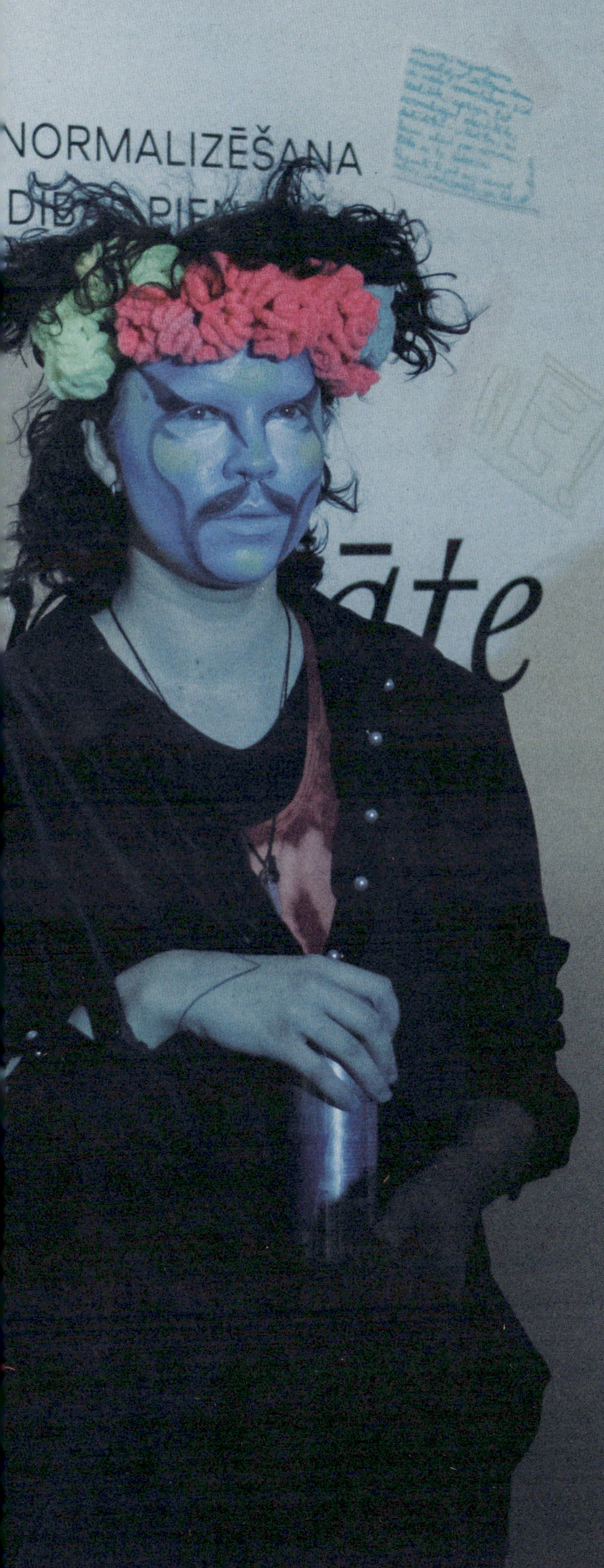

NORMALIZĒŠANA
VAI TEV IR BIJIS
PARTNERIS, KURŠ IR SKA
KĀ TAS TEVI IETEKMĒJ
Skapi
VAI IZNĀKT NO SKAPJ
IR PIENĀKUMS?

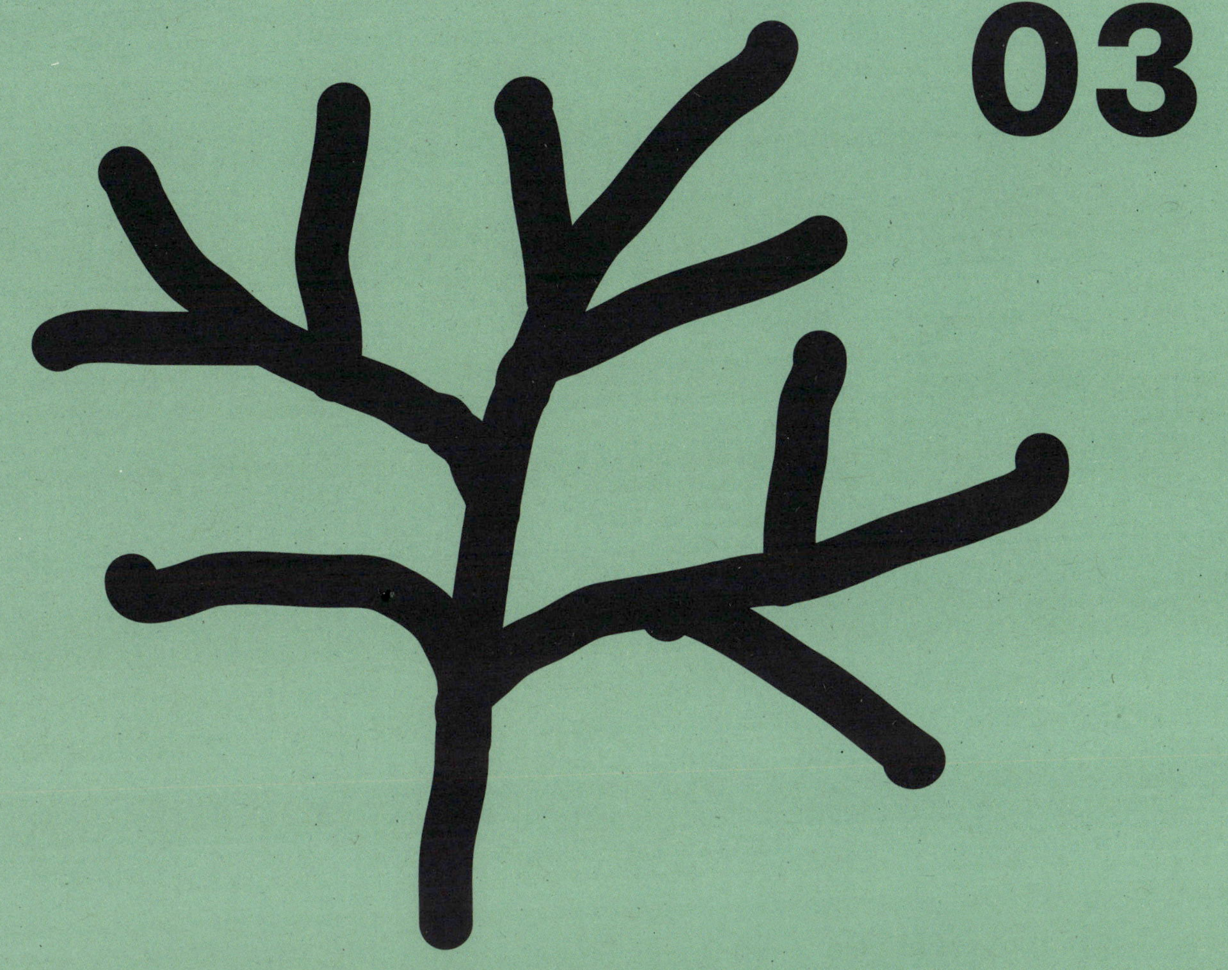

Beyond Ecology

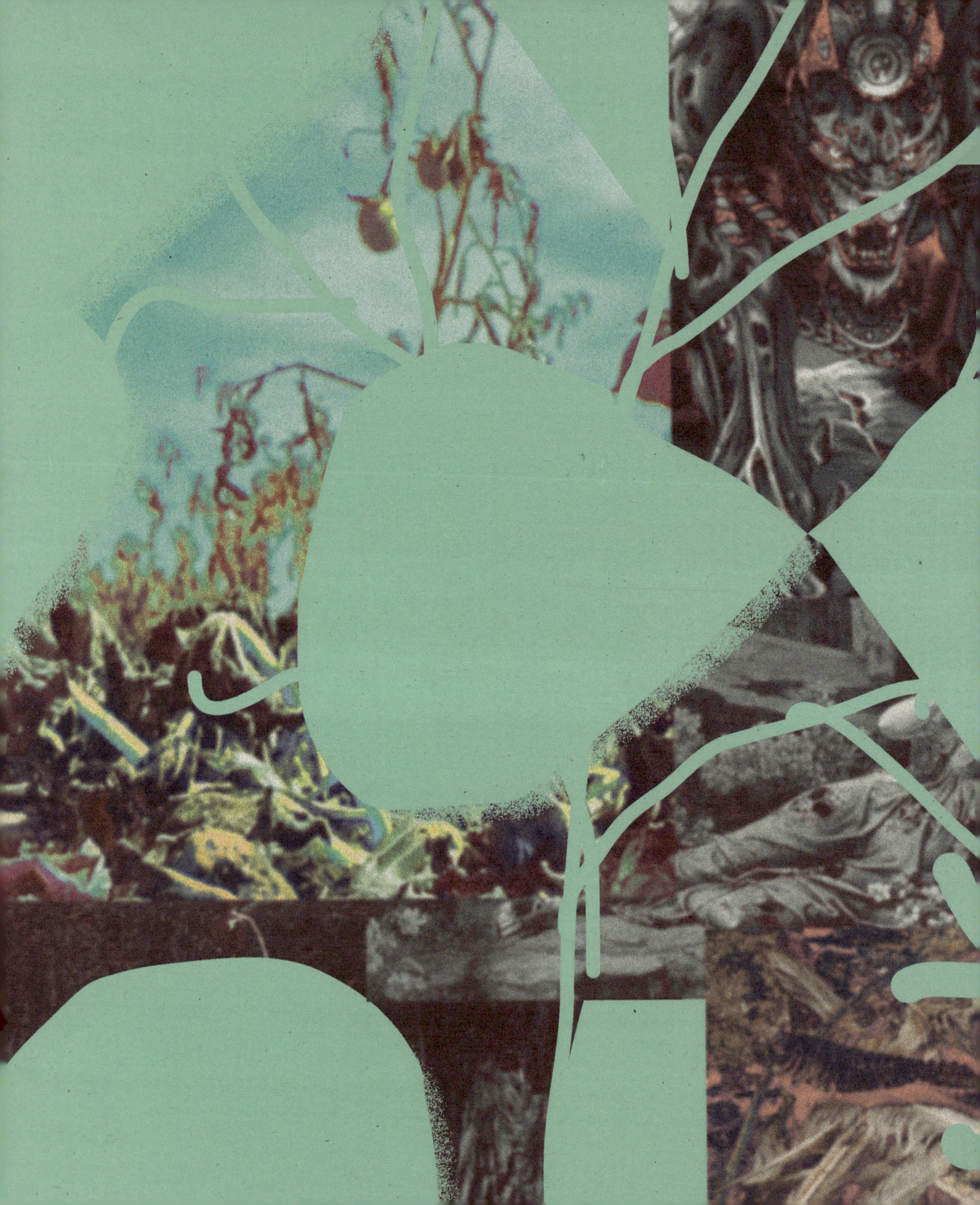

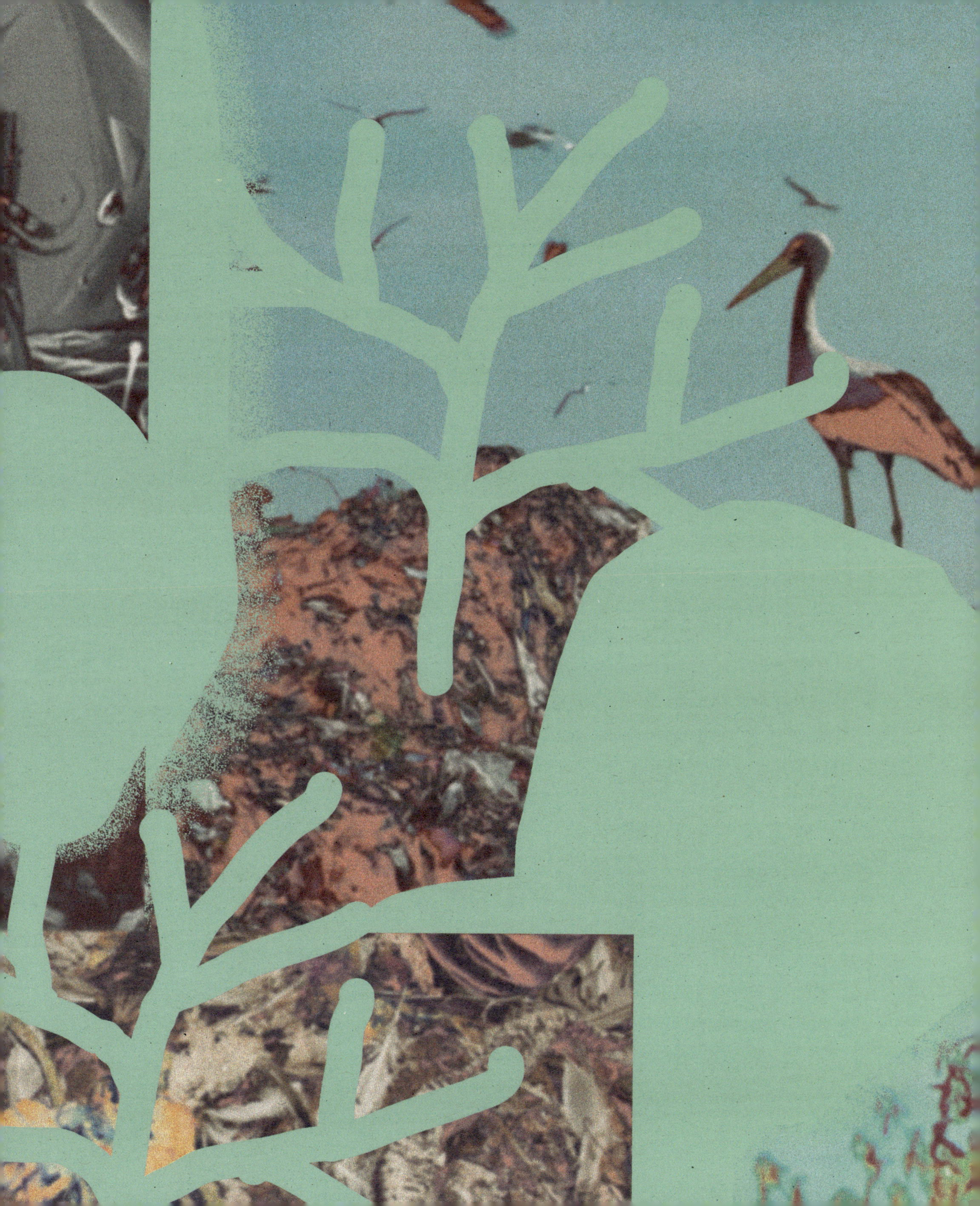

This program line focuses on the ecological crisis and possible future scenarios, advocating for more just relations between people from diverse geographies and socioeconomic backgrounds, between humans and other species, between urban landscape and nature. It also addresses the potential of civic movements, grassroots initiatives, and communities striving

to create livable future for all human and nonhuman beings.

213

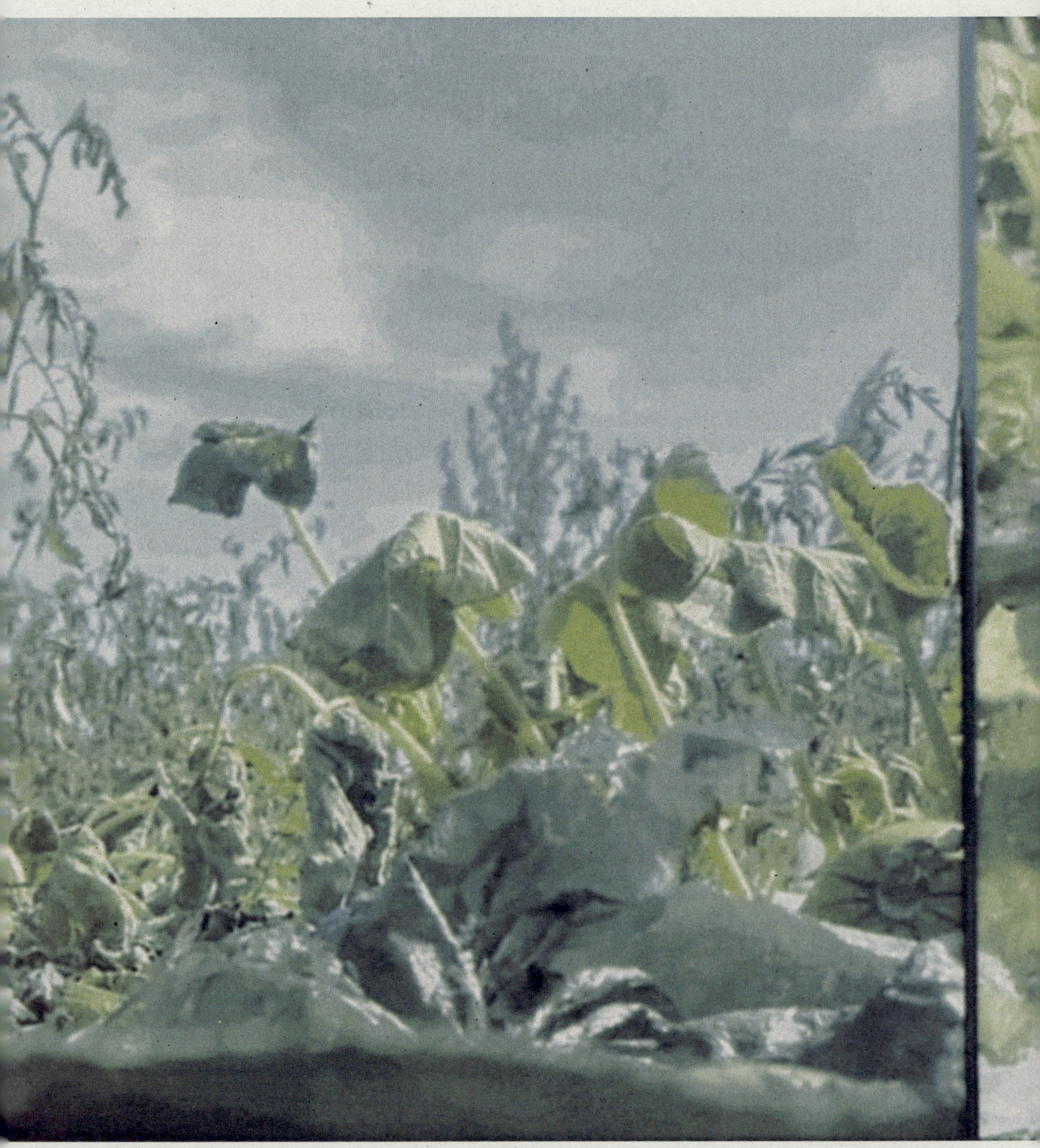

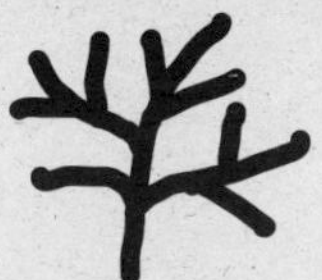

Beyond Ecologies: Solidarity, Decoloni-ality, and System Change

Ieva Astahovska

How can we work with ecological solidarity as an artistic practice? Can advocacy for the equality of nature be combined with political demands for system change? How can today's political and environmental crises help to understand and possibly address the consequences of the problems of the past, including the consequences of political and natural colonialism? And how can changes in strengthening diverse and inclusive societies influence understanding, responsibility, and engagement in environmental and climate crisis responses?

These issues were at the heart of the events that formed the thematic line Beyond Ecology of the Islands of Kinships project, which focused on the topics of ecological crisis and future scenarios, the relation between humans and other species, and the potential of civic movements. It included the exhibitions *Decolonial Ecologies* in Riga, *Hay, Straw, Dump* in Prague, *Imagine a Breath of Fresh Air* in Warsaw, and Ines Doujak's solo show *Every Courageous Life Is a Song to the Future* in Cologne, as well as the summer school *Care of Earth, Care of People* in Smiltene, Latvia.

The very name of this thematic line shows that ecology, like environmental and climate crises, cannot be thought of as a separate issue today, because it is first and foremost a political crisis, the result of societies prioritizing economic and financial gain over a shared and sustainable future. Ecology has become an existential condition that calls for a rethinking of the relationship between humans and environment and a reversal of the dominant, consumptive influence of human beings on it, both in individual choices and decisions and in systemic changes to shift social and political life. It makes us realize that in order to survive on the planet damaged by humans (to quote Donna Haraway), we need to start noticing the world around us and learn from other beings and forces. This requires a fundamental shift in our conceptions of nature, human and nonhuman, and building new solidarities between them, linking ecological issues to posthumanist ideas, contexts of community, participation, solidarity, and sustainability.

Even though ecology is of course an important framework for identifying and addressing environmental problems, it first developed as a colonial discipline and its concept of nature as a resource to be either exploited or preserved as a valuable wildlife sanctuary were part of colonial ideology. There is a continuity between colonial thinking and today's anthropocentric utilitarian view of nature as a source to sustain capitalist societies and as an exoticized and idealized value that ought to be preserved for the benefit of humankind. Natural resource depletion, irreversible loss of natural habitat, and environmental degradation are all consequences of modern societies' idea of unrelenting growth and materialist orientation. These effects are felt both locally and globally. Not only must we be aware of the current situation, but we must also recognize that our current relationship with the environment has been shaped by historical developments and ideological frameworks that continue to exist in modern societies, as well as by particular localized collective experiences and connections to other contexts, including global ones. Only then can we begin to design change.

For example, in the Baltic region and the larger former Eastern Bloc, of which the partner institutions were a part, the ecological damage caused by Soviet socialism has continued to leave footprints in human-nature relationships. Moreover, the consequences of the environmental problems of the past have often been invisibly transformed into the environmental ignorance of today's neoliberal world dominated by petrocapitalism, and into the ecological and climate crisis caused by pollution, deforestation, and other degradation and depletion of natural resources, and the loss of biodiversity and many species.

However, this daily harm becomes seemingly trivial compared to a tragedy such as the Russian Federation's neocolonial war in Ukraine, now in its third full year, the real reason of which is the resumption of colonial policies in order to gain control over this country and its resources. Europe has not seen such military conflict since World War II, with the aggressor brutally destroying not only people but also the environment. By ravaging and fatally polluting land, forests, water, and air, the war is exposing people, animals, and plants to toxic pollution and causing daily devastation, the consequences of which will continue to be fought for decades. The impact of this catastrophe, including on climate change, is only partially grasped and will have to be dealt with for decades also far beyond Ukraine's borders. In Eastern Europe, and especially in the Baltic States, this war is perceived as a direct threat, an unexpected return to a violent and totalitarian past, still a vivid memory for many. This brought tension to the more universal reflection on the critical relationship between humans and the environment in the age of Anthropocene, urging immediate engagement in resistance to the devastating violence perpetrated not only against people but also against the environment, and a much clearer and regionally focused perspective.

This perspective—how to rethink and act critically and anew to free ourselves from the influence of the colonial past, and how to revise and deconstruct the structures, systems, and foundations based on its logic in order to imagine and build a different present and possible future—is activated by the position of decoloniality. To decolonize thinking, perception, memory, and ways of life is a political, ethical, and knowledge-based position. Being an analytical viewpoint rather than a historical or geographic one, decolonization aims to establish new ways of thinking and doing while confronting the legacy of hegemonic power and its discourses.

The Eastern European and post-Soviet region was, until recently, rarely represented in global debates surrounding postcolonialism and decoloniality. That being said, when studying the changes in these countries, scholars make a connection between the experiences of colonialism and Soviet political and cultural domination of the region, using the theoretical framework of postcolonialism and the concept of decoloniality. It not only highlights the covert continuation of Soviet colonial practices in the area but also raises the question of how to break free from the oppressive power that seemed to have faded with the fall of the Soviet Union.

Moreover, since Russia's war in Ukraine and the resumption of imperial policy clearly manifested there, the understanding of the relevance of the postsocialist regional experience for decolonial thinking has given it a much more politically pressing meaning. It has also muddied the conventional line between the Global North and South, which interprets colonialism as offenses against the so-called developing countries by the Western advanced economies, while ignoring the abuses of power and interventions in the so-called semi-periphery, i.e. the socialist bloc. The complex historical context of Eastern Europe as a postsocialist region, in which the past continues to actively influence the present, calls for a more nuanced analysis and for new multiple decolonial perspectives on the colonial subject and object. It also calls for a revision of universalizing, stereotyping notions of the West and East, the Global North and South.

Along with political decolonization, we need to embrace decolonization of nature. To achieve environmental justice, we must first comprehend the scope and depth of environmental damage, and then implement systemic change at the social, political, and economic levels. The global crisis of climate change and the environment is proof of its urgency, and the most important solutions needed are to produce and consume less, to reduce extractivism and the emissions of natural resources, and to develop alternative, renewable forms of energy. These solutions are necessary to reverse the global dominance of fossil resources in energy production and consumption, which is still linked to the manifestations of imperial violence in many regions of the world.

The intertwining of post- and decoloniality and postsocialism is also essential to the exhibitions and artworks created within the framework of the *Beyond Ecology* thematic line, which were seeking new points of view, creative collaborations, and alternative ways of knowing about specific contexts and historical and current aspects and scenarios of possible futures. For example, in the exhibition *Decolonial Ecologies*, which brought together realistic and imaginative perspectives on the intertwined aspects of social, political, and ecological change in the past, present, and possible future, the artistic research assemblage consisted of themes such as the meaning and experience of place, questions of identity and belonging, contradictory and complex discourses of memory, environmental activism, infrastructural landscapes affected by technology and industry, cultural meanings and social practices of ecological issues, and alternative strategies for coping with the challenges of environmental crisis and climate change. The spectrum of ecologies was extended in these, thinking both about direct environmental damage and about social and mental ecologies, including the impact of the environment on mental health and well-being, and issues of sustainability. The exhibition also addressed themes such as environment and consumption, the life and afterlife of things, the impact of the waste industry on the living nature around us, gardening practices and alternative methods of growing food, and a return to nature as an opportunity to renew mental and emotional resources. The themes highlighted concrete and specific ecosystem and environmental stories that take us beyond the human-centric perspective and make us recognize that human forms of knowledge are only a very small part of wider forms of knowledge. Rooted in both everyday experience and more general sociopolitical memory, these stories invited us to imagine a different world and to engage in what Haraway has called sympoietic practices of living on a "damaged planet," the coexistence of living and nonliving beings, and creation-as-becoming-together. These specific stories—for example, of beavers occupying drainage ditches in Lithuania, or the feeding habits of white storks in the largest Baltic landfill—formed a decolonizing vision of potential resistance both to the power of neoliberal capitalism, and socialist past and present. At a time when the region is experiencing new colonial violence and disaster, these environmental narratives exposing the complex relationships between the past and present have sparked new solidarity in ecological thought to open the door for a different future.

Intro

One of the artworks featured in both the *Decolonial Ecology* exhibition in Riga and *Hay, Straw, Dump* exhibition in Prague was Diana Lelonek's video installation *Stork, a Sacred Bird.* Lelonek also authored "The Landfill Stork Manifesto" which completes the video installation and is reproduced in this publication. The essay "Building a Community around Food Waste," also published in this edition, goes into greater detail about Lelonek's artwork. Lelonek's work focused on how living nature not only resists but also adapts to man-made environmental changes. White storks are a symbol of blessing and happiness in several Eastern European cultures, and their image is closely linked to an idealized view of nature. However, in her video installation, these birds inhabit the dystopian landscape of the largest Baltic landfill hill, Getliņi. Searching for answers to the question why in recent years the number of storks that use the landfill for feeding has increased, and what this reveals about the interconnectedness of the life of these birds and humans, she draws connections between the industrial monocultures of today, the waste industry, and climate change, all of which have compelled humans and other living things to adapt and modify their ways of living. This work vividly exposed the decolonial potential in the relationship between humans and nature, calling for a deconstruction, decolonization, demythologization, and critical re-evaluation of intertwined notions of culture and nature. Despite the stork being a "national" bird, today it could be seen more as a symbol of migrants, nomads, and refugees, because, as a migratory bird, it connects with other lands and countries, and confronts national sentiment with transnational experiences. This, in turn, correlates with the relationship of contemporary waste management to the global economy and neocolonial practices, where consumer societies in the Global North dispose of their waste by sending it to developing countries, including Africa, one of the destinations on the storks' migration route. Lelonek's work also reminds us that waste management is one of the most worrying environmental problems, where local and global realities are intertwined: waste is growing at an incredible rate everywhere and its inefficient management is exacerbating the climate crisis as a major contributor to greenhouse gases, but the solutions cannot be isolated or localized.

By connecting the environmental contexts of the past, present, and future, the artists and curators of this project not only ask how we can continue to live in a world in ecological crisis, but they also make it clear that it is vital to be aware of the possibilities of these future scenarios now, while reflecting on the traces left by the past and striving to overcome their impact. They therefore engage both a critical perspective on the current reality and imagine a world in which nature and the ecosystems around us are much more than just a resource for satisfying human wants and needs, since the relationship with these ecosystems is a multifaceted and symbiotic web in which human beings are among, not above, other environmental beings.

Artworks play an important role in this reflection: unlike the natural sciences, which describe and explain human involvement in the ecologies of many species “from the outside,” art helps us realize and understand it “from the inside.” It uncovers intertwinings and insertions, and forges new connections where there seems to be nothing in common. It expands the collective imagination and engages new narrative forms and territories, where the voices given to nature and the environment make us recognize that they are not just “settings” for people’s stories, but active forces that shape our lives. Telling these kinds of environmental stories is more important than ever because they link to a multitude of other stories and expose a shared “pluriverse,” or universe of multiple worlds connected by differences and a shared desire to coexist.

Knowing full well that in light of the present ecological and environmental catastrophe, imagination and critical analysis are insufficient, a political stance of artworks is a crucial component. Because it is both an ecological and a political concern, the environmental crisis politicizes the connection between art and ecology and demands a new kind of politics that puts the shared interests of many worlds front and center. Politicization translates to revisiting the region's socialist history and narratives of liberation and transformation by confronting them with environmental narratives. Further, decolonization of art fosters an awareness of the inseparability of aesthetic, ethical, social, material, and political elements in these stories.

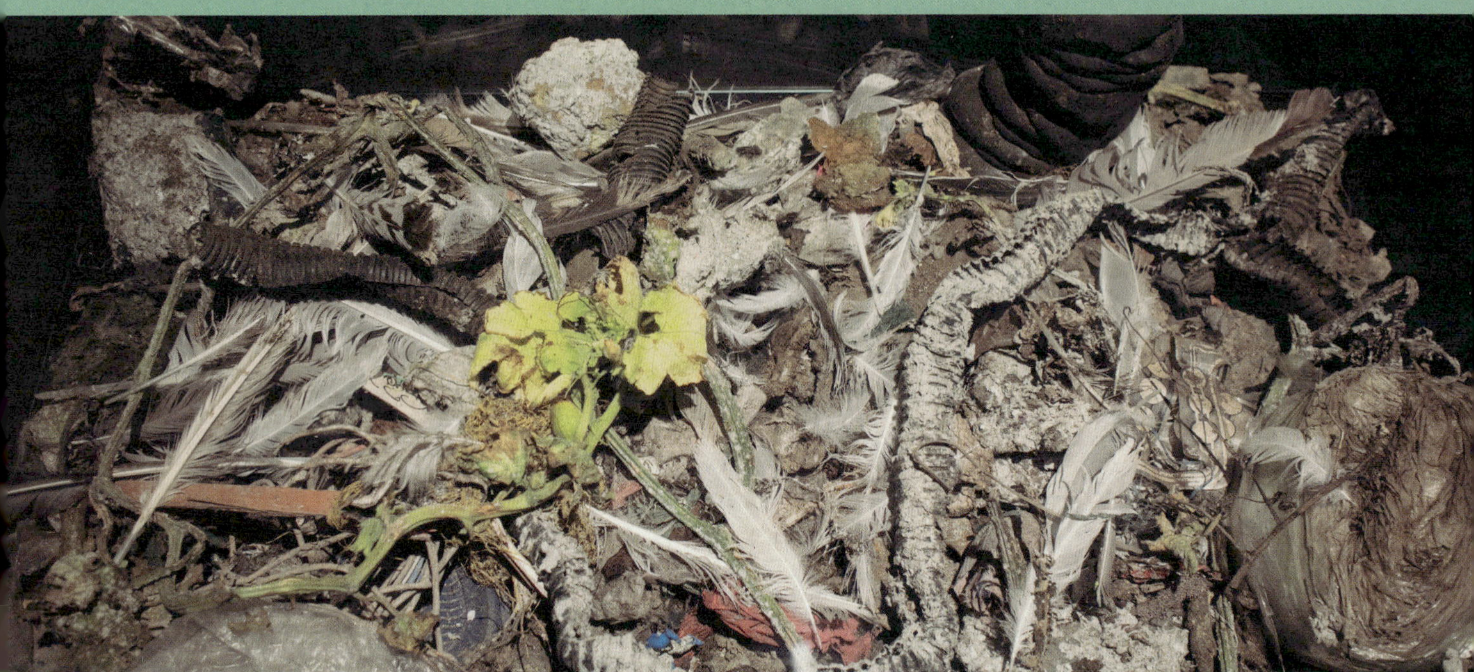

Diana Lelonek: Stork, a Sacred Bird

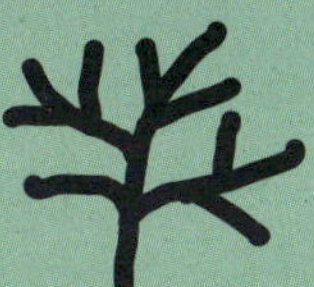

The Landfill Stork Manifesto

1. The white stork is a cultural construct created by the system of patriarchy and anthropocentrism—this construct must be overthrown so we can look at the stork as it is and accept it as a species in all its complexity.

2. The image of a stork on a green meadow, deeply rooted in European culture, especially in Eastern Europe, is a fiction. It is a tool to maintain an idealized vision of nature and cover its true complexity, toxicity, and ambiguity.

3. Interspecies coexistence in the era of the Anthropocene is associated with working through, demythologizing, and overthrowing the existing paternalistic approach to other beings.

4. Idealizing the white stork species—as a beautiful bird swallowing a green frog in idyllic nature—is a false image, infantilizing and depriving it of subjectivity, its own decision-making, and agency.

5. Looking with respect at the stork as it is also implies accepting the uncomfortable truth about what nature is in the era of the Anthropocene—with all its entanglement, toxicity, and multilayered connections.

6. Storks have learned to use open garbage dumps and this fact should not be sad or indignant, this fact should be taken with relief, because there is a liberating and revolutionary potential in it.

7. The stork in the landfill can no longer be a symbol of a romantic vision of nature.

8. A garbage-swallowing stork does not fit into nationalist narratives, so it can be liberated from being a national bird, as is the case in Latvia, Poland, or Lithuania.

9. The stork swallowing garbage does not necessarily fit the vision of the bird “bringing” children, in this sense, the garbage dump also frees it from the system of patriarchal control.

10. The dump is visited more often by storks that have not started families and do not feed chicks, in this sense, the dump can also be a way out of the heteromatrix.

11. A stork that doesn't bring babies is still a real stork. Parenting is a choice, not a compulsion. My body, my choice!

12. Garbage, so it is a chance to overthrow not only a false vision of nature, but also patriarchy, which is the cause of climate change and the destruction of the earth.

13. The dump provides food for old storks, sick storks, storks with disabilities, which would lose in the fight for dwindling amphibian resources.

14. A landfill is only seemingly a desert of biodiversity. Many species use its resources on a daily basis. Living in a landfill is often the only option when there are not enough amphibians and small rodents to feed on.

15. Whoever learns to use garbage will survive. In the era of the sixth great extinction, this is an important skill.

16. The Anthropocene forces all living beings, both non-human and human, to change their behavior. Living in a toxic, polluted, and littered landscape is a fate shared by all (albeit to varying degrees).

17. The possibility of living outside contaminated areas has undoubtedly become a privilege. A privilege that belongs to a few and is a luxury. Some species are privileged to live in a closed, strictly protected wildlife reserve, while others live within the affluent, closed, and also strictly protected borders of nation-states. In this context, the stork as a "national symbol" requires critical deconstruction and decolonization.

19. A garbage dump can be read as a horizontal structure on which new interspecies communities of the future, new meanings and ontologies are created.

20. Do not look away from storks in landfills, watch them closely. It's time to start learning from multispecies and complex garbage dump ecosystems!

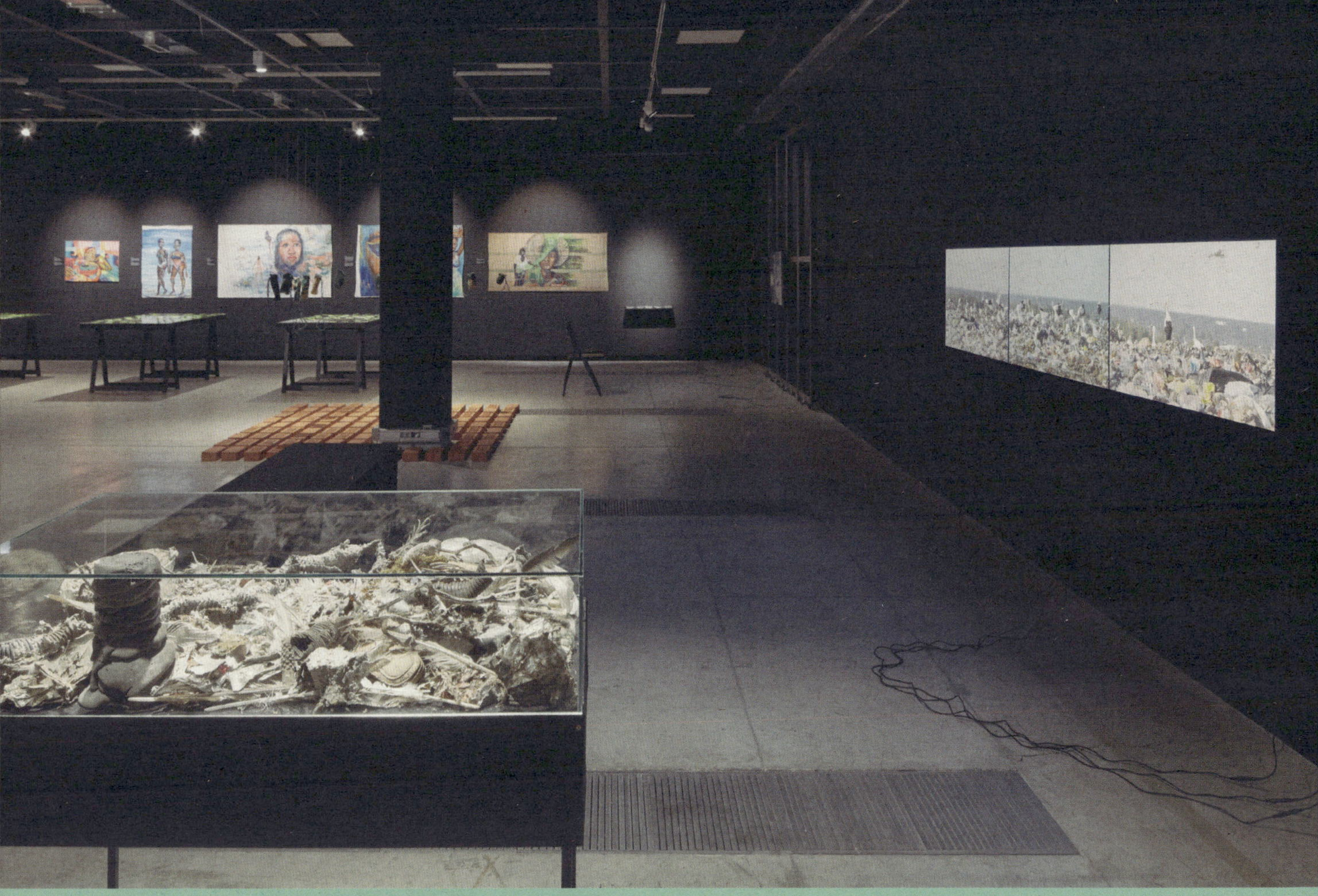

DIANA LELONEK:
STORK, A SACRED BIRD

video, 10 mins
2022

The commission was presented as part of exhibitions:

- **DECOLONIAL ECOLOGIES: UNDERSTANDING POSTCOLONIAL AFTER SOCIALISM**, Riga Art Space, Latvia, November 2, 2022 – January 15, 2023, organized by Latvian Centre for Contemporary Art
- **HAY, STRAW, DUMP**, Václav Špála Gallery, Prague, Czech Republic, March 28 – May 3, 2023, organized by Jindřich Chalupecký Society

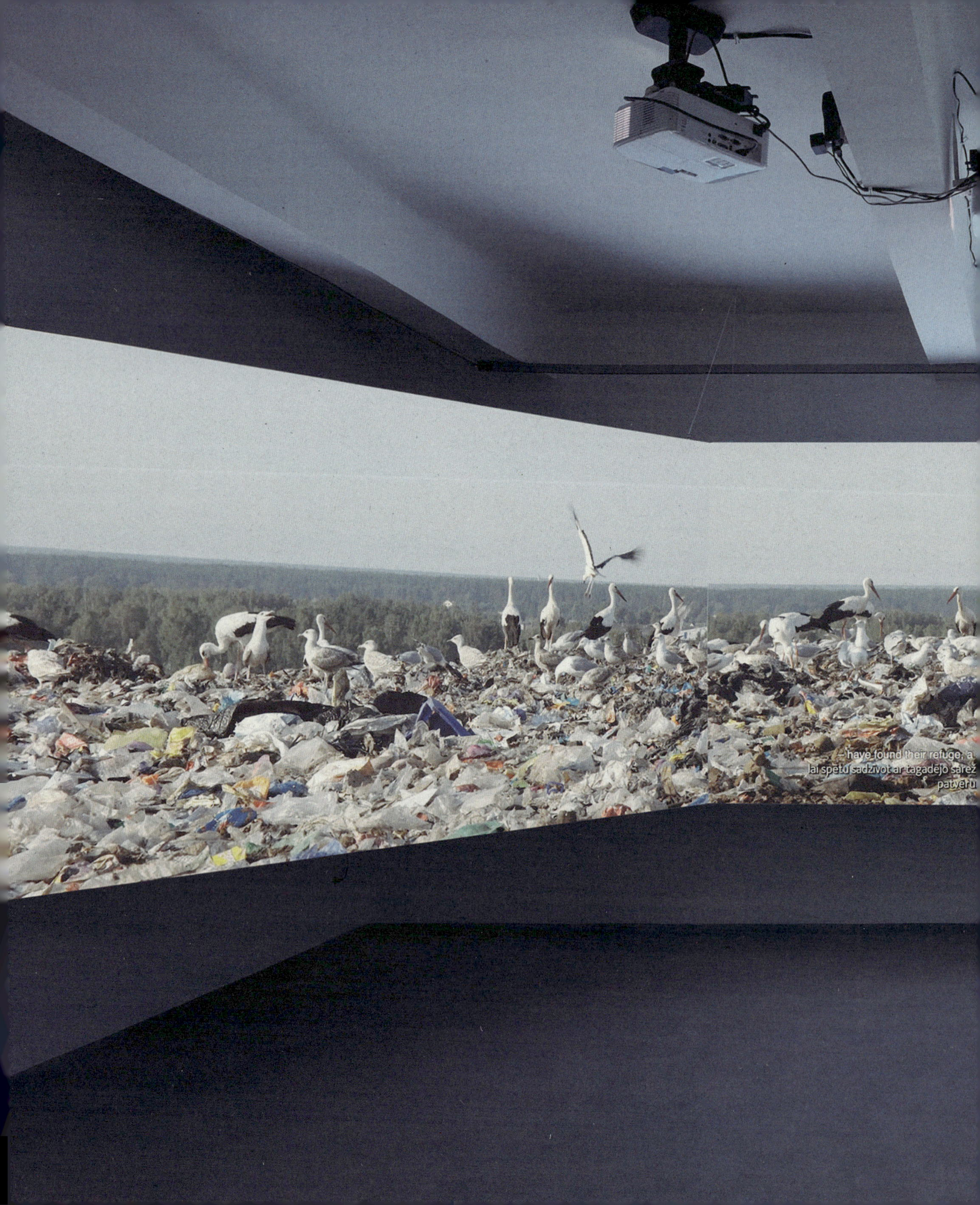
– have found their refuge, a
lai spētu sadzīvot ar tagadējo sarež
patvēru

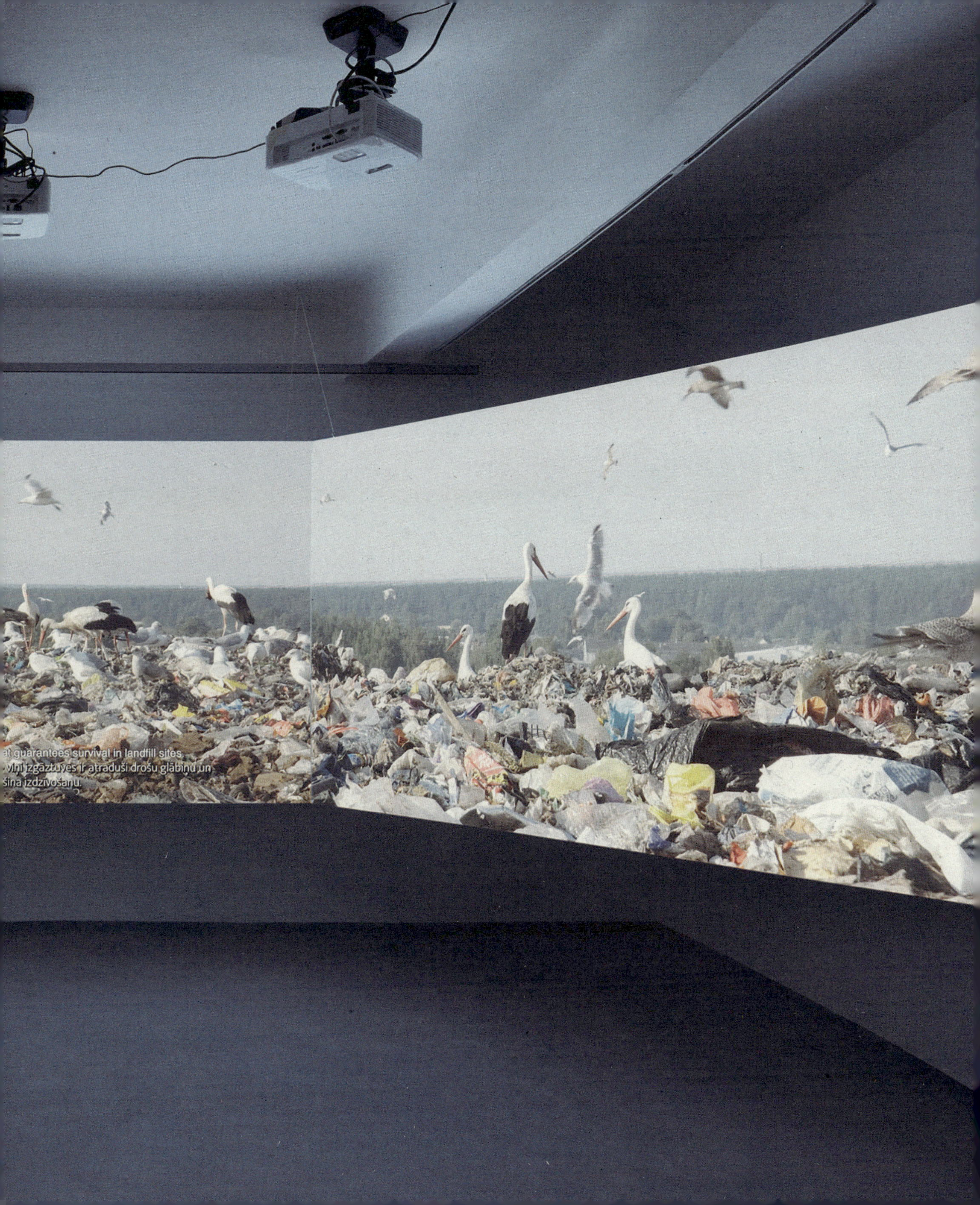
at guarantees survival in landfill sites.
viņi izgāztuves ir atraduši drošu glābiņu un
šina izdzīvošanu.

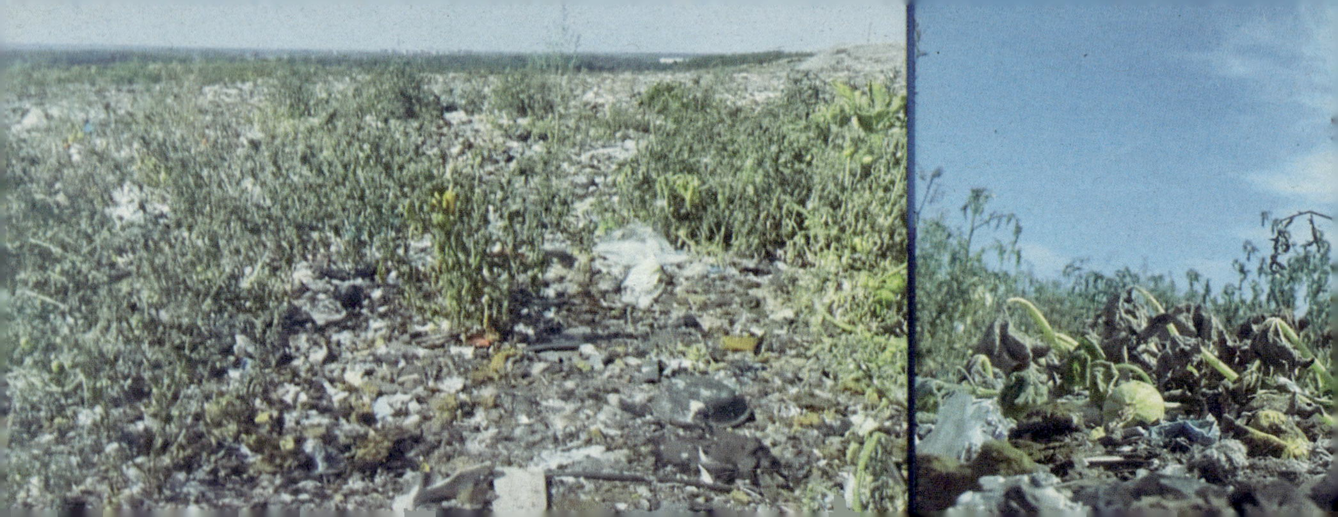

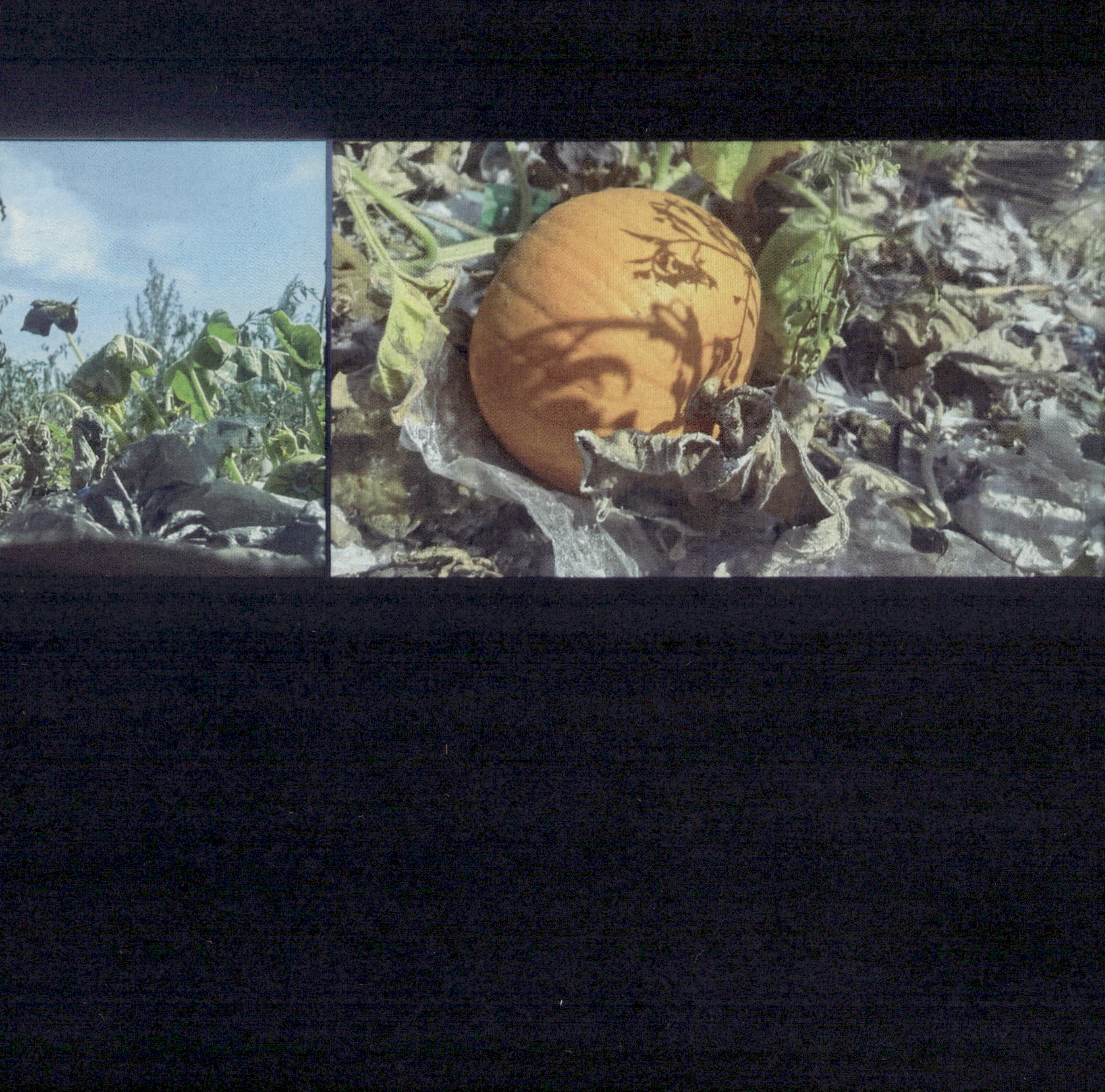

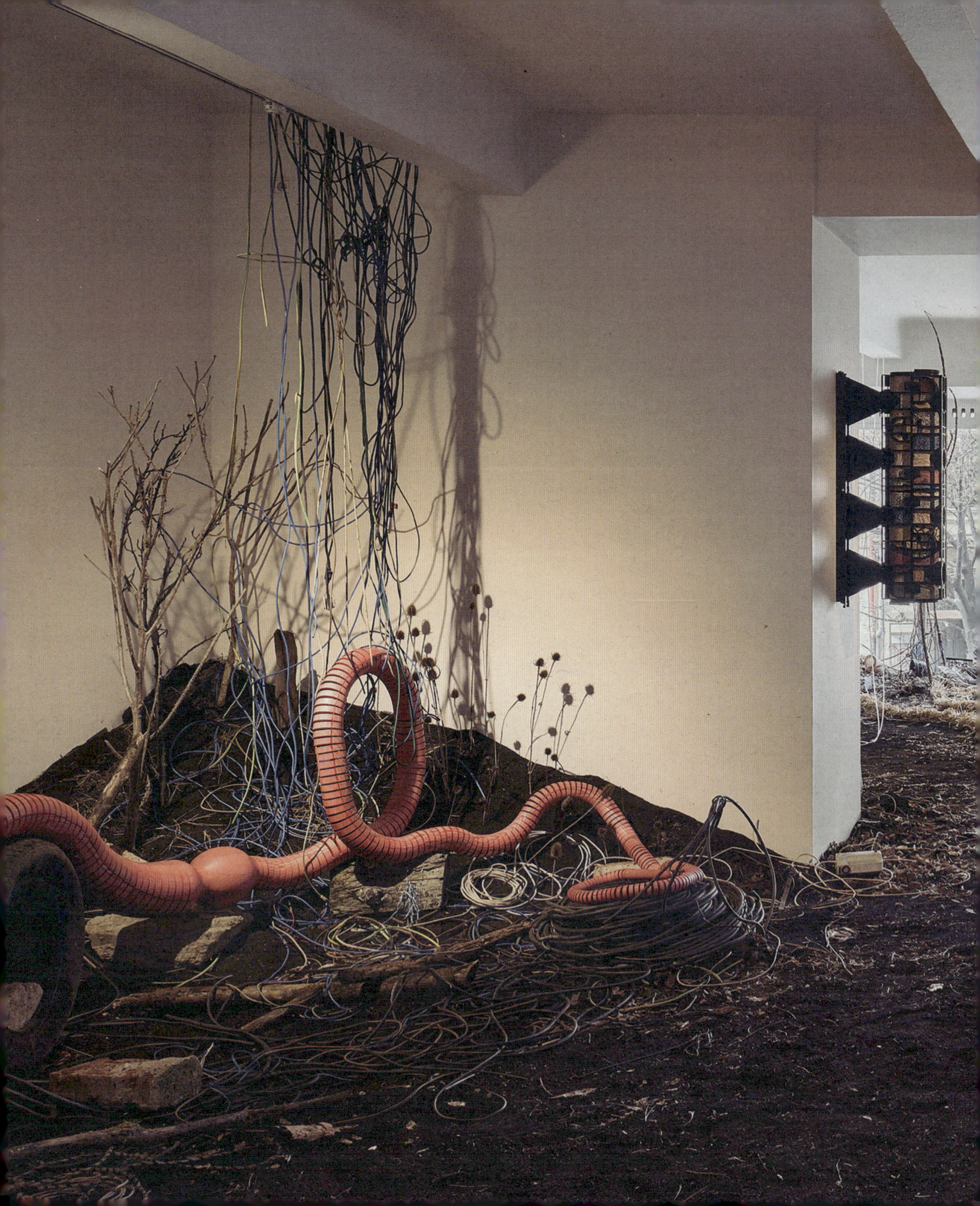

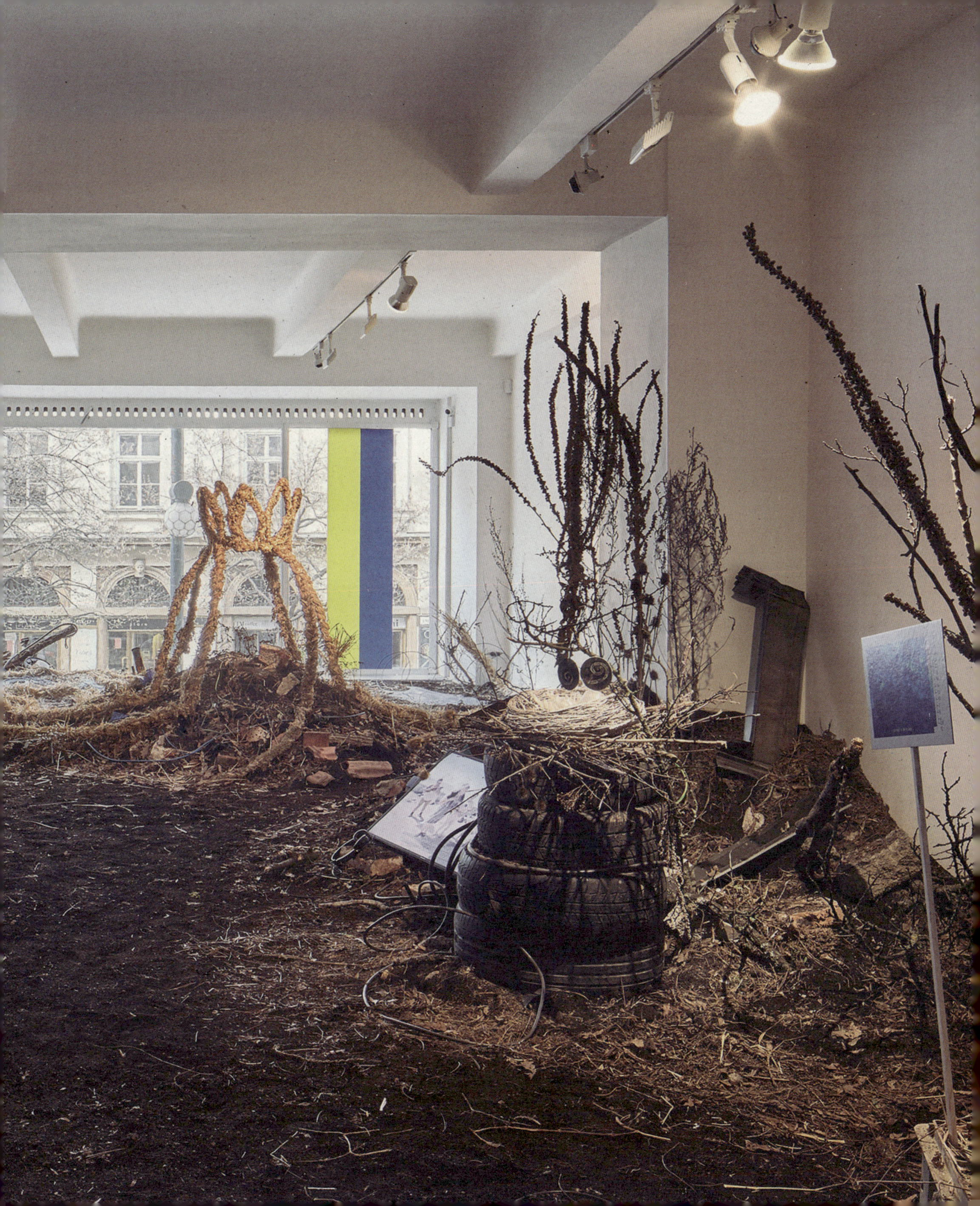

Eloïse Bonneviot & Anne de Boer: A Devoured Hedge Burrows Deep II

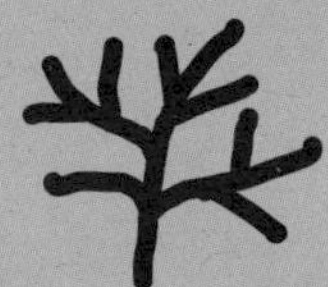

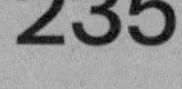

DECAYING INSTITUTION IDENTITY CREATOR

Welcome to your new institutional identity creator. By filling in one of the identity creators you agree to become part of the Decaying Institution Ensemble. As a first step you will have to select which category your institute is affiliated to:

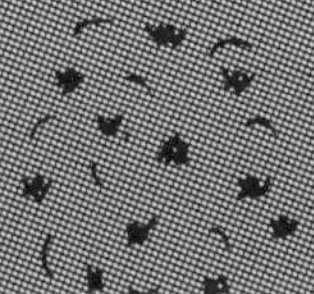

FRAGMENTIZER

You are a fast-paced institution taking care of the initial stage of decay. Your institution is capable of shredding large amounts of information and content, partly obscuring their meaning but simultaneously leaving grains of insane clarity. Your institutional framework makes use of mechanisms of weathering, abrasion or attract other organisms that feed on dead organic material. These activities will expose a larger surface area to the decaying institution and attract a rich variety of audiences within the shredded remains of thoughts and notions.

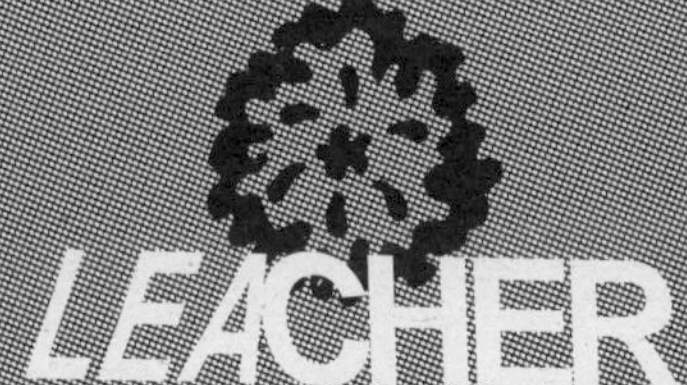

Everything is liquid, and so are you! The foundation to your existence is a complete solubility into anything that is willing to absorb. No need to think outside the box, as no box is capable of holding you hostage inside. Your concepts and radical undertakings have a far reach and are reappearing spontaneously around the globe. As such you need to find gratification in the fact that your capacities lie deep within institutional pathways as nutrient.

CATABOLIZER

Slow processes and deep focus are the interests that lay close to your heart. Throughout your existence you focus on enabling space and infrastructures that allow for deceleration while truly digesting and absorbing information that matters. This constitutes a guidance in breaking down matter into smaller components that in turn provide a source of energy for a collective audience to nurture and grow.

HUMIFICATER

Your institution creates so to say humus, a dark, stable, and nutrient-rich substance as a foundation to fungal architectures, congregations of mold or insect curators that live only a short amount of time. These foundations are highly resistant to decomposition and can resist worst commotions over time. Your physical appearance can change over time, knowing that the true importance lies within the bonding networks that you have harboured and let flourish.

MINERALIZER

You are the institution that is concerned with leaving a legacy. Perhaps a bit too often and somewhat perpetually in existential crisis. You do find yourself often in an argument with the other decaying institutions, that feel an unease towards your attitude of breaking anything into solid compounds. However, there is a joy to that debate, entering it from a solid point of view of forebearers that too have carved their histories in stone. You have put yourself to the task to provide grains and snippets of fossilized knowledges that can be released as nutrients for many generations of decay to thrive.

Now that you have chosen your ***Institutional Category***, fill in the ***Identity Sheet*** on the following page:

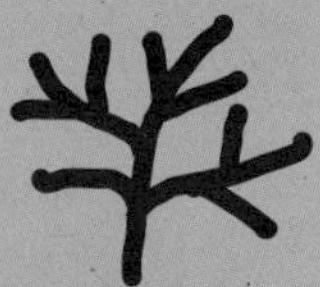

Insitituitonal Identity Sheet

Portrait

Name:

Institutional Profile:

Obsession:

Fear:

Mission:

Decaying Institution Ensemble

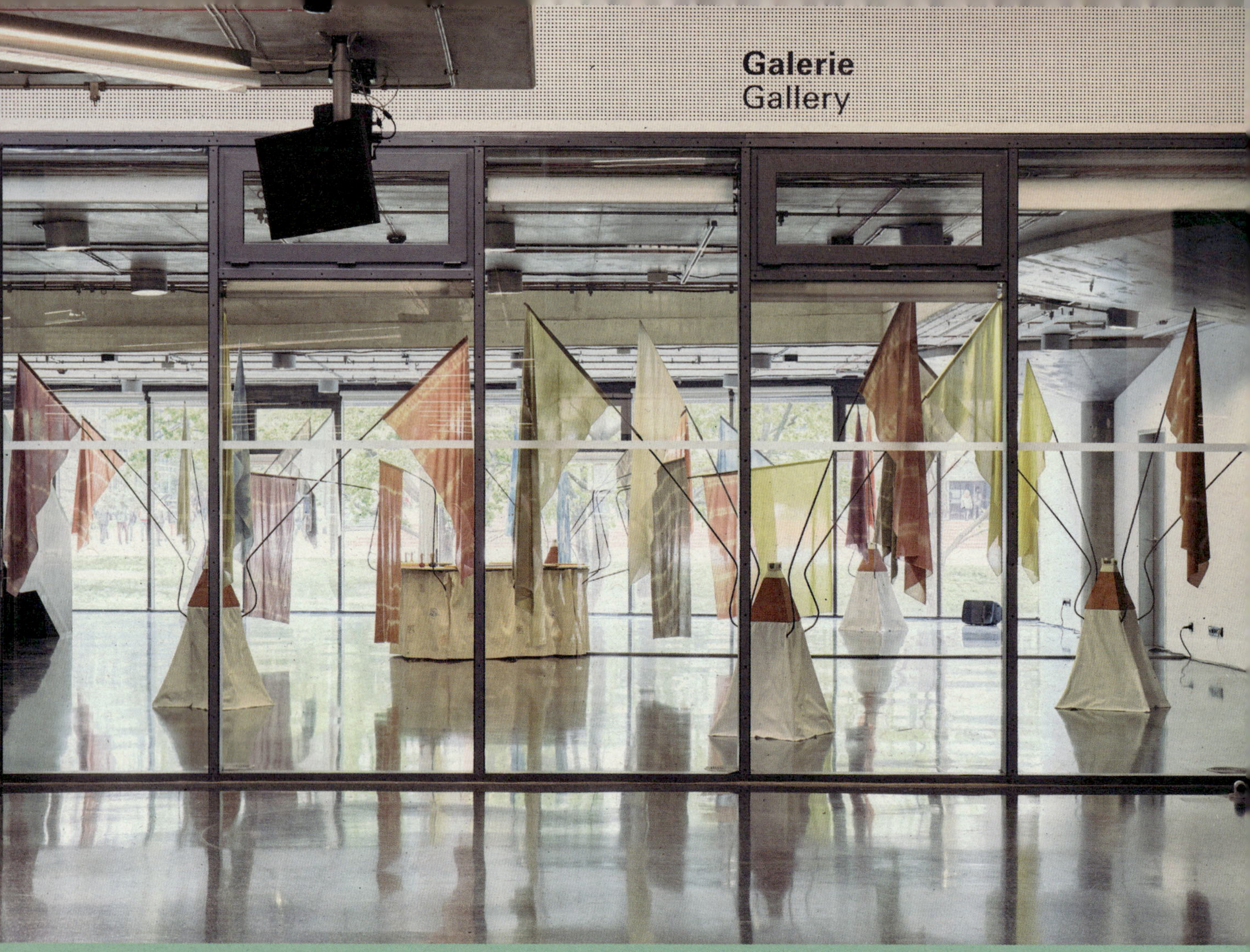

**ELOÏSE BONNEVIOT & ANNE DE BOER:
A DEVOURED HEDGE BURROWS DEEP II**

interactive spatial installation,
virtual game, live game sessions
2024

The commission was presented as part of exhibitions:

- **A DEVOURED HEDGE BURROWS DEEP II,** Czech National Library of Technology in Prague, Czech Republic, April 19 – May 2, 2024, organized by Jindřich Chalupecký Society
- **URBAN REWILDING IN A POST-WILD WORLD,** organized by Temporary Gallery in Cologne, hosted by NeuLand Urban Garden, Cologne, Germany, July 20 – 28, 2024

239

Share
Give some of what you have to others so you can thrive together.
Teile
Gib etwas von dem, was du hast, an andere weiter, damit ihr gemeinsam vorankommen könnt.

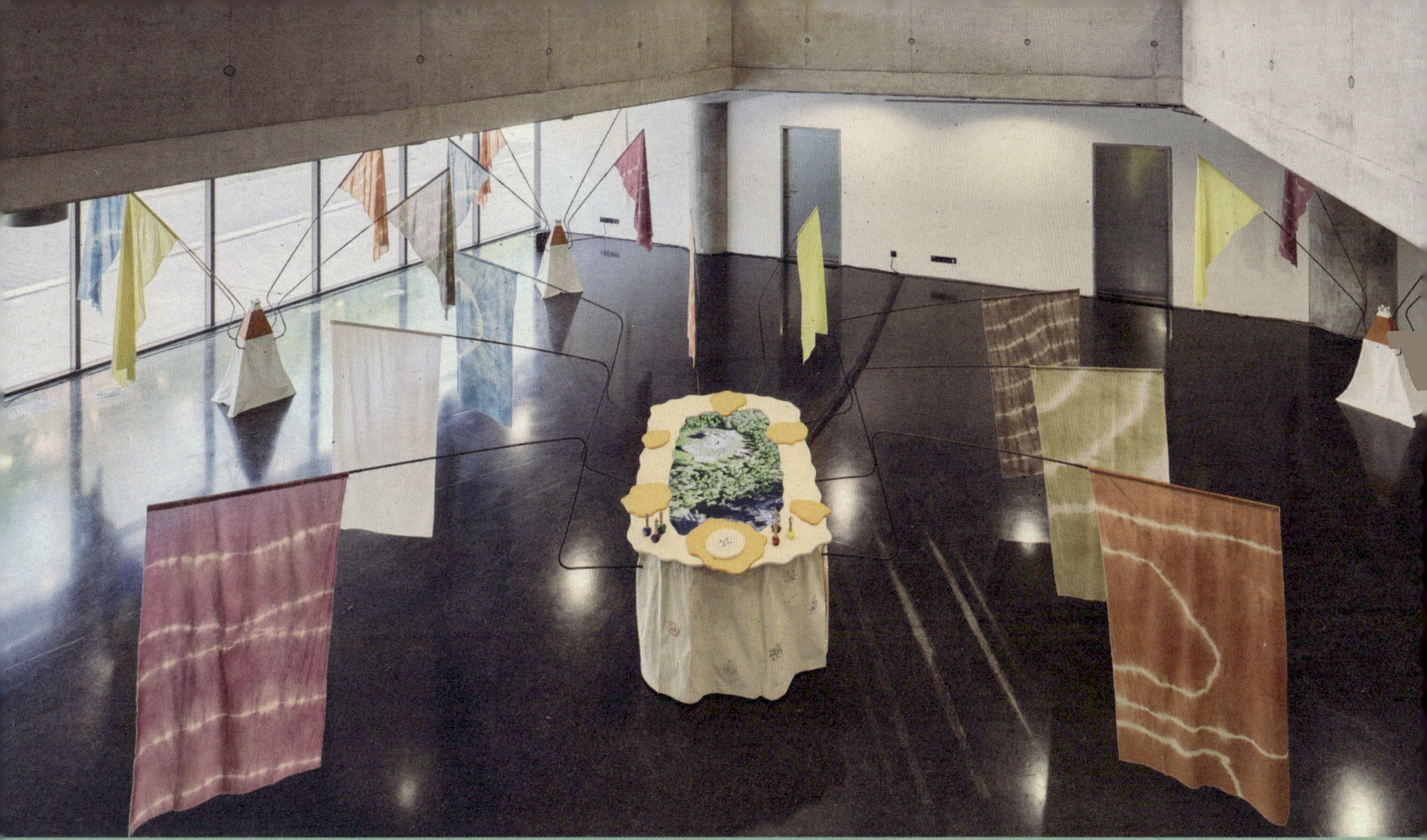

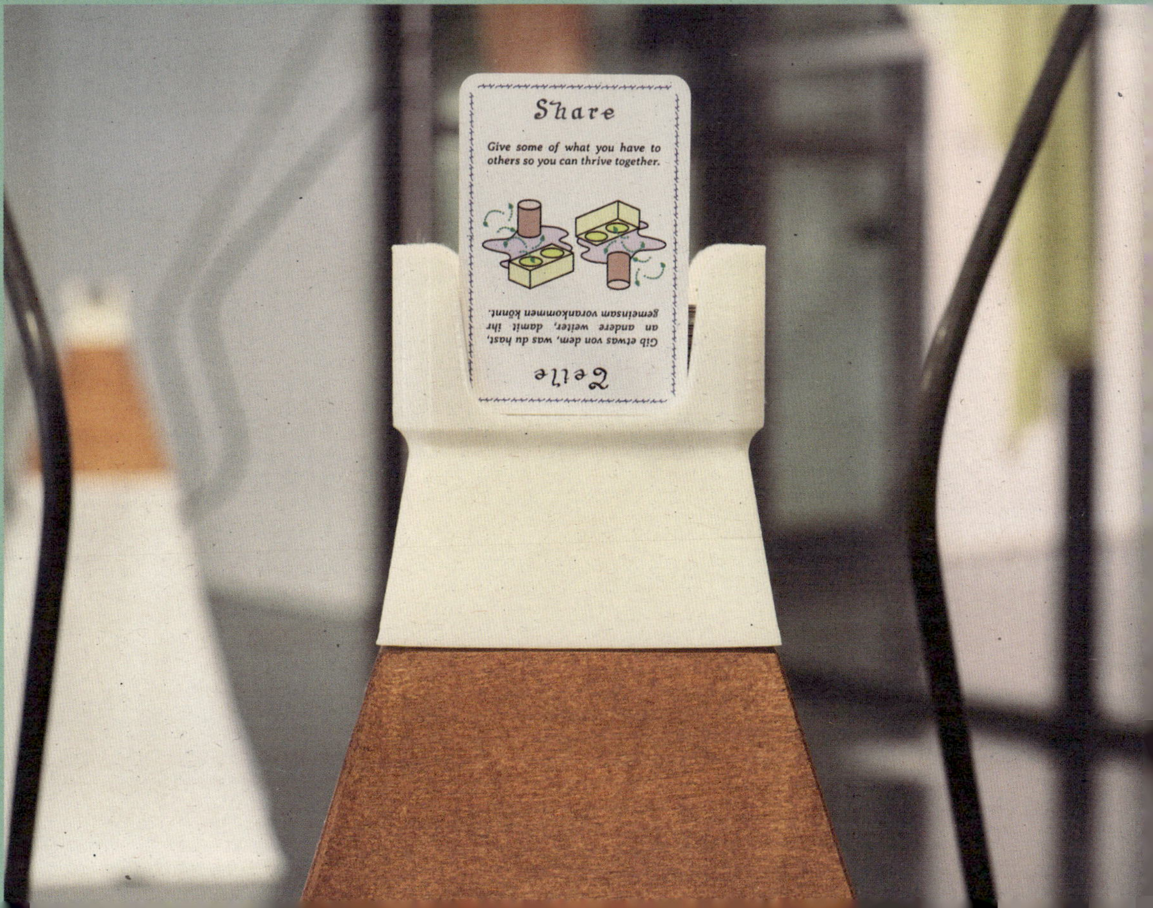

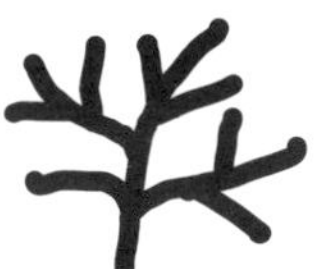

Digital Healing: From Ecofeminism to Data Feminism and Creating Civil Society with Nature

Michal Klodner, Květa Nguyen

Techno-eco-feminism inquires into the role technologies play in the restructuring of our diverse relationships with human and more-than-human beings in entangled techno-mediated-ecologies. In this text, we invite you to explore how the foundations of feminist science and feminist technology meet the environmental approaches of ecofeminism. On these foundations, facing the climate and social reality, feminist collectives and broader alliances of organizations based on ethical values are creating and sharing the practice of change.

Turning Points in Ecofeminism History

Stereotyping Gender—Essentialism

Charlene Spretnak in *Ecofeminism: Our Roots and Flowering*[1] describes one path to ecofeminism as the study of political theory. Cultural feminists used the framework of dominance theory. Dominance of male over female was the key to comprehending every expression of patriarchal culture as hierarchical, mechanistic, industrialist, or militaristic forms. Antiwar and antinuclear political movements of the 1960s and early 1970s considered science and technology as industrial, governmental, or militaristic practices, associated with masculinity.

Lacking any feminist discourse, feminist scholars analyzed the Scientific Revolution, and stated that the resulting science was based on the (masculine) ideology of exploiting the Earth and control. During this time, nature and scientific inquiry were modeled after misogynous relationships to women. Femininity was associated with nature and considered as something passive to be objectified.

Charlene Spretnak's second path to ecofeminism originated from nature-based spirituality, which placed the Goddess and the healing Divine immanent in and around us at its core. Through historic and archeological sources, the sacred link between the Goddess

1 Charlene Spretnak, "Ecofeminism: Our Roots and Flowering," in *Reweaving the World: The Emergence of Ecofeminism*, ed. Irene Diamond and Gloria Feman Orenstein (San Francisco: Sierra Club Books, 1990), 3–14.

and totemic animals and plants as teachers, moon rhythms of renewal and regeneration, ecstatic dances, the experience of knowing Gaia giving life was revealed. Of course, these attributes of ecological wisdom were associated to women.

In her article in *Feminist Formations*, Greta Gaard reviews how ecofeminism, as formulated in the 1980s, was later critiqued as essentialist and effectively discarded. As we can see, it was unilaterally stereotyping gender so feminists working on the intersections of feminism and the environment thought it better to rename their approach. While celebration of goddess spirituality and the critique of patriarchy advanced in cultural ecofeminism, poststructuralist and other third-wave feminisms inclined to urban anthropocentric view and portrayed ecofeminism as a solely essentialist equation of women with nature, ethnocentric and anti-intellectual, linking to the "traditional" social role of woman as nurturer and caregiver. Further, the feminists have not regarded the category of animals and interspecies justice as relevant for feminist analysis and practice. Environmental activists and theorists used the same antiessentialist rhetoric to dismiss the significance of gender and sexuality to environmental thought and politics. Nonetheless, this critique was unable to see ecofeminism's valuable contribution to diversity of arguments and standpoints of structuralist insight that associated patterns of environmental degradation with women's oppression, culture—nature dualism, and drew attention to colonialism and environmental racism which are the underlying ideologies and forces behind legitimization and proliferation of hazardous waste, military bomb tests, coal mining, nuclear storage, hydropower construction, and toxic chemical contamination.[2]

The contemporary path to ecofeminism leads through environmentalism and public policy, public-interest environmental organizations, environmental studies programs in universities, careers

2 Greta Gaard, "Ecofeminism Revisited: Rejecting Essentialism and Re-Placing Species in a Material Feminist Environmentalism," *Feminist Formations* 23, no. 2 (Summer 2011): 27, 31.

in science and technology, climate justice, cooperative eco-economics, trans, queer, and more-than-human gender theory. With prevalence of social ecofeminism, grounded in social ecology and materially based analysis, we can also identify liberal ecofeminism and spiritual/cultural ecofeminism. One of the answers to the illusion of essentialism, that of Vandana Shiva, is that women have a special connection to the environment through their practical daily interactions. According to her, women produce wealth in partnership with nature, and have been experts in holistic and ecological knowledge of nature's processes. These modes of knowledge, oriented to the social benefits and sustenance needs, have been underestimated and not recognized by the reductionist paradigm, because it fails to perceive the interconnectedness of nature, or the connection of women's lives, work, and knowledge with the creation of wealth.[3]

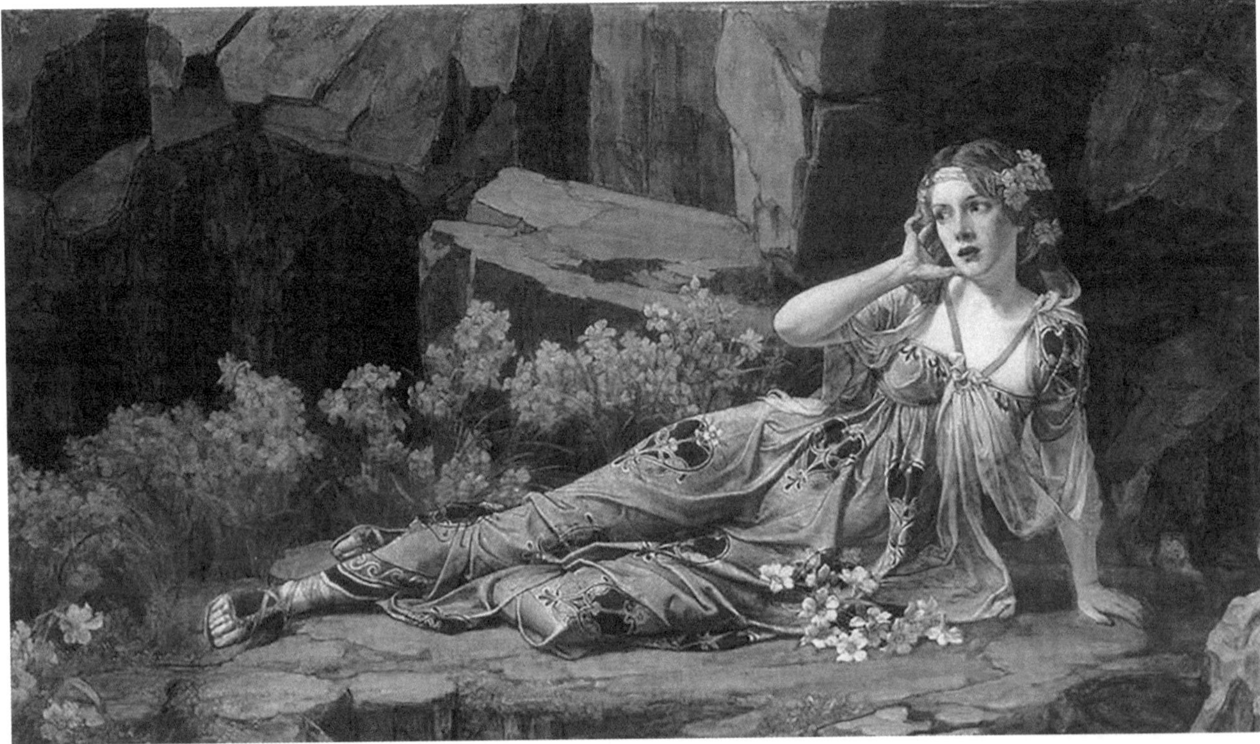

European romantic symbolism of the female fairy. Mountain nymph Echo from Greek mythology. Image by Talbot Hughes.

3 Vandana Shiva, *Staying Alive: Women, Ecology and Development* (London: Zed Books, 1988).

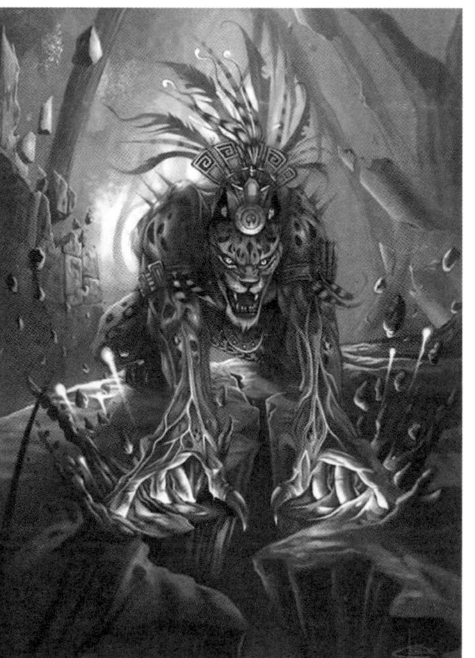

Tepēyōllōtl, "heart of the mountains," the indigenous god(dess) of darkened caves, earthquakes, echoes, and jaguars. Image by Carolina Eade aka infraberry, Chile.

In *Art and Sustainability* (2011), Sacha Kagan explains how efficient and rational implementation of technology and technocratic decisions throughout the whole society is deeply rooted in the positivism of Enlightenment. Such Technological System accepts only one common logic that is based on representation by numbers, while anything outside this reasoning is seen as a sheer fantasy. The pure reason of positivist science is driving technical progress, and thus it is required to be free of any mythical thought and to become a universal instrument in the all-encompassing economical apparatus.

The debate on the position of artists and their role in environmental discourse added to the critique of art as a kind of religion inherited

from the 19th century with its cult of the genius Great Artist.

Art does not fit into the system of the "most efficient method" of Enlightenment and artists as dreamers belong to quite an opposite invention of the 19th century: subjectivity and individualism of Romanticism. Thus Romantic Order is where all intuition, imagination, attention to feelings, and admiration of nature reside. Artists in Romantic Order are gifted to create works of exceptional beauty by their hands, they are independent and free from influences from others. This dichotomy, as a result, creates an artist pushed outside of the Technological System, locked in their romantic realm of individual genius, and in this escapist ghetto freed from the structural hold of formal rationality.[4]

Of course, this criticism is not new. Just recall the book *Has Modernism Failed?* (1984), a provocative critique of the commodified

4 Sacha Kagan, *Art and Sustainability. Connecting Patterns for a Culture of Complexity*, 2nd ed. (Bielefeld: Transcript, 2013).

modernist and postmodernist art world by Suzi Gablik. In the revised edition from 2004, updated with inspiring trends of contemporary art at the beginning of the 21st century, Gablik highlighted commitment to socially meaningful and spiritually informed art. Sacha Kagan, belonging to a new generation of art theorists, analyzes in his remarkable piece the foundations of Enlightenment and disciplinary science, and especially the science of the second half of the 20th century. The paradigmatic shift in thinking and initial concerns about the human ability to maintain the biological livability of the earth were marked by the formation of systems art in 1960s, when artists started combining technological, biological, and social systems, and whose approach continues to inspire contemporary artists of environmental practice.

Ecofeminism and Knowledge: Forming New Science

I Would Rather Be a Cyborg than a Goddess

As we have already noted, feminist theory in the 1970s and 1980s was marked by what Mari Mikkola calls "classificatory gender essentialism." It is an assumption that some common social characteristics exist that define gender, for example that something experienced by all women, such as gender socialization or sexual objectification, consequently defines womanhood.[5]

Many feminists took an issue with this position, including Donna Haraway, who in her fundamental and viral *Cyborg Manifesto* (1985) argued that "there is nothing about being 'female' that naturally binds women."[6] Another problem that she tried to counteract was the technophobic nature of feminist theory of the time,

5 Keira McCarthy, "Cy-Candy," https://edspace.american.edu/cy-candy/homepage/.

6 Other contributions to antiessentialist feminist scholarship include Audre Lorde's *Sister Outsider* (1984), Elizabeth V. Spelman's *Inessential Woman: Problems of Exclusion in Feminist Thought* (1988), or Judith Butler's *Gender Trouble: Feminism and the Subversion of Identity* (1990).

seeing technology and science as instruments of patriarchal oppression. She argued that it was in the eroding boundary between human beings and machines, and especially in the integration of women and machines, that we can find liberation from old patriarchal dichotomy. Referencing Rachel Grossman's (1980) use of the phrase "women in the integrated circuit," she described how relations of women are deeply and intimately structured through science and technology.

Donna Haraway wanted to develop a political strategy that could take the power of technology to liberate women without promoting an essentialist conception of womanhood, taking responsibility for the social relations of science and technology means. For Haraway, the cyborg was a symbol of dismantled postmodern collective and a personal self. It represented a body and self reassembled from fragments, reflecting the interconnected postmodern human experience. She redefined the ritual as a spiral dance of building and destroying machines, identities, categories, relationships, as a coming out of the maze of dualisms. The idea of a cyborg, whose

gender was changing and changeable, was radically new and explicitly complicated gendered boundaries.

It is substantial to note that the cyborg theory was inherently materialistic. It is no way about losing or overcoming the body and becoming a pure digital mind. Cyborg body is a body of labor, situated in social reality.

Donna Haraway's next most influential text was published a few years later, explaining what she called "situated knowledges."[7] This concept, developed in conversation with feminist philosophers and activists such as Nancy Hartsock, centers on how truth is constructed. Haraway argued that truth is created by the particular practices of particular people. Scientists in the laboratory, for example, do not merely observe or run a clearly objective experiment on a cell,

7 Donna Haraway, "Situated Knowledges: The Science Question in Feminism and the Privilege of Partial Perspective," *Feminist Studies* 14, no. 3 (1988): 575–599.

but they cocreate what a cell is: by ways of measuring, naming, and manipulating it. Similar ideas have a long history in pragmatism, but they became politically charged during the so-called science wars of the 1990s—debates between "scientific realists" and "post-modernists" that have echoes in today's disputes over bias and objectivity in academia.[8] In contemporary ecofeminism and data feminism, this situatedness is the basis of the emphasis on practice, or on the practice--based art research, which we will explore later on.

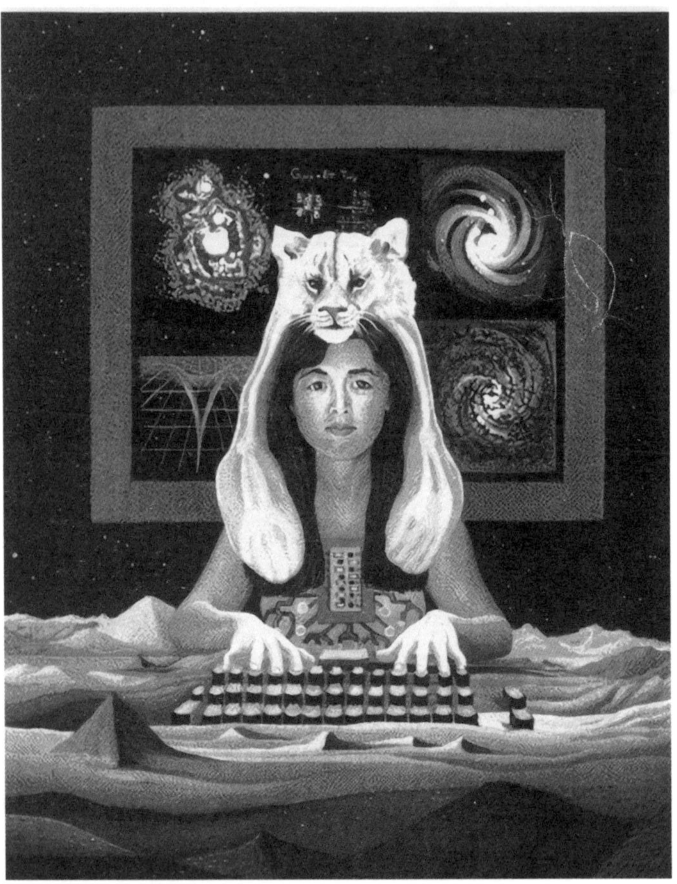

"A Cyborg Manifesto" was republished in 1991 in the collection of essays *Simians, Cyborgs, and Women*, subtitled The Reinvention of Nature. Cover image of the book.

8 Moira Weigel, "Feminist cyborg scholar Donna Haraway: 'The disorder of our era isn't necessary,' *The Guardian*, June 20, 2019, https://www.theguardian.com/world/2019/jun/20/donna-haraway-interview-cyborg-manifesto-post-truth.

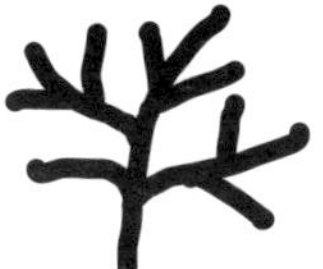

Automated Inequality

In her interview, Cornelia Solfrank, artist in digital media and networks, recalls how the term "cyberfeminism" fits best in the 1990s, the time of the advent of the Internet, net-art, the euphoric time when everyone went to cyber-cafés.[9] It was the imaginary coforming of new media, net-art, networked art, and virtual communities. The perception of the Internet in the 1990s was somewhat naive, as a new space, a territory not yet structured by traditional power dynamics, and there was a certain expectation that something new could be created there, including new art practices. But this was apparently due to the fact that the Internet was initially only available in academia. Being important in exploring and developing new digital spaces and related social practices, the term is often still used in these contexts.

In recent years, we have witnessed how new media have become corporate, monetized, and weaponized spaces. *The Anatomy of a Viral Tweet*[10] is the series of Caroline Orr Bueno, where she analyzes social media culture war issues. Rage Farming of the corporate platforms produces viral content, particularly when the engagement is framed as a way for cultural warriors to signal which side of the battle they're on. When content is positioned as ammunition to use against the other side, it becomes irresistible bait. The reason this tactic works is that both sides are willing to engage with bad-faith posts and outrage bait. And the reason both sides are willing to engage with this content is that rage farming promises benefits for those who put out the bait as well as those who take the bait. There is no cultivation of arguments, both sides can just bury themselves forever in destructive fights, organized by monetization algorithms to amplify hierarchies and replicate social divisions.

9 Son[i]a #384, Cornelia Sollfrank, *Radio Web MACBA 2023*, https://rwm.macba.cat/en/sonia/sonia-384-cornelia-sollfrank.
10 Caroline Orr Bueno, "The Anatomy of a Viral Tweet: Rage Farming Edition," https://weaponizedspaces.substack.com/p/the-anatomy-of-a-viral-tweet-rage.

One of the technofeminist concerns is the inherent relationship between gender and technosphere, including historical and societal norms, technology design and how it is implemented. The unnoticed biases and inequities ingrained in systems regarding gender, socioeconomic status, race, sexuality, body politics, and others. It was Judy Wajcman in *Technofeminism* (2004)[11] who helped to establish the term and a new transdisciplinary research field called feminist technoscience.

Overcoming another naivety, namely the assumption that science always works for the common interests of society, science is suggested to be held to the same level of political and ethical accountability as the technologies which develop from it. Feminist technoscience thus focuses less on intrapersonal relationships between men and women, and more on broader issues concerning knowledge production and how bodies manifest and are acknowledged in societies.

Judy Wajcman points out that feminist approaches of the 1990s and today adopt an optimistic perspective on the nature of digital technologies and their implications for women. They tend to view and present an image of new technology as radically distinct from older technologies and, as such, positive for women. In looking forward to what these new technologies could make possible, they elaborate a new feminist "imaginary" detached from the material reality of the existing technological order. While attributing technological determinism to the past and emancipatory features to the present, paradoxically, such approaches infer a new form of technological determinism. But as they distinguish new technologies from the infamously established ones and downplay any continuities between them, obviously the need for feminist technopolitics arises.

11 Judy Wajcman, "Technofeminism," https://openlibrary.org/books/OL7956549M/TechnoFeminism.

Leaving aside the current digital technology for a moment, an important role in reconfiguring norms and social conventions in cultural systems in the 1970s and 1980s was played by feminist performance and video art practice. The video camera was used to interrogate the politics of representation in maintaining hegemonic power structures. In Martha Rosler's *Vital Statistics of a Citizen*, *Simply Obtained*, from 1974, the performer poses to be "objectively" measured and represented by data by male-dominated science. Instructed by medical examiners, the artist gradually undresses so they can measure the different parts of her body.[12]

Martha Rosler, *Vital Statistics of a Citizen, Simply Obtained*, reformulated and turned into a video piece in 1977, MACBA Collection. Barcelona City Council long-term loan. © Martha Rosler, 2023.

12 Catherine Long, *A Feminist Dialogue with the Camera: Strategies of Visibility in Video Art Practices* (London: University of the Arts, 2016).

This particular work of Rosler criticizes and illustrates the social construction of science, pointing to the gendered cultural and political assumptions and agendas underlying its concepts and methods. Here, Rosler primarily deals with the broader theme of scientificization of societies and medicalization of the bodies for the sake of disciplining and governing the citizens. She exposes how "the data" whose credibility and authority is derived from the power-status of their producers gain the power to represent and therefore socially situate and determine the position and opportunities of subjects. In contemporary digital society, our knowledge is predominantly shaped by the data. The questions of data feminism are: "What are the bodies these technologies support, which ones does it harm? What are the territories paying the expenses, and which are the ones reaping the benefits?" Many people and politicians argue with data to make a point, but where do the data come from, how complete are they, how were they collected, and how are they interpreted?

Over the past decade, Critical Data Studies has emerged as a field, and we see it in the works by Virginia Eubanks' *Automating Inequality*, Safiya Noble's *Algorithms of Oppression*, Ruha Benjamin's *Race after Technology*, Shoshana Zuboff's *The Age of Surveillance Capitalism*, Emiliano Treré and Lina Dencik's *Data Justice*, Nick Couldry and Ulises Mejias *The Costs of Connection*, in Paola Ricaurte's article "Data Epistemologies, the Coloniality of Power, and Resistance," or finally *Data Feminism* by Catherine D'Ignazio and Lauren Klein, among many others.

Much work has advanced to identify the harmful and discriminatory effects of data and intelligence, data extractivism, colonialism, the New Jim Code. The New Jim Code is an acronym of Ruha Benjamin for a systemic bias in data and algorithms, which replaces any other means of trustworthiness with a range of discriminatory designs that encode inequity. Even in academic publications, obscure and overhyped algorithms are posed as ultimate proof of truth, while being poorly designed and deeply flawed by assumptions without including any historians, artists, or independent assessment.

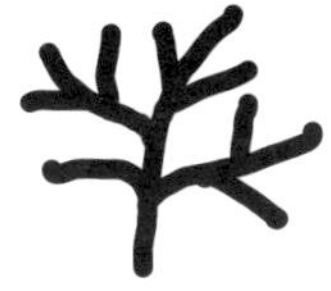

This type of research may be the 21st century version of pseudoscience dressed up as machine learning and artificial intelligence.[13]

Today, data science is a form of power. These works show convincingly how data sets, systems, AI are automating and accelerating social inequalities—sexism, racism, discrimination. Power and politics are concentrated through data, particularly as AI systems are permeating all sectors including medical services, access to education and housing. In this situation, mainstream data science is encumbered with extracting, dominance logics, and it purports views that would be rejected by a lot of scholars.

A slide from Data + Feminism Lab and Tierra Común at Data, Bodies, Territories: A Conversation on Global Majority Challenges to Data Colonialism with Paola Ricaurte.

13 Sarah E. Bond and Nyasha Junior, "How Racial Bias in Tech Has Developed the 'New Jim Code,'" https://hyperallergic.com/593074/how-racial-bias-in-tech-has-developed-the-new-jim-code/.

14 Mariel García-Montes, "Data + Bodies + Territories—A Data + Feminism and Tierra Común event," https://medium.com/data-feminism-lab-mit/data-bodies-territories-a-data-feminism-and-tierra-comun-event-cca0cd0a3f23.

Devastation Supercharged by a Myth

Increasing Doses of Techno-Anesthetics

Timnit Gebru, an ethical AI researcher, began to warn about a group of ideologies that she coined as the TESCREAL Bundle. The letters stand for Transhumanism, Extropianism, Singularitarianism, Cosmism, Rationalism, Effective Altruism, and Longtermism: TESCREALism is basically the worldview that arises from this group of ideologies. Those who subscribe into these beliefs envision a technologically utopian future, where humanity, as purely high IQ population, discovers practical ways to live in outer space, and is capable of effectively colonizing all parts of the universe.

That sounds like a promising development coupled with awaited economic growth. Until we recognize certain problematic aspects, like the widespread increase in intelligence is in fact not about to be achieved by equal access to education, but in their belief with genetic engineering founded on the principles of eugenics and racism. Tescrealist thinking works routinely with reducing unwanted population by expected nuclear war or climate catastrophe, because only a fraction of the population with a high IQ is needed to populate space. So, the protection of nature is unnecessary because we will leave the Earth for other planets anyway, and in devastating energy consumption, needed for high-tech global computation claiming to surpass human brain, the environmentalists are just annoying mosquitoes standing in the way.[15] Unfortunately, these ideologies are behind numerous tech startups massively funded by investment finance and maintaining large media influence over the tech field and increasingly in politics. While promising global cognitive infrastructure, no proprietary AI company is interested in building networks of sensors for data needed. Such networks exist

15 Émile P. Torres, "Eugenics in the Twenty-First Century: New Names, Old Ideas," https://www.truthdig.com/dig-series/eugenics/.

for quite some time already. They are built by individuals on the principle of citizen science or as research funded by public money.

Aiming to run global extractive systems based on inequality, they can use all kinds of manipulation. One of the most common is the utopian narrative of future technology, used for breaking any rational discussion on sustainability. For such an amazing mystical technology, solving any problem, we should give up our rights, social responsibility and justice, or any other possible solution and give our money and beliefs without any guarantees to individualist advantages of private companies. To make any argumentation impossible, the promised technology must be portrayed in advanced and complex terminology inaccessible to broad understanding. And if such a debate arises, influencers act as sole experts, defaming others with fabricated data-based arguments, pushing to bypass rational thinking with emotional and affective shortcuts fueled by both utopianism and fear.

It comes in handy for unsustainable business models to intentionally prevent any education on the subject, keeping the decisions irrational, emotional, while abusing democratic principles by manipulative techniques. Some media and even academics paid by public money act as influencers of corporate businesses, avoiding providing complete information, facts, and critical inquiry on the social and environmental consequences of technology, being thus deployed in favor of billionaires and pyramid investment schemes.

Félix Guattari in *Three Ecologies* draws attention to capitalistic subjectivity, seeking to gain power by controlling and neutralizing the maximum number of existential refrains, being intoxicated with and anaesthetized by a collective feeling of pseudo-eternity. Rosi Braidotti reflects this systemic undoing of the ties that bind the human to nature and disconnection of the territorial, planetary as well as social ties. This “undoing” of the bonds between human life and nature postulated rational consciousness as the flight into transcendence, projecting the burden of physical materiality—and consequently the natural world—unto the bodies of the “others.”

These discriminated, sexualized, racialized, and nonhuman "others" have paid a heavy price, in both material and symbolic terms, for their supposed association with the natural order.[16]

We should question the possessive individualism and its aggressive view of evolution and replace it with a cooperative vision of human relationality as the true evolutionary capacity. Reciprocity and mutuality and emergence of cooperation is a central issue in behavior and evolution research. Not individual strength but cooperation and care in groups in human—environment coupling mechanism is an evolutionary stable strategy, the key factor for human survival in critical moments of evolution.

As the state of digital technologies and media raises serious questions, Critical Infrastructure Lab was opened in 2023 at the University of Amsterdam,[17] with the aim to research power and contestation in transnational media infrastructures and to create space to codevelop alternative infrastructural futures that center people and planet over profit and capital. Also, Critical Change Lab of Ars Electronica Festival[18] and several universities and organizations had set themselves on the crossroad of democracy and arts, building resilient democratic cultures through creative and narrative practice.

16 Rosi Braidotti and Rick Dolphijn, "After Nature," in *Philosophy After Nature* (Washington: Rowman & Littlefield, 2017).
17 Critical Infrastructure Lab, https://www.criticalinfralab.net/.
18 Critical ChangeLab, https://criticalchangelab.eu/en/.

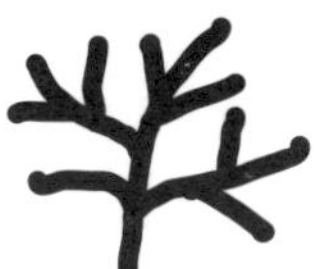

Publicly Governable Stacks and Civil Society

Small, Ethical, and Sustainable

As digitalization has become almost indispensable, more and more cultural actors have recognized the need to actively shape its path. This has led to the emergence of a variety of sustainable alternatives based on principles of civil society, such as democratic control, equitable access, and commons-based models for operating digital infrastructures.

As the counterpart of the global corporate surveillance megastructure and dystopic geopolitical architecture, which Benjamin Bratton entitled The Stack (2016), Waag | technology & society formulated a mission for digital public spaces called the Public Stack in 2019.[19] The difference in the Public Stack lies in the core values embodied in the principles and design process it encourages. The Public Stack departs from the private and state-centric conception upon closed design processes resulting in proprietary technology, the base layer of the Public Stack is built on common values of fundamental rights and socioeconomic considerations, which are embodied in the open design processes involving all stakeholders to provide democratic governance of digitalization. The resulting tech layer is open-source and ethical. There are no powerless "users" but digital citizens with their digital rights.

1. All stakeholders are involved and it is clear why we optimize.
2. Human rights are guaranteed and public values respected.
3. Society as a whole keeps a grip on digitalization.
4. The financial-economic model takes human and planet into account.

19 Waag | technology & society (2019), Public Stack, https://publicstack.net/.

Public stack layers and one of the tools for cocreation, published on the project website. Open design focuses on the question of how to design products to make collaboration as easy as possible.

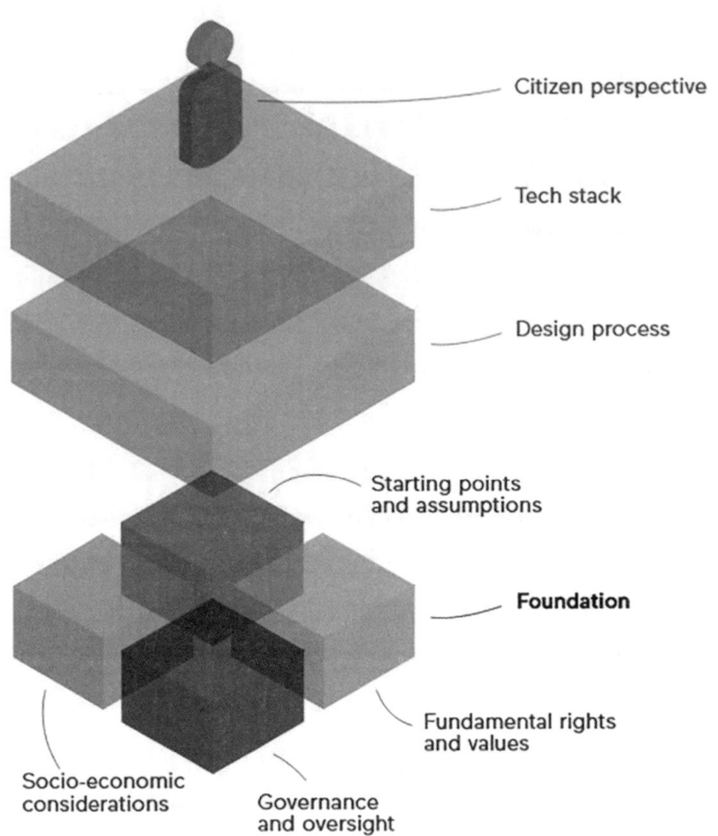

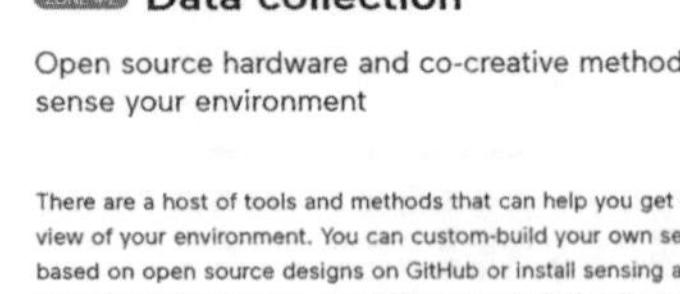

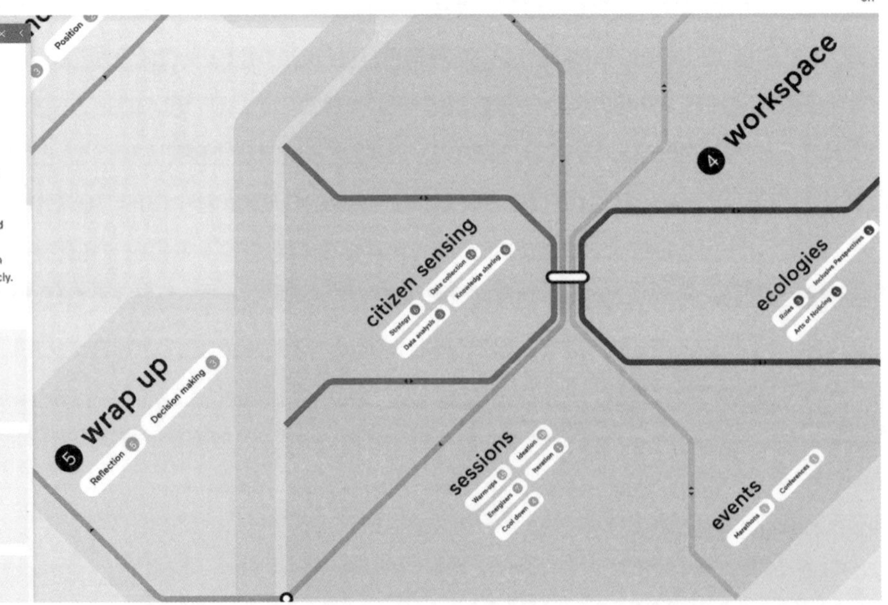

A broad coalition of media and academic institutions was also formed in the Netherlands under the name Public Spaces,[20] supporting public transition to an open software, whose operations are based on civic values. The coalition includes more than 40 libraries, public TV broadcasters, audiovisual archives, media art organizations and festivals, NGOs, and software developer organizations. They run their citizen social media instance, PeerTube videoportal, and an annual Public Spaces conference.

The Digital Kitchen Sink is the name of a methodology developed by Public Spaces, which was made as a tool to answer the simple question: Are the digital tools you employ reflecting your values? This question may not be a priority for private commercial organizations yet, but it is valid and important for public organizations with responsibilities beyond profit making. These organizations, which can be labeled as values-led organizations,[21] include municipal governments, state agencies, public broadcasters, educational or research institutions, libraries, archives, healthcare institutions, cultural organizations, and NGOs. They are expected and often required by law to adhere to and protect values such as transparency and accountability.[22]

This methodology provides an organization with insight into the extent to which the software and tools used by members comply with the values set out in the Public Spaces manifesto, which consist of Openness, Transparency, Accountability, Sovereignty, and User Centrism.[23]

Those who embrace these core public values and express this, among other things, in the choice of software tools they use, contribute to the ultimate goal of a more transparent, open, sovereign, and human-centric digital environment, and eventually the Internet in general. They often have a set of applications from various suppliers and it is not always possible to turn this ethical and sustainable overnight.

20 Public Spaces, https://publicspaces.net/.
21 Bogaerts et al., 2023.
22 Björn Wijers, The Digital Powerwash, in: Bits und Baume.
23 Manifesto, Public Spaces, https://publicspaces.net/english-section/manifesto/.

There are situations in which instant replacement of products or services from Big-tech is not possible. However, it is possible to assess to what extent the values of the application correspond to desired organizational values or energy and carbon emissions.

Ethical and sustainable apps are available. This status earns to a tool or service which uses open source code and thus meets the requirement for public verifiability of its algorithms and can be operated by a provider of choice who is transparent as concerns their energy use or social responsibility. Free or Libre open source software (FLOSS) can be developed cooperatively and no license fees are incurred. There is no need for any pioneering hard work nowadays, many organizations already went this way before. FLOSS-based infrastructure guarantees individuals, companies, and the public sector control over access to their information. Some examples of the basic software includes:

- Linux operating system instead of Windows or MacOS
- LibreOffice document editors replacing Word, Excel, or Powerpoint, Gimp and Inkscape for graphics installed quickly and effortlessly in place of expensive Photoshop or Illustrator subscriptions.
- Nextcloud instead of Google Docs, Dropbox, OneDrive, or iCloud: documents can be stored and managed by different user groups. It can be integrated into the desktop and also has mobile apps.
- JitsiMeet for online meetings and BigBlueButton for more complex online workshops and education instead of Zoom, Skype, or Webex.
- PeerTube for videoportal replacement of YouTube.
- Fediverse social networking like Streams, Mastodon, Pixelfed, and others instead of (or in addition to) Instagram, X, TikTok.
- Other alternatives can be found in Delightful curated lists of free software, open science, and related information sources.[24]

24 Delightful, https://codeberg.org/teaserbot-labs/delightful.

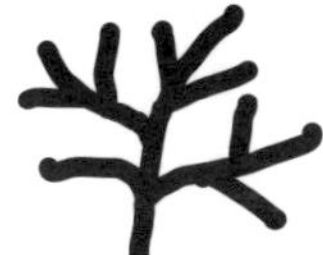

For online apps based on open-source software, the following applies. There is no single service or owner, you can choose from many providers, running the software in different places, under various financing models. It can be free service, paid service, cooperative, donation-based, or public infrastructure.[25] Jumping into Jitsi chat or sharing those photos from Nextcloud, there's no hassle, it's just sending a link as everyone is familiar with.

Monoskop.org published a wiki page[26] of small, ethical, and sustainable providers, feminist servers, online galleries, or autonomous digital collectives. If you need help or want to join existing infrastructure of your choice, you can turn to any of them. The first publication listed together with servers on the wiki, which is from Art Servers Unlimited conference, goes back to 1998.

25 For example, with Jitsi meet, you don't need to use only the service run by the development company (https://meet.jit.si), but also the service of an internet domain administration organization (https://meeting.nic.cz/), university (https://meet.sh.cvut.cz/), sustainable cloud provider (https://meet.greenhost.net/), or many others.

26 Community Servers, https://monoskop.org/Community_servers.

Feminist Servers: Networks of Care and Trust

WTF? Women, Technology, and Freedom!

In Lisa Gitelman's *Always Already New* (2006), she seeks to uncover the strict dichotomy of production and consumption, which characterizes most of the history and conceptions of media technology. We are told the story of a brilliant lone inventor in a garage, who invents the technology, masses of people consume it, they have their experiences mediated by it, while soon they inhabit a different world.

When we descend to the layer of materiality, we find people and practices underneath: populations of "superusers" who operate "close to the metal," including system and net administrators also with hackers, all of them in complex relationships. Hardware always includes designed institutional and structural potentials and constraints for various purposes. Users and superusers take material objects with many levels of agency and get them rhetorically and discursively packaged, especially through mass media.

Lisa Gitelman and feminist community practices thus bring in the "users" as diverse, dynamic, and disaggregate groups who are actively involved in shaping the features, the values, and the future of the systems they use.

Open source hardware and open design are enablers of a sustainable circular economy. For approaches such as degrowth, sufficiency, and circularity, we need nonbinary thinking and a fruitful dialogue. That requires spaces, both physical and digital, that are free from divisive manipulation and bot networks. We need safe spaces to nurture sensible information.

refuse; rethink; reuse; repair; refurbish; remanufacture; repurpose; recycle; recover[27]

27 Julian Kirchherr et al., Conceptualizing the Circular Economy: An Analysis of 114 Definitions, available at SSRN: https://ssrn.com/abstract=3037579.

Feminist hardware is a strategy and method of making hardware coming from feminist hacking practices. Collective intensive knowledge sharing, workshops, and do-it-together sessions are part of getting close to the metal, which means getting close to the narratives and the people telling them.

One of the thinkers and practitioners in feminist hardware is Mz*Baltazar's Lab[28] collective in Vienna, founded in 2008 by artist and researcher Stefanie Wuschitz. Their makerspace is investigating opportunities that would facilitate regional, inclusive access to making and expand making beyond educated, young men towards underrepresented groups—especially including women and girls. Their Female Artist Index Vienna is an online platform and directory which amplifies the visibility of female artists working within the intersection of science, technologies, and feminism, specifically the artists working on/with developing hardware, tools, or alternative materials for their artistic practices. Computing can be carried out by mud batteries, pottery, cutlery, or embroidery. Stefanie Wuschitz describes feminist hardware and material principles as follows:

- Without mining in harmful ways
- Environmentally friendly
- Fair working conditions
- Manufactured from ubiquitously available materials
- Not generating e-waste

We can also take a look at some feminist servers and thinking through digital spaces in a situated way—how they contribute to distributing and sharing knowledge in local communities, finding collectives setting up and maintaining online shared infrastructures with queer and marginalized groups. For interviews and details on Rosa's ecofeminist dictionary, you can read through the article by Marloes de Valk at Solar Protocol website,[29] here are two examples.

28 Mz * Balthazar's Lab, https://www.mzbaltazarslaboratory.org.
29 Marloes de Valk, Rosa's Ecofeminist Dictionary, http://solarprotocol.net/sunthinking/index.html#devalk.

Systerserver, which "offers services to its network of feminist, queer, and antipatriarchal folks," was launched in early 2005 by Genderchangers, a group of women and women-identified minorities. In 2002, Genderchangers started the Eclectic Tech Carnival, "a gathering of feminists who critically explore and develop everyday skills and information technologies in the context of free software and open hardware."[30] Through systerserver, they are connected to mur.at, a grassroots "art server farm" in Graz, they run their Fediverse Mastodon instance and PeerTube videoportal.

Varia, a community in Rotterdam, runs a space for long-term, sustainable, critical, artistic, hands-on, dialogical learning about technology. For the collective, demystifying the complexities of technical objects is a way to find how to adapt them to the needs of different communities. Developing critical understandings of everyday technologies around us and experimenting with tools for building physical and digital infrastructures in a collective way unfolds in series of activities like Read & Repair, Feminist Hack Meetings and many others, combining social and technological aspects in the form of research worksessions.

Designer and researcher Mindy Seu has put together Cyberfeminism Index,[31] a list of more than 700 cyber and technofeminist manifests, radical techno-critical activist and academic articles, entries on hackerspaces or net art projects. The index shows a vast amount of thinking on techno-social systems informed by feminist discourse. Starting with first entries in 1985, we can continue reading through Cyberfeminist Manifesto of VNS Matrix in 1991: "Women who hijack the tools of domination and control introduce a rupture into highly systematized culture by infecting the machines with radical thought, diverting them from their inherent purpose of linear top-down mastery." Then move on to Old Boys Network in 1997, first international Cyberfeminist alliance founded in 1997 in Berlin,

30 About the Eclectic Tech Carnival, /ETC. Available from: https://eclectictechcarnival.org/ETC/about/.
31 Mindy Seu (ed.), Cyberfeminism Index, https://cyberfeminismindex.com/.

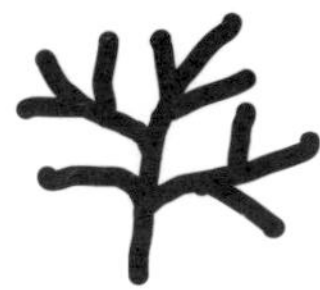

which contributes to the critical discourse on new media, especially focusing on its gender-specific aspects. And not to miss A Hacker Manifesto of McKenzie Wark in 2004: “We are the hackers of abstraction. We produce new concepts, new perceptions, new sensations, hacked out of raw data. What code we hack, be it programming, language, poetic language, math or music, curves or colorings, we are the abstracters of new worlds. Whether we come to represent ourselves as researchers or authors, artists or biologists, chemists or musicians, philosophers or programmers, each of these subjectivities is but a fragment of a class still becoming, bit by bit, aware of itself as such.”

GENDERCHANGERS.ORG

free skills from scratch

DATE 13-14 JANUARY 07

220V ~ 700W

SAT:
10AM HARDWARE COURSE
2PM LINUX INSTALL PARTY
6PM ORGANIC VEGAN MEAL
8PM LECTURE / DEMONSTRATION
THE TURING TEST
SUN:
11AM SOLDERING WORKSHOP
2PM WEBSITE FROM HTML TO CSS

PROGRAM

THERMOSTAT - 80° C

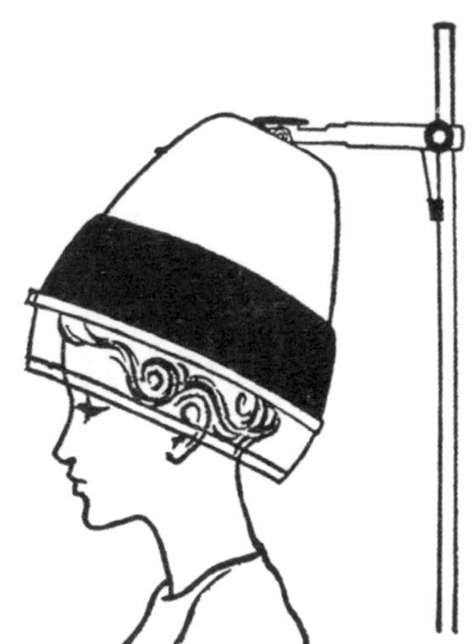

WORKSHOPS FOR WOMEN ONLY; TURING TEST LECTURE OPEN TO THE PUBLIC

de Peper, Overtoom 301, Amsterdam

020-4122954 or info@genderchangers.org

Genderchangers flyer, 2007

To avoid making the impression that these strategies can be applied only by privileged white Europeans, it can be pointed out that cheap hardware, reuse, and cooperative participation also help in the Global South. Especially there, they may help to create an important infrastructure. In a world where our digital lives reside on servers owned by global conglomerates, the feminist server is a way to reclaim ownership and management of our data. Cocreating digital infrastructure with local communities ensures agency in the knowledge creation and storage process.

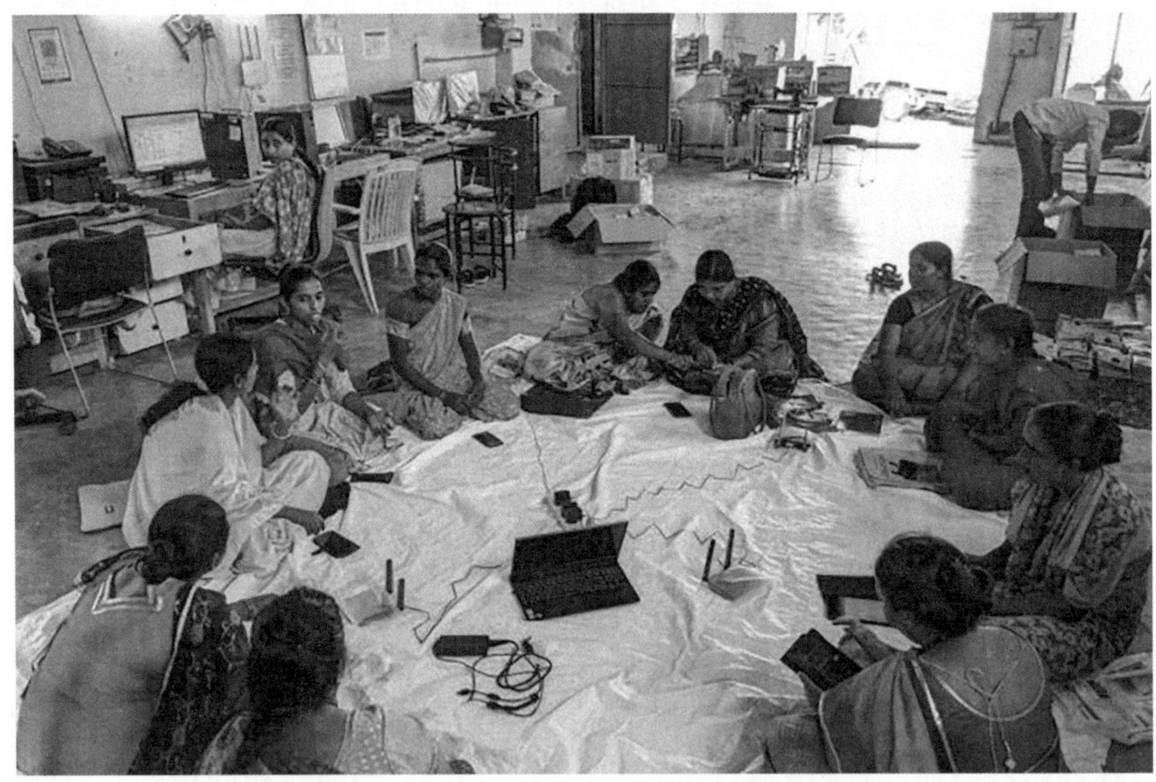

The Health Navigators using LTE routers to upload the narratives they collected during the week to online Channapatna Health Library, while discussing and annotating in smaller groups.

"For example, in Channapatna, a town about 80 km southwest of Bangalore, Design Beku is engaging with health worker communities to not only codevelop a local health knowledge archive but also to codesign and set up a stand-alone, decentralized digital infrastructure. This has taken the shape of a Community Owned Wireless Knowledge Infrastructure that enables communities to cocreate local knowledge repositories and offer meaningful digital services,"[32] writes Padmini Ray Murray with her collaborators, who focuses on research-led practice of challenging acts of infrastructural and algorithmic violence in India, and creating alternative digital spaces and imaginations that are characterized by feminist values, specifically ethics of care.

Biophysical, Biocultural, Biodigital... and the Postdigital

Curating and Computing with Nature

From "artists in laboratories" in 2000s, who were supposed to be visually illustrating scientific work to make it more understandable to the public or to showcase the capabilities of high-tech devices and help establish centers of excellence, art research progressed to a true interdisciplinary science. Art research is involving inquiry through the methods of humanities and synthesizes new knowledge by bridging separate disciplines. The outcome can be used not only for ecosystem care and sustainable technology design, but involves urban planning and social actors in the process.

As far as philosophy is concerned, one cannot fail to mention the ecosophy of Félix Guattari, formulated in his *Three Ecologies* (1989). Ecosophy consists of social ecology, mental ecology, and environmental ecology which all work together. Having specific value systems, they should not be put on the same plane of equivalence like material assets, cultural assets, or wildlife. Neither should they be explained by simple pseudoscientific paradigms. The three ecologies are governed by a different logic. While the logic of discursive sets endeavors to statically position and delimit its objects, the logic of intensities, or eco-logic, concerns the movement, flux, potential, and intensity of evolutive processes.

32 Padmini Ray Murray et al., A 'Feminist' Server to Help People Own Their Own Data, https://thebastion.co.in/politics-and/tech/a-feminist-server-to-help-people-own-their-own-data/.

Luciana Parisi in 2004 outlines the notions of the biophysical, the biocultural, and the biodigital to de-privilege the human body as a discrete organic thing. In these contexts, the body does not end at the skin. We breathe in and metabolize what others breathe out, we leave traces of our DNA everywhere we go, we live with other organisms within us, microbes and bacteria, we are enmeshed in forces, affects, energies, we are composites of information. These assemblages do not privilege bodies as human, nor as residing within a human animal / nonhuman animal binary. Along with a de-exceptionalizing of human bodies, multiple forms of matter can be bodies—bodies of water, cities, institutions. The original French term for assemblage is "agencement," which means design, layout, organization, arrangement, and relations. Biodigital co-evolution with its transdisciplinary research context has incorporated a diverse range of perspectives that engage complex bio-informational, socio-material, socio-political, and eco-social assemblages that undergrid the production, creation, and mediation of knowledge. In recent artistic practice anthology *Plants by Numbers*,[33] Jane Prophet and Helen V. Pritchard suggest a variety of modes of reverting old narratives by proposition of practices of categorization and numbering that reside within the computation of plants as new ethical-political engagements that are decolonial, queer, and feminist.

However, extractivist exploitation by biodigital capitalism has led to a concept of postdigital that diverts from utopic techno-deterministic accounts of increasingly problematic human-technology associations in pursuit of more agreeable biodigital futures.

Postdigital philosophy understands biology and digital information as interconnected fabric of bio-informational ecosystem, positioning us in "new knowledge ecologies," nested within an overarching technoscience. Recognition of culturally bounded ways of

33 Jane Prophet and Helen V. Pritchard, eds., *Plants by Numbers: Art, Computation, and Queer Feminist Technoscience* (Bloomsbury Visual Arts, 2023), https://www.bloomsburycollections.com/monograph-detail?docid=b-9781350351042.

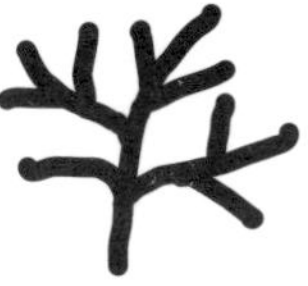

knowing is required to establish trust within and between communities of practice—plurality of knowledge partners that co-create and co-apply knowledge based on practical engagement with the world. The need to recognize the value, validity, and significance of knowledge as "fundamentally social and dependent on an evolving community of inquiry" has been incorporated within a postdigital understanding that the digitization, speed, and compression of communication "has led to the spread of global cultures as knowledge and research networks."[34]

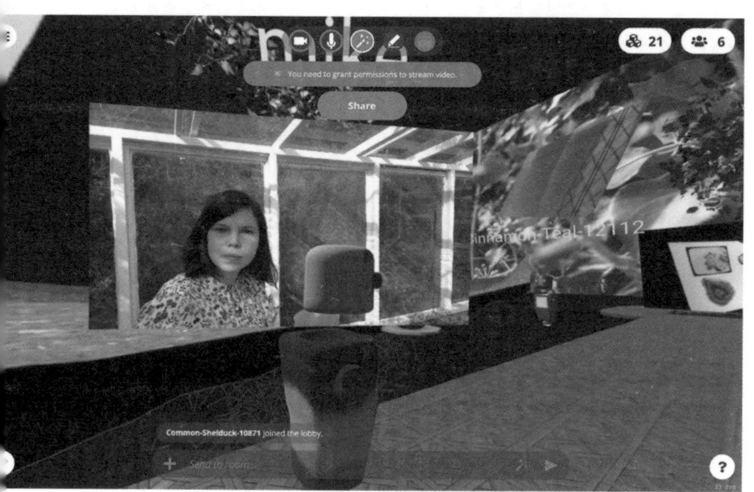

Irina Andreeva, Nikola Brabcová, Michal Klodner, children. Waterlily Tea: Performance during Art Meets Radical Openness festival 2020, combined butoh dance, tea ceremony, fediverse social channel, and online streaming to open source virtual meeting space with solar energy from the environmental forest care project of node9.org livinglab.

Cathy Fitzgerald in her thesis, explicitly titled "The Ecological Turn: Living Well with Forests to Articulate Eco-Social Art Practices Using a Guattari Ecosophy and Action Research Framework,"[35] asks a simple question. When eco-social art practitioners perform art and nonart practices over extended timeframes, sometimes years, and do not prioritize the production of singular artworks, the most familiar response is: "But is it art?", while this being the long-standing argument also against social art practice.

Care for living ecosystems is reflected in gallery and museum spaces from the second half of the 20th century. Part of the exhibitions can be chemical processes, water systems, bioreactors,

34 Michael A. Peters, Tina Besley, Petar Jandrić, Postdigital knowledge cultures and their politics, ECNU Review of Education, 1(2), 2018, https://doi.org/10.30926/ecnuroe2018010202.

35 Cathy Fitzgerald, *The Ecological Turn: Living Well with Forests to Articulate Eco-Social Art Practices Using a Guattari Ecosophy and Action Research Framework*, PhD by Practice, National College of Art and Design, Dublin 2018.

plants and animals, social engagement. In *The Living Exhibitions* book,[36] the editors consider exhibition as living in different ways. Those can be exhibiting and integrating living creatures or situating them in living environments, outside of white cube: in parks, forests, or open landscapes. There are influences of the environment, like rain, sunshine, organisms. Part of the experience is the movement and complexity that cannot be completely controlled, which is complex and evolves under its own rules, which can be contradictory to expectations or plans, unlike the human designed garden. The environments are shaped by human presence and interactions, technical parameters, accompanied by workshops and performances, interwoven into exhibition matter.

In the same book, Dorothea von Hantelmann develops the concept of time based exhibition as "individualized experiential space." Not only Suzi Gablik, also Margaret Mead in her essay *Art and Reality* from 1943 formulates a standpoint against modern concept of art and its institutions. Margaret Mead considers the modern emphasis on the visual reflection unsatisfactory and lacking spiritual and transcendent energies. Compared to a ritual, an exhibition does not intermediate the experience of the sensuous being as a whole. The collectivity created in exhibitions is limited and temporal, it does not constitute full collective body.

A possible response to this critique is that historically, it was emancipatory to break from the ties of involuntary bonds and obligations of traditional societies, families, religions, and nationality. Modern age brought freedom through the process of distancing which is inherent in the format of individualized exhibitions. Art institutions are the places of industrialized liberalism and the cultural and historical achievement lies in the breaking away from holistic experiences as cosmologies of feudal societes. The exhibition format was specifically meant to be modern, liberal, democratic, and personal, incapable

36 Thomas Oberender and Paul Rabe, eds., *The Living Exhibition* (Leipzig: Spector Books, 2021).

and with no intention to replicate holistic collective thinking. It ritualizes the rationalist approach, fundamental and also extremely productive in modern societies. That, in Enlightenment, led also to emancipation from nature, leaving it out as something inferior, as a resource.

The living exhibitions as individualized experiential spaces are essentially a hybrid form of exhibition and performance. The separations of nature from culture, product from process, the individual from social ties are being reconnected beyond conventional concepts of collectives. We now think in systems of connections and reciprocity instead of systems of separation and liberalization, giving attention to living forms, to their answers of our activity and inhabitation. The wealth and prestige lies not in the accumulation and statutory consumption, but in the variety of encounters with nature, the uniqueness of our place, and the many ways in which we expand our horizons by stepping from this place to another.

There is a movement and a vast network of organizations and collectives, formal and informal, involved in environmental and ethical digital practice in arts, public sphere, or education. I could only write about a few of them to give some examples. They've already built Fediverse, community-owned, decentralized, and privacy-centric social networks. Techno-eco-feminism is not just a theoretical stance, it's a practice. As Félix Guattari writes, "It seems to me essential to organize new micropolitical and microsocial practices, new solidarities, a new gentleness, together with new aesthetic and new analytic practices regarding the formation of the unconscious."

In my view of the ecosystem metaphor, big-tech platforms are like monocultures of weeds that have by fast-growth strategies taken over the internet meadows, shaded and smothered the blooms of various kinds of little healing herbs. But these haven't died yet. They are hidden, resilient and when the monoculture stage passes and we start tending the internet meadows again, the flowers will bloom with many colors, smells, and tastes.

This paper (Vergemit Yellow, 120 g/m²) was used from surplus stock normally destined for disposal. Manufactured in Štětí, Czech Republic.

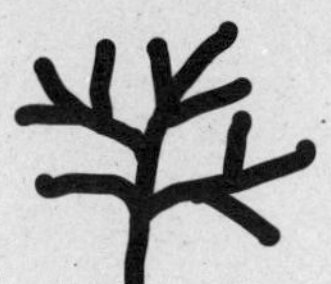

Aneta Rostkowska

Towards Perma-cultural Institution

Introduction

In this text, I would like to draft a proposal of an alternative institutional model for the art system. The proposal is based on my curatorial work in the last twelve years as well as my observations concerning the work of various art institutions. It is also based on countless conversations with people I often collaborated with, like Nada Rosa Schroer, Kris Dittel, Paulina Seyfried, Paloma Nana, Agustina Andreoletti, Alicja Rogalska, Mateusz Okoński, Jakub Woynarowski, Cecylia Malik, and other colleagues, many of them participants of the Islands of Kinship network.

Although I have a weakness for art theory and definitely try to be up-to-date concerning the newest developments in this field, I'm foremost a cultural practitioner: I develop various activities and reflect on them on the go, my thoughts are formulated mostly during discussions and interviews and rarely take form of a theoretical or scientific text. This essay is written from this, mostly practical, perspective, so forgive me some simplifications or theoretical inconsistencies. I hope that after this initial "report from the work field," a more theoretical analysis will follow that will place my thoughts in a more elaborate historical context.

While I use the term "institutional model," I'm entirely aware of the problems related to formulating any "models." As we know, each context is different and it would be a mistake to claim that one's ideas have any kind of universal validity. Still, in many conversations with cultural practitioners from all over the world, I was surprised how many common points we would find and how many solutions from very different contexts could be applied in other ones. Since the current art system is spread almost everywhere in the world, its problems and pitfalls tend to repeat themselves even if contexts differ. The disillusionment with the system and the need to find alternatives seem to be almost universal. In this text, I will try to formulate some more general statements, although they obviously have to be confronted within local contexts and adjusted accordingly. The same applies to the scale of the art institution you work with and the type of funding you deal with in your work. My perspective is formed by the experience of working in mid-scale and small-scale art initiatives, first in Poland, then in Germany. I never worked in a big museum although I collaborated with some of them. In both countries, institutions rely mostly on public funding while the dependence on private funding is relatively low. This, of course, heavily influences the conclusions in my text. I encourage the readers to critically examine this aspect while still considering a possible "translation" from context to context.

This text draws from many activities I undertook in the last years whose goal was to reflect on the state of the cultural sector, most of them developed within the institution I'm running since January 2019—Temporary Gallery: Centre for Contemporary Art in Cologne. In June 2020, together with Nada Rosa Schroer, I began addressing the topic of sustainability with the event The Curatorial Unknown: About Ecology and Sustainability in Art Institutions. A second step followed in May 2021 with the 6-month online course Under the Paving Stones, the Soil! Permaculture, Art and Social Change. Led by permaculture designer and environmental activist Alfred Decker, over 90 cultural practitioners from around the world came together to explore the principles of permaculture and its application in the art field. The course was continued for the participants from Cologne as a permaculture working group in cooperation with the Neuland community garden. With the series Instituting in Cycles: Ecological Approaches in Art and Art Institutions in 2022, curated by Nada Rosa Schroer, this programmatic pillar was continued within the framework of artistic-ecological workshops through approaches such as ecofeminism, urban gardening, and multispecies democracy. In July 2022, the institution also organized a seven-day summer seminar in collaboration with the Stiftung Künstlerdorf Schöppingen, entitled Towards Permacultural Institutions: Exercises in Collective Thinking (curated by me, Nada Rosa Schroer, and Julia Haarmann). In autumn 2023, a series of workshops on the topic of socioecological transformation processes in art institutions (with focus on allyship/climate justice, degrowth, and grounding) was organized together with Medienwerk NRW. The reflection was enhanced through various gatherings of Creative Europe Programme Islands of Kinship: A Collective Manual for Sustainable and Inclusive Art Institutions (2022—2024). Drawing from these experiences, in 2022, I was able to formulate preliminary conclusions through several lectures I gave, for example at the Academy of Media Arts in Cologne (Moss Time. Towards Vegetal Curating), Art Academy in Düsseldorf (Plant-Thinking in Art Institutions), and Art Academy in Münster (Towards "Vegetal Curating").

All these activities were informed and fueled by various programs I curated, starting from my initial interest in monuments, activist art, and public art, continuing through my first bigger curatorial project called After Capitalism (2012), including many reading groups, and then taking the form of Floraphilia, a series of research and exhibition projects dedicated to the relations between plants, botany, and politics. Currently, my practice continues in the context of the CCA Temporary Gallery, aiming at a hybrid institutional identity which combines an appreciation for art, including its most "traditional" forms like painting or sculpture, with a sociopolitical awareness.

Historical Context: The Neoliberal Art System

In our daily work as curators and artists, we are submerged in a system of predefined concepts and structures. Constantly overworked, we move within this specific environment, gradually taking all its elements for granted. We focus on efficiency without questioning the basic framework of our projects. At the same time, we become increasingly aware that the system has fundamental flaws and needs to be changed. I believe that what could help us here is to become more aware of the historicity of the art system we are experiencing now. After all, what we are dealing with on a daily basis is one specific constellation of institutions and concepts that emerged in a particular economic and social reality. For the sake of simplicity, I call it the "neoliberal art system," however, we could naturally use other names as well. Fifty or one hundred years ago, art functioned in a different way, as there were other institutional forms and other concepts at play. A deep recognition of this fact allows us to distance ourselves from the status quo and treat is as contingent. In the second step, we can venture into reimagining the situation: rethinking various elements of the system and implementing alternatives: art institutions of different scales, art academies, funding structures, residency programs, art prizes. This is encouraged by the multiple crises we are facing now: the climate crisis, the political crisis, the crisis of welfare state in Western societies as well as a growing need to tame/modify/replace capitalism. It is clear that the conditions of our work fundamentally changed and will continue to do so. We all know that a systemic change is needed on various levels. Is it utopian to think in this way and demand systemic change, in general and in the art sector? Following David Harvey, we could ask "can we afford not to be utopian?" Even if this kind of change seems impossible, history—including art history—shows us that carving spaces of freedom in a corrupt system is always possible, even though these are geographically and temporally limited.

Possible Allies

There are many allies in the journey of redesigning the art system. One of them might be coming back to the critical reflection on modernity, as it is modernity that built the pillars of what we are confronted with now. Modernity, understood as a historical epoch as well as a conglomerate of ideas like individualism, scientific approach, rationalization, specialization/compartmentalization, secularism, emergence of bureaucracy and nation states, or urbanization,[1] together with their "dark sides" like colonialism, racism, or eugenics. Here we can come back to the writings of postmodern thinkers like Jean Francois Lyotard or draw from newer approaches like the fascinating book *Hospicing Modernity. Facing Humanity's Wrongs and the Implications for Social Activism* by Vanessa Machado de Oliveira

1 https://www.britannica.com/topic/modernity

(North Atlantic Books, Berkeley California 2021). The last one is in fact a set of exercises and tools whose goal is to "hospice" the idea of modernity—mourn its pitfalls (human exceptionalism/anthropocentrism, coloniality, cultural supremacy, denial of violence/limits of the planet/entanglement/magnitude, and complexity of the problems we face) and create space for change. It is clear that the modernity will never leave us, but maybe since we are its children (and the neoliberal art system is definitely one of them), we can "adopt" other "parents" and become, for example, as Donna Haraway says, "Children of Compost."[2]

In the field of art theory, we can re-examine the heritage of institutional critique, new institutionalism, or look at alternative proposals inspired by activist art, like for instance the book *Toward a Lexicon of Usership* by Stephen Wright, published on the occasion of the exhibition Museum of Arte Útil in Vanabbemuseum in Eindhoven.[3] The results, however, might not always be satisfying. Although institutional critique brought us many fascinating artistic projects examining how art institutions work, it didn't result in substantial changes or proposal for changes concerning the art system itself. Wright's book can be much more inspiring, however, its radicality (visible in, for example, its call to deactivate art's aesthetic function and open it up to other functions) might narrow our perspective too much (after all, our vision for a different art system can accommodate a variety of approaches to art without privileging its activist forms). New institutionalism—understood as an attempt to widen institutional practices beyond the traditional exhibition programs[4]—generated many interesting curatorial projects, but did not change the ways of working "behind the scenes" in a systemic way.

2 The name "Children of Compost" comes from Haraway's science-fiction short story published in her book *Staying with the Trouble. Making Kin in the Chthulucene* (Duke University Press, 2016) and describes future communities which make kin with endangered species by adopting some of their genetic characteristics. It can be treated as a symbol of a close relationship to natural environment and willingness to transform one's life in order to make nature thrive.

3 https://museumarteutil.net/tools/

4 https://www.on-curating.org/issue-21-reader/new-institutionalism-revisited.html

Other potential allies in the quest for a better art system might be theories and beliefs that position themselves as alternatives to modernism or its modifications. In the art scene of the past years, we could observe a fascination with Indigenous worldviews, a rise of ecofeminism, various strains of ecological thought advocating for nonanthropocentric perspectives. I'm deeply convinced that, in order to confront the system which became a "hardware" of our brains, we need a strong anchoring of a different kind. In other words, we have to develop strong ideological "roots" that will allow new ideas to grow and flourish. In my work, I found several approaches particularly useful: permaculture, writings of such authors as Robin Wall Kimmerer and Michael Marder, and turning to artists and people regularly working with plants. In all of these approaches, we can find valuable practices and thoughts, while some of them—for instance permaculture—also offer a quite coherent and comprehensive worldview, including a specific ethical and political positioning. They definitely possess a guiding potential that can—in the next step—be used to inspire particular structural solutions for the art field.

In the end, what we can do is not reject modernity altogether (which would be not only useless but also impossible) but rather build a new ideological base using a part of modernity's heritage. It is clear that there are no easy and definitive answers here, rather a set of intellectual and practical tasks to try out, hopefully forming a fragmented worldview entailing in itself a capacity for self-critique.

Finally, our allies, naturally, can be art practitioners, institutions, and initiatives that have been or *already* are working differently. Here, however, we should not be too demanding—after all, they all operate in a hostile environment of the neoliberal art system which means being constantly subjected to various ideological and practical constraints. Nevertheless, if we look long enough, we will find inspiring examples, in art history as well as in contemporary times. What definitely makes sense here is to look beyond standard Western geographies and to look for actors working on the cross section of art, social work, and activism.

Permacultural Institution

In the next paragraphs, I will try to sketch an institutional model that I call "permacultural institution." It is by no means a coherent and complete proposal, rather a set of observations that I made in the last years. A permacultural institution is an institution guided by the reflection on sustainability. In general, sustainability is "a property of any activity, practice, process, or institution that has the capacity to be continued in more or less the same way indefinitely,"[5] more specifically, it means "preserving the earth's capacity to 'sustain,' to 'support' the weight of mankind."[6] "Sustainability addresses the question of 'how societies can shape their modes of change in such a way so as to ensure the preconditions of development for future generations, it refers to the viability of socially shaped relationships between society and nature over long periods of time."[7]

Sustainability divides into various kinds like an environmental one and social one. The first is already quite present in the art system in the form of guidelines ensuring a minimalization of CO2 emissions. The social dimension has been relatively neglected though. In a normative sense, it refers to the social goals of sustainability strategies.[8] "Social sustainability occurs when the formal and informal processes; systems; structures; and relationships actively support the capacity of current and future generations to create healthy and liveable communities. Socially sustainable communities are equitable, diverse, connected, and democratic and provide a good quality of life. Social sustainability is a process for creating sustainable successful places that promote well-being, by understanding what people need from the places they live and work. Social sustainability combines design of the physical realm with design of the social world—infrastructure to support social and cultural life, social amenities, systems for citizen engagement, and space for people

5 https://www.rep.routledge.com/articles/thematic/sustainability/v-1
6 Encyclopedia of Quality of Life and Well-Being Research, ed. by Alex C. Michalos, Springer Science+Business Media Dordrecht 2014, 6484.
7 Op. Cit., after Becker et al., 1999, 4.
8 Op. Cit, 6178.

and places to evolve."[9] Please, note that in this perspective, the issue of diversity is part of the effort towards making our institutions contribute to social sustainability. The question that can be posed here then is:

How can an art institution contribute to the creation and existence of an "equitable, diverse, connected, and democratic" community that provides "a good quality of life"?

There are many approaches to sustainability and I support the ones in which both environmental and social aspects are discussed together. I follow here the approach of Malcolm Ferdinand, author of *Decolonial Ecology. Thinking from the Caribbean World* (Polity Books, 2021). Ferdinand writes about the "double break" that permeates modernity: the separation of ecological questions from the history of colonialism and slavery. He identifies this double break in the Western environmental tradition and in the anticolonial/antislavery traditions. The former focuses on environmental destruction, but cannot connect it with colonialism, land expropriation, and racial slavery. The latter neglects environmental issues in the fight against colonialism and slavery. Ferdinand's approach is an attempt to incorporate anticolonial and abolitionist genealogies in order to connect and synthesize movements and traditions that fight against the destruction of the environment. In this way, the book addresses the "apolitical" environmental protection of the global North, which rarely considers the empire, questions of colonial and neocolonial value transfer, and the white supremacy on a global scale. Ferdinand calls for a revival of anticolonial and antiracist internationalism and world shaping in the fight against climate change.

What I would like to underline is that the permacultural institution is *not* an art institution that focuses on environmental issues.

9 (Source: WACOSS, Western Australia Council of Social Services) and (Source: Social Life, a UK based social enterprise specializing in place based innovation) https://www.adecesg.com/resources/faq/what-is-social-sustainability/.

The permacultural aspect refers primarily to the way the institution operates, not to the topics it pursues. Permacultural institutions are not institutions that only show activist art or pursue political themes (!).

What is definitely characteristic for my proposal is that it puts equal importance to what is happening within the program of the institution and what is happening "behind the scenes"—in the structure of the institution itself. As my colleagues put it in their code of practice of a feminist art institution: "The ethics of its own internal operations are as important to a feminist art institution as the program by which it presents itself to the public."[10]

Below you will find a sketch of aspects that are important in the work of a permacultural institution. It is by no means comprehensive or complete. I'm fully aware that they are not uncontroversial and definitely deserve a separate debate and text. My main goal here is to provide some kind of vision, an outline, a proposal that can be considered by the others. For better understanding, I added a few examples from the work of the CCA Temporary Gallery and the Islands of Kinship project.

10 http://feministinstitution.org/code-of-practice/ Importantly, the concept of feminist art institution is also developed by Elke Krasny, for example in her book *Das moderne Museum als Anthropozän-Institution. Für feministisches Kuratieren im Zeitalter des Massensterbens* (Kunstpädagogische Positionen 57, 2022).

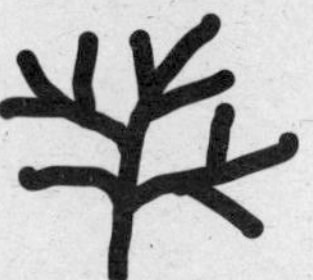

Permacultural Institution Is:

HYBRID

It combines art with a social approach. Sophisticated exhibitions are presented next to community art projects or socially engaged art practices. Moreover, the sophistication does not exclude a consistent effort towards mediating the content to various groups of people. The education department is not separated from the curatorial one, which means that the educators are involved in the curatorial process from the very beginning and can create mediation strategies adequate to the particular exhibition, going beyond standard mediation tools like simple guided tours and workshops.[11] Diversity coordinators are members of curatorial teams from the very beginning, taking care of making the program accessible (our Islands of Kinship project taught us that this is the best solution). The roles within the institution are flexible and so are divisions between the departments: educators can sometimes come up with curatorial ideas, curators can develop interesting mediation ideas. PR and promotion might be playgrounds for curatorial/artistic ideas.

A permacultural institution remains flexible in terms of responding to the needs of its changing environment. In this aspect, it resembles a community center. It sees art and artists as members of a larger societal mechanism, always in relation and dialogue with it. It is aware that the times of multiple crises require from us more resilience, and creating resilience can also be one of the institutional goals. For several years, CCA Temporary Gallery has run a group whose goal is to combat the alienation of cultural workers. The group became a space to share anxieties, ups and downs. It is led by Dr. Daniel Meyer and revolves around learning "narrative exposure therapy,"

11 This reminds me how many years ago when I worked at the CCA Bunkier Sztuki in Kraków, we convinced our director Piotr Cypryański to merge the curatorial and educational departments. This resulted in many unique mediation projects, like games in the exhibition spaces or special activity boxes for children visiting the exhibition.

"an empirically based, brief intervention designed to help individuals navigating the fallout of traumatic experiences and chronic stressors."[12] Until now, the group was relatively hidden, yet we are planning to publish accounts from our meetings and provide assistance to institutions that would like to organize similar gatherings.

(TRANS)LOCAL

It builds up a web of local, national, and international connections. Here I would like to stress the importance of local rooting or "grounding" strategies, thanks to which the institution responds to the local context and the needs of the local community and brings this community into relation with the national and international ones. The crucial question in this context would be: how can the institution become a better neighbor? At the CCA Temporary Gallery, Paula Erstmann and Lisa Klosterkötter initiated a mobile kitchen project in the course of which they collaborate with different actors in our neighborhood and organize cooking sessions in public space.

An important aspect here is also the idea of solidarity and sharing resources with institutions in the Global South, responding to the existence of "climate debt." This can result in long term collaborations with actors from the Global South. My institution initiated for example a long-term collaboration with the curatorial collective Sour Grass from Barbados. The collective participated in our summer seminar in 2022, then came for a residency to Cologne in 2023, and this year curates a solo exhibition of Alberta Whittle in our space. We hope that in the future, they will also collaborate with other institutions from our city or region.

DEMOCRATIC

It disperses and decentralizes the notion of curatorial authority. Here different levels of radicalization are possible, some are compatible with existing organizational structures within art institutions,

12 https://www.cologne-counseling.com/

some are more demanding (among the latter ones, we can recall the sociocratic model that involves consent- based decision-making processes).[13] What I would like to try out at the CCA Temporary Gallery in the next years is a partial democratization of the program: several working groups receive their own budgets, then each group decides autonomously what they will do. This organically ensues from the current situation of the institution as in fact, we already have several groups working with us: the mobile kitchen group, the narrative exposure therapy group, the community garden group.

COMMUNAL

In the Islands of Kinship gatherings, we often speak about not using the term "audience" but rather the term "community." "Audience" implies passivity, being subjected to targeting by marketing experts and instrumentalization. Striving to build a community around the institution means developing relation to people and engaging them in the work of the institution. It means cultivating different forms of conviviality and hospitality within the institution. At the CCA Temporary Gallery, I gave up organizing exclusive dinners for our artists after exhibition openings. Instead, we work with artists that cook—at each opening, we serve food for free to everyone that comes. This simple change introduced a very different atmosphere at our openings (and made them much longer). Unfortunately, most of the funding bodies in Germany do not cover expenses for hospitality.

DIVERSE

It strives towards having a diverse team in terms of identities and social classes involved as well as towards those those invited to construct and experience the program: collaborators and audiences. Since 2023, the CCA Temporary

13 https://thesociocracygroup.com/4-principles/

Gallery is running a residency program whose guests visit different institutions in Cologne that support artists with disabilities. Our goal is for these places to become normal places of curatorial research and enable artists working there to participate in the art system, not only through separate exhibitions of "outsider art." Apart from that, my colleague, Paloma Nana, initiated an educational program for young people whose access to contemporary art is not very good. Through different activities, sometimes in collaboration with schools, the participants learn more about art institutions, also as potential future work places.

WORKERS-ORIENTED

It actively supports the self-organization of workers, and if there isn't a body representing the workers at the institution, it initiates other structures that provide necessary internal feedback concerning the organization of work. It actively works towards the emancipation of its employees and an ongoing dialogue on improvement of working conditions. It seeks at least partial dehierarchization of work relations. An interest in contemporary management theories could be useful here, for example the ones by Frederic Laloux, who has spent several years developing the "teal organization" model, in which management is based on worker autonomy and peer relationships.[14] What we urgently need in the art system is surveys aimed at identifying problems encountered in the work of various types of workers—assistants (curatorial, artistic, gallery), directors, producers, and technical teams. These surveys should also include proposals for solutions.

SELF-REFLECTIVE

It actively supports self-organization of cultural workers and different forms of activism within the art system aiming at its critique and transformation. It remains autonomous in terms of its functioning,

14 https://www.reinventingorganizations.com/

keeping a distance towards the harmful routines of the art system. In the last years, the Temporary Gallery initiated a series of events presenting progressive practices related to different elements of the art system ("and only the birds fly first class...").

SLOW

Annalee Davis from Sour Grass collective is using the term "slow cultural work." I really like it and I think it expresses well what a permacultural institution does. It tries to avoid overproduction of exhibitions and events, develops long-term projects, and adapts the program to the capacities of its team. It is not afraid of repeating programs that made sense, actively opposing the capitalist ideology of the "new."

QUESTIONING THE WHITE CUBE

Although the usual white-cube presentation of contemporary art seems to be a neutral approach to exhibition design, a closer examination of its history (provided for example in the seminal text of Brian O'Doherty *Inside the White Cube*) proves that this structure is far from neutral. Appearing in a certain historical context of modernism and embodying its ideology, this type of exhibition space wants to isolate itself from the external world. It is a space in which time is suspended in an effort of achieving total cleanliness, perfection, and purity. I would even say that it is an unhuman or nonhuman space, as to be human means to be imperfect, physiological, and random. The only materiality that is allowed here is the materiality of the artwork exhibited within the space. The traditional space of the white cube is also a space of control. It starts with the effort of painting the walls white in a perfect way and culminates in the effort of cleaning the exhibition after the process of installing the artworks. The walls have to be absolutely white and no dust is allowed. The exhibition design with its rigid simplicity resembles minimalist sculptures and minimalist interior design in general. We have to finally admit that it is an aesthetic of a certain social class. (Probably the one that can afford buying Macs in Mac stores). The flow of visitors is to be controlled (in time of Covid-19 even more than usual) and their path has to be determined (even if it's determined as an "open structure"). Moreover, the visitors themselves have to control their own behavior. The exhibition guards (very often forced to stand for many hours in order to protect the artworks) together with security cameras are like an embodied panopticon, you are never sure when you are being observed or not (so better behave!). Is it hospitable? No. As a visitor, you often feel like you are not in the right place. Your shoes are dirty and you leave traces on the perfectly polished floors. The seats are scarce as they "contaminate" the visual appearance of the space. You are not wanted and you are made aware of it.[15] Questioning this would mean many things: to ease the control, to create a space that is friendly, to make seats comfortable to different kinds of audiences, in general: to experiment with exhibition designs.

In the course of my curatorial practice, I started to treat the exhibition design as equally important to the artworks that are presented within it. Together with my long-term collaborator—sculptor, collector, and exhibition designer—Mateusz Okoński, we developed exhibitions in which the design actively contributed to the exhibition's content, created a hospitable and audience-friendly atmosphere, and highlighted features of artworks that would be less accessible in the traditional white-cube environment—after all, the white cube appeared not by itself but by means of emergence of a certain type of art (O'Doherty gave the example of Frank Stella's works). Such exhibitions as *Heart of an Old Crocodile Exploding Over a Small Town* (CCA Temporary Gallery, 2019), *Floraphilia. Plants as Archives* (Academy of the Arts of the World, 2018), *Floraphilia. Revolution of Plants* (Warsaw Biennale, 2019, Temporary Gallery, 2020), *Alicja Rogalska. From Ground to Horizon* (CCA Temporary Gallery, 2021—2022),

15 Astonishingly, I heard from a British curator that what visitors leave in exhibition spaces, and what is collected by a cleaning team are, watch out, pieces of human skin! So the visitors are literally making the exhibition space more human.

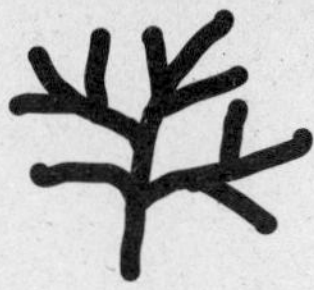

Ines Doujak. Every courageous life is a song to the future (2023) successfully questioned the logic of the white cube.[16]

ACCESSIBLE

It creates and follows protocols enabling it to become more accessible for people with different needs (people with disabilities, people of different ages, parents, children). If possible, it employs an accessibility coordinator who works closely with the curatorial team.

ENVIRONMENTALLY FRIENDLY

It applies as many rules of environmental sustainability as possible. Here we already have plenty of guidelines and manuals specifying what exactly can be done. To widen our perspective, we can also use the twelve principles of permaculture.[17] What is particularly important is to apply the environmental thinking to different levels of work: not only to production of exhibitions and events but also, for example, to curatorial lifestyles (which are still very much based on extensive international mobility involving long-distance flights) and different program elements, for example rethinking residency program or biennales (for instance, could biennales be more accessible online for the ones that want to avoid flying?). An interesting question arises whether art institutions could take on a more active role in taking care of nature around them—becoming its guardians, initiating gardens. What happens to an institution when its employees together with the community around it start to take care of a garden?

16 In this context, I would also like to mention two other exhibitions where an extraordinary design was created by other people than Okoński: *Cooking as Performance* (cocurated with Agustina Andreoletti) with design by artist Daniel Basso and *Blue Binding Ribbon* (cocurated with Lisa Klosterkötter) with design by stage designer Jakob Engel. The documentation of all exhibitions mentioned in this section is accessible on the website of the CCA Temporary Gallery (https://www.temporarygallery.org/en/archive/exhibitions/).

17 https://permacultureprinciples.com/permaculture-principles/

The Mycelium Movement

In the text above, I focused on a singular institutional unit but it is obvious that—if we aim to challenge the existing system and push it into another direction—we have to rethink all other elements of it: art funding, art academies, art residencies, art prizes, stipends, curatorial studies. All these elements constantly condition and influence one another, so changing one of them will never be enough. For example, if our institutions work differently, then we need curatorial studies to change in order to educate future staff in a matching way, and also we need artists that understand the way we work. How can we proceed in this ambitious endeavor to reimagine all elements of the art system?

Let me start with an organizational framework within which these thoughts crystallized: Islands of Kinship is a temporary project funded by Creative Europe program. It connects several institutions that want to work differently and that in the course of the project tried out different solutions related to the issues of sustainability and inclusion. For the ideas formulated in this text to spread, gain significance, and grow, however, they cannot be contained within a network of an institution, they have to form a base of a movement. This movement would apply permacultural thinking to other elements of the art field and bring us towards a different form of the art system, beyond the neoliberal one we experience now.

The Mycelium is an international movement of individuals and cultural organizations who share these values and are taking steps towards a different art system. We call it a Mycelium, taking inspiration from the root-like structure of a fungus consisting of a mass of branching, thread-like elements. Mycelium symbolizes the notions of interconnectedness, symbiotic communication, grassroots and organic forms of organization and strength. It is an underground network (after all, many progressive ideas had to develop first without much visibility) that, however, from time to time generates a beautiful outcome—like a mushroom—an institution, an event, an art project. It is a web of connections without any clear center, respectful to a great variety of nuances dependent on particular contexts in which art practices take place, rather than any "universal" values and measures.

The Mycelium as a social movement in the domain of the art system challenges the traditional, modernist model of an art institution as an entity separated from social and political struggles. In our mind, this model is no longer relevant in times of multiple crises and has to be questioned and reshaped. An art institution of the future is a hybrid between a vehicle of presentation and dissemination of art and a community center, attuned to the needs of various communities that use it, including its direct neighborhood. It is much more diverse, inclusive, and democratic than the art institutions we have known so far. It is driven by a deep understanding of the social tissue of the society within which it operates and takes an active role in making this tissue stronger and more resistant. This also means taking into account various class divisions that the contemporary art system thrives on and consciously fighting for more equal access to experience and production of contemporary art. An underlying intention here is to ensure a variety of perspectives in the field of artistic production so that it reflects the whole society and not only its most privileged parts.

Karina Kottová

Cyclical Curating

Manual #7

I am fascinated by communities that can align their life rhythm with the changing seasons and natural cycles, which means, in the geographic conditions of Central Europe, prepare everything at the beginning of the year, sow in the spring, farm in the summer, harvest and process in the fall, and get some rest in the winter to recharge for the next round. In theory, the Czech art scene could also work like that, yet its cycles are completely different: grueling grant reports at the beginning of the year, then maybe a little break, but no later than spring, once the funds from the ministry or city hit the account, comes the marathon of exhibitions, events, and projects, peaking before the summer. In June, everyone wants to open one more exhibition, art schools present end-of-term and final art projects, we are busy meeting tasks and visiting events, but the weather's nice and the bustle still quite joyful. In the summer, we used to take a breather, but in the past years, it felt shorter and shorter—with the big events of the fall getting into the groove, preparations already disrupting the out-of-office mode, texts needing to be written, as it seems that there would finally be time for that (which in fact there never will). In late August, a new exhibition is often already being installed. Then, the fall is the new June. One festival follows another, all institutions and independent spaces present their main projects, to which they are mostly forced by the grant calendar (yes, most of us have prepared exhibitions that were opened before the grant results were even announced, thus without the certainty of funding). Also, fall is usually the time for another round of grant proposals for the next year. The light and energy are waning, but work is not. Those who can get all done before Christmas without dragging it into the holidays are heroes of the year. I think that many of my friends working outside the art field see my job as sitting around coffee shops, having long conversations with artists, and hanging up the occasional painting. In reality, it often feels like a marathon with a paralyzing amount of multitasking.

The concept of slow curating has been discussed for some time in the international context, and it has also entered the Czech scene. However, so far rather theoretically. With the team of Jindřich Chalupecký Society, even before the launch of Islands of Kinship, we were part of the collective of Feminist (Art) Institutions which seeks the fulfillment of a collectively formulated code. The code focuses on the ethics of art institutions *both* internally and externally, the feminist approach to work, the need of institutions to be self-critical, inclusive, fair, and open-minded. However, if I was to be truly self-critical, I would have to admit that we at the Society are doing a much better job of meeting the code in all other respects but taking care of ourselves, which definitely involves the current need to slow down. I will guess that my colleagues working in other institutions who have subscribed to the code feel the same way. The word care has been thrown around so much lately that it's getting kind of empty. Yet it is still not clear what it really means in the changing art scene, who is taking care of whom or what, and under what circumstances. As we know, the very term of curating comes from the Latin *curare*, which means to take care of someone or something. In the original context of museums, it primarily related to caring for collections and the collected objects. In contemporary art, care is shifting to the interpersonal level, and curating largely means taking care of the collaborating artists and creating optimal conditions for their work. The curator should be a good dialogue partner, sometimes even a cocreator, yet it is often her who is responsible if there isn't sufficient support for the exhibition or artwork creation, and enough assurance of the comfort of the artist, in material, psychological, intellectual, ethical, and other terms. All that is swell and all, yet to maintain balance, there should be a similar amount of care for the curator (and her colleagues in production, promotion, and all other related professional roles). But from where shall it come? I'd guess that the curator spends a large chunk of her time at work, then at exhibitions, openings, lectures, and performances, which essentially also means at work, and then, probably as much as she can, with her family and friends, sometimes traveling (usually at least partly for work). Possibly all she can do with the little time off she can get is kill it on Instagram and Netflix. Can self-care then be reduced to the occasional bath, yoga lesson, or massage? It seems like a pretty small band-aid for the systemic imbalance. Rather than seeking cracks of time (and a little extra money) for some sort of instant wellness, we must strive to redefine this and similar jobs, so the pros outweigh the cons, and so it doesn't have to be exhausting to be considered meaningful.

I heard about supervision from one of my friends who works in the social sector many years ago. To her, it is a common thing. Since her job is emotionally, intellectually, and physically demanding, as she has to tackle the difficult life situations of her clients on a daily basis, trying to help them find new ways in their lives while working on structural changes, it is completely automatic for her and her team to consult their work with supervisors who are ready to address organizational as well as psychological issues. When we first wrote to a supervisor that we would like to hire him as the team of Jindřich Chalupecký Society, he probably took it as a slightly bizarre rarity and took us in his "care." For several years now, we have been going to supervision every six weeks, dealing with internal issues, telling things to each other that may not be nice to hear but shouldn't be swept under the rug, lamenting problematic collaborations, whether with individuals or institutions, and rethinking how to make our collective work more effective. Sometimes we come there to let out some steam and facilitate conflicts, sometimes to fine-tune and plan. They are things that wouldn't receive enough time or attention at our work meetings. While it is not a panacea for all woes, I think that this carefully moderated "time out" helped us pull a few skeletons out of the closet, resolve many practicalities, and get a better grip on a situation in which a group of closely knit people creates a professional art institution largely based on the principles of fair collaboration and collectivism. Especially for the more horizontally structured organizations like ours, it is (among other similarly oriented practices) a great tool to sort out some fluctuating competencies, to constantly redefine the position of each team member within the whole, to define shared goals, as well as to learn to say that I seriously cannot do all this right now, or that some of my colleagues really ticked me off.

While I'm immensely grateful for our supervision meetings, it clearly cannot be the only prevention of fatigue. After all, one of the most recurrent themes in our sessions is why we took on too much again this year, how come we have three major projects going on at once, with the team scattered all over the place, and submitting grant applications worth millions at the last minute. In the end, we don't even know who is to blame for all that. That brings me to the eternal dilemma—is the problem with the system that dictates the pace, or with us who shape the system? Exhausting ourselves with countless projects about (self)care, anxiety, healing, and unlearning a busy lifestyle in late capitalism is really a vicious circle. But how to get out of it? As I have written before, I find it important that the vocabulary of "critical" institutions adopts more positive terms such as "kind," or that these terms even fully replace the appeal for (self)criticism: critical institution → kind institution. This kindness must then, as with criticism, go not only outward, into the care for others (artists, viewers) but also inward. Not only curators but entire institutions can start putting their research topics into practice, initiating and experiencing the mantra of slowing down and healing. However, it still begs the question what can be done by a single institution, and what must be done collectively within a broader whole or network. I have to say that we at Jindřich Chalupecký Society do stand and strive for mutual care and kindness, it is not an empty concept for us. We can even treat ourselves to those instant forms of help like a sauna or a good dinner. But we cannot really slow down. Because of inertia? For fear that we'll get less money from the funders? That we can't sustain the current team, that our activities will be less visible? That we won't tickle our egos, that we won't be good enough?

One of our—and my personal—motivations for entering the collective of Feminist (Art) Institutions was the possibility of sharing. For ten years, Jindřich Chalupecký Society has been striving for a structural transformation of an institution that once organized an art award but has grown to become a curatorial and production platform supporting contemporary art in a much broader sense. With representatives of other like-minded institutions, we wanted to discuss the changes we were going through—how (un)successful we were with our transformation from a hierarchical organization to a horizontal one, how we came up with the idea of a different person running the meetings each week and ultimately failed to sustain it, how we managed our first collectively curated project and what we have (un)learned in the process. We wanted to listen to what other institutions are dealing with, hear each other out, and inspire each other. Unfortunately, with a few exceptions, that never really happened. As a kind of an uber-collective, bringing together several collectively minded organizations, the feminist institutions rather became a good communication and activist tool, but again mostly externally (sharing the code in local and international contexts, the Art for Climate initiative, the 10-women collective application for the post of General Director of National Gallery Prague, and more). I believe that through these avenues, we managed to open up a broader debate over various burning issues, and in many cases, we reached clear practical results. Yet we didn't slow down while doing it, but rather took on extra unpaid work.

The international Islands of Kinship project was born precisely out of this need for collective sharing and cocreating institutional practices focused on (both internal and external) sustainability and inclusivity. Merely the fact that the project has its own funding and thus a more clearly defined structure has allowed us to really focus on this exchange, embedding it as a fundamental pillar of the whole agenda. Thus, alongside the regular things that we do, like organizing exhibitions and art projects, it also left us more space for various transformational institutional experiments. However, even in this situation, it was not easy to take a slower and careful pace. Each of the participating institutions has a specific situation given by the sociopolitical climate and conditions for culture and art in their country, and each struggles with the constant justification of its own existence, the precarity of funding, and the related stress and exhaustion. While hugely helpful in our joint endeavors to fight this and set out new, livable, sustainable, meaningful, and joyful standards, a single EU grant simply won't save the day.

Art is often perceived as a rather individualistic field (compared to theater, film, music). In the Czech art scene, this is also obvious in the lack of a professional platform to defend the interests of visual arts in interdisciplinary discussions and strategies concerning the entire sector of culture and its position in society. To some extent, this agenda is advocated by the Skutek association, however, its reach and representation of various actors across the art scene is limited in comparison to similar organizations in other fields. Hopefully, the situation will improve with the emerging Cultural Federation, which will bring together individual fields instead of each trying to push their own agenda. Even the much-discussed turn towards collaboration and collectivism across more than just the local art scene has not changed the fact that as much as they often cheer each other on, or at least try not to compete too much, art institutions also don't particularly share or collaborate. Again, we can blame the system (we all apply for the same grants, and though we like each other, in the end we still fight for points and money), but that won't get us too far. While systemic change seems necessary and it is our mission to constantly try to achieve it, it probably won't come right away in the current conditions, and we must somehow survive until then. We can fight together for unconditional basic income (which sounds like another externally focused agenda for feminist institutions), but in the meantime, even without it, tired, vulnerable, yet still motivated by the unique charm of the art world, we shall try to bring to fruition our ideas about sets, networks, and octopuses, about supportive platforms that may eventually help us relax. Start with small changes for which we still have energy, and which may lead up to big shifts. However, without a deeper knowledge of the positions and needs of others, not only within our teams but also in our "neighboring" organizations, this will be hard to achieve. We need allies, naturally not only in the field of art institutions.

It may also be important to admit that curating, especially in the field of contemporary art, will never be really slow. It is too full of curiosity, the will to do something, to explore, create, share. A certain sense of incompletion, witnessing something that is only being born, being able to cocreate it, trying to describe and formulate it, and shift it further. It is linked to a desire to change the world around us, to become active, to face challenges, to fight with indifference. To inspire, to call for dialogue, to include, to engage ourselves and others. However, this list implies that to maintain a basic balance, we also need to listen, learn, look, get some good sleep, or also go to the park, eat ice cream, swim, play, go dancing. Say nothing, write nothing, and even think about nothing for a while. Not only from a feminist point of view, passivity is just as important as activity. So, if curating can't be slow, it could at least be cyclical. With the joys of ovulation and the depressions of PMS, hyperactive springs and long winters, and all those phases in between. Knowing that each phase of the cycle is important, each has its unique qualities, and that after a weekend (or week) spent in bed, with warm socks and a chocolate bar, we will again be happy to go out to the world and change it for the better. A motivational book about female cycles by British author Miranda Gray has been going around some circles for quite a few years now. Although it is unfortunately anchored more in the productivity logic of late capitalism, it aptly deals with the individual (and hugely different) phases of the menstrual cycle and their suitable connection to the dynamics of our own work and personal life. Simply said, it is better to speak at an exhibition opening when I'm in my expressive phase than in my bed week. At the beginning of the cycle, I will be better at logical tasks and the pace will be high, while at the end, I will be much more creative and slower. While this unfortunately can't be fully respected in today's society, the book advises that if we can learn more about our cycle and align it with our activities, our life and work will be easier. Obviously, not everyone in the art scene menstruates, but I believe that we all go through some cycles and phases. And again, this raises the question of individual cycles versus a more general rhythm that could be followed across the community. As known from various purely female collectives, women can perfectly (and completely unconsciously) align their cycles, and it would be interesting if art institutions could do the same, at least to some extent. If only no one called you on that bed weekend that you owe them a text. Could cyclically structured work be that exit from the wheel of productivity and exhaustion, and could we really align ourselves? Don't we already follow the grant cycles, and notice that spring has finally come after the long winter? Not only a collective slowdown but also collective cyclicality could work like a form of resistance to the vicious circles in which we may be spinning. It doesn't necessarily mean that there would be no exhibitions all winter because all the curators were asleep. For starters, we could agree on a shared month of gallery holidays and learn to recognize and respect our individual and institutional cycles to pull out other possibilities for synchronization. Perhaps they could also be aligned with the lunar calendar. Anyway, many curators already had to admit that they are actually a little bit (or quite a lot) witchy.

P.S. When reflecting on this text, I made a list of pros and cons of being a curator. It is based on the classic binaries of good—bad, active— passive, and so on. Nothing really comes out of it, as each pro has its con. Next time, I will try to make a cyclical list, as I believe it will be much less black-and-white.

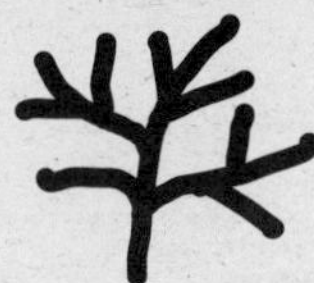

PRO	CON
Collaboration with artists	Collaboration with overly demanding artists
Collaboration with interesting institutions	Collaboration with dysfunctional institutions
Very social work	Too social work
Creative work	Constant administration
Writing texts	Writing grants
Research and conceptual work	Lack of time for research and conceptual work
Diversity	Uncertainty
Freedom	Precarity
Self-development	Self-exploitation
Opportunity for grants and scholarships	Projects tailored to grants and scholarships
Traveling and learning new things	FOMO, neurotic need not to miss out on anything
Activism and overlaps with other fields	Exhaustion and feeling like I do and know nothing properly
Sharing my work with the public	Inability to reach wider public
Creating autonomous systems and safe spaces	Inability to step out of my own bubble
Openings, events, and parties	Too much gossip
Connection across the art scene	Constant comparison and criticism (often behind one's back)
Satisfaction	Feeling not good enough
Enthusiasm	Permanent exhaustion
Summer	Winter

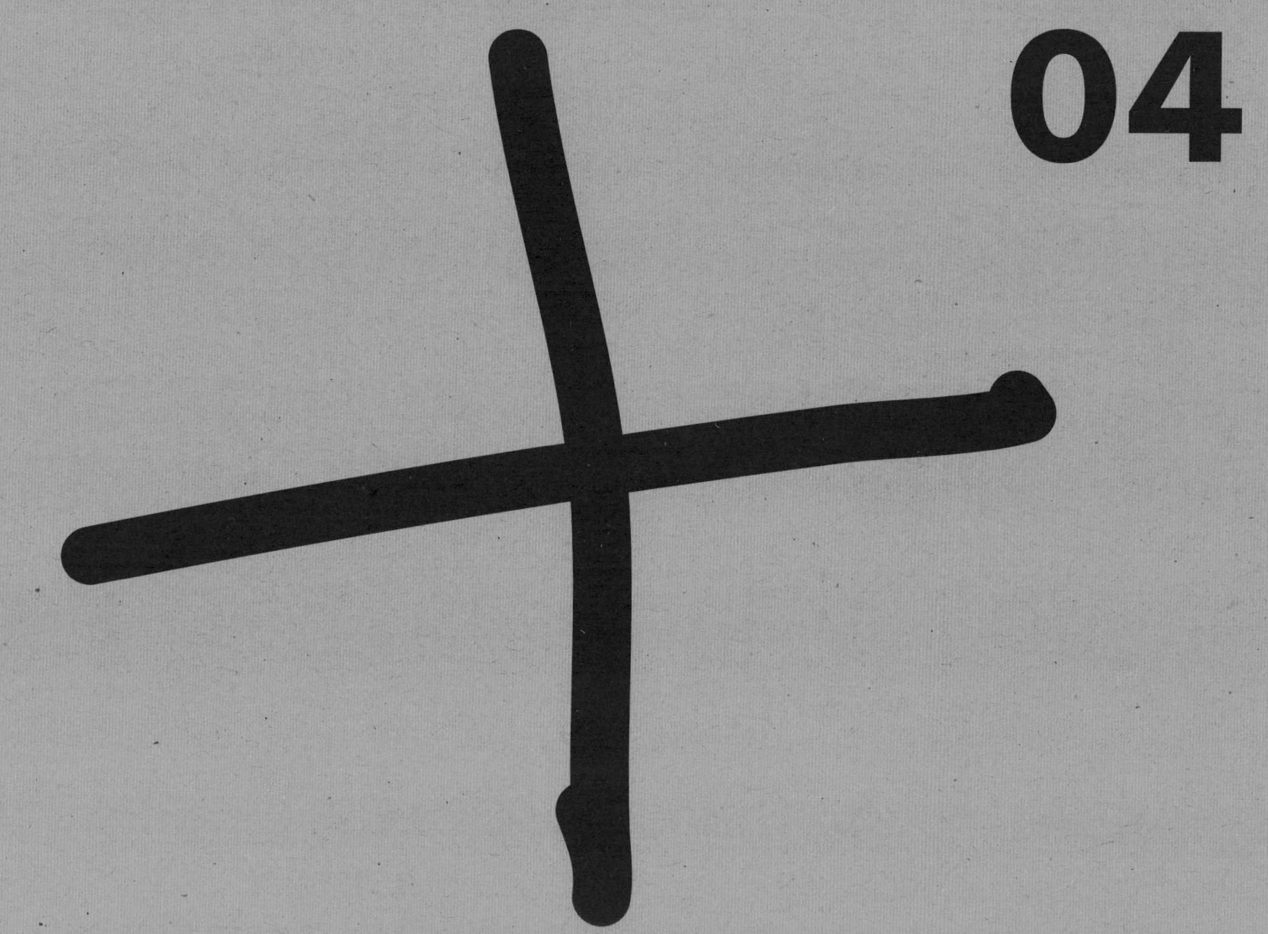

04

Inclusive (Curatorial) Strategies

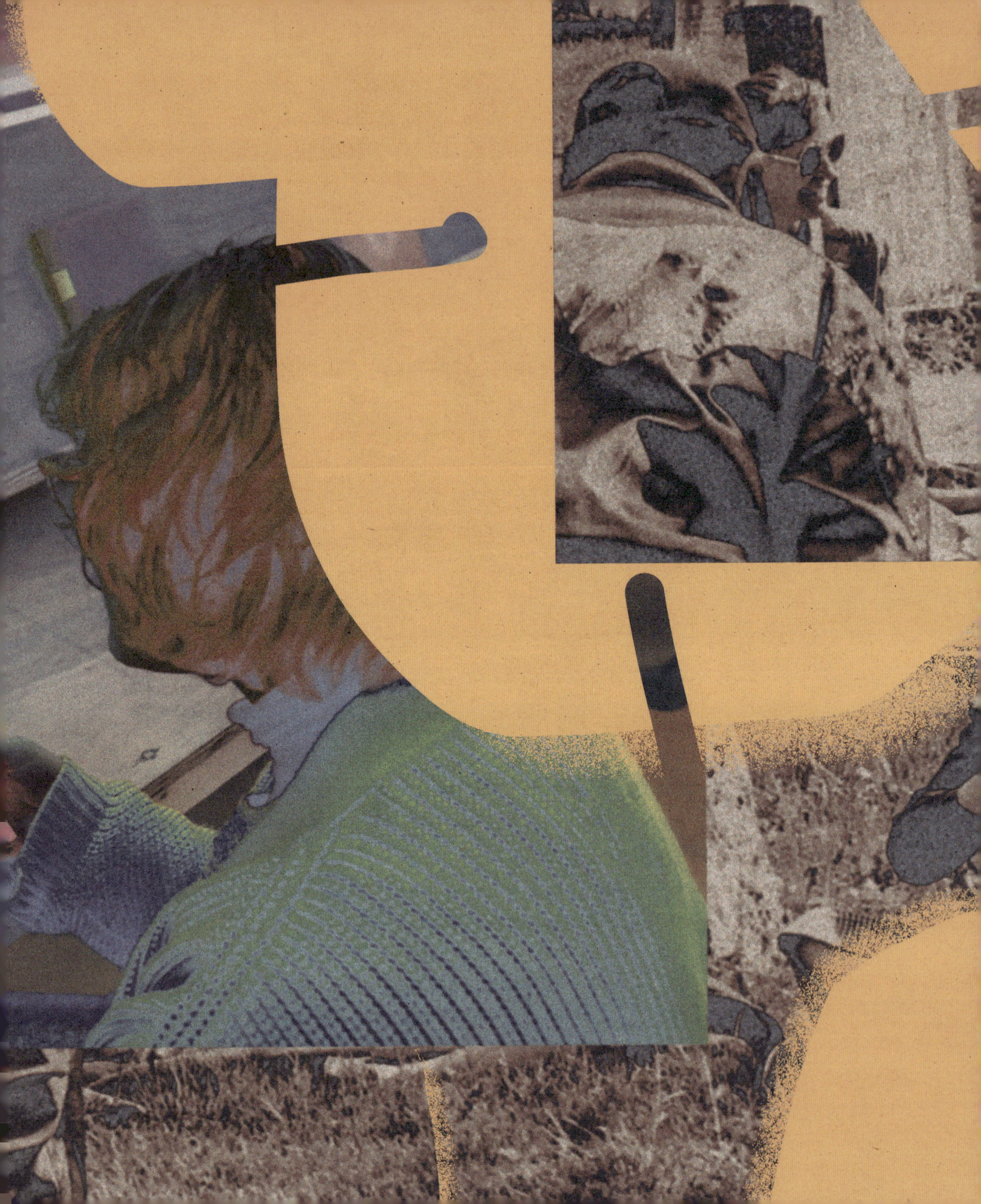

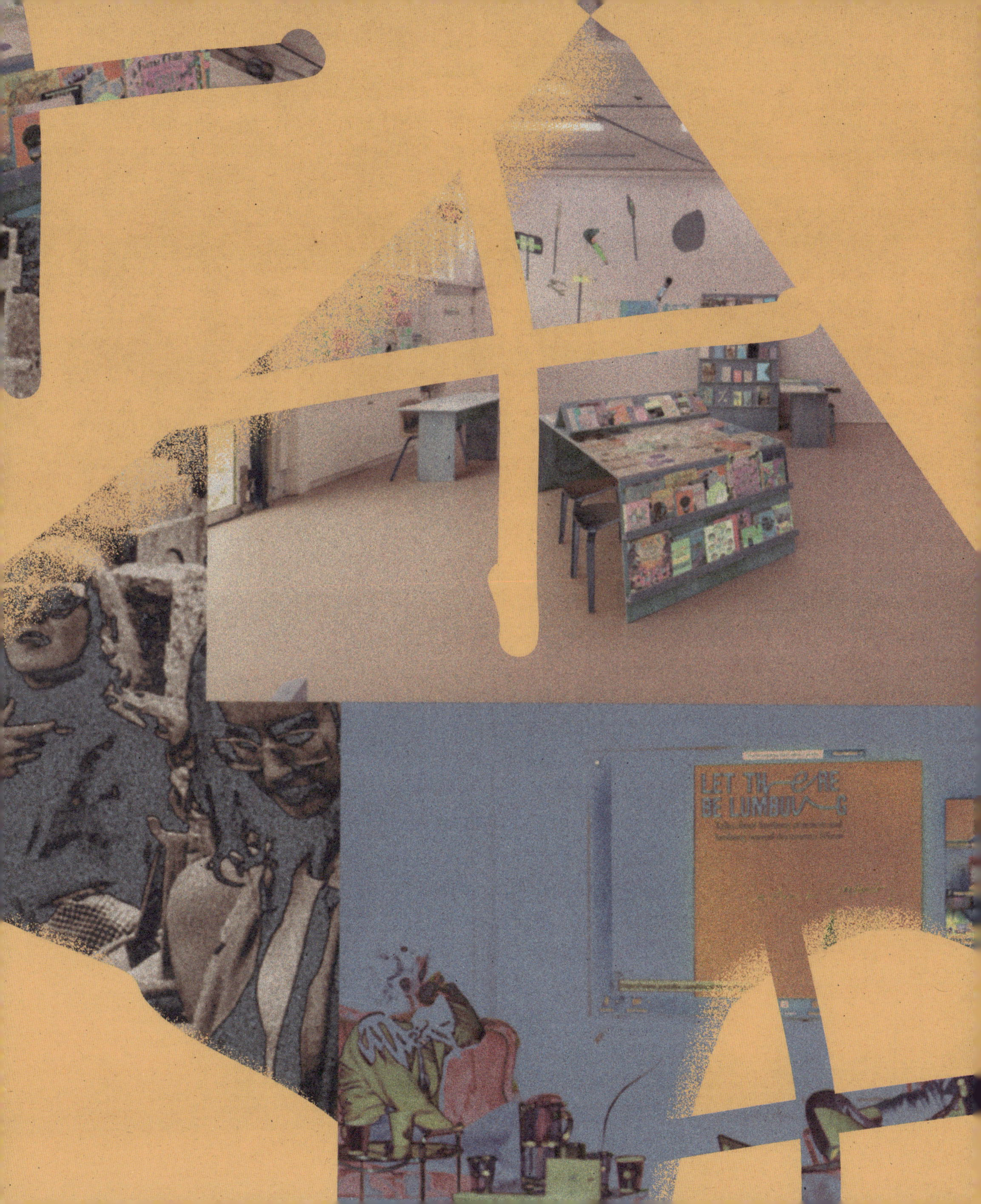

This thematic line is focused on learning and sharing direct strategies of inclusion with a strong intersectional accent. It addresses the questions of (re)distributing power, knowledge, visibility, and resources within contemporary curatorial and institutional practices. Its aim is to also gradually shift our perspective

beyond inclusion towards equality, equity, justice, and liberation. It focuses on experimentation in the development of tools increasing accessibility and care, be it in the realm of language, space, or programming itself.

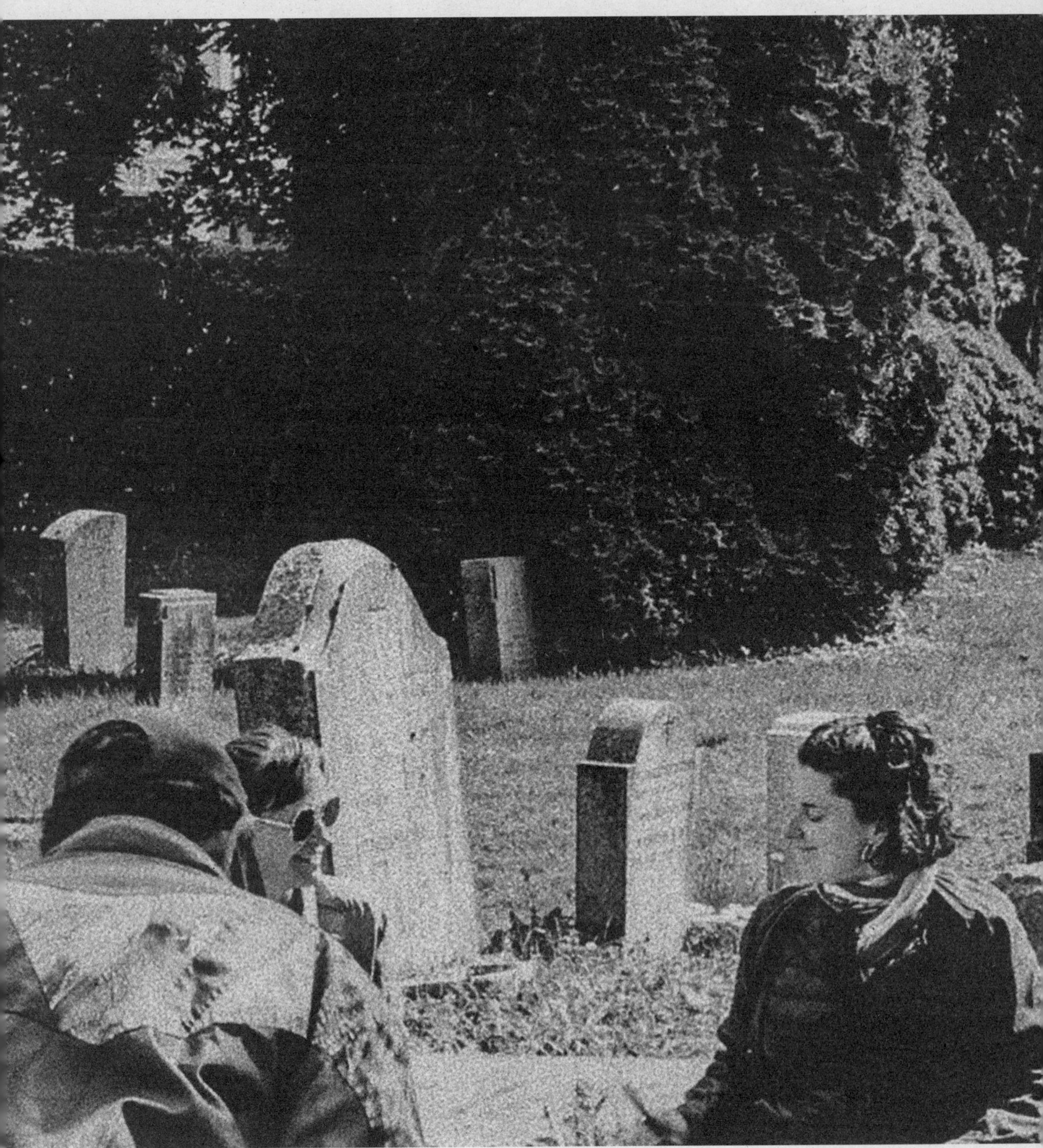

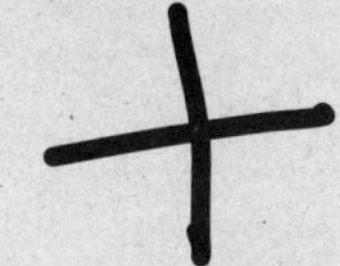

Jussi Koitela

Divisions and Expectations That Shape Inclusion

Inclusive is a term that is currently popping up in many places and situations when art institutions' activities are discussed and critiqued. It seems that it can be used in discussion to speak about many different kinds of injustice that the institution is involved with. It almost feels like an overcompassing solution to all the possible challenges and power-related troubles in the activities of art institutions. But if the institution is just inclusive to different marginalized forms of art, bodyminds, participation, and cultural backgrounds, is that enough for more socially and ecologically sustainable art organizations' practices or is there something else needed?

When speaking and thinking about inclusion, the immediate question is: inclusion of who and what and where? The field of contemporary art is full of various ways of managing institutions and organizations that serve versatile aims and motives. It is full of different kinds of power relations and networks where inclusion and exclusion are granted and obstructed, depending on their roles and mandates in the art field. For example, we expect different inclusive institutional practices from publicly funded art organizations and from commercial galleries. Many times, we also expect museums to represent larger groups of artistic practices than small art centers. Yet we don't tend to expect the inclusion of marginalized artist communities from commercial galleries.

Jessie Bullivant and Jemina Lindholm, Access Riders publication, 2021, published by Frame Contemporary Art Finland

Also, broader understandings of publicness, communication culture, and economic conditions dictate what is expected from art organizations and individuals. We might expect institutions to be inclusive similarly and universally for everybody while they must show off and tick boxes for audiences, stakeholders, and partners, but inclusion means different things for different individuals and groups. Similarly, institutions expect that activists and community groups develop inclusive practices, and bigger institutions should learn from them and bring their knowledge and better practices to the institution's context. In these exchanges, institutions easily expect one individual and/or activist to represent larger communities of people and offer them inclusive practices that work in all possible situations.

Another aspect that shapes the practices of inclusion is the division of inside and outside. Something that is, of course, elemental to the whole concept of inclusion. This dichotomy that almost automatically expects those assumed to be "inside" the institution to have privileges and automatically power and impact on the activities and practices of the institutions. On the other hand, this division into inside and outside hints that those who are not part of the institution's staff or shaping its activities don't have any agency whatsoever within the arts field. This is constantly repeated.

If we are looking at the factual and historical conditions of art institutions, such as their origin in ethnographic racism and the ongoing sexism and classism where people, objects, and entities are divided into something that is included and something that is excluded from the institution, it is, of course, a valid way to critique existing power structures. Still, in order to give space for new forms of agency to develop, there is a need to challenge the different dichotomies and differences that dictate the imaginaries of how relations between institutions, communities, and individuals are narrated. That helps to develop structures that allow forms of participation and inclusive spaces of art in broader society.

There need to be shared and decentralized ways of accountability and access. Sustainable, inclusive practices need to be collectively shaped and maintained, not only the work of communities of activists or institutions with a public mandate.

Inclusive Curation—Intersecting Struggles and Processes

Regarding everything mentioned above, what is inclusive curation? Who and what is being included, at what time, and how? Who is actually the one who includes who? Can curating and institutional work at art organizations create space and a breeding ground for collaborations and collective work that allow different forms of inclusion to emerge?

In the Islands of Kinship project, we tested and developed multiple forms of collaboration and practices of inclusion. We have worked with, for example, how to create accessible language within the art context, permaculture and institutions, ableism and neurodiversity in art institutions.

Frame's programming within the project built around the long-term Rehearsing Hospitalities public program, looking at politics of hospitality and collaboration. We connected artists, curators, and other practitioners in the field of contemporary art and beyond to build up and mediate new practices and engagements with diverse hospitalities. Rehearsing Hospitalities was a far-reaching collaborative process that nurtured the emergence of new practices and paradigms of political and cultural hospitality. We were trying to see hospitality and inclusion as an open-ended skill spreading among multiple social struggles that need to be constantly rehearsed.

During Autumn 2022 in Helsinki, week-long programming looked at how to redistribute resources and power in sustainable ways. The program highlighted institutional, curatorial, and artistic practices that go beyond offers of hospitality and transgress unbalanced forms of power distribution, such as those instilled in host and guest dynamics. Rather than simply working through "inclusion" and "invitation"—which often privileges the host—we were trying to imagine what decentralization and redistribution of institutions, land, and public life and the power they hold might do to support a more equal and just arts ecology. How might redistributing power and wealth remove some of the access barriers which block marginalized communities from participating in and (re)forming the fields of arts and culture?

Intro

In January 2023, the Editorial Tables—Reciprocal Hospitalities exhibition organized with The Showroom celebrated the production and dissemination of knowledge through the act of independent, experimental, and artist-led publishing, with a focus on intersecting feminist and decolonial perspectives. The project involves a range of publishing, archiving, print, and distribution practices by artists, curators, and art workers, bringing these into relation and dialogue in the lead-up to the realization of the exhibition. The exhibition space aims to open up new connections through live processes of encounter and exchange around the printed matter, where visitors can engage and think with the material in the space. The project challenged who is allowed and has resources to produce, disseminate, and archive knowledge.

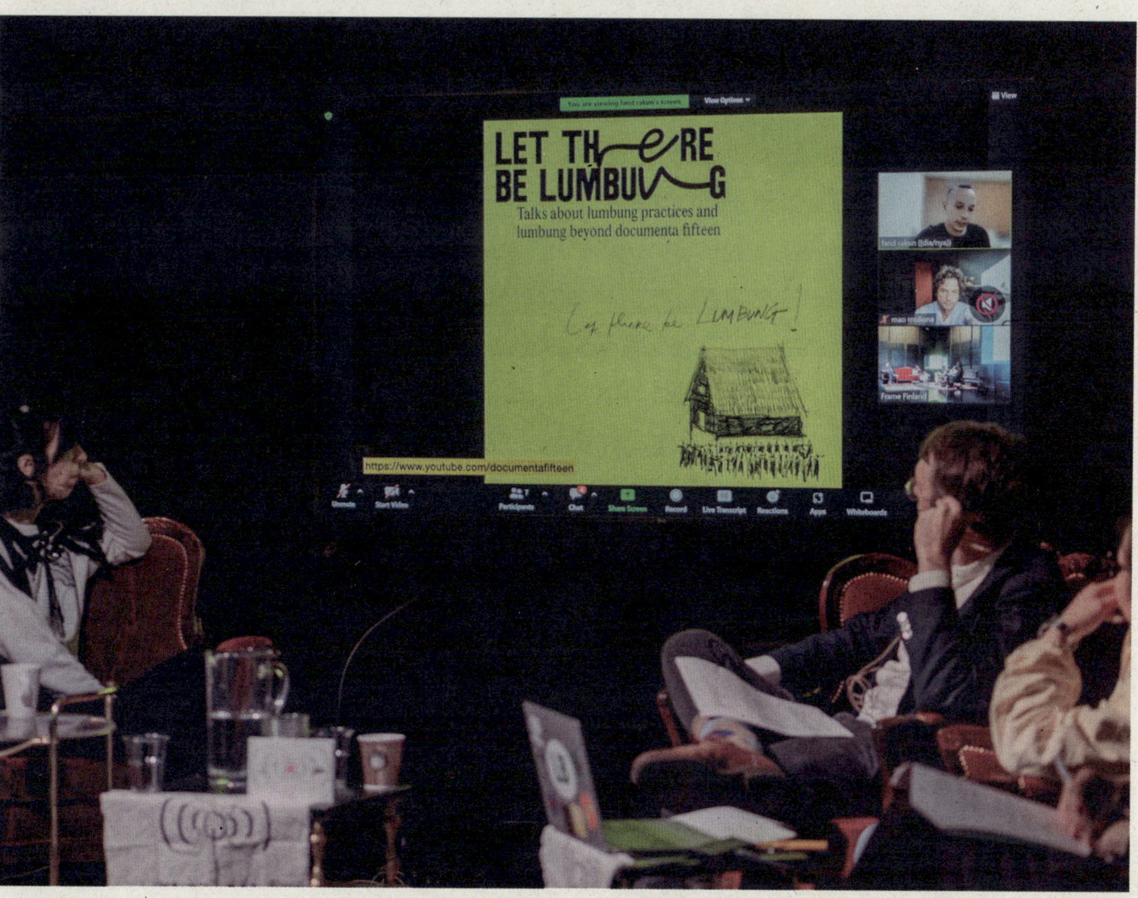

Gathering for Rehearsing Hospitality, Promise of Collectivity Session, 2022

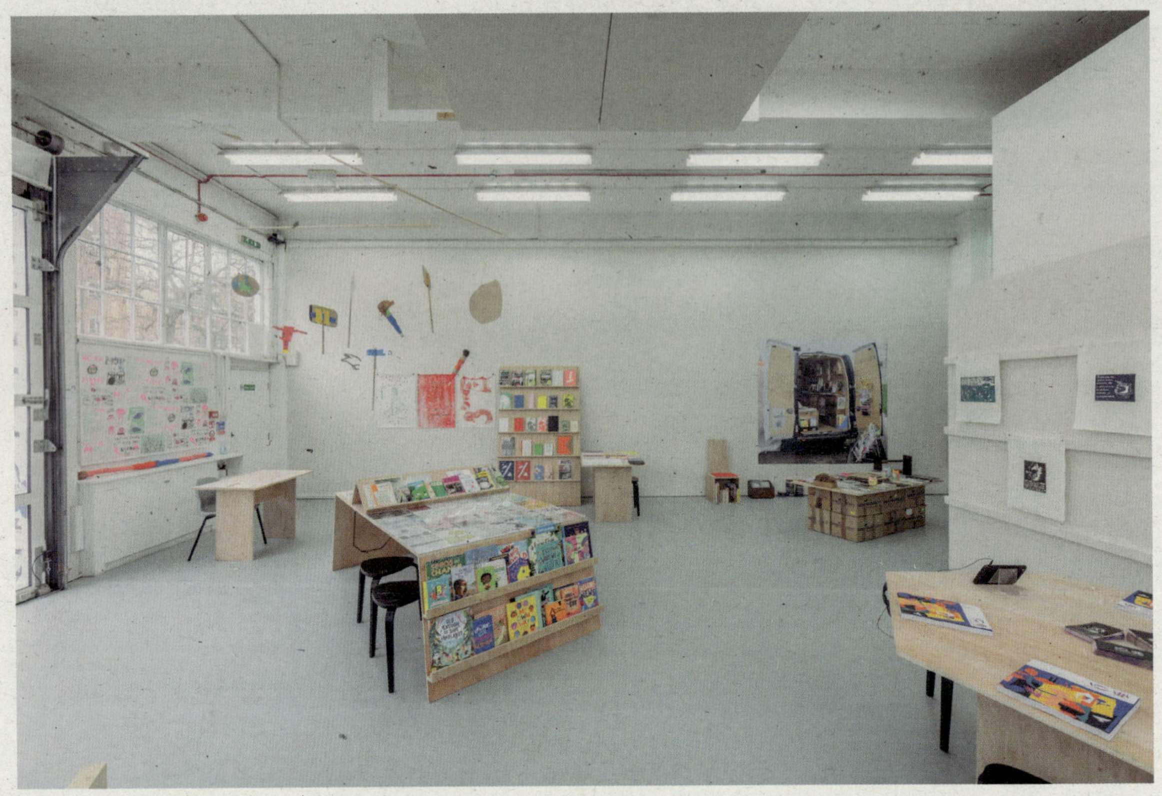

Editorial Tables—Reciprocal *Hospitalities—installation* view at The Showroom, 2023

Since the inception of Rehearsing Hospitalities, Indigenous perspectives on matters of hospitality and inclusion—and acknowledging the various forms of social, cultural, and political inhospitality that Sámi people experience—have been critical to the program and the dialogues it fosters. With Vera List Center for Art and Politics and the Finnish Culture Institute in New York, we organized the Conflicting Relations event in March 2023. The event was built around the work and research by artist Matti Aikio on the so-called "neo-Lapp movement" in Finland and settler-colonial attempts at claiming Indigenous identity. Taking into consideration Indigenous sovereignty and self-determination, Aikio looked past individual violations to question the structural and large-scale implications of this movement as a counterstrategy to the political mobilization of the Sámi. His practice considers the ongoing conflict between the Sámi culture and the Nordic nation-states' use of natural resources.

Intro

In the final part of the Rehearsing Hospitalities program in May 2023, we focused on consent, intimacy, and emotional labor as tools of inclusion in the art field in collaboration with the UKS (Young Artists Society) in Oslo. The exhibition *Moon in Your Mouth,* curated by Max Hannus, thought of consent in artist-curator relationships, asking how to think about consent as a methodological tool and how to host or mediate different agencies in relation to the presentation of artistic work. *Moon in Your Mouth* looked at processes of desire and intimacy in relation to questions of access.

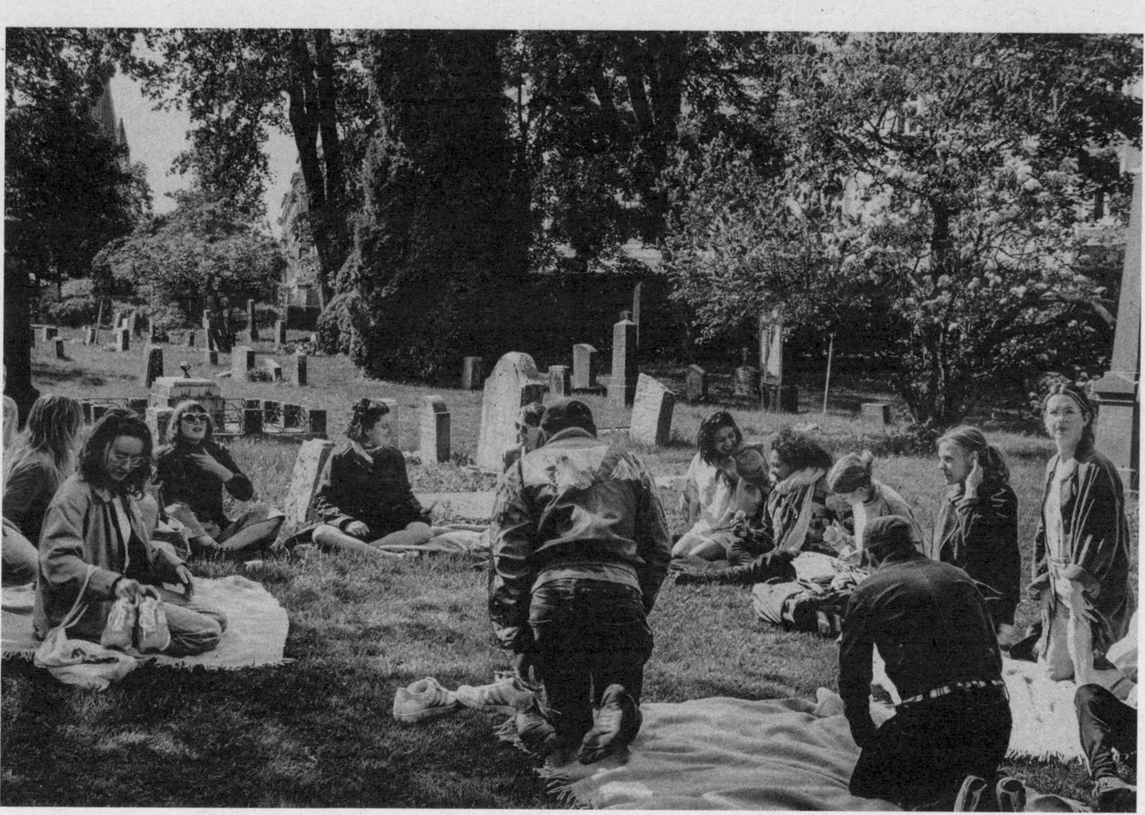

I CONSENT Summer School,
UKS (Young Artists Society), 2023

Parallel to the exhibition, we organized together with Bedside Productions *I CONSENT*, a three-day summer school in Oslo. Convening around consent, complaint, and intimacy, this multiday program offered a tender environment to explore alternative, safe, and loving ways of relating, particularly in the context of arts institutions and cultural production.

The curriculum is framed by a series of questions that softly guided the program and discussions without placing emphasis on arriving at direct answers:

How might we welcome structures, principles, and practices of consent within creative processes and working relationships? Can consent be instituted?

Can we embrace "complaint" as a generative and generous act? Can we understand complaint as a shared project?

If we think of intimacy as seeing and being seen, what is required for the "seeing" to take place? How does one access intimacy?

In October 2023, we gathered in Helsinki with the partners and participants from the local art scene to understand how climate, social, and transformative justices intersect and how art institutions can implement practices of justice in their daily operations and working models. Discussions and workshops dealt for example with unequal distribution of natural and economic resources in areas affected by the climate crisis, with the poor population being most vulnerable to its effects. When addressing our institutions' responsibilities and activities, we need to think of strategies that do not reinforce this imbalance. What is eco crispness and what could that offer for more sustainable cooperation? What does transformative justice mean for the community (specifically the arts)? How is transformative justice not only a tool for developing strategies to solve problems collectively through nonpunitive actions but also a call to recognize how inequality must be addressed intersectionally, including by fighting about emerging forms of discrimination, such as eco-ableism?

While trying to learn and unlearn from artists and activists and from other organizations and trying to turn these learnings into sustainable institutional practices, we have experienced how hard it is to collaborate from the beginning with different aims and mandates of the partners and their sociopolitical and cultural contexts. While there have been significant focuses, for example on inclusive languages and spatial conditions, and representation and participation of intersection of marginalized queer, racialized, and artists with disabilities—inclusive curating and institutional collaboration is also about understanding the effects of different broader sociopolitical, historical, economic, and cultural conditions in Europe and globally.

So inclusive curating operates among multiple intersecting processes which might be in conflict with each other but can also frequently form useful allies between struggles and political concerns that might not have so much in common with each other. Simultaneously, it needs to create conditions to work beyond harmful divisions of inside—outside, ecological justice—social justice, and center—periphery. In inclusion, we are all in together, but everyone can have different forms and levels of agency and effect. Acknowledging your situation and position from which you can contribute to the collective.

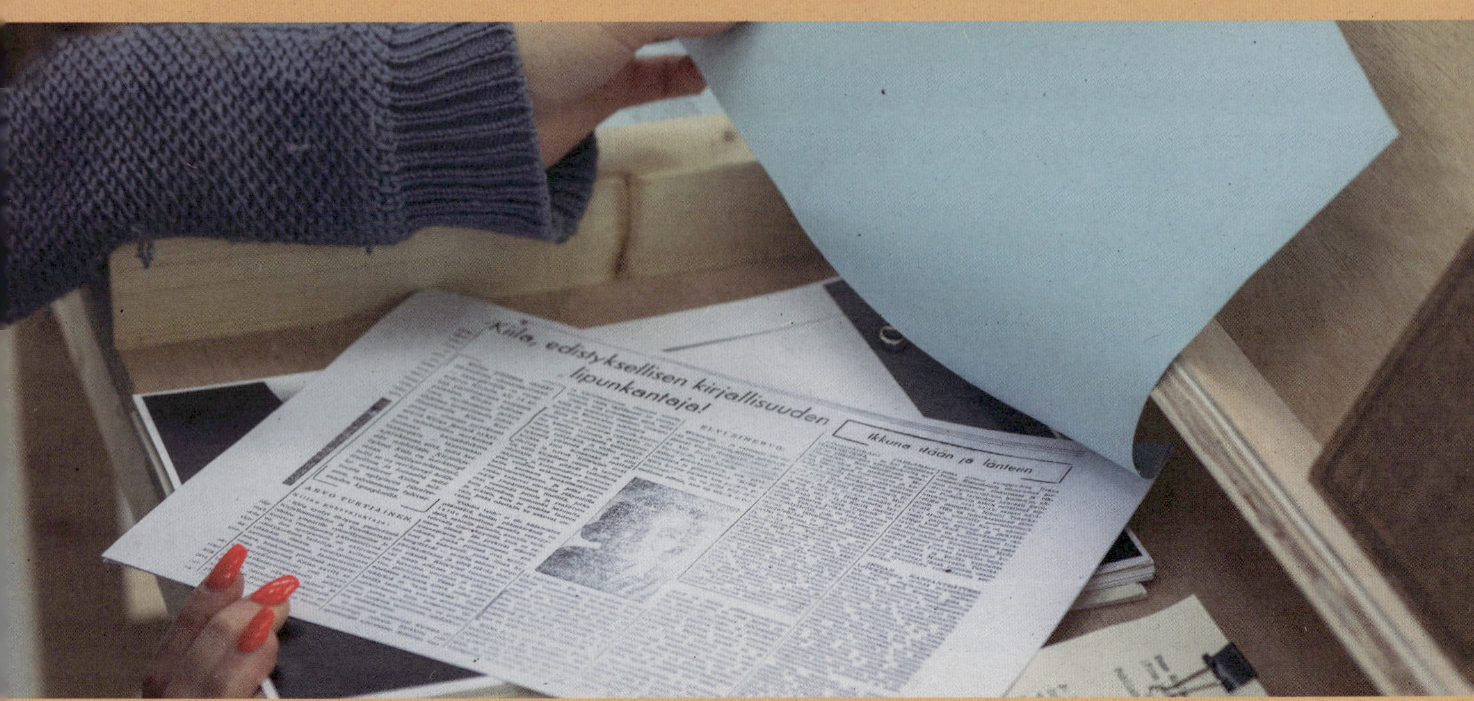

Minna Henriksson: The Kiila Feminist Archive

The Kiila Feminist Archive / The Wedge is an archive-as-artwork by artist Minna Henriksson. The work involves a long-term and ongoing process of research into the early years of the Kiila artists' and writers' association in Finland, which has been running for over eighty years.

A new version of the artwork was commissioned in the context of Frame Contemporary Art Finland's Rehearsing Hospitalities program and Islands of Kinship project. It was also part of Together Again, a program by the Finnish Cultural and Academic Institutes. It was presented in Editorial Tables: Reciprocal Hospitalities at The Showroom during spring 2023.

The Kiila Feminist Archive is compiled of materials which foreground intersecting feminist issues which were fundamental to the founding of Kiila, but which have since been obscured, lost, or edited out of its official histories. As an active current member of Kiila, Henriksson continues retracing, translating, and subjectively situating these feminist orientations through the fiction writing—novels, poems, and short stories—of the organization's founding female members.

National and global politics significantly influenced the course of Kiila. In 1935, they aligned with the First International Congress of Writers for the Defense of Culture, held in Paris as a reaction to the burning of books in Nazi Germany. At this time, Finland was politically far-right and laws had been put in place to effectively ban procommunist organizations or activities. It was also a time of increasing militarization, and it was clear early on that Finland would side with Nazi Germany in the forthcoming war. Founded in this heightened environment, Kiila was grounded in values of socialism, antifascism, and pacifism. During World War Two, forty percent of Kiila members were put into prison; deemed by the State as a preventive measure against the potential sabotage of the war effort.

Four out of seven founding members of Kiila were women: sisters Aira and Elvi Sinervo, Tyyne Maija Salminen, and Katri Vala. Many other female writers and critics were also active in the early years of the organization. After the Second World War, the history of Kiila was written by its notable male members but omitted the role of the women. For Henriksson, the aim of compiling this archive has been to observe the connections between socialist and feminist tendencies in the collective act of organizing between artists and cultural workers.

Henriksson's table presents a selection of books by writers Tyyne Maija Salminen, Elvi Sinervo, Iris Uurto, and Katri Vala, members of the Kiila association in the 1930s. Copies of memo documents from the Kiila archive and linocut prints illustrating Henriksson's translations from pages of the books are dispersed throughout the exhibition space.

**MINNA HENRIKSSON:
THE KIILA FEMINIST ARCHIVE /
THE WEDGE: ARCHIVE-AS-ARTWORK**

installation and linocuts
2023

The commission was presented as part of the exhibition and public program:

- **EDITORIAL TABLES: RECIPROCAL HOSPITALITIES, The Showroom, London, UK, January 25 – March 18, 2023, organized by Frame Contemporary Art Finland**

Commission #7

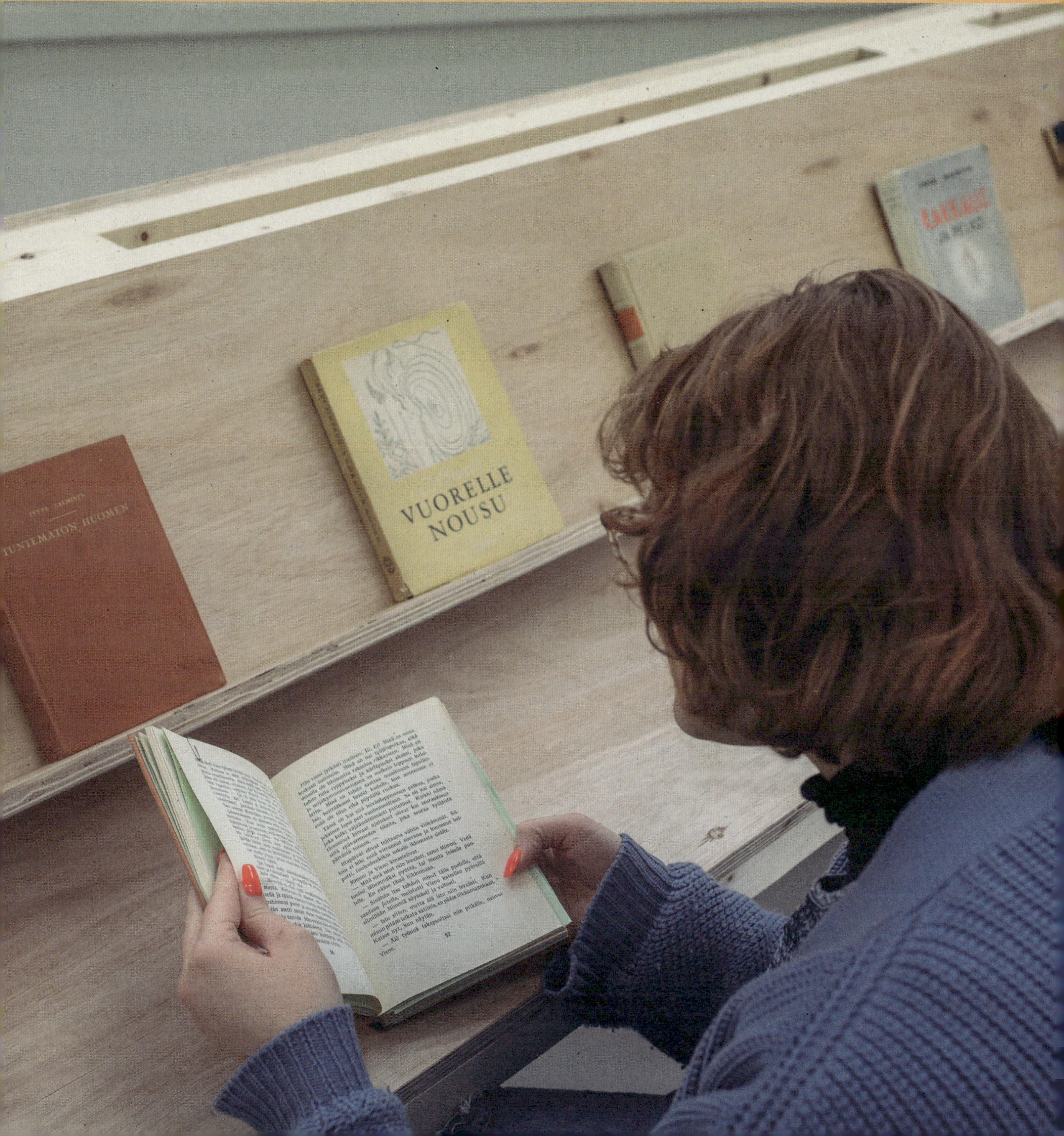

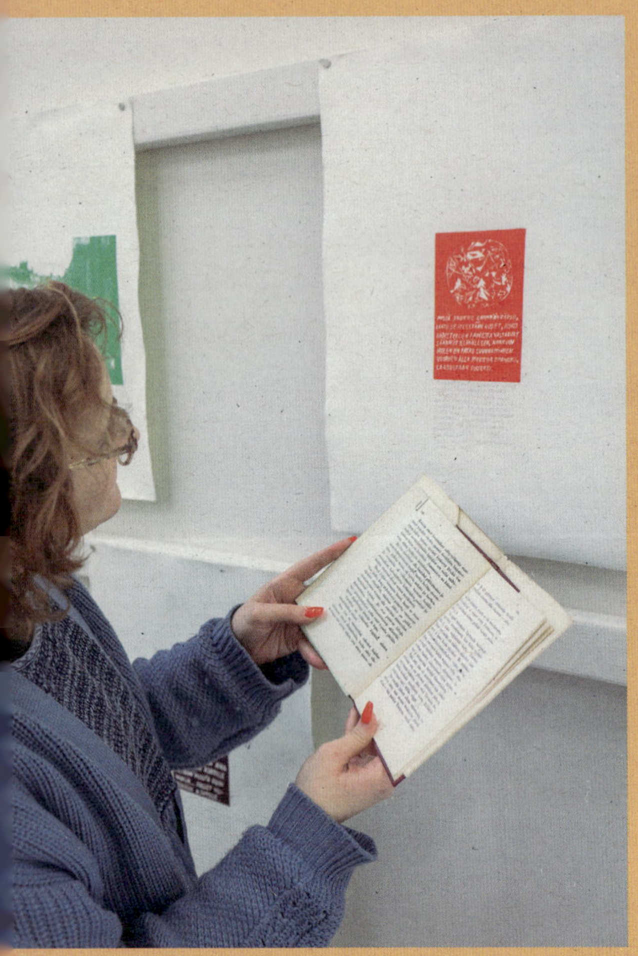

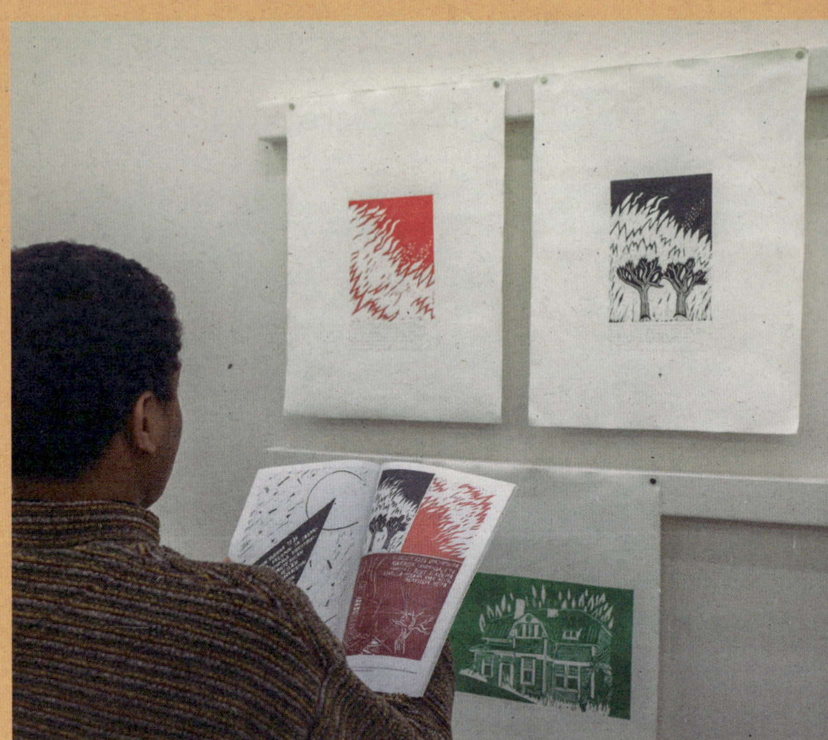

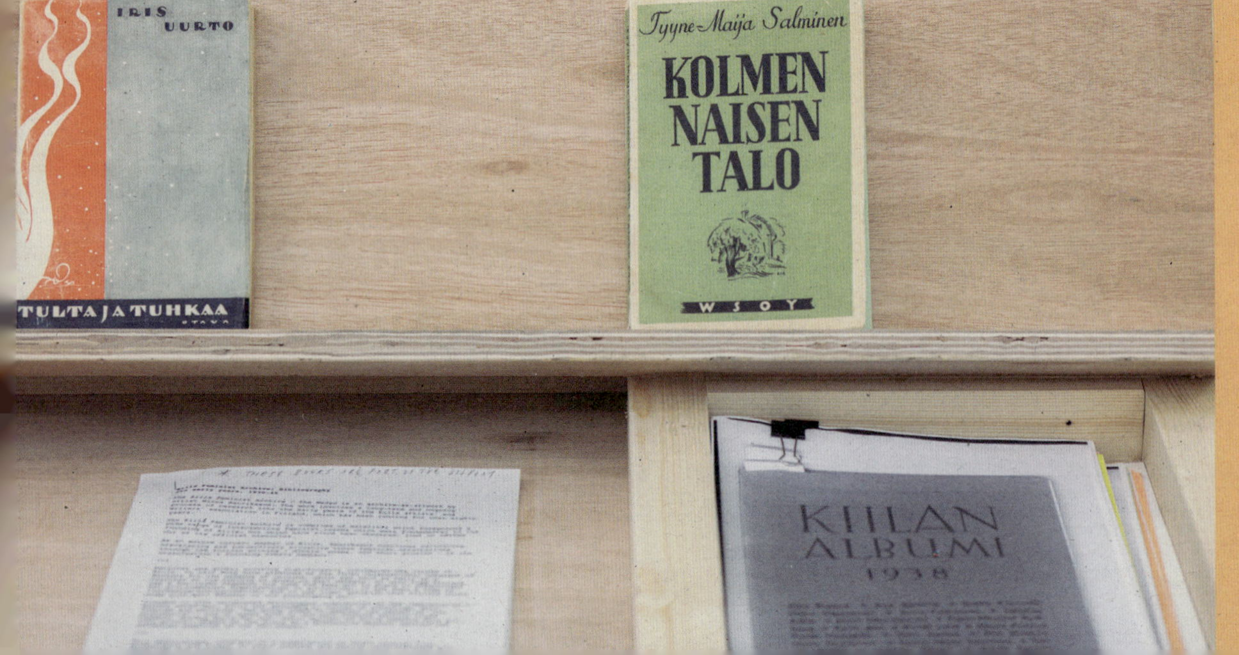
IRIS
UURTO
TULTA JA TUHKAA
Tyyne-Maija Salminen
KOLMEN
NAISEN
TALO
WSOY
KIILAN
ALBUMI
1938

Commission #7

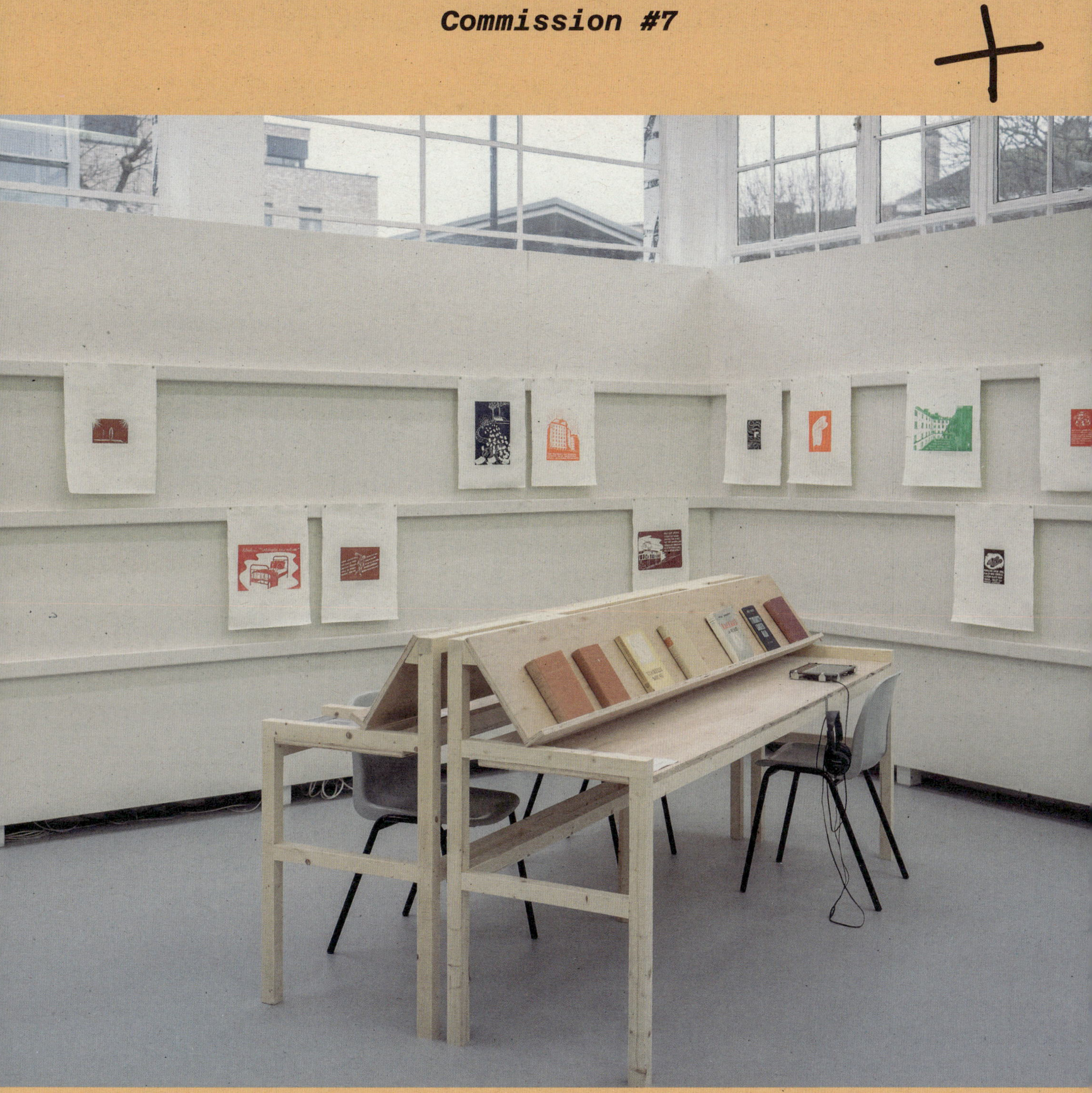

Blu Doppe, Agnieszka Habraschka, Gina Jeske, Rafia Shahnaz: Inclusivity and Awareness

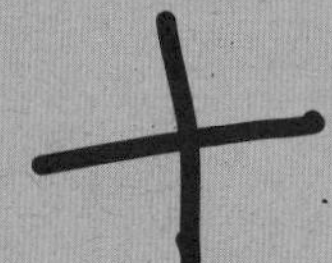

Workshop on Critical Whiteness and Privileges with Rafia Shahnaz
Wednesday, October 18, 2023, 5–8:30 p.m.

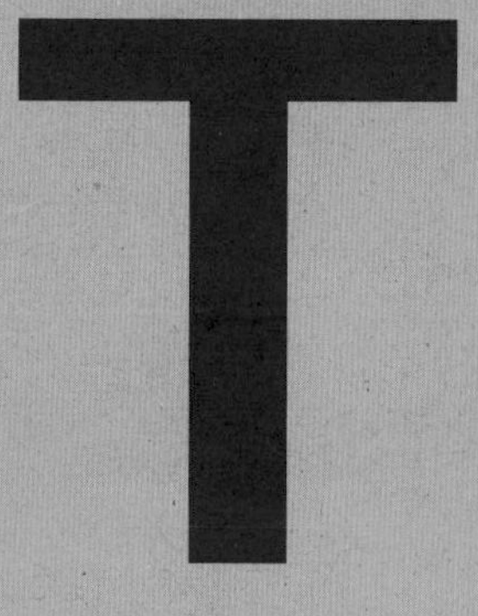

he workshop offered an introduction to the discussion of racism and whiteness. It provided a space to reflect on one's position as a white person in racist systems and what privileges are associated with it. The aim was to understand whiteness in an interactive way, to question systems of power, and to open up to a critical approach to racism. This workshop put a special focus on language as an instrument for reproducing white systems as well as on the strategies that we can develop to deconstruct this reproduction. How can we use language to include and expand the spectrum of life realities that function outside of a "white" mindset? The workshop was particularly aimed at people who want to actively position themselves against racism and are willing to recognize and deconstruct white dominance culture.

Rafia Shahnaz is a trainer and consultant with several years of experience focusing on topics such as intersectionality, critical whiteness, antiviolence and antidiscrimination, diversity and awareness oriented organizational development. They also facilitate empowerment spaces for communities facing structural discrimination in the form of racism, sexism, queerphobia, and classism.

Paloma Nana, Paulina Seyfried

Workshop on Antiableist Cultural Work with Agnieszka Habraschka and Gina Jeske
Tuesday, November 28, 2023, 4–7:30 p.m.

In the 3-hour workshop, we got an understanding of disability and ableism and learned why access is a human right as well as why it is a matter of mindset in the first place. We uncovered ableist norms, expectations, and stereotypes as well as the differences between integration and inclusion in order to create safe(r) and welcoming spaces for disabled people in our events, work culture, and program structure.

Agnieszka Habraschka is a production manager, consultant, and dramaturgist specializing in accessibility and antiableist cultural work/performance art and intersectional antidiscrimination. Agnieszka is neurodivergent, has invisible disabilities, and has experience of migration and poverty. Gina Jeske works in public relations for performance and dance, as audio describer, and as workshop leader for antiableist cultural work and accessibility in theater. Gina is white, hearing, and nondisabled. She understands her work as an ongoing learning process of how to make use of one's own privileges to reduce barriers and exclusions.

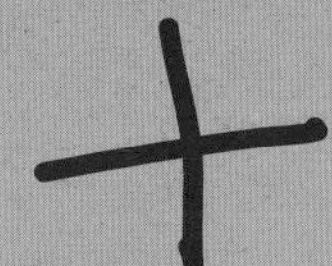

Workshop on Awareness with Blu Doppe
Wednesday, January 10, 2024,
5–8:30 p.m.

Recognizing Entanglements—A Workshop about Discriminations, Intersectionality, and Own Privileges

In this workshop, we wanted to deal with our own entanglements. To do so, we addressed the following questions: What are the different forms of discrimination and how do I benefit from them? How are different forms of discrimination intertwined? How can I deal with my own privileges and use them to make a better life possible for all? How can I make my institution more inclusive?

Blu Doppe has been a freelance trainer for 7 years and has gained knowledge autodidactically, in activist communities, and at university. Blu's own experiences also play a big role for their knowledge. Blu has a degree as social justice and radical diversity trainer, a degree as theater of the oppressed and Betzavta trainer, and is a sex educator. Blu regularly gains further qualifications around the topics of sexual, amorous, and gender diversity, sexuality, gender roles, and all other intersections. Blu also works for Dissens—Institut für Bildung und Forschung e.V.

INCLUSIVITY AND AWARENESS

online workshop #1

Critical Whiteness and Privileges

with Rafia Shahnaz

Wed, October 18th, 5—8:30 p.m.

INCLUSIVITY AND AWARENESS

online workshop #2

Anti-ableist Cultural Work

with Agnieszka Habraschka & Gina Jeske

Tue, November 28th, 4—7:30 p.m.

BLU DOPPE, AGNIESZKA HABRASCHKA, GINA JESKE, RAFIA SHAHNAZ: INCLUSIVITY AWARENESS

- CRITICAL WHITENESS AND PRIVILEGES with Rafia SHAHNAZ October 18, 2023, 5 – 8:30 p.m.
- ANTI-ABLEIST CULTURAL WORK November 28, 2023, 4 – 7:30 p.m.
- AWARENESS by BLU DOPPE January 10, 2024, 5 – 8:30 p.m.

online workshops 2023, 2024

The commission was organized by CCA Temporary Gallery

INCLUSIVITY AND AWARENESS

online workshop #3

Workshop on Awareness

by Blu Doppe

Wed, January 10th, 5—8:30 p.m.

Manual #8

A Short Manual on Ableism and Neuro-diversity for Art Institu-tions

Fran Trento

Introduction. What Is This about?

This text compiles information from academic and nonacademic sources and observations from the institution's daily practices. Upon reading, the reader can understand how to avoid ableist practices and support neurodiversity within their organisations as much as possible, understanding that it is a process that requires constant assessment. Some recommendations may seem too obvious to some arts-based institutions but new to others. That is why this manual starts from the very basics.

Ableism is a system of marginalization based on causality that feeds microaggressions. Ableism reifies and classifies populations (Campbell, 2019), instituting the normative divide between the able and the nonable bodies. This means the separation between normal and nonnormal bodies is artificial and arbitrary. Nevertheless, it refers to an old history of colonization and whiteness, and a universal yet changeable design must be implemented. All our institutional premises and organizations are ableist, even if they name themselves "accessible," because accessibility encompasses access and comfort to numerous bodily arrangements. The fight against ableism shall happen in many levels and layers, and this manual has a particular focus on ableism against modalities of disability that are often disregarded as the invisible ones in the spectrum of neurodiversity/neurodivergence.

Neurodiversity is a term coined by autism activists focusing on guaranteeing rights for people who have different neurological configurations from the established norm. The neurodiversity movement defines some mental health conditions—the ASD spectrum, ADHD, and others—not as deficits but as expressions of human variability. These conditions are known as invisible disabilities because they are not easily "recognized" at first glance or at all. The fact that they are "invisible" also interferes with the way they are handled in many art institutions, where accessibility is mostly thought concerning visible disabilities. Even when these are addressed, they fail to embrace necessary measures beyond having an accessible bathroom for a person in a wheelchair. However, accessibility must be thought of in a broader sense. Neurodiversity, like other positive approaches to disability, fits the social model of disability, which aims to undo the ableism in society by adapting it to differently-abled persons, not labeling disabled bodies as defective.

Language on Neurodiversity and Gender

Neurodivergent persons often do not identify with binary pairs of gender. There is widely spread misinformation about autistic people that categorize them as "extremely male" persons. Some protocols may enhance the practices toward neuroqueer bodyminds in art institutions, and they happen in the intersection between neurodiversity and queerness:

1. Regardless of their physical appearance, ask somebody their pronouns before engaging in any activity.
2. If you do not have the opportunity to ask for their pronouns, use gender-neutral pronouns (they/them/hän), but change to the preferred pronoun as soon as you know the answer.
3. Never assume that somebody is able or disabled. Do not question a person's affirmations or ask for an official diagnosis. Diagnoses are not often accessible to marginalized communities (BIPOC, LGBTQIAP+ folks).
4. A person in the spectrum of neurodiversity is neurodivergent or neurodiverse/neuroqueer. Use the terms they inform you about, or ask them how they prefer to be called.

Moreover, using words such as "crazy" and "lame" should be avoided in the artistic pieces and the daily working life of an art institution. These terms reinforce the stigmatization of persons in the spectrum of neurodiversity. Being a disabled person is different from having a disease in the sense that a disability may or may not be a short-term disease.

Therefore, it is prudent never to assume somebody is sick or has any disease because they are not neurotypical. Avoid generalizing that a person with a disability is courageous or inspiring simply because they are living their lives. This kind of language can reinforce negative assumptions about people with disabilities and lead to an unrealistic idealization of all people who experience any impairment. These last two recommendations were inspired by suggestions present in Sierra Club's *Equity Language Guide*.

Hiring Practices

Some hiring practices can be reformulated to make them more inclusive. There is abundant research on how the phrasing of an open call for a job application can interfere with the lack of diversity of the applicants. As Davies et al. (2023) mentioned, employers rebrand their open positions with vague job postings that emphasize nonspecific "baseline skills" like "teamwork" and "communication" rather than "specialized skills" necessary for the position. Some neurodivergent people may interpret language more literally than neurotypicals, which is a problem because they feel they need to gain the skills necessary to work there. The existence of so-called good communication skills implies that there are not-so-good communication skills or modalities of communication that need to be validated because they do not fit into the basis of normative understandings of oratory.

Following Davies et al. (2023) article, prompt recommendations for the improvement of hiring practices include:

1. Remove reference to nonessential skills in job descriptions.
2. Make interview questions less ambiguous.
3. Provide clear documentation regarding the tasks that candidates will complete, the time the hiring process will take, and who will be involved. (Davies et al., 2023)

4. Provide clear deadlines regarding when candidates will hear the outcome of the hiring process. (Davies et al., 2023, p. 13; modified)
5. Explain clearly what they want from the employees and what the employers can expect. (Hamilton & Petty, 2023; modified)
6. Think of ways to reduce the time spent in places that are too crowded, bright, or loud, such as waiting rooms. (Hamilton & Petty, 2023)

Other suggestions include providing a space for decompression and soft gatherings in events organized by our organisations, as people can often feel sensorially overwhelmed; using forms instead of asking people to register for events via email messages, as these can be demanding and understood as a social task that costs too much energy or generates anxiety; keep in mind the duration of the events or meeting with collaborators, understanding that not all bodies can endure many hours of activity in a given day, especially without any breaks.

Organisational Practices within the Network

If the artist/curator/visitor/partner has an access rider, ask for it.

An access rider is a document that contains their requirements for traveling, hosting, food, payment, and work environment. Please note that writing an access rider constitutes a form of what disability and transformative justice activist Mia Mingus denominates "access intimacy." Writing an access rider can be extremely overwhelming and emotionally consuming; therefore, do not oblige anybody to ask to write in advance. Frame Contemporary Art Finland has participated in developing the *Access Riders* project, which can be read online on the website https://frame-finland.fi/en/resources/access-riders/.

Misunderstandings *will* happen during cross-neurotype communication.

Nobody should be personally blamed. When people with different neurotypes interact, the neurodivergent person is frequently blamed for the confusion, even if both parties have limitations in understanding each other, and there is the hidden, ableist assumption that neurodivergent individuals are the ones responsible for communicating in neurotypical standards, without highlighting that neurotypicals should also become interested in neurodivergent communication. This practice of imputing the guilt into disabled bodies needs to be avoided. Researcher Emily Stones (2023) suggests the necessity of developing cross-neurotype communication competencies by adapting one's communication and behavior to a variety of situations based on one's understanding of oneself, one's interpersonal goals, the other person, the environment, and the relationship (Wilson & Sabee, 2003). The qualities associated with communication competence include but are not limited to supportive and empathetic communication (Wiemann, 1977), communication that promotes equality and dialogue (Baxter & Montgomery, 1996), motivation to understand the perspectives of others (Spitzberg & Cupach, 1984), and the awareness of identity and cultural values on communication preferences.

1. For Scheduling—

I require all of the below to be confirmed and agreed upon by contract at least three weeks before the event takes place. Trust me, the more time there is to work out all the logistics, the better. Accessibility takes a really long time and it's messy af!

(For the commission of new work, or an event that requires a more long-term relationship, we'll need to have a conversation about time.)

I require at least 48 hours after arriving to acclimate before I can participate in any public events. I'll need to fly home the day after the event.

2. For the Entirety of the Trip—

I require a care person to assist me. I cannot travel alone. I prefer to bring a care person with me, because we will already have a relationship and they will know what is needed. Their travel, lodging, food, and transportation must be paid for by the host, as mine are.

3. For Air Travel—

The flight cannot depart before 15:00. The airport cannot be more than one hour away from my house. Nonstop is preferred. If a layover must happen, it cannot be longer than two hours. I need to be picked up from, and taken to, the airport. I must have an aisle seat on the flight, because I use a cane. This has to be booked in advance. On transatlantic flights, I require an economy seat with extra leg room, premium economy, or business class. Depending on my health, sometimes I require wheelchair assistance at the airport. Please check with me about this before booking flights.

Take the requirements and access riders seriously. If they are there, it is for a reason.

See, for instance, the excerpt of the publicly available access rider by artist, activist, and scholar Johanna Hevda.

For organizations that host exhibitions/ performances or indirectly fund them, a suggestion is to organize activities in which:

Individuals can leave and come back if needed; some people may need pauses in the activity even if its duration is not long.

Different opportunities to access the experience: sitting up, lying down, with the eyes closed.

Rounds of self-presentation can be exhausting for some persons in the spectrum of neurodiversity. Give somebody the right not to present themselves.

Antiableism Artists and Collectives in Finland and Abroad

- **https://www.instagram.com/justanothercripgroup/ Group of Finnish crip activists.**
- **https://www.stophatrednow.fi/isa-hukka / Finnish disability activist and artist.**
- **Rampa co. at Baltic Circle Festival.**

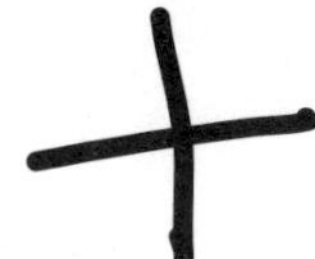

References

Campbell, F. K. (2019). Precision ableism: a studies in ableism approach to developing histories of disability and abledment. In *Rethinking History* (Vol. 23, Issue 2, pp. 138–156). Informa UK Limited. https://doi.org/10.1080/13642529.2019.1607475

Davies, J., Heasman, B., Livesey, A., Walker, A., Pellicano, E., & Remington, A. (2023). Access to employment: A comparison of autistic, neurodivergent and neurotypical adults' experiences of hiring processes in the United Kingdom. *Autism*, online first. https://doi.org/10.1177/13623613221145377

Hamilton, L. G., & Petty, S. (2023). Compassionate pedagogy for neurodiversity in higher education: A conceptual analysis. *Frontiers in Psychology*, v. 14, online first. https://doi.org/10.3389/fpsyg.2023.1093290

Stones, E. (2023). Cross-Neurotype Communication Competence. In *The Palgrave Handbook of Disability and Communication* (pp. 45–65). Springer International Publishing. https://doi.org/10.1007/978-3-031-14447-9_4

Sierra Club. (2021). *Equity Language Guide* [PDF document]. Retrieved from https://www.sierraclub.org/sites/default/files/sce-authors/u12332/Equity%20Language%20Guide%20Sierra%20Club%202021.pdf

This paper (Lux Cream, 90 g/m²) was
used from surplus stock normally destined for
disposal. Manufactured in Inkeroinen, Finland.

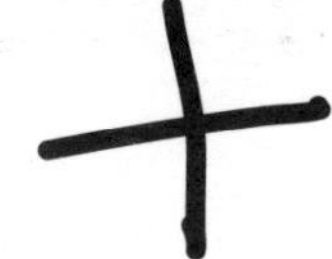

Paulina Seyfried

(In)Accessibility of Language in the Art Field

Prologue

Memory log: There's a diversity explosion on the opening panel of some random conference on diversity in culture and the arts happening in Germany.[1] *A Black person, one in a wheelchair, and two grown-up working-class children discuss the urgent need to make the art world more accessible, that it needs more money and other resources (what does that mean? Where from?). It is communicated in German spoken language and translated into German sign language.*

If you look around the audience, you see a collection of formally dressed, mostly white, healthy bodies nodding in agreement. Contradictory? So what? On stage, the names of thinkers are thrown around and reference is made to the connections of inclusion, decolonialism, participation, and social justice. Intersectionality and the deconstruction of encrusted structures are also loudly proclaimed and, finally, they say it's about "just doing things and talking less." After 45 minutes, the podium ends and the guests, now participants, split into workshop groups. There is no translation here and so-called diversity criteria are no longer considered. Instead, representatives of cultural institutions talk about their best practices in terms of integrating marginalized communities into existing structures and how they open doors. It seems as if the problem of the homogeneous, exclusive cultural industry has long since been penetrated by all those present, everyone agrees—it can't go on like this.

Introduction

It is easy for us academics to keep the scenario described in mind, to understand it as a lens through which the following is viewed. We are used to communicating in metaphors, making connections between sometimes highly contrasting topics and fields, such as applying scientific analyses to works of art or theoretically analyzing complex issues and imagining solutions.

1 As I am living and mostly working in Germany, this is my reference. Therefore, a lot of my sources are in German and translated by myself.

Most of the time, this does not apply to neurodiverse people, people with learning difficulties, people with other first languages, nonacademics, or simply people not from the art field. For others, reading "our" texts is no easy task, they have no sense of belonging, contexts and specialist discourses are alien to them. The language of the art field is to be understood as a common language—it includes and excludes. In "International Art English," Alix Rule and David Levine write about the extent to which it is a language of its own that consciously distinguishes itself from everyday English—more words, more metaphors, and in particular the right codes and buzzwords need to be used.[2] "When we sense ourselves to be in proximity to something serious and art related, we reflexively reach for subordinate clauses."[3]

From an institutional critique perspective, this mechanism of inclusion and exclusion is nothing out of the ordinary, as it has always been part of the art world and in particular the principle of collecting and preserving.[4] Still, although language is so basal and it is so obviously problematic, the discourse around it is quite marginal. In response to Alix Rule and David Levine's text, Hito Steyerl states: "Clearly, as with any other resource, access needs to be restricted in order to protect and perpetuate privilege.

2 Alix Rule/David Levine, *International Art language*, Triple Canopy 2018; short version online: https://canopycanopycanopy.com/contents/international_art_english (last access: 10.1.2024).

3 Ibid.

4 Ex. Manual on Archiving in this book. Without going into institutional critique discourses in depth here, it is worth briefly mentioning that Pierre Bourdieu and Alain Darbel, for example, were already examining museums and their audiences from a sociological perspective in the 1960s. See also: Joachim Baur/ schnittpunkt (ed.), *Das Museum der Zukunft: 43 neue Beiträge zur Diskussion über die Zukunft des Museums*, Bielefeld: transcript 2020; Nora Sternfeld, *Das radikaldemokratische Museum*, Berlin: De Gruyter 2018; Oliver Marchart, *Hegemonie im Kunstfeld: die documenta-Ausstellungen dX, D11, d12 und die Politik der Biennalisierung*, Cologne: König 2008; Andrea Fraser, "From the critique of institutions to an institution of critique", in: *Artforum*, September 2005, Vol. 44, No.1, pp. 278-283; Pierre Bourdieu/Alain Darbel/Dominique Schnapper, *The Love of Art: European Art Museums and Their Public*, Stanford: Polity Press 1990.

Interns and assistants the world over must be told that their domestic—and most likely public—education simply won't do."[5]

So how can an academic write about mechanisms of exclusion through language? I would like to start by positioning myself in order to explain why I am concerned with this issue. Then, after an introduction to the topic of easy and simple language, I will put forward some theses on why the art world communicates in the way it does internationally: academically, in English, and above all with a multitude of codes and metaphors, and how this approach could be changed.

I describe myself as white, German, cis-female, queer and (physically) disabled. The parenthesis is important for this text because it has led me to train my head, to perceive my cognitive "intactness" as the best way to participate in "normal life" as inconspicuously as possible, to educate and qualify myself, especially by reading and studying in an academic context, in German and English. I quickly realized that, contrary to my disabled body, my head is very fast and efficient, and I used this to position myself in the art field, to network, but also, and this will become clear in the following, to move casually in the specialist language jargon. I know how to talk about art, especially in the art world, which foreign words are used to convey affiliation, and which buzzwords secure funding. *Passing.* What I want to say is that language was never my barrier, but on the contrary: my self-created door opener. And that's why the problems behind it became all the clearer to me.

The Basics of Easy and Plain Language

In addition to the basic distinction between spoken and sign language, there are different language levels within spoken language, from which our written language also derives.[6]

5 Hito Steyerl, "International disco latin", in: *Eflux Journal* 45 "Language and Internet", 2013, online: https://www.e-flux.com/journal/45/60100/international-disco-latin (last access: 10.1.2024).

6 Common European Framework of Reference for Languages (CEFR), "Official translations of the CEFR Global Scale", Council of Europe, online:, https://www.coe.int/en/web/common-european-framework-reference-languages/official-translations-of-the-cefr-global-scale (last access: 10.1.2024).

These can also be used to roughly determine the classification of plain and easy language, whereby easy language corresponds to language level A1 but is bound to a set of rules and is therefore considered an accessibility measure. Easy language also requires a larger typeface and high luminance contrast. Texts are first translated into easy language according to fixed rules and must then be checked by people with learning disabilities.[7] Plain language, on the other hand, is comparable to language level A2 and can be translated by anyone.

This is what the Hamburg Lebenshilfe office writes: “Long texts, lots of technical terms, small letters: For many people, everyday texts are full of barriers. This is especially true for people with learning or intellectual disabilities. They often need help from others in everyday life to understand letters from authorities or contracts. Easy-to-read language is a tool for providing barrier-free information and enabling participation.”[8]

Put simply, from an accessibility point of view, Easy Language is aimed at people with learning difficulties and some kinds of neurodiversity. Plain Language is primarily for people with reading difficulties and language learners or nonnative speakers (A2 level), but it is also generally regarded as a language for communicating specialist content to a large part of society that has no specialist knowledge or academic background and thus offers a good basic orientation for writing exhibition texts or similar formats of institutional communication.

7 Bundesfachstelle Barrierefreiheit (Federal accessibility center), „Glossary“, Bundesfachstelle Barrierefreiheit Deutschen Rentenversicherung Knappschaft-Bahn-See, online: https://www.bundesfachstelle-barrierefreiheit.de/DE/Presse-und-Service/Glossar/Functions/glossar.html?lv2=b2b3ed55-94c9-48c1-a6ef-2d5089709a5e&lv3=75a8df97-da59-4c61-8b6b-85e1ec72ac11 (last access: 10.1.2024).

8 Büro für leichte Sprache, „Einstieg leichte Sprache“, Lebenshilfe Landesverband Hamburg e. V., online: https://ls.lhhh.de/einstieg-leichte-sprache/ (last access: 10.1.2024).

So, if you implement even just a few of the recommendations of Plain Language, you can ensure that the content to be conveyed is accessible to more people. The basic rules listed here are to be understood as a kind of guideline and apply to most languages with an alphabet! In general, the following maxim/recommendation applies: Do not assume any knowledge that the reader cannot have without qualification.

PLAIN LANGUAGE	EASY LANGUAGE
Simplified written language: ● Make only one statement per sentence and one train of thought per paragraph. ● A sentence should not have more than 15 to 20 words. ● Avoid interpolations and nested sentences. ● Write active verbs, avoid the passive voice. ● Clear sentences, avoid irony and metaphors. ● Avoid synonyms and stick to one term.	Very easy written language, means of accessibility: ● Short sentences, no subordinate clauses ● Simple, short words should be used, and the same words should always be used for the same things. ● Technical and foreign words should be avoided entirely or explained. ● No abbreviations or special characters ● No idioms or figurative language ● Only a selection of the rules
No fixed set of rules, customizable for specific purposes	Fixed rules

Information from the handout for the introductory course Office for Plain Language Hamburg, Lebenshilfe Landesverband Hamburg e.V. 2023 and from the website of the Office for Plain Language Bonn.

9 See Constanze Lopez, “Einfache Sprache Bonn”, online: https://einfachesprachebonn.de/grundregeln_einfache_sprache.html (last access: 10.1.2024).

10 German network for easy language updated the guidelines in 2022, there are no international guidelines yet, but in 2010 the law of plain writing was installed in US and therefore the government established a first binding version in English: U.S. General Services Administration, “Federal plain language guidelines”, online: https://www.plainlanguage.gov/guidelines (last access: 10.1.2024) and ISO (International Organization for Standardization) is constantly updating an English version, International Organization for Standardization, “Plain language — Part 1: Governing principles and guidelines”, online: https://www.iso.org/standard/78907.html (last access: 10.1.2024); as well as an international reading list by The International Plain Language Federation “Bibliography” online: https://www.iplfederation.org/plain-language/bibliography/ (last access: 10.1.2024).

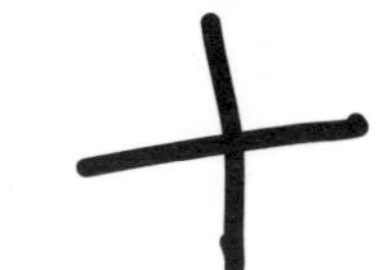

Problematization: Language in the Art Field

Over the last decade, more and more agencies have been set up to provide translation and proofreading services for plain and easy language.[11] Initially mainly used by state organizations and authorities outside the art field, the art world has also become aware of this service in the last few years. Although major institutions, such as Documenta 15 in 2022, also offered a translation of their website into easy language,[12] even the dissemination of this service-based measure is progressing very slowly. While the translation of core information, such as the physical accessibility of the institutions, into easy language does occur from time to time,[13] the background and interpretation of the artworks and productions is still largely conveyed in academic language with many art-specific technical terms, even though it only requires the commissioning of external service providers, such as the translation work from first language into English. Despite the findings on language comprehension and the relatively simple use of easy and plain language (although outsourcing as a service presumably does little to change the fundamental considerations of exclusion and inclusion mechanisms),

11 Triggered by the enactment of the Act on the Equality of Persons with Disabilities (Behindertengleichstellungsgesetz – BGG), Section 11 Intelligibility and Plain Language by German Federal Ministry of Justice in 2022, which obliges public authorities to provide translation services. Online: Bundesamt für Justiz, „Gesetz zur Gleichstellung von Menschen mit Behinderungen (Behindertengleichstellungsgesetz – BGG) § 11 Verständlichkeit und Leichte Sprache“, https://www.gesetze-im-internet.de/bgg/__11.html (last access 10.1.2024).

12 See also documenta und Museum Fridericianum GmbH, “Easy read. About documenta fifteen”, online: https://documenta-fifteen.de/en/easy-read-home/ (last access 10.1.2024).

13 Ex. Berliner Festspiele, “Gropius Bau—Über das Ausstellungshaus”, online: https://www.berlinerfestspiele.de/leichte-sprache/gropius-bau; Haus der Kunst München, „Barrierefreiheit“, online: https://www.hausderkunst.de/barrierefreiheit; KW Institute for Contemporary Art Berlin, “Einfache Sprache”, online: https://www.kw-berlin.de/einfache-sprache/ (here also exhibition texts in simple language); Museum Für Moderne Kunst Frankfurt, „Plain Language“, online: https://www.mmk.art/en/leichte-sprache; Center for Art and Urbanistics (ZKU) Karlsruhe, „Plain Language“ online: https://www.zku-berlin.org/plain-language/ (last access to all of these 10.1.2024).

it must be noted that little has changed in the basic understanding of high culture, in which academic language is the norm with a distinguishing function and in whose circles the belief still prevails far too often that the supposed complexity of art can only be conveyed through complex language.

> "[...] because the exhibition text still remains one of the most widely used communication platforms in museum exhibitions, it seems obvious that contrary to all the new communication elements that enable differentiation of the communication in order to reach diverse audiences separately, the exhibition text must do just the opposite. It must reach and function for all the different types of users simultaneously and be accessible to every single person entering the exhibition, no matter what educational, social, or cultural background he or she may bring."[14]

In addition to this option, which requires monetary resources in particular, I would like to suggest another, more fundamental approach, which in my opinion is long overdue and could contribute to a hegemonic shift in the self-image of art and cultural institutions. While easy language has to be translated by professional translators, the guidelines of plain language can be used by people without further training at any time. There are various tools available for this, such as checklists, exercises, and the like.

14 Anna Karina Kjeldsen/Matilde Nisbeth Brøgger, "When words of wisdom are not wise", in: *Nordisk Museologi* No. 1 (2015), Oslo 2015, p. 95, https://doi.org/10.5617/nm.3002.

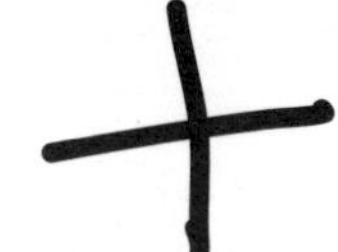

An example:

"Top 10 Principles for Plain Language

Plain language is clear, concise, organized, and appropriate for the intended audience.

1. Write for your reader, not yourself. Use pronouns when you can.
2. State your major point(s) first before going into details.
3. Stick to your topic. Limit each paragraph to one idea and keep it short.
4. Write in active voice. Use the passive voice only in rare cases.
5. Use short sentences as much as possible.
6. Use everyday words. If you must use technical terms, explain them on the first reference.
7. Omit unneeded words.
8. Keep the subject and verb close together.
9. Use headings, lists, and tables to make reading easier.
10. Proofread your work and have a colleague proof it as well."[15]

15 National Archives, "Top 10 Principles for Plain Language", online: https://www.archives.gov/open/plain-writing/10-principles.html (last access 10.01.2024).

As with many forms of discrimination and isms, change is also very slow in terms of power asymmetries through language and employees of art and cultural institutions often work on the surface—supposedly due to a lack of resources or expertise—by doing something for the external effect with the least possible effort. Unfortunately, this approach all too often appears to be ticking off topics à la tick politics and tokenism, without having any impact on the internal structure.

> Article 30 of the UN Convention on the Rights of Persons with Disabilities—Participation in Cultural Life states:
> "States Parties recognize the right of persons with disabilities to take part on an equal basis with others in cultural life and shall take all appropriate measures to ensure that persons with disabilities [...] enjoy access to [...] theatre and other cultural activities, in accessible formats."[16]

So why is it that, despite this legal regulation and a clear decline in audience numbers, it is only now that more attention is being paid to exclusion mechanisms through language levels? Based on this question, I conducted a survey among the partner institutions of the Islands of Kinship project. This concerned both communication within the respective team, the use of language in public texts, and the background of the employees.

In general, only spoken and written language is used as a means of communication. While four out of six institutions communicate internally in the national language and only two speak English due to international composition, meetings are generally held informally and at eye level, according to self-description. In general, it became clear that internal communication plays a very important role: regular meetings in various constellations, sometimes with fixed,

16 United Nations: Department of Economic and Social Affairs (Social Inclusion), "UN Convention on the Rights of Persons with Disabilities 2008", online: https://social.desa.un.org/issues/disability/crpd/convention-on-the-rights-of-persons-with-disabilities-crpd (last access 10.01.2024).

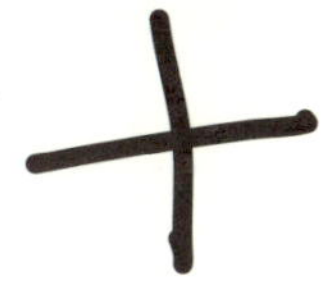

sometimes changing moderation, as well as communication via tools such as Slack, WhatsApp, email, or SMS were mentioned.

In comparison, it is noticeable that texts for external communication, such as exhibition texts, are mostly written by the curators in English.[17] Informal communication, as well as within the team, takes place on social media and also serves as a tool for reaching alternative (young, subcultural) target groups.

Depending on the participatory, activist level of the project, some texts are also written collectively. All teams mention the attempt or desire to write texts in a “more comprehensible,” “less academic,” and “more collective” way.[18]

Nevertheless, only one of the six institutions mentioned a formulated communication strategy that defines the tone of all texts and aims to be as clear and understandable as possible, although it differs depending on the target group (e.g. artists or politicians).

At the same time, all the others state that metaphors are used as a common stylistic device in exhibition or publication texts,

one interviewee indicates the understanding that these could facilitate access to the artworks and another that it is difficult to avoid the use of figurative, complex language or metaphors in the explanations of the artworks, as this threatens the integrity and complexity of the artwork. In addition, an audience is often imagined here that already has prior knowledge while at the same time formulating the desired opening.

Neutral descriptions, on the other hand, tend to be used for practical information, such as accessibility. In general, the more the project aims to be participatory or to specifically address marginalized groups, the more informal and collective the drafting process of the texts seems to be.

17 An institution is run collectively, so the texts are also created collectively. Sometimes coauthors / cocurators play a role.

18 This was a nonrepresentative survey of the project partners, which anonymized individuals but not institutions.

In summary, the use of academic language depends on the desired target group of the texts to which certain media are attributed: Exhibition visitors are unconsciously associated with a higher level of education or language than people on social media. Although all but two or three of the project participants come from nonacademic families and only encountered this type of language through their studies or entry into the art world, the art field-specific language with metaphors and references to theories and thinkers characterizes everyone's everyday working life and thus also their self-image. Even though plain or easy language (the distinction between the two is not known) was discussed as part of this project or in some cases beforehand from an institutional critique or inclusive perspective, and in some cases specific workshops were also held on the subject, no clear routines or procedures seem to have been established yet as to how a text could be written or peer-reviewed in a more accessible way. In addition to the self-reports of the participating institutions, the texts speak for themselves. Most of them have a small font size and are long, peppered with metaphors, quotations, anecdotes, and philosophical theories.[19]

Conclusion

In conclusion, it can be said that the Islands of Kinship project led to all six institutions taking a closer look at mechanisms of exclusion in the art world, their own practice and language. This is the first step, and in addition, smaller changes were tested on various levels.

19 Temporary Gallery, "Every Courageous Life Is A Song To The Future", online: https://www.temporarygallery.org/en/every-courageous-life-is-a-song-to-the-future-ines-doujak-2; Július Koller Society, "Luki Essender: Of Yous", online: https://juliuskollersociety.org/luki-essender-of-yous-2; Faculty of things that can't be learned, "PRECARITY HAS A CHANCE: Public spaces in movement (toward)", online: https://akto-fru.org/en/precarity-has-a-chance-public-spaces-in-movement-toward_group-exhibition/; Frame Contemporary Art Finland, "public programme for 2019-2023", online: https://frame-finland.fi/en/programme/rehearsing-hospitalities/, Jindřich Chalupecký Society, "Imagine a Breath of Fresh Air", online: https://www.sjch.cz/en/imagine-a-breath-of-fresh-air/; Latvian Centre for Contemporary Art, "A Visionary Drawing Riddle", online: https://lcca.lv/en/exhibitions/exhibition-dedicated-to-the-artist-maris-bisofs/#izstade (last access to all of them 10.01.2024).

Anchoring a continuous engagement and lasting change in dealing with external communication is a fundamental shift that has not yet taken place or is not considered essential at the majority of art institutions.

The following paradox often seems to exist: On the one hand, there is a lack of resources (time, money, personnel) to deal with issues of accessibility and participation of other people besides the art audience; on the other hand, there is a lack of expertise in the team, but the necessary consequences are not taken in either case—rather, many employees seem to be in a state of shock. The discussion provided here is just one of many measures that break down barriers without requiring more resources beyond a rethink. The conservative linking of art and academic language, and the associated mechanisms of distinction, could be counteracted in the longer term by cultural actors questioning themselves and by focusing on the 10 principles cited above. In the worst-case scenario, this would lead to so-called art lovers being able to read more comprehensible texts.

Finally, I would like to give an outlook with a spontaneous list of possible questions for writing a text:

- What is the intention and aim of the text?
- Is there a specific target group?
- Can I assume special prior knowledge or knowledge of terms?
- In what context do the readers receive the text and what action should follow from it? (For example: invitation to participate, knowledge transfer)
- Where will the text be published? (Print or Internet, everywhere or at a specific location)

Sources

- Constanze Lopez, "Einfache Sprache Bonn," online: https://einfachesprachebonn.de/grundregeln_einfache_sprache.html (last access: 10. 1. 2024).
- Baur, Joachim/schnittpunkt (ed.), *Das Museum der Zukunft: 43 neue Beiträge zur Diskussion über die Zukunft des Museums*, Bielefeld: transcript 2020.
- Berliner Festspiele, "Gropius Bau—Über das Ausstellungshaus", online: https://www.berlinerfestspiele.de/leichte-sprache/gropius-bau (last access: 10. 01. 2024).
- Bourdieu, Pierre/Alain Darbel/Dominique Schnapper, *The Love of Art: European Art Museums and Their Public*, Stanford: Polity Press 1990.
- Büro für leichte Sprache, „Einstieg leichte Sprache", Lebenshilfe Landesverband Hamburg e. V., online: https://ls.lhhh.de/einstieg-leichte-sprache/ (last access: 10. 01. 2024).
- Bundesamt für Justiz, „Gesetz zur Gleichstellung von Menschen mit Behinderungen (Behindertengleichstellungsgesetz – BGG) § 11 Verständlichkeit und Leichte Sprache", https://www.gesetze-im-internet.de/bgg/__11.html (last access 10.01.2024).
- Bundesfachstelle Barrierefreiheit (Federal accessibility center), „Glossary", Bundesfachstelle Barrierefreiheit Deutschen Rentenversicherung Knappschaft-Bahn-See, online: https://www.bundesfachstelle-barrierefreiheit.de/DE/Presse-und-Service/Glossar/Functions/glossar.html?lv2=b2b3ed55-94c9-48c1-a6ef-2d5089709a5e&lv3=75a8df97-da59-4c61-8b6b-85e1ec72ac11 (last access: 10. 01. 2024).
- Center for Art and Urbanistics (ZKU) Karlsruhe, „Plain Language" online: https://www.zku-berlin.org/plain-language/ (last access: 10. 01. 2024).
- Common European Framework of Reference for Languages (CEFR), "Official translations of the CEFR Global Scale", Council of Europe, online:, https://www.coe.int/en/web/common-european-framework-reference-languages/official-translations-of-the-cefr-global-scale (last access: 10.1.2024).
- documenta und Museum Fridericianum gGmbH, "Easy read. About documenta fifteen",online:, https://documenta-fifteen.de/en/easy-read-home/ (last access 10. 01. 2024).
- Faculty of things that can't be learned, "PRECARITY HAS A CHANCE: Public spaces in movement (toward)", online: https://akto-fru.org/en/precarity-has-a-chance-public-spaces-in-movement-toward_group-exhibition/ (last access 10. 01. 2024).
- Frame Contemporary Art Finland, "public programme for 2019–2023", online: https://frame-finland.fi/en/programme/rehearsing-hospitalities/ (last access 10. 01. 2024).
- Fraser, Andrea, "From the critique of institutions to an institution of critique", in: *Artforum*, September 2005, Vol. 44, No.1, pp. 278-283.
- Haus der Kunst München, „Barrierefreiheit", online: https://www.hausderkunst.de/barrierefreiheit (last access 10. 01. 2024).

- **International Organization for Standardization, "Plain language — Part 1: Governing principles and guidelines", online: https://www.iso.org/standard/78907.html (last access: 10. 01. 2024).**
- **Jindřich Chalupecký Society, "Imagine a Breath of Fresh Air", online: https://www.sjch.cz/en/imagine-a-breath-of-fresh-air/ (last access 10. 01. 2024).**
- **Julius Koller Society, "Luki Essender: Of Yous", online: https://juliuskollersociety.org/luki-essender-of-yous-2 (last access 10. 01. 2024).**
- **Kjeldsen, Anna Karina/Matilde Nisbeth Brøgger, "When words of wisdom are not wise", in:** *Nordisk Museologi* **No. 1 (2015), Oslo 2015, p. 95, https://doi.org/10.5617/nm.3002.**
- **Latvian Centre for Contemporary Art, "A Visionary Drawing Riddle", online: https://lcca.lv/en/exhibitions/exhibition-dedicated-to-the-artist-maris-bisofs/#izstade (last access 10. 01. 2024).**
- **KW Institute for Contemporary Art Berlin, "Einfache Sprache", online: https://www.kw-berlin.de/einfache-sprache/ (last access: 10. 01. 2024).**
- **Marchart, Oliver, *Hegemonie im Kunstfeld: die documenta-Ausstellungen dX, D11, d12 und die Politik der Biennalisierung*, Cologne: König 2008.**
- **Museum Für Moderne Kunst Frankfurt, „Plain Language", online: https://www.mmk.art/en/leichte-sprache (last access: 10. 01. 2024).**
- **National Archives, "Top 10 Principles for Plain Language", online: https://www.archives.gov/open/plain-writing/10-principles.html (last access 10. 01. 2024).**

357

- **Rule, Alix/David Levine, International Art language, Triple Canopy 2018; short version online: https://canopycanopycanopy.com/contents/international_art_english (last access: 10. 01. 2024).**
- **Sternfeld, Nora,** *Das radikaldemokratische Museum*, **Berlin: De Gruyter 2018.**
- **Steyerl, Hito, "International disco latin", in:** *Eflux Journal* **45 "Language and Internet", 2013, online: https://www.e-flux.com/journal/45/60100/international-disco-latin (last access: 10. 01. 2024).**
- **Temporary Gallery, "Every Courageous Life Is A Song To The Future", online: https://www.temporarygallery.org/en/every-courageous-life-is-a-song-to-the-future-ines-doujak-2 (last access: 10. 01. 2024).**
- **The International Plain Language Federation "Bibliography" online: https://www.iplfederation.org/plain-language/bibliography/ (last access: 10. 01. 2024).**
- **United Nations: Department of Economic and Social Affairs (Social Inclusion), "UN Convention on the Rights of Persons with Disabilities 2008", online: https://social.desa.un.org/issues/disability/crpd/convention-on-the-rights-of-persons-with-disabilities-crpd (last access 10. 01. 2024).**
- **U.S. General Services Administration, "Federal plain language guidelines", online: https://www.plainlanguage.gov/guidelines (last access: 10. 01. 2024).**

This paper (Vergemit Yellow, 120 g/m²) was used
from surplus stock normally destined for disposal.
Manufactured in Štětí, Czech Republic.

List of Participants and Collaborators

Basel Abbas
Noor Abed
Ruanne Abou-Rahme
Dan Acostioaei
Safet Ahmeti
Nick Aikens
Matti Aikio
Yin Aiwen
Deniz Ajdarevic
Venuše Al Ali Tesner
Robert Alagjozovski
Nora-Swantje Almes
Kocho Andonovski
Andrea
Angel
Lena Anouk Philipp
anto_nie
Architects without Frontiers
Ljubisa Arsić
Mothers Artlovers
Ieva Astahovska
Nicole Baginski
Alex Bailey
Boris Bakal
Nada Baković
Karolina Balcer
Đorđe Balmazović
Khairani Barokka
Canan Batur
Shiraz Bayjoo
Ruth Beale
Ana Beatriz Sepúlveda
Daniela Berger Prado
Elza Bērziņa
Yvonne Billimore
Catherine Biocca
Gabriela BK
Jonathan Blackwood
Remco van Bladel
Linda Boļšakova
Zlata Borůvková
Sezgin Boynik
Nikola Brabcová
Jānis Brizga
Liene Brizga-Kalniņa
Jana Brsakoska
Tatiana Buženková
Oriol Cabarrocas
Cansu Cakar
Triple Candie
Krzysztof Candrowicz
Cihad Caner
Barbora Ciprová
Joshua Citarella
Zoë Claire Miller
Family Connection
Anita Ćulafić
Pauline Curnier Jardin

Nemanja Cvijanović
Lamija Čehajić
Veronika Čechová
Marina Čelebić
Martina Danailovska
Lizza May David
Sára Davidová
Cian Dayrit
Stan de Natris
Aleksandr Delev
Vlasta Delimar
Maija Demitere
Vladimir Deskov
Gjorgji Despodov
Simona Dimkovska
Kriṡ Dittel
Zvonimir Dobrović
Thora Dolven Balke
Ines Doujak
Veerle Driessen
Martina Drozd Smutná
Ivan Durgutovski
Tamara Dzerkov
Lina Džuverović
Clementine Edwards
Vika Eksta
Krišjānis Elviks
Eva Ellereit
Emilia Epštajn
Inga Erdmane
Eri
iSaAc Espinoza Hidrobo
Luki Essender

MATERNAL FANTASIES
Barbora Fastrová
Feel Good Cooperative
Kristina Fingerland
Mark Fridvalszki
Květoslava Fulierová
Robert Gabris
Seana Gavin
Matej Gavula
Nikola Gelevski
Giuliana
Marjan Gjorgjiev
Antonio Gjorgjiev
Justyna Górowska
Alva Gotby
Nadine Gouders
Anna Griķe
Igor Grubić
Daniel Grúň
Annemarija Gulbe
Viktor Gurov
Ruben Hamelink
Hanna-Maria Hammari
Max Hannus
Tereza Haspeklová
Minna Haukka
Minna Henriksson
Johannah Herr
Jitka Hlaváčková
annette hollywood
Ondřej Houšťava
Anna Hulačová
Ellie Hunter

Participants and Collaborators

Martin Hurych
Binelde Hyrcan
Siniša Ilić
Merve Iseri
Bojana Isijanin
Biljana Isijanin
Ljupcho Isijanin
Bojan Ivanov
Ana Ivanovska Deskova
Jovan Ivanovski
Atis Jakobsons
Petra Janda
Vladimir Janchevski
Janez Janša
Lucie Jarkovská
Eva Jaroňová
Ewelina Jarosz
Charlotte Jarvis
Vladan Jeremić
Tereza Jindrová
Signe Johannessen
Emily Johnson
Agnė Jokšė
Gjorgje Jovanovik
Filip Jovanovski
Aleksandar Jovanovski
Rūta Jumīte
Miodrag Kuch
Nam June Paik
Krõõt Juurak
Marija Kaeva
Violeta Kachakova
Maria Kapajeva

Kristijan Karadjoski
Kinga Kiełczyńska
Michal Kindernay
Lucy Kirkwood
Lenka Klodová
Petr Kněžek
Ana Knežević
Jussi Koitela
Július Koller
Miriam Kongstad
Oliver Kostic
Eva Koťátková
Věra Kotlárová-Chovancová
Karina Kottová
Katarína Kováčová
Marko Kovachevski
Filip Kraus
Līva Kreislere
Karolína Kripnerová
Márton Kristóf
Paul Kuipers
Siniša Labrović
Tarek Lakhrissi
Ieva Laube
Borko Lazeski
Diana Lelonek
Kristina Lelovac
Jakub Lerch
Michelle Levy
Raffıa Li
Katya Libkind
Claudia Liebelt
Alexandra Lopez

Nikola Ludlová
Marie Lukáčová
Kristin Luke
Agita Lūse
Mary Maggic
Markéta Magidová
Aurelija Maknytė
Nora Malles
Jumana Manna
Alexandra Mapuchina
Cara Marsh Sheffler
Francisco Martinez
Haralds Matulis
Emma McCormick-Godhart
Elza Medne
Teja Merhar
Dimitar Milev
Aaron Moulton
Tamara Moyzes
Sethembile Msezane
Burju Musli
Oliver Musovik
Olia Mykhailiuk
Persefoni Myrtsou
Paloma Nana
Wanda Nanibush
Rosalind Nashashibi
Branislav Nikolov
Sandra Nikolovska
Chiara No
Rose Nordin
S.J. Norman
Martina Nosková

Alanis Obomsawin
Mateusz Okonski
Serena Olcuire
Paulina Olszewska
Boris Ondreička
OPA
Tanja Ostojić
Camilo Pachón
Zlatko Paković
Nina Paszkowski
Amol K. Patil
Martina Petreska
Ingrīda Pičkukānes
Nela Pietrová
Rory Pilgrim
Katarína Pirháčová
Bojana Piškur
Tadeáš Polák
Darinka Pop Mitić
Darja Popolitova
Mirko Popov
Luiza Proença
Dragan Protić Prota
Laure Prouvost
Anni Puolakka
Ruta Putramentaite
Rebeka Rácz
Vojtěch Radakulan
Rena Rädle
Elham Rahmati
Milan Ressel
Tabita Rezaire
Leon Romanow

Participants and Collaborators

Jakeline Romero Epiayú
Ali Rosa-Salas
Liz Rosenfeld
Ieva Rosne
Aneta Rostkowska
Janek Rous
Adam Rzepecki
Mētra Saberova
Artan Sadiku
Egill Sæbjörnsson
Jan Ságl
Zorka Ságlová
Ivana Samandova
Grace Samboh
Inari Sandell
Denis Saraginovski
Vidha Saumya
Ľubica Segečová
Dubravka Sekulić
Selma Selman
Luna Shalamon
Tai Shani
Elizabeta Sheleva
Anna Shkodenko
Ivana Sidjimovska
Vojtěch Sigmund
Jonne Sippola
Jiří Skála
Jirka Skála
Katarína Slezáková
Maja Smrekar
Ebun Sodipo
Adéla Součková

Ljubica Spaskovska
Ondřej Spiritza
Līga Spunde
Jonas Staal
Joanna Stange
Gilda Star
Evgenija Stojanova
Denica Stojkovska
Hyun Suk Seo
Superflux
Sophia Süßmilch
Iga Świeściak
BCAA Systém
Bálint Szabó
Borbála Szalai
Ezra Šimek
Branko Šimić
Rasa Šmite
Raitis Šmits
Zuzana Šrámková
Terezie Štindlová
Michal Štrompach
Dagmar Šubrtová
Jakub Tajovský
Marija Taleska
Jay Tan
Stefan Tankov
Biljana Tanurovska-Kjulavkovski
James Taylor-Foster
Minh Thang Pham
Nenad Tonkin
Igor Toshevski
Susanne Treister

Ondřej Trhoň
Karoline Trollvik
Marie Tučková
Mila Turajlić
Stanislav Turina
Sophie Utikal
Nikola Uzunovski
Jozef Vančo
Ivana Vaseva
Boris Vasileski
Ana Vasileva
Dejan Vasilevski
Ivancho Velkov
Karin Vicente
David Vojtuš
Ivan Vrtev
Natalija Vujošević
Elina Waage Mikalsen
Stanislaw Welbel
Miriam Wistreich
Baiba Witajewska-Baltvilka
Ruth Wolf-Rehlfeldt
Jakub Woynarowski
Geo Wyex
Shlomi Yaffe
Barnabás Zemlényi-Kovács
Klelija Zhivkovikj
Konstantīns Žukovs
Marwa Arsonios
Anastasia Artemeva
Alemanji Aminkeng Atabong
Federica Bueti
Birgit Ærenlund Bundesen
Florian Carl
Mary Conlon
Dahlia El Broul
Ida Enegren
Gemma Medina Estupiñán
Farbod Fakharzadeh
Noah Fischer
Johanna Hedva
Sigrid Holmwood
Isa Hukka
K-oh-llective
(Nada Elkalaawy,
Engy Mohsen,
Mohamed Al Bakeri,
Soukaina Joual,
Rania Atef)
Pilvi Kalhama
Milla Kallio
Xenia Kalpaktsoglou
Kaise Karvinen
William Keohane
Raija Koli
Karolina Kucia
Jenni Laiti
Anissa R. Lewis
Jemina Lindholm
Steve Maher
Massimiliano Mollona
Iida Niisinen
Eoin O’Dowd
Paul O’Neill
Vishnu Vardhani Rajan
Farid Rakun (ruangrupa)

Participants and Collaborators

Kaura Raudaskoski
El Reid-Buckley
Anna Rieder
Sandra Ruiz
Ailie Rutherford
Alessandra Saviotti
Station of Commons
(Grégoire Rousseau,
Minerva Juolahti &
Eddie Choo Wen Yi)
Anna Talasniemi
Minna Tarkka
Meenakshi Thirukode
Arlene Tucker
Hypatie Vourloumis
Mike Watson

We are extremely grateful to all artists and collaborators who took part in this project. For a detailed lists of teams and participants, please see the individual events at **islandsofkinship.org**.

TEXTS:
Ieva Astahovska, Jana Brsakoska, Veronika Čechová, Kris Dittel, Daniel Grúň, Michal Klodner, Eloïse Bonneviot & Anne de Boer, Jussi Koitela, Karina Kottová, Diana Lelonek, Nikola Ludlová, Aneta Rostkowska, Paulina Seyfried, Katarína Slezáková, Taka Taka, James Taylor-Foster, Fran Trento, Ivana Vaseva

ART COMMISSIONS:
Inclusivity and Awareness workshops (Blu Doppe, Agnieszka Habraschka, Gina Jeske, Rafia Shahnaz), Luki Essender, Minna Henriksson, Pauline Curnier Jardin & Feel Good Cooperative, Diana Lelonek, Eloïse Bonneviot & Anne de Boer, Jonas Staal, Taka Taka

AUTHORS OF COMMISSIONED BOOKMARKS:
Cultural Community Center (Marcela Capoušková, Helena Dolečková, Alena Kunčíková, Alena Prosečová, Iva Šafandová, Blanka Vetešníková)

GRAPHIC DESIGN: Petr Knězek (vonsaten.net)

TYPEFACES: Azeret, Azeret Mono

PAPER: Recycled Lettura, 60%, 80 g/m^2 and a mix of surplus paper

EDITORS: Barbora Ciprová, Tereza Jindrová, Karina Kottová, Nikola Ludlová

EDITORIAL COLLABORATION: Lamija Čehajić, Tereza Chocholová, Aneta Rostkowska, Fran Trento

TRANSLATIONS AND PROOFREADING: Tereza Chocholová

PRODUCTION: Barbora Ciprová

PRODUCTION COOPERATION: Sára Davidová

PHOTOS:
Leontína Berková, Radek Brousil, Jacob Dahlin, Ján Kekeli, Jan Kolský, Madara Kupla, Šimon Lupták, Kristīne Madjare, Katri Naukkarinen, Denis Saraginovski, Ján Skaličan, Sanita Sparāne, Michal Ureš, Simon Vogel, Dan Weill, Sheung Yiu

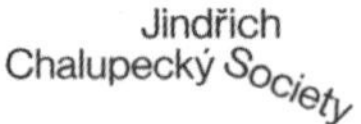

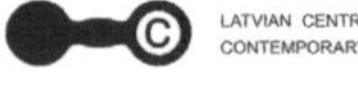

frame finland

Stroom Den Haag

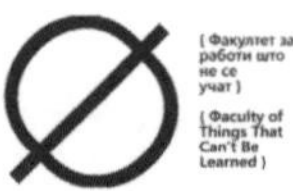

JÚLIUS KOLLER SOCIETY

Temporary Gallery

The bookmarks with personal messages to the public art institutions feature the original artwork by our collaborating senior artists from the Cultural Community Center residing in Prague, Czech Republic.

In 2023 and 2024, we engaged attendants of this Center in various capacities as consultants, feedback providers to our programs, as well as speakers at our public event. Reciprocally, the Jindřich Chalupecký Society employees and collaborating artists participate as guest speakers at the Center's public events.